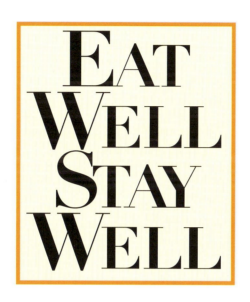

Reader's Digest

EAT WELL

Over 450 delicious South African recipes made with healing foods

STAY WELL

The Reader's Digest Association, Southern Africa

Project Team, South Africa

EDITOR
Pat Kramer

ART DIRECTOR
Gusti Prohn

PICTURE AND TEXT RESEARCHER
Rose-Ann Martini

PROJECT MANAGER
Grant Moore

PROOFREADER
Pat Brennan

PHOTOGRAPHER
Henrique Wilding

COOKERY CONSULTANT AND RECIPE DEVELOPER
Marina Searle-Tripp

NUTRITIONIST
Edelweiss Wentzel RD (SA), MSc Dietetics,
Dipl. Hosp. Dietetics.

Project Staff, United States

Reader's Digest Cooking, Home, Consumer Books

GROUP EDITORIAL DIRECTOR
Carol A. Guasti

GROUP DESIGN DIRECTOR
Joan Mazzeo

RESEARCH EDITOR
Linda Ingroia

Project Development Staff

DESIGN DIRECTOR
Perri DeFino

SENIOR EDITOR
Lee Fowler

EDITOR
Judith Cressy

Reader's Digest General Books

EDITOR-IN-CHIEF
David Palmer

EXECUTIVE EDITOR
Gayla Visalli

MANAGING EDITOR
Christopher Cavanaugh

Visit us on the World Wide Web at www.readersdigest.co.za

ISBN 1-874912-68-8

PRODUCED BY REBUS, INC.

PUBLISHER
Rodney M. Friedman

DIRECTOR, RECIPE DEVELOPMENT & PHOTOGRAPHY
Grace Young

EDITORIAL DIRECTOR, FOOD GROUP
Kate Slate

WRITER
Bonnie J. Slotnick

ASSISTANT EDITOR
James W. Brown, Jr.

ART DIRECTOR
Timothy Jeffs

DESIGN ASSISTANT
Yoheved Gertz

SENIOR RECIPE DEVELOPER
Sandra Rose Gluck

RECIPE DEVELOPER
Paul Piccuito

RECIPE TESTERS
Iris Carulli, Michelle Steffens

PHOTOGRAPHERS
Beatriz daCosta, Mark Ferri, Lisa Koenig, Steven Mark Needham

PHOTOGRAPHERS' ASSISTANTS
Alix Berenberg, Todd Chalfant, Phill Chevalier, Katie Bleacher
Everard, Christopher Lilly, Inbal Nahari, Robert Piazza, Robert
Presciutti, Lisa Silvestri, Tanya Stroedel

FOOD STYLISTS
A.J. Battifarano, Roscoe Betsill, Delores Custer, Paul S. Grimes, Helen
Jones, Karen Pickus, Diane Simone Vezza

ASSISTANT FOOD STYLISTS
Margarette Adams, Charles Davis, Tracy Donovan, Danielle Gorman,
Julie Grimes, Amy Lord, Cara Morris, Eric Robledo, Megan
Schlow

PROP STYLIST
Debrah Donahue

DECORATIVE BACKGROUNDS
Sue Israel

NUTRITION CONSULTANT
Jeanine Barone

NUTRITIONISTS
Hill Nutrition Associates

EATING WELL IS THE KEY TO GOOD HEALTH

Nearly every day, researchers announce another exciting discovery regarding the foods we eat and how they affect our health. We now know, for instance, that vitamins and minerals add up to more than we thought: some help fight heart disease, cancer and cataracts. And some vitamin- and mineral-rich foods—fruits, vegetables, legumes, grains and seeds— also contain newly-discovered compounds, called phytochemicals, which have surprisingly powerful health-preserving properties. Meat, poultry, fish, eggs and dairy products also supply health-giving and, possibly, life-extending, nutrients. *Eat Well, Stay Well* tells you about the foods which can help you avoid illness and achieve optimal health. Our recipes offer delicious ways to serve these foods—from appetizers to desserts; each food and every recipe is accompanied by a nutritional analysis. And in the front of the book you'll find a comprehensive nutrition glossary, as well as a chapter of photo-illustrated cooking techniques.

The Heart Foundation of South Africa encourages everyone to follow a healthy lifestyle and an integral part of this is to eat well. Good eating habits involve a low-fat, high-fibre diet which includes plenty of fruit and vegetables and a good variety of foods. Eat Well Stay Well *shows us how to do this and makes it easy for us to make well informed choices which are healthy, interesting and tasty.*

Shân Biesman-Simons, Director of Nutrition and Education, Heart Foundation of South Africa.

Contents

Nutrition
A-Z

A **ALLYL SULPHIDES:** These PHYTOCHEMI-CALS are found in onion-family plants —onions, leeks, spring onions, chives, shallots and garlic. Allyl sulphides are sulphur compounds that seem to suppress cholesterol production and lower blood pressure; they may also have cancer-fighting properties in that they may deactivate certain hormones which promote tumour growth.

AMINO ACIDS: The building blocks of PROTEIN. Of the 21 amino acids, nine are *essential.* Your body cannot produce enough essential amino acids to meet its needs: you must get your supplies of these amino acids from food. The essential amino acids are histidine, isoleucine, leucine, lysine, methionine, phenylalanine, threonine, tryptophan and valine. Some amino acids—cysteine, tyrosine, arginine, proline and glycine—are considered 'conditionally essential' because the body can produce them only under certain circumstances.

ANTICARCINOGENS: Substances that fight cancer. Research has shown that many substances in food may be anticarcinogenic. They include VITAMIN C, VITAMIN E, BETA CAROTENE and a host of PHYTOCHEMICALS, such as ELLAGIC ACID, ISOFLAVONES and SULPHORAPHANE.

ANTIOXIDANTS: Compounds that deactivate and repair the damage caused by FREE RADICALS, thus preventing the onset of certain diseases. A number of antioxidants are found in food. For instance, VITAMINS C and E and BETA CAROTENE are known to be antioxidants. Scientists are currently researching the antioxidant capabilities of the many different plant compounds called PHYTOCHEMICALS.

ASCORBIC ACID: *see* VITAMIN C

B **BETA CAROTENE:** The most common of the 600 or more CAROTENOIDS, beta carotene gives colour to carrots, spanspek and other orange and yellow fruits and vegetables. It's found in dark-green vegetables, too, but its orange colour is obscured by the green colour of chlorophyll. Beta carotene is a vitamin A precursor; that is, the body converts available beta carotene into as much vitamin A as it requires. Beta carotene is a cancer fighter and may also help prevent cataracts, in both cases partly through its ANTIOXIDANT function. Beta carotene also seems to enhance immune function.

BETA GLUCANS: The type of soluble DIETARY FIBRE found in barley and oats. Beta glucans have been shown to lower blood cholesterol levels.

BIOTIN: One of the B vitamins, biotin is made by the human body, so deficiencies of it are virtually unknown. Biotin plays a role in the metabolism of proteins and fat. Good food sources include egg yolks, liver, mushrooms, bananas, grapefruit, watermelons and strawberries.

BORON: A trace MINERAL that works in conjunction with CALCIUM and MAGNESIUM to build strong bones. Boron is found in most fruits; peaches are a good source, as are dried fruits, mushrooms and cucumbers.

BRASSICA: The cabbage family of vegetables, which includes cabbage, broccoli, Brussels sprouts, cauliflower and mustard greens. These plants are also called CRUCIFEROUS VEGETABLES.

C **CAFFEINE:** A natural stimulant found in coffee, tea, colas and, to a lesser extent, chocolate. Caffeine increases the heart rate and enhances mental alertness. Taken in moderation, caffeine can help wake you up or keep you alert; if you're not accustomed to it, however, it can make you irritable and anxious. Caffeine promotes calcium loss and may increase the risk of osteoporosis. And there is some evidence that caffeine may increase the risk of miscarriage. Although not all experts agree, it's probably a good idea to cut down on caffeine if you are pregnant.

CALCIUM: A major dietary MINERAL that builds and restores bones and teeth and is essential in the pre-

Food	Amount	Calcium (mg)
BROCCOLI, FRESH, COOKED	150 grams (250 ml)	54
BUTTERMILK, LOW-FAT	250 millilitres	216
CHEESE, CHEDDAR	30 grams	236
CHEESE, MOZZARELLA	30 grams	155
CHEESE, PARMESAN	30 grams	413
CHEESE, RICOTTA	125 grams (125 ml)	259
MILK, LOW-FAT	250 millilitres	305
MILK, SKIM	250 millilitres	307
PILCHARDS, TINNED	150 grams (2 medium)	495
SALMON, TINNED, DRAINED, EATEN WITH BONES	100 grams	239
SARDINES, TINNED, DRAINED, EATEN WITH BONES	50 grams (2 large)	191
SESAME SEEDS, UNHULLED	20 grams	26
SPINACH, FRESH, COOKED	180 grams (250 ml)	196
WATERCRESS, RAW	80 grams (250 ml)	96
YOGHURT, LOW-FAT PLAIN	250 millilitres	373
YOGHURT, LOW-FAT SWEETENED, FRUIT	250 millilitres	363

vention of osteoporosis, the 'brittle bone disease' which can cause bone fractures in older people, especially women. Adequate calcium intake is especially important before age 35—when your body is still building bone—but also after age 35, to maintain strong bones for a lifetime. Another function of calcium is that it helps regulate muscle contractions, including heartbeat. Some research indicates that an adequate supply of calcium may help counteract high blood pressure. Many dairy foods, especially milk and yoghurt, are excellent sources of calcium; some dark-green leafy vegetables, such as broccoli, are also good sources, as are the types of tinned fish (pilchards and salmon) that are eaten bones and all.

CAPSAICIN: A PHYTOCHEMICAL found in hot peppers (chillies) and concentrated in the seeds and ribs. Aside from the 'heat' it adds to foods, capsaicin may act as an anticoagulant, preventing blood from clotting and sticking to blood-vessel walls. Researchers believe that capsaicin may protect DNA from CAR-

CINOGENS, and may help kill *Helicobacter pylori*—the bacteria now known to cause most stomach ulcers. The hotness of capsaicin can also help clear up nasal congestion (think of how a spoonful of very hot salsa seems to go right through your head) and can be useful when you have a cold. Capsaicin is potent enough to burn skin, so when you are cooking with chillies, wear rubber gloves or else be sure to wash your hands with soap and water afterwards. Never touch your eyes after handling chillies.

CARBOHYDRATES (SIMPLE OR COMPLEX): Along with PROTEIN and FAT, one of the three MACRONUTRIENTS—the major components of foods.

Carbohydrates—which are either sugars (simple carbohydrates) or starches (complex carbohydrates)—are carbon compounds that the body turns into GLUCOSE, its basic fuel. Carbohydrates are found in all foods from plant sources—fruits, vegetables, legumes and grains. Foods rich in complex carbohydrates should make up a large part of your diet: they supply energy and usually also contain other valuable nutrients, such as vitamins, minerals and fibre. Foods that contain large amounts of simple carbohydrates may supply little else of redeeming nutritional value.

Naturally sweet fruits are a notable exception: they contain valuable nutrients in addition to sugar in the form of fructose or sucrose.

CARCINOGEN: A substance that causes the growth of cancer.

CAROTENOIDS: These PHYTOCHEMICALS are the yellow, orange and red pigments found in fruits and vegetables. There are 600 or more carotenoids. The body converts some carotenoids, including BETA CAROTENE, into vitamin A. Other carotenoids include LUTEIN, LYCOPENE and ZEAXANTHIN. Scientists are researching the antioxidant and other cancer-fighting properties of foods containing carotenoids.

CHLORINE: An element that in its compound forms (chlorides) is a mineral essential to maintaining the acid balance in the body's cells. Most of our dietary needs for this mineral are met by table salt (sodium chloride).

CHOLESTEROL: A waxy, fatlike substance present in every cell in animals, including humans. Cholesterol is essential to several of the body's functions, including the manufacture of vitamin D, hormones and skin oils, so we need a certain amount of cholesterol. But when excess cholesterol circulates in the blood, it adheres to the artery walls, forming a substance called plaque that can limit blood flow and contribute to stiffening of the arteries—a condition called atherosclerosis. This can eventually lead to a heart attack or stroke.

The body produces all the cholesterol it requires, but there is also cholesterol in some foods; this dietary cholesterol does not go directly into your bloodstream. If you do consume a lot of dietary cholesterol, however, it will have the *indirect* effect of elevating your blood cholesterol level; but consumption of saturated fat actually does much more to raise blood cholesterol—especially LDL cholesterol (*see page 13*)—than does consumption of cholesterol. Only foods from animal sources (meat, poultry,

GOOD SOURCES OF BETA CAROTENE

Food	Amount	Beta Carotene (mcg)
APRICOTS, DRIED	60 grams (125 ml)	310
APRICOTS, FRESH	105 grams (3 medium)	425
BROCCOLI, RAW	70 grams (250 ml, florets)	275
BUTTERNUT, COOKED	210 grams.(250 ml, cubed)	3392
CARROTS, RAW	60 grams (1 medium)	9540
ENDIVE, RAW	120 grams (500 ml)	1788
KALE, RAW	80 grams (500 ml, chopped)	5315
MANGO	160 grams (250 ml, sliced)	624
PUMPKIN, FRESH, COOKED (BOERPAMPOEN)	210 grams (250 ml)	2646
SPANSPEK	160 grams (250 ml, diced)	1104
SPINACH, RAW	100 grams (250 ml)	2790
SWEET POTATO (WHITE FLESH)	285 grams (1 medium)	29
SWEET POTATO, RAW (YELLOW FLESH)	285 grams (1 medium)	37312
WATERCRESS, RAW	60 grams (250 ml)	2222

seafood, eggs and dairy products) contain cholesterol. There is no cholesterol in foods from plant sources—and that includes fatty foods like nuts, avocados and coconuts, as well as vegetable, seed and nut oils.

Cholesterol circulates in the bloodstream in units, called lipoproteins, which also contain fat and protein. There are two types of lipoproteins:

• *Low-density lipoprotein,* or LDL, carries cholesterol from the liver to other parts of the body. This is the cholesterol that leaves deposits on blood vessel walls. Sometimes referred to as 'bad' cholesterol.

• *High-density lipoprotein,* or HDL, performs the reverse task, carrying cholesterol from the body's tissues back to the liver—which includes removing some of the cholesterol deposits from the blood vessels. Hence, HDL is sometimes called 'good' cholesterol.

Your goal should be a low *total* blood cholesterol level (under 5 mmol per litre), but the *balance* of lipoproteins is equally important: A high level of HDL (above 1,2 mmol per litre) and a low level of LDL (below 3,0 mmol per litre) is desirable. A diet low in total fat, and, more important, low in saturated fat, will help you toward this goal. Eating plenty of fibre, especially soluble fibre, is also a good idea. An exercise programme can also help lower your blood cholesterol.

CHROMIUM: A trace MINERAL that helps the body turn GLUCOSE into energy, chromium also helps regulate the action of the hormone insulin. Some experts believe that chromium deficiency is fairly common, but it's easy to get an adequate amount of this mineral: chromium is found in green, red and yellow peppers, meat, seafood, eggs, nuts, whole grains, dairy products, sweet potatoes and potatoes (be sure to eat the skin).

COBALAMIN: *see* VITAMIN B12

COPPER: A trace MINERAL that aids in the formation of genetic matter, red blood cells, bones and connective tissue. Copper also supports the functioning of the immune system. Copper deficiencies are rare. Among the best

sources are shellfish (especially oysters), sunflower seeds, nuts, liver and cacao.

CRUCIFEROUS VEGETABLES: The word 'cruciferous', which means 'cross-shaped', describes a family of vegetables with cross-shaped flowers. Cruciferous vegetables are also called brassicas, or cabbage family vegetables. They include cabbage, broccoli, Brussels sprouts, cauliflower and kale, as well as mustard greens and turnips. These vegetables contain PHYTOCHEMICALS called INDOLES which seem to offer protection against some forms of cancer. Cruciferous vegetables are also rich in vitamin C and most are good sources of DIETARY FIBRE. Those that are dark green or yellow, such as broccoli, also contain BETA CAROTENE.

D **DIETARY FIBRE:** The parts of foods from plant sources (fruits, vegetables, legumes, grains, nuts and seeds) that we eat, but, for the most part, cannot digest. Though indigestible, fibre performs some vital functions in the body. There are two basic types of fibre: insoluble (insoluble in water) and soluble.

Insoluble fibre, which used to be known as roughage, is bulky material that helps move waste through the digestive tract. This promotes regular bowel function and may also reduce the risk of colon cancer. Some good sources of insoluble fibre are wheat bran and whole grains, the skins of apples and pears and vegetables such as potatoes, carrots and broccoli. Soluble fibre is found in oats, barley, beans and many fruits and vegetables. Some types of soluble fibre have been found to help lower blood cholesterol. Soluble fibre also helps control blood-sugar levels.

Many health experts agree that South Africans should at least double their fibre consumption, for a total of 30 to 40 grams per day. In addition to the known benefits of fibre itself, foods that are naturally high in fibre (i.e. foods from plant sources) are rich in other important nutrients.

GOOD SOURCES OF DIETARY FIBRE

Food	Amount	Dietary Fibre (g)
APPLE, WITH SKIN	220 grams (1 large)	5
ASPARAGUS, GREEN, COOKED	180 grams (250 ml)	5
BARLEY, PEARL, COOKED	130 grams (250 ml)	5
BROWN RICE, COOKED	140 grams (250 ml)	2
BUTTERNUT, COOKED	210 grams (250 ml)	4
FIGS, DRIED	80 grams (125 ml)	7
GUAVA, RAW	160 grams (1 large)	10
KIDNEY BEANS, COOKED	270 grams (250 ml)	19
LENTILS, WHOLE, COOKED	180 grams (250 ml)	13
OATMEAL, COOKED	250 grams (250 ml)	4
ORANGE, PEELED	180 grams (1 medium)	6
PEAS, COOKED	85 grams (125 ml)	6
POTATO, BAKED, WITH SKIN	125 grams (1 medium)	3
PRUNES, DRIED	100 grams (125 ml)	7
WHEAT BRAN	11 grams (60 ml)	5
WHEAT PEARL, COOKED	160 grams (250 ml)	4

E ELLAGIC ACID: Found in strawberries, raspberries, cranberries and some other fruits, nuts and vegetables, this PHYTO-CHEMICAL shows promise as a cancer preventive through its ability to inactivate CARCINOGENS and inhibit the formation of FREE RADICALS.

ENDOSPERM: The inner kernel of a whole grain, which contains most of the starch and protein.

ENRICHMENT: According to new draft legislation, enrichment means the addition of one or more nutrients to a food whether or not these are normally present in the food. The sole purpose of enrichment is to add nutritional value to the food. Typically, enriched foods are breakfast cereals, flours and bread. The added nutrients in these products are usually iron, riboflavin, thiamin, niacin and folate. Margarine and milk are usually enriched with vitamin A and vitamin D and some of these products also contain vitamin E. See also FORTIFICATION.

F FAT: One of the three MACRONUTRIENTS found in the foods we eat. Dietary fats are vital to many of the body's functions; for instance, vitamins A, D, E and K are fat-soluble and will not be absorbed by the body in the absence of sufficient dietary fat. And fats are important in cooking: they carry flavour, lock in moisture and help keep baked goods tender.

Although some dietary fat is necessary, excessive fat intake can lead to obesity and also increase the risk of heart disease, diabetes and cancer.

Fats are composed of chains of fatty acids, of which there are a number of different types. These fatty acids are classified as either saturated or unsaturated, according to the number of hydrogen atoms they contain.
- *Saturated fatty acids* carry a full complement of hydrogen atoms.
- *Monounsaturated fatty acids* are missing one pair of hydrogen atoms.
- *Polyunsaturated fatty acids* lack two or more pairs of hydrogen atoms.

Fats are classified according to the proportions of fatty acids they contain: e.g. highly saturated, highly polyun-saturated, etc. Highly saturated fats are mostly animal fats, such as those found in butter, lard, meat and poultry; palm, palm kernel and coconut oil are also highly saturated. Saturated fats are usually solid at room temperature. Highly polyun-saturated fats include corn, sunflower and sesame oils, while olive and canola oils are highly mono-unsaturated fats.

Hydrogenated fats form another category. These are vegetable oils that have been specially treated with hydrogen to make them solid at room tempera-ture and resistant to rancidity. Hydrogenation cre-ates what are called 'trans fatty acids' by saturating unsaturated fatty acids and changing their structure.

The different types of dietary fat have different effects on the body. Mono- and polyunsaturated fats have been shown to lower total cholesterol levels. Highly saturated fats raise total blood cholesterol and, in particular, LDL or 'bad' cholesterol. Trans fats have a similar, and possibly worse, effect: they raise overall cholesterol and LDL, and perhaps also lower HDL. So from a health standpoint, liquid fats (cooking oils) are a better choice than solid fats (butter, lard, shortening or margarine).

Of course, overall fat intake is important, too. Health authorities recommend that adults get no more than 30 per cent of their daily energy from fat;

some researchers call for an even lower fat intake. (Note that this recommendation applies to food intake over the course of a day or a week, and not to a single dish or meal.) But most South Africans need to to cut down on saturated fat as well: it should account for no more than one-third of your total fat intake. The most effective way to do this is to eat smaller portions of lean red meat and to eat chicken (no skin) and fish more often. The first step in cutting down on trans fats is to read labels: hydrogenated fats are often used in margarines, sweet and savoury biscuits, rusks and potato chips. Solid vegetable shortening sold for cooking and baking is also a hydrogenated fat and this type of fat is widely used to cook fast-food french fries. Some margarines, however, do not contain any trans fatty acids.

FIBRE: *see* DIETARY FIBRE

FLAVONOIDS: These PHYTOCHEMICALS are found mostly in fruits and vegetables, including cherries, apples, red grapes, onions, soya beans, carrots and broccoli, as well as rooibos tea, tea and wine. The antioxidant properties of tea are probably lost when milk is added. Flavonoids act as ANTIOXIDANTS. High flavonoid intake has been linked to reduced risk of coronary heart disease; one

COMPARING COOKING OILS

Type of Oil	% Poly-unsaturated	% Mono-unsaturated	% Saturated
CANOLA	31	62	7
CORN (OR MAIZE)	47	37	16
OLIVE	9	77	14
PEANUT	36	43	21
PALM	11	39	50
SOYA BEAN	58	22	15
SUNFLOWER	68	19	13
BUTTER (FOR COMPARISON)	2	30	68
SOFT MARGARINE (40% POLY-UNSATURATED) (FOR COMPARISON)	51	21	27

Note: Some percentages do not add up to 100% because water and other substances make up the total composition of the oil.

of the known effects of these phyto-chemicals is that they keep platelets from clumping together and blocking blood vessels. Flavonoids may also inhibit enzymes responsible for the spread of malignant cells.

FLUORIDE: This mineral contributes to the formation of bones and teeth. The Department of Health is finalizing regulations regarding the fluoridation of water in South Africa. Tinned salmon and sardines, eaten with their bones, are good sources of this mineral, as are black and green tea.

FOLATE: This B vitamin—also called folacin or folic acid—is vital to tissue growth and thus plays a role in the prevention of certain birth defects, so it is particularly important that women of childbearing age get enough of this nutrient. Folate may also help prevent cancer of the cervix. And folate is one of three B vitamins that help fight heart disease by lowering levels of HOMOCYSTEINE, an AMINO ACID that may contribute to arterial blockage. Folate is found in leafy vegetables, but also in legumes, whole grains, nuts, pork and shellfish. Because of this vitamin's importance, cereals and many other refined grain products are also enriched with folate.

FORTIFICATION: In new draft legislation for labelling, fortification means the addition of one or more nutrients to a food whether or not these are normally present in the food. The purpose of fortification is to prevent or correct a demonstrated deficiency of one or more nutrients in the population or specific population groups by the relevant authority. A good example is the fortification of table salt with iodine to prevent and correct iodine deficiency or 'goitre' in South Africa. The Department of Health is also investigating the possibility of fortifying foods to prevent and correct vitamin A and iron deficiencies in a large proportion of the South African population.

FREE RADICALS: These are unstable compounds (oxygen compounds, among others) formed in the body during normal metabolic processes. These unstable, highly reactive molecules attempt to bind with other elements, creating even more unstable molecules and setting up a chain reaction that can

GOOD SOURCES OF FOLATE

Food	Amount	Folate (mcg)
ARTICHOKE, COOKED	120 grams (1 medium)	61
ASPARAGUS, WHITE, COOKED	180 grams (250 ml)	270
AVOCADO	100 grams (half a medium)	29
BEANSPROUTS, (LENTIL), RAW	20 grams (250ml)	60
BROCCOLI, RAW	150 grams (250 ml)	74
BRUSSELS SPROUTS, COOKED	160 grams (250 ml)	22
CHICKPEAS, COOKED	170 grams (250 ml)	82
GRANADILLA, PULP	125 millilitres	113
GREEN PEAS, FRESH, COOKED	170 grams (250 ml)	75
LENTILS, COOKED	180 grams (250 ml)	326
MAIZE, BABY SWEETCORN, COOKED	60 grams (4 small spears)	180
ORANGE JUICE, FRESH	250 millilitres	75
PEANUTS, ROASTED	30 grams	38
SPINACH (SMALL LEAF), RAW	100 grams (500 ml)	194
SUGAR BEANS, COOKED	200 grams (250 ml)	280
WHEAT GERM	20 grams (60 ml)	70

damage basic genetic material (DNA) as well as other cell structures and tissues. This cellular damage, if uncorrected, can eventually result in cancer and other diseases (free radicals are suspected of playing a role in heart disease, cataracts, arthritis and neurological diseases). External factors can promote the formation of free radicals: these include exposure to heat, radiation, environmental pollutants, including cigarette smoke and drinking alcohol. The body has its own mechanisms for self-repair but certain nutrients, which function as ANTIOXIDANTS, can also aid in repairing the damage caused by free radicals.

G GENETICALLY MODIFIED ORGANISMS (GMOS) AND BIOTECHNOLOGY: A

genetically modifed organism (GMO) is any living organism which contains genes not normally found in it. This genetic material will have been transferred into the organism using genetic modification technology (biotechnology). The main purpose of food biotechnology is to increase the quality and quantity of food. The South African Department of Agriculture has given approval for the planting of two GM crops—insect-resistant cotton and insect-resistant maize. Some of the benefits are that considerably fewer insecticides will be used and a better quality food will be produced since there is less fungal infection, less insect damage and less residual insecticide. The SA Committee for Genetic Experimentation (SAGENE) has advised government, industry and the public over the last 10 years on the safety of GMOs. The GMO Act (No 15, 1997), which makes provisions for new biosafety structures, has been implemented. Imported genetically modified crops (e.g. some soya products) are included in certain manufactured foodstuffs in South Africa.

GENISTEIN: This compound belongs to the category of PHYTOCHEMICALS called ISOFLAVONES. Genistein, found in soya beans and soya products, may block the formation of new blood vessels; this in turn slows the growth of tumours. Genistein is currently being studied as a potential anti-cancer drug.

GLUCOSE: Your body turns most of the CARBOHYDRATES you eat into its basic energy source, glucose. Glucose is carried in the bloodstream for distribution to the cells when energy is required, or stored as GLYCOGEN.

GLYCOGEN: Excess GLUCOSE not utilized by the body is converted into glycogen, a form in which it can be stored in the muscles or liver.

H

HDL: *see* CHOLESTEROL

HAEME IRON: *see* IRON

HOMOCYSTEINE: An AMINO ACID that circulates in the blood. People with elevated homocysteine levels are at increased risk of arterial blockage, resulting in a heart attack or stroke. Normally, three of the B vitamins (FOLATE, VITAMIN B6 and VITAMIN B12) assist in the conversion of homocysteine into other non-damaging amino acids; however, if these vitamins are in short supply (due to dietary deficiency or a genetic problem) the homocysteine in the bloodstream will continue to pose a risk.

I

INDOLES: Nitrogen compounds found in CRUCIFEROUS VEGETABLES. Indoles seem to have the ability to convert the active form of oestrogen (which can promote the growth of breast tumours) into an inactive form. Indoles may protect against other cancers as well.

IODINE: Required for normal cell metabolism, this mineral is essential to the functioning of the thyroid gland. Most of our dietary iodine comes from iodated salt, but the mineral is also found in seafood and dairy products, among other foods.

IRON: This mineral plays a key role in the blood's distribution of oxygen to the body. A serious shortage of iron—iron-deficiency anaemia—produces fatigue and impaired immunity. Iron is found in red meat, poultry, fish, egg yolks, legumes, nuts, dried fruits, leafy greens and enriched foods such as breakfast cereals. There are two types of iron in food: haeme and nonhaeme iron.

• *Haeme iron,* found in meat and other foods from animal sources, is easily absorbed by the body.

• *Nonhaeme iron,* found in foods from plant sources, is less readily absorbed, but you can enhance absorption by consuming some vitamin C-rich foods along with the vegetarian iron sources. Some examples are beans (nonhaeme iron) with cabbage (vitamin C); prunes or raisins (nonhaeme iron) with orange juice (vitamin C); and kale (nonhaeme iron) with tomatoes (vitamin C). You can also add iron to your diet by cooking in iron pots; if the food you cook is acidic (tomatoes, for example), the food will pick up even more iron from the pot.

ISOFLAVONES: PHYTOCHEMICALS found in legumes, including soya beans. Isoflavones are phyto-oestrogens—plant substances that mimic oestrogen's action in the body. Some researchers believe that a diet rich in isoflavones may protect against 'hormone sensitive' cancers, such as those of the breast and prostate. Isoflavones also lower total cholesterol while raising HDL, the 'good' cholesterol.

ISOTHIOCYANATES: The class of PHYTOCHEMICALS, found in CRUCIFEROUS VEGETABLES which includes SULPHORAPHANE. Isothiocyanates stimulate anti-cancer enzymes.

K **KILOJOULES:** A unit used to measure the energy potential in food and the amount of energy used by the body. Technically, a kilojoule is defined as the work done by a force of one newton acting through a distance of one metre (mechanical energy). We get energy from the carbohydrates, proteins and fat in the foods we eat. Carbohydrates and protein have 17 kilojoules per gram, while fat has 38 kilojoules per gram. (One calorie is equal to 4,184 kilojoules.)

The basic rule for weight maintenance in terms of energy is that 'kilojoules out' should equal 'kilojoules in': if you consume just the amount of energy that your body needs to maintain itself and to power your daily activities, your weight will remain fairly constant. However, if you consistently consume more energy than you need, it will be stored as fat and you will gain weight.

L **LDL:** *see* CHOLESTEROL

LACTOSE: The type of sugar found in milk. Some people, called lactose-intolerant, have difficulty digesting lactose but such people can more easily digest cheese (most of the lactose is removed in processing) and cultured dairy products, such as yoghurt and buttermilk. Specially treated milk, in which the lactose is fermented through the addition of bacteria, is widely available. Good examples are yoghurt and amasi.

LEGUMES: A family of plants characterized by the seed-bearing pods that grow on them. All beans and peas, as well as lentils and peanuts, are members of this group of plants. Legumes are very healthy foods, being good sources of protein, iron, B vitamins and fibre.

LIMONENES: Compounds found in the peels of citrus fruits that may deactivate certain CARCINOGENS.

LIPOPROTEINS: *see* CHOLESTEROL

LUTEIN: A CAROTENOID found in kale, spinach, parsley, red peppers, plums and other fruits and vegetables. This PHYTOCHEMICAL may protect against age-related macular degeneration, the leading cause of blindness in the elderly.

LYCOPENE: One of the CAROTENOIDS, this PHYTOCHEMICAL is found in tomatoes and tomato products, waterblommetjies, watermelon, guavas, apricots and some other fruits and vegetables. Studies have shown that a diet that includes plenty of tomato products can be protective against prostate cancer. The lycopene is best absorbed by the body if the tomatoes are cooked, as they are in tomato sauce, paste or purée. Lycopene also seems to have

IMPORTANT MINERALS AT A GLANCE

Mineral	The roles it plays	Where to find it
CALCIUM	Builds and maintains bone strength and density; helps regulate heartbeat and muscle contraction	Dairy products, sardines and pilchards eaten with bones, dark leafy vegetables
CHLORINE	Helps maintain fluid and acid balance	Table salt
CHROMIUM	Metabolism of carbohydrates and fats	Peppers, sweet potatoes, potato skins
COPPER	Formation of red blood cells; for healthy bones, nerves, immune system	Shellfish, nuts, beans, sunflower seeds, cacao
FLUORIDE	Keeps teeth and bones strong	Fluoridated water; sardines and salmon (with bones); black or green tea
IODINE	Necessary for function of the thyroid gland, cell metabolism	Iodated salt; fish; produce grown in iodine-rich soil
IRON	Essential to formation of haemoglobin; component of enzymes and proteins	Red meat, eggs, legumes, nuts, fortified cereals; foods cooked in iron pots
MAGNESIUM	Aids in bone growth, nerve and muscle function	Whole grains, leafy vegetables, nuts, soya beans, bananas, figs, avocados
MANGANESE	Aids in reproduction and energy production; helps build bones	Nuts, whole grains, legumes, tea, spinach
MOLYBDENUM	Helps build strong bones and teeth	Whole-grain cereals, dark leafy greens
PHOSPHORUS	Helps build bones and teeth and form cell membranes and genetic material	Meat, poultry, fish, dairy products, legumes, nuts
POTASSIUM	Helps regulate muscle contraction, nerve impulses, function of heart and kidneys, fluid balance	Bananas, potatoes, avocados, dried fruits, cheese, legumes, spinach, tomatoes, dates
SELENIUM	Component of an enzyme that acts as an antioxidant; detoxifies toxic metals	Brazil nuts, fish, shellfish, red meat, grains, chicken, garlic, kidneys, liver
SODIUM	Helps regulate fluid balance and blood pressure	Table salt, salt and sodium compounds added to prepared foods, MSG
ZINC	Involved in activity of enzymes for cell division, growth and repair as well as proper functioning of immune system; maintains taste and smell acuity	Oysters, crayfish, meat, eggs, peanuts, pumpkin seeds

protective effects against other types of cancer, including tumours of the colon, cervix and bladder.

LYSINE: *see* AMINO ACIDS

MACRONUTRIENTS: The food components—PROTEIN, CARBOHYDRATES and FAT—from which we get energy.

MAGNESIUM: This mineral works with its allies, CALCIUM, MOLYBDENUM, POTASSIUM and PHOSPHORUS, to build and maintain bones and teeth; magnesium also contributes to the functioning of the nerves and muscles. Magnesium is found in whole grains, leafy vegetables, meat, fish, dairy products, nuts, seeds, legumes, avocados, figs and bananas.

MANGANESE: A trace mineral, manganese plays a role in reproduction and in the production of energy. It is also a component of ANTIOXIDANT enzymes. Good sources include whole grains, nuts, legumes and spinach.

MINERALS: Inorganic elements that originate in the soil; some minerals act as nutrients. Of the 16 nutrient minerals, seven—CALCIUM, COPPER, IODINE, IRON, MAGNESIUM, SELENIUM and ZINC—have been assigned RDAs, and five other minerals—COPPER, MANGANESE, FLUORIDE, CHROMIUM and MOLYBDENUM—have been assigned 'estimated safe and adequate dietary intakes'. The *macro-minerals,* of which we need to consume relatively large amounts, are calcium, chloride, magnesium, phosphorus, potassium, sodium and sulphur. The other minerals, which our bodies require in minute amounts, are called *trace minerals.* Minerals are required for formation of bones, teeth and nails, as well as other parts of the body. They are components of enzymes and play roles in the regulation of the nervous and digestive systems and in heart function. Unlike vitamins, minerals cannot be destroyed by overcooking food. But if you boil mineral-rich foods (such as vegetables) for a long time and then discard the cooking liquid, you will be pouring some of the minerals down the drain. To conserve the mineral content when cooking vegetables, steam, braise or microwave them whenever possible; if blanching in a large quantity of water, do it quickly— in a matter of seconds or minutes. *See also* BORON, CHLORINE, CHROMIUM, FLUORIDE, MAGNESIUM, MANGANESE, MOLYBDENUM, PHOSPHORUS, POTASSIUM and SODIUM.

MOLYBDENUM: This trace MINERAL is a component of various enzymes; it also helps strengthen bones and teeth. Molybdenum deficiency is almost unknown. Legumes, whole-grain cereals and dark leafy green vegetables are all good sources.

MONOTERPENES: PHYTOCHEMICALS that function as ANTIOXIDANTS and seem to protect against heart disease and cancer. Monoterpenes are found in citrus fruits, berries, parsley, broccoli and cabbage.

MONOUNSATURATED FAT: *see* FAT

NIACIN: One of the B vitamins (vitamin B3), niacin is important in the body's production of energy from food. It is also required for normal growth and the synthesis of DNA (genetic material). In addition, niacin helps keep the skin, nerves and digestive system healthy. The best sources of niacin are liver, peanuts and peanut butter. Lean meat, poultry and seafood are also good sources.

NUTRITIONAL INFORMATION ON LABELS: When the proposed new Regulations are legislated or printed in the Government Gazette, nutritional information will be mandatory whenever nutritional information is provided on a label. The serving size and the following nutrients must be given for labels.

EXAMPLE
Serving size 30 g

		Per 30 g serving	Per 100 g	% RDA per serving*
Energy	kJ	408	1362	–
Protein	g	2,2	7,4	4,4
Carbohydrate	g	24,3	81,0	–
Total fat	g	0,1	0,4	–
Dietary fibre**	g	0,9	3,1	3
Sodium**	mg	300	1000	10

* RDA-Recommended Dietary Allowances for labelling purposes
** SA Prudent Dietary Guidelines

Health claims, nutrient content claims and nutrient function claims will be allowed provided that they meet the conditions set out in the Regulations. The words 'health', 'healthy', 'wholesome' or 'nutritious' or words that imply that a foodstuff has health-giving properties may not be used as part of the name or description of the foodstuff. Products may not be labelled as suitable for diabetics. Statements using 'heal' or 'cure' or 'restorative' or any other medicinal or theapeutic claim are also not permitted.

O **OMEGA-3:** This term describes two types of polyunsaturated fatty acids (*see* FAT). The preeminent source of omega-3 fatty acids is seafood. Omega-3s are unique in their ability to lower levels of TRIGLYCERIDES in the blood. In addition, omega-3s function as blood thinners, lessening the likelihood of a heart attack or stroke. Omega-3s also seem to protect against certain forms of cancer and, because they have anti-

GOOD SOURCES OF OMEGA-3 FATTY ACIDS

Type of food	Fat (g)*	Omega-3 (mg)*
ANCHOVY, TINNED (DRAINED)	9,7	2070
HIGH FAT FISH, GRILLED**	11,6	2150
KIPPER, BAKED	12,4	2290
MEDIUM FAT FISH, GRILLED***	4,5	1030
MACKEREL, TINNED	11,3	2320
PILCHARDS, TINNED	5,4	1490
SALMON, FRESH, STEAMED	13,0	2340
SALMON, RED, TINNED (DRAINED)	7,3	1240
SARDINES, TINNED (DRAINED)	11,5	1480
SOLE, GRILLED	1,5	520
TROUT, RAINBOW, GRILLED	4,3	800
TUNA, TINNED IN WATER (DRAINED)	0,8	270
CRAB, FRESH, COOKED	1,8	490
CRAYFISH, BOILED	1,9	490
MUSSELS, BLACK, BOILED	4,5	830
OYSTERS, TINNED	2,5	480
OYSTERS, RAW	2,5	480
WALNUTS, DRIED	61,9	6810
SOYA BEANS, DRIED, COOKED	9,0	600
SOYA BEAN OIL	100,0	7740

* PER 100 GRAMS

** HIGH FAT FISH (11-30% FAT)—BARACUDA, BUTTERFISH, EEL, HERRING, MACKEREL, SWORDFISH

*** MEDIUM FAT FISH (3-11% FAT)—GALJOEN, HARDER, MAASBANKER, SNOEK, YELLOWTAIL, TROUT, TUNA

inflammatory powers, may be effective against rheumatoid arthritis. The best sources of omega-3 fatty acids are fatty fish, such as salmon, mackerel, anchovies, sardines and herring; many leaner fish and shellfish are also good sources. Three portions of 100 grams fatty fish per week are recommended.

OXALIC ACID (OXALATES): A natural compound found in some vegetables, including spinach, Swiss chard, beetroot leaves and rhubarb. Oxalic acid binds with calcium and iron, thus limiting the body's absorption of these minerals. Vegetarians should not depend on these vegetables for iron and calcium.

PANTOTHENIC ACID: This B vitamin helps the body convert food into energy; it also plays a role in synthesizing hormones and other body chemicals. Deficiencies of pantothenic acid are virtually unknown.

PECTIN: A type of soluble DIETARY FIBRE, pectin is found in apples, citrus fruits, berries, bananas and grapes, as well as other fruits, vegetables, legumes and nuts. (Pectin is also sold in powdered form for use in making jams and jellies.) Pectin helps reduce cholesterol and thus may help prevent heart disease. Pectin also helps regulate intestinal function.

PHOSPHORUS: This bone-building MINERAL is important for energy production and the formation of cells. Phosphorus is found in a great variety of foods, notably fish, meat, poultry, dairy products, eggs, peas, beans and nuts. Phosphorus deficiencies are rare.

PHYTOCHEMICALS: Plant-derived foods that are biological non-nutrient compounds but have biological activity in the body. Ongoing research demonstrates that some phytochemicals also boost immunity and help fight diseases, including cancer and heart disease. Phytochemicals include ALLYL SULPHIDES, BETA CAROTENE and other CAROTENOIDS, CAPSAICIN, ELLAGIC ACID, FLAVONOIDS, GENISTEIN, INDOLES, ISOTHIOCYANATES, LIMONENES, LUTEIN, LYCOPENE, RESVERATROL, SAPONINS, SINIGRIN, TRITERPENOIDS and ZEAXANTHIN.

PHYTO-OESTROGENS: These compounds, found in plants, mimic the action of the oestrogen produced by the human body. Phyto-oestrogens may protect against both cancer and heart disease. Soya beans are rich sources of phyto-oestrogens.

POLYPHENOLS: PHYTOCHEMICALS that show promise as disease-fighters in several different arenas. They act as antioxidants and, in the laboratory, have been shown to have antiviral and anticarcinogenic properties. FLAVONOIDS, ISOFLAVONES and ELLAGIC ACID are all polyphenols.

POLYUNSATURATED FAT: *see* FAT

POTASSIUM: This MINERAL is crucial to the regulation of muscle contraction and nerve impulses and thus helps regulate heart contractions. It also helps control fluid balance in the cells as well as blood pressure. Some studies have indicated that a diet rich in potassium may reduce the risk of high blood pressure and stroke. The RECOMMENDED DIETARY ALLOWANCES do not include potassium, but the estimated minimum requirements of a healthy person is 2000 mg. Potassium is found in most foods: white and sweet potatoes, bananas, avocados, dried fruit, spinach, tomatoes, cheese and dates are some particularly good sources. Legumes also supply good amounts of potassium.

PROTEIN: The basic building material of our bodies, protein consists of chains of AMINO ACIDS. Some foods provide complete protein; that is, they have a full complement of essential amino acids. Foods from animal sources—meat, poultry, seafood, eggs and dairy products—fall into this category. Among plant-derived foods, only soya beans contain complete protein; all other plant foods are deficient in one or more essential amino acids. Still, even if you are a vegetarian (or eat little meat), you needn't worry about getting complete protein as long as you eat a wide range of foods over the course of each day. For instance, the amino acids that are in short supply in grains are found in legumes, so a combination such as peanut butter on bread or bean chilli con carne with rice will help restore the balance. If you consume sufficient protein, you needn't monitor your amino acid intake; it will take care of itself. For vegetarians, eating whole grains and legumes will increase protein intake, as will eating dairy products.

PYRIDOXINE: *see* VITAMIN B6

R

RECOMMENDED DIETARY ALLOWANCES (RDAs): Established by the National Academy of Sciences, USA, the RDAs are standards that specify the amount of nutrients required daily for the maintenance of good health. That is, they set the minimum intakes of vitamins, minerals and protein needed for the average person to stay healthy. There are different RDAs for infants, children, men and women of different ages, as well as special standards for pregnant and lactating women. These RDAs are widely used in South Africa.

RECOMMENDED DIETARY ALLOWANCES FOR THE PURPOSES OF LABELLING: These RDAs are the average nutrient intake values recommended for healthy individuals 10 years and older. They are used as a uniform set of reference values for the purpose of labelling against which foodstuffs are compared. It therefore provides a basis for consumers to calculate the nutritional value of a foodstuff in relation to the recommended daily nutrient intake. These values are also used as the reference values in the rest of this book.

RESVERATROL: A PHYTOCHEMICAL found in grapes, grape juice, and wine—and also in peanuts. It may lower cholesterol and seems to protect against coronary artery disease.

RIBOFLAVIN: This B vitamin (B2), found in dairy products, lean meats, eggs, nuts, legumes, leafy green vegetables and enriched breads and cereals, plays essential roles in the production of red blood cells, energy production and growth. Studies show that older women seem to need more riboflavin than other people, and researchers believe that many elderly people do not consume enough riboflavin.

S

SALT: *see* SODIUM

SAPONINS: PHYTOCHEMICALS found in potatoes, onions, leeks, garlic and other vegetables, as well as legumes. Saponins are ANTIOXIDANTS which may reduce blood cholesterol and fight cancer.

SATURATED FAT: *see* FAT

SELENIUM: This trace MINERAL may have cancer-fighting properties: it forms a part of an enzyme, glutathione peroxidase which is an ANTIOXIDANT. Selenium also helps detoxify poisonous metals, such as mercury. Selenium is found in Brazil nuts, fish, oysters, chicken, avocados, dried beans and garlic.

SINIGRIN: A PHYTOCHEMICAL found in CRUCIFEROUS VEGETABLES that gives them their slightly bitter flavour. Brussels sprouts are especially rich in

RECOMMENDED DIETARY ALLOWANCES (RDAs) FOR THE PURPOSES OF LABELLING*

FIGURES GIVEN FOR ADULTS AND CHILDREN OVER THE AGE OF 10 YEARS.

Nutrient	Amount
PROTEIN	50 g
VITAMIN A	800 mcg* RE
VITAMIN C	60 mg◆
CALCIUM	1 200 mg
IRON	14 mg
VITAMIN D	10 mcg
VITAMIN E	10 mg TE
THIAMIN	1,4 mg
RIBOFLAVIN	1,6 mg
NIACIN	18 mg
VITAMIN B6	2 mg
FOLATE	400 mcg
VITAMIN B12	1 mcg
BIOTIN	100 mcg
PANTOTHENIC ACID	6 mg
PHOSPHORUS	800 mg
IODINE	150 mcg
MAGNESIUM	300 mg
ZINC	15 mg
DIETARY FIBRE**	30-40 g
SODIUM**	300 mg

* as proposed in new draft legislation ** SA Prudent Dietary Guidelines ◆ milligrams ★ micrograms RE = retinol equivalents TE = alpha tocopherol equivalents

sinigrin. In the laboratory, sinigrin has been shown to suppress the development of precancerous cells.

SODIUM: A MINERAL that is vital for maintaining proper fluid balance in the body. The problem for most people, however, is getting *too much* sodium. This mineral is found not only in table salt, but also (as a part of various chemical compounds) in most processed foods, particularly tinned foods, fast foods, cheese and smoked meats. Sodium occurs naturally in fresh foods as well, although usually at moderate levels. Excess sodium elevates blood pressure in many people (however, not everyone with high blood pressure is sodium-sensitive), and it can also contribute to such problems as osteoporosis.

SOLANINE: A bitter natural compound in potatoes that can rise to mildly toxic levels if the potatoes have been improperly stored (in too warm a place or exposed to light). Potatoes that have sprouted or taken on a greenish tinge have high levels of solanine; either peel the greenish skin off (solanine only goes about two millimetres deep) or discard the potatoes.

STARCH: *see* CARBOHYDRATES

STEROLS: PHYTOCHEMICALS found in monounsaturated and polyunsaturated vegetable oils, some vegetables (including cucumbers) and some shellfish. Sterols have a cholesterol-lowering effect.

SUGAR: *see* CARBOHYDRATES

SULPHORAPHANE: A PHYTOCHEMICAL found in CRUCIFEROUS VEGETABLES such as broccoli, cabbage and Brussels sprouts. Sulphoraphane stimulates the production of enzymes that rid the body of CARCINOGENS.

T THIAMIN: One of the B vitamins (B1), thiamin helps the body transform food into energy. Pork is a leading source of thiamin; fish, sunflower seeds, rice and pasta also supply good amounts of this vitamin. Some breads and breakfast cereals are enriched with thiamin.

TOCOPHEROL: *see* VITAMIN E

TRACE MINERALS: *see* MINERALS

TRANS FAT: *see* FAT

TRIGLYCERIDES: Triglycerides are fats that circulate in the bloodstream. Some come from food we eat, but the body also assembles its own triglycerides. High blood triglyceride levels usually accompany low levels of 'good' CHOLESTEROL (HDL) and are often present in people who are overweight. Blood triglycerides can often be lowered through weight loss, decreased consumption of saturated fat, refined carbohydrates and alcohol and exercise. The omega-3 fatty acids found in seafood have also been shown to help lower triglycerides.

TRITERPENOIDS: Found in citrus fruits, grains and cruciferous vegetables, these PHYTOCHEMICALS help deactivate certain hormones that promote tumour growth; they also slow down the rapid cell division that is characteristic of malignant tumours.

V VITAMINS: These nutrients, required by the body in minute amounts, are organic compounds that regulate reactions taking place in the body. They enable the body to convert food to energy and help the body to protect itself from disease and to heal itself when injured. We get most of the vitamins we need from foods (or from supplements); the body produces a few vitamins, but not in the quantities it actually requires.

The B-complex vitamins and vitamin C are water soluble; any excess of these vitamins is excreted in urine, rather than stored. So it's important to replenish your body's supply of these vitamins regularly.

Water-soluble vitamins, especially vitamin C, can be lost if foods that contain them, such as vegetables and fruits, are cooked too long, over too high heat or in too much liquid. Try steaming or microwaving and always cook these foods as quickly as possible.

The fat-soluble vitamins—A, D, E and K—are stored in the liver and in body fat, so you don't need

Vitamin	The roles it plays	Where to find it
BIOTIN	Important in the metabolism of protein, carbohydrates and fats	Egg yolks, liver, mushrooms, bananas, grapefruit, watermelon, strawberries
FOLATE (FOLACIN, FOLIC ACID)	Fights heart disease; adequate intake reduces risk of birth defects and some cancers	Leafy green vegetables, asparagus, broccoli, beans, orange juice, enriched cereals
VITAMIN A	Important for healthy eyes; also maintains health of skin, teeth, bones	As beta carotene (which the body converts to vitamin A) in yellow, orange and dark-green produce; as vitamin A in eggs, enriched milk, margarine
VITAMIN B1 (THIAMIN)	Conversion of carbohydrates into energy; brain, nerve cell and heart function	Pork, liver, fish, sunflower seeds, rice, breads and breakfast cereals
VITAMIN B2 (RIBOFLAVIN)	Conversion of food to energy; growth; red blood cell production	Dairy products, meat, poultry, fish, leafy green vegetables, nuts
NIACIN (VITAMIN B3 OR NICOTINIC ACID)	Conversion of food to energy; health of skin, nerves, digestive system	Liver, peanuts, peanut butter, lean meat poultry, fish
PANTOTHENIC ACID (VITAMIN B5)	Conversion of food to energy; production of essential body chemicals	Found in nearly all foods
VITAMIN B6 (PYRIDOXINE)	Important in chemical reactions of proteins and amino acids in the body; production of red blood cells	Poultry, beef, fish, bananas, beans, nuts, enriched cereals
VITAMIN B12 (COBALAMIN)	Essential for development of red blood cells, nervous system function	Meat, poultry, seafood, eggs, dairy products, fortified soya milk
VITAMIN C (ASCORBIC ACID)	Antioxidant; helps reduce risk of cancer, cataracts; also essential for healthy gums and teeth, wound healing; enhances iron absorption	Citrus fruit, guavas, red peppers, chillies, strawberries, kiwifruit, spanspek, broccoli, potatoes
VITAMIN D	For strong bones and teeth; also seems to reduce risk of colon cancer	Milk, dairy products, fatty fish, enriched milk and margarine
VITAMIN E	Antioxidant; helps prevent heart disease	Nuts, vegetable oil, avocados, leafy green vegetables, almonds, enriched margarine
VITAMIN K	Essential for normal blood clotting; may aid in calcium absorption	Broccoli, Brussels sprouts, cabbage, spinach, milk, eggs

to renew your supply as often. These vitamins are less likely to be lost in cooking, although high heat (as used in frying) can destroy the vitamin E in vegetable oils.

VITAMIN A: Known as a vision enhancer, vitamin A is also important for healthy skin, teeth and bones. This vitamin may have some anticarcinogenic powers, but many of the disease-fighting properties formerly attributed to it actually belong to BETA CAROTENE and the other CAROTENOIDS that are precursors of vitamin A (that is, the body converts them into vitamin A). The best sources of vitamin A, in the form of beta carotene, are dark green, orange or yellow fruits and vegetables, such as apricots, mangos, spinach, kale, carrots, pumpkin and sweet potatoes (yellow flesh or 'borrie'). Preformed vitamin A is found in egg yolk, dairy products, fish and organ meats.

VITAMIN B COMPLEX: BIOTIN, FOLATE, NIACIN, PANTOTHENIC ACID, RIBOFLAVIN, THIAMIN and VITAMINS B6 and B12 make up this group of vitamins.

VITAMIN B1: *see* THIAMIN

VITAMIN B2: *see* RIBOFLAVIN

VITAMIN B3: *see* NIACIN

VITAMIN B5: *see* PANTOTHENIC ACID

VITAMIN B6 (PYRIDOXINE): This vitamin aids in the body's utilization of protein and in the production of red blood cells. Pyridoxine works with other B vitamins to help keep levels of HOMOCYSTEINE low. Vitamin B6 plays a role in antibody production, so an adequate supply of this nutrient strengthens immunity. Many elderly people do not get as much of this vitamin as they should for optimal health. Some good sources of B6 are chicken, beef, fish, beans, bananas and enriched cereals.

VITAMIN B12 (COBALAMIN): Vitamin B12 plays a role in the formation of red blood cells and in the functioning of the nervous system. A very

GOOD SOURCES OF VITAMIN C

Food	Amount	Vitamin C (mg)
ASPARAGUS, GREEN, FRESH, COOKED	180 grams (250 ml, pieces)	38
BROCCOLI, FRESH, COOKED	150 grams (250 ml, chopped)	38
BRUSSELS SPROUTS, FRESH, COOKED	160 grams (250 ml)	46
CABBAGE, FRESH, RAW	80 grams (250 ml, shredded)	24
GREEN PEPPER, RAW	120 grams (1 medium)	92
GRAPEFRUIT JUICE, FRESH SQUEEZED	250 millilitres	95
GUAVA, RAW	160 grams (1 large)	451
HONEYDEW MELON	160 grams (250 ml, cubed)	43
MARULA, RAW	100 grams (5 medium)	194
MANGO	160 grams (250 ml, sliced)	50
ORANGE JUICE, FRESH SQUEEZED	250 millilitres	125
ORANGE	160 grams (1 medium)	95
PAWPAW	140 grams (250 ml, cubed)	122
POTATO, WHITE, BAKED, WITH SKIN	150 grams (1 large)	20
RED PEPPER, RAW	55 grams (125 ml, chopped)	105
SPANSPEK	160 grams (250 ml, cubed)	62
STRAWBERRIES, FRESH	160 grams (250 ml, sliced)	93
TOMATO, FRESH, FULLY RIPE	120 grams (1 medium)	24

important role of vitamin B12 is that it enables the body to utilize FOLATE, thus helping to keep HOMO-CYSTEINE levels down. This vitamin is plentiful in meat, poultry, fish, eggs and dairy products—that is, foods from animal sources. Strict vegetarians can get B12 from soya products, such as soya milk, which are fortified with this vitamin.

VITAMIN C (ASCORBIC ACID): This water-soluble vitamin is an important ANTIOXIDANT. It helps the body build new cells and repair damaged ones and promotes the absorption of dietary iron. Researchers are investigating vitamin C as a line of defence against many diseases, including several types of cancer, heart disease, cataracts and the common cold. The body does not produce vitamin C and does not retain stores of the vitamin for very long, so you should eat C-rich foods often. Most fruits and vegetables have some C and the following are particularly rich in this important nutrient: guavas, citrus fruits and juices, strawberries, kiwifruit, melon, cabbage, peppers, broccoli and potatoes.

VITAMIN D: A fat-soluble vitamin, D works in concert with calcium and phosphorus to build and maintain strong bones and teeth. This makes it a crucial nutrient in the prevention of osteoporosis. Vitamin D may also reduce the risk of colon cancer. When your skin is exposed to sunshine, it causes your body to produce vitamin D. You can also get vitamin D from foods, notably milk and margarine, which has vitamin D added to it. This vitamin is also found in fatty fish, such as salmon, mackerel and herring and in some enriched breakfast cereals.

VITAMIN E (TOCOPHEROL): A potent ANTIOXIDANT, vitamin E is a fat-soluble vitamin. Research indicates that vitamin E helps prevent heart disease, in part by reducing the harmful effects of LDL CHOLESTEROL and by preventing blood clots. Vitamin E is also under investigation as a treatment for osteoarthritis. Vitamin E is found in some fatty foods, including vegetable oils, avocados, nuts and seeds, but also in brown rice and dark leafy vegetables. However, it is almost impossible to get sufficient vitamin E from food to have an antioxidant effect; therefore, some health authorities recommend supplements.

VITAMIN K: This fat-soluble vitamin facilitates blood clotting; it may also play a role in calcium absorption, thus helping to prevent osteoporosis. The body makes most of the vitamin K it needs, but K is also found in dark leafy greens, broccoli, Brussels sprouts and many other fruits and vegetables.

W

WATER: Although not a nutrient, water plays a vital role in many body processes, making possible the functions of every cell and organ. Water lubricates the joints, rids the body of waste, and regulates body temperature. You need two to three litres (eight to twelve 250-millilitre glasses) of water just to replace what's lost through normal body functions. Of course, you don't need to take in all this liquid by drinking water: you also replenish fluids with other beverages, such as milk or juice, and by eating foods (such as soups and most fruits and vegetables), which have a high water content. Because fibre absorbs water, anyone who eats lots of fibre (and almost everyone should) also needs to drink plenty of fluids.

Z

ZEAXANTHIN: One of the CAROTENOIDS, zeaxanthin, like LUTEIN, may help prevent age-related macular degeneration, the leading cause of blindness in the elderly. Kale and broccoli are two good sources of zeaxanthin.

ZINC: An important MINERAL with many functions, zinc is involved in cell division, repair and growth, as well as immune function. It also keeps your senses of taste and smell working properly. A Dutch study suggests that high zinc levels are associated with a reduced risk of cancer. Zinc deficiency is rare, although it is sometimes seen in vegans (vegetarians who eat no animal products at all, including dairy products and eggs). Slight zinc deficiencies have also been noted in elderly people. Good sources of zinc include oysters, crayfish, meat, eggs and peanuts.

FOODS THAT FIGHT ILLNESS

Since ancient times, food has been used to prevent and cure disease. Recently, this concept has been seen in a whole new light, thanks to research that has shown that many substances in foods—from vitamins and minerals to fibre and phytochemicals—play roles in disease prevention. The recommendations in this chart are for foods that have proven or possible disease-fighting qualities. It is not meant as a prescription and definitely not as a list of cures for diseases. Consult your doctor or a dietician for personal advice before making dramatic changes in your diet.

Disorder	Consume plenty of
ACNE	Carrots, spanspek, dark leafy greens for vitamin A. Poultry, nuts, fish for zinc. Yoghurt for active cultures. Fruit and vegetables for vitamin C.
ANAEMIA (IRON DEFICIENCY)	Liver, meat, poultry, fish, legumes, dried fruit, dark leafy green vegetables, fortified cereals for iron. Citrus fruits, cabbage, broccoli, red peppers, strawberries, kiwifruit for vitamin C, which enhances iron absorption. Avoid drinking tea with meals.
ARTHRITIS	Sardines, pilchards, salmon, kob for omega-3 fatty acids (for rheumatoid arthritis only). Citrus fruits for vitamin C and flavonoids. Dark leafy greens, orange and yellow fruits and vegetables for beta carotene.
CANCER	Orange and yellow vegetables, tomatoes, red peppers, chillies; dark leafy green vegetables, cabbage family vegetables (broccoli, Brussels sprouts, cauliflower), garlic, onions, orange fruits (apricots and nectarines), citrus (including red grapefruit), guavas, grapes, watermelon, whole grains, legumes (especially soya), nuts, seafood, lean poultry, low-fat dairy products. These foods supply beta-carotene, lycopene, indoles, ellagic acid and other phytochemicals; folate, vitamins C and E, calcium and selenium; and omega-3 fatty acids.
CATARACTS AND OTHER EYE DISORDERS	Kale, spinach, parsley, green peas, celery, carrots, sweet potatoes, potatoes, citrus fruits, kiwifruit, bananas; wheat germ and whole grains; lean meat, poultry and fish. These supply the antioxidants lutein and beta carotene, as well as vitamins C and E, the B vitamins, zinc and selenium.
COLDS	Citrus fruits, strawberries, kiwifruit, red peppers, broccoli, and cabbage for vitamin C. Chillies for capsaicin. Onions and garlic as decongestants. Whole grains, legumes, seafood, and meat for zinc.
CONSTIPATION AND OTHER INTESTINAL ILLS	Water, whole-grain breads, oats and cereals, fruits (including prunes, figs and other dried fruits) and vegetables (especially root vegetables) for insoluble fibre.
DIABETES	Plenty of whole grains, fruits, vegetables; moderate portions of lean meat, poultry and fish—these add up to a low-fat, high-fibre diet and weight control is a prime factor in diabetes prevention. Eat regularly.

Disorder	Consume plenty of
HEART DISEASE	Fruits (including citrus, berries, apples), vegetables (including dark leafy green vegetables), legumes, wheat germ, whole grains (including oats), nuts, unsaturated oils, low-fat dairy products, tofu, seafood. These supply the antioxidant vitamins C and E, as well as soluble and insoluble fibre, calcium and omega-3 fatty acids. Garlic, ginger, onions, chillies, grapes and wine supply heart-healthy phytochemicals.
HIGH BLOOD PRESSURE	Low-fat dairy products (including vitamin D-fortified milk), dark leafy green vegetables and tofu for calcium. Fruits and vegetables (including bananas, avocados, dried apricots, potatoes and tomato sauce) for potassium. Citrus fruits, strawberries, kiwifruit and red peppers for vitamin C. Garlic, onions and celery for their phytochemicals. Fish and shellfish for omega-3 fatty acids. Follow an overall low-fat high-fibre diet for weight control.
HIGH CHOLESTEROL	Fruit (including citrus fruits, apples, guavas strawberries, raspberries, bananas, dried apricots and figs), oat bran, barley, carrots and legumes (especially soya beans) for soluable fibre. A wide variety of other fruits and vegetables for their antioxidant powers. Low-fat dairy products for calcium; milk fortified with vitamin D. Unsaturated vegetable oils (sunflower, canola and olive) (in place of—not in addition to—saturated fats). Garlic, onions and their relatives also seem to lower cholesterol. Alcohol—in moderate amounts—raises HDL, or 'good' cholesterol.
HIGH TRIGLYCERIDES	Fish and seafood for omega-3 fatty acids. Chillies for capsaicin.
OSTEOPOROSIS	Dairy products, tinned fish with bones and dark leafy green vegetables for calcium. Peaches, nectarines and cucumber for boron. Whole grains and nuts for magnesium and manganese. Fortified milk, fish and enriched cereals for vitamin D and phosphorus. Poultry, lean meat and beans for phosphorus.
STROKE	Fruits and vegetables for vitamin C and other antioxidants. Fish for omega-3s. Nuts and seeds for vitamin E. Fruit for potassium and soluble fibre. Garlic for its phytochemicals which lower blood pressure.
TOOTH DECAY AND GUM DISEASE	Dairy products, tinned salmon, sardines and pilchards (with their bones) for calcium. Citrus fruits and guavas for bio-flavonoids (phytochemicals). Cheddar cheese, cherries, apples, tea and grape juice help fight decay after you eat sugary foods. Crisp fruits and vegetables act as natural 'toothbrushes' and supply vitamin C.
URINARY TRACT INFECTION	Cranberry juice and blueberries contain substances that fight UTIs. Eat other fruits and vegetables for vitamin C. Drink plenty of water.
WEIGHT CONTROL	Complex carbohydrates and fresh fruits and vegetables for energy, vitamins, minerals and a feeling of fullness without fat. Small portions of low-fat dairy products, lean poultry, lean meat and fish for protein. Drink plenty of water.

ROASTING PEPPERS

1 ▶

It's easy to roast and peel peppers if you cut them into flat sections. Start by cutting off the top and bottom.

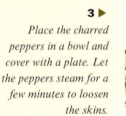

◀ 2

Cut the pepper into flat panels; remove the seeds and ribs from the inside of each piece. Place the pieces, skin-side up, on a grilling pan and grill until the skin is well charred.

3 ▶

Place the charred peppers in a bowl and cover with a plate. Let the peppers steam for a few minutes to loosen the skins.

◀ 4

After steaming, the charred skin will pull off easily. If not, scrape the pepper with a knife.

PEELING TOMATOES

◀ 1

To peel tomatoes, drop them into a big pot of boiling water; blanch for about 20 seconds or until the skin splits.

2 ▶

Lift the tomatoes out of the boiling water and let stand for a minute or so to cool; then peel off the loosened skin with your fingers.

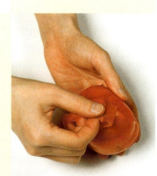

SOFTENING SUN-DRIED TOMATOES

◀ 1

Reconstitute sun-dried tomatoes by soaking them in boiling water. Let stand for 5 to 10 minutes or until softened.

2 ▶

Drain the tomatoes; save the liquid for use in the recipe or in a soup or sauce. Use scissors to cut the tomatoes into strips or cubes.

CUTTING CARROTS INTO JULIENNE

1 ▶

First cut the carrot (or baby marrow, celery, etc.) into 5-centimetre lengths.

◀ 2

Then cut the 5-centimetre pieces lengthwise into slices which are 3 millimetres thick.

3 ▶

Finally, cut the slices into julienne strips that are about 3 millimetres wide.

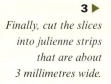

MAKING BABY MARROW RIBBONS

◀ 1

Slice baby marrow into ribbons with a vegetable peeler. To serve, steam or blanch the ribbons, then sauté briefly.

STEAMING VEGETABLES

◀ 1

Steaming is one of the most healthy ways to cook vegetables. This inexpensive collapsible steamer is widely available.

2 ▶

This is an Asian bamboo steamer. It comes with its own lid and is used over a wok. Place a shallow layer of vegetables in the bottom of the steamer; don't fill it.

CARAMELIZING ONIONS

◀ 1

Cook thinly sliced onions, covered, over medium heat, stirring often, for 10 minutes, or until very soft.

2 ▶

Uncover the pan and cook, stirring occasionally, for 10 minutes longer, or until the onions are nicely browned but still soft. Adding a pinch of sugar to the onions will speed the process.

PREPARING ASPARAGUS

1 ▶

To remove the tough end from an asparagus stalk, bend the stalk not far from the bottom. The tough part will snap off.

SHREDDING CABBAGE

◀ 1

Start by halving the head lengthwise through the core. Then cut each half in half again, lengthwise.

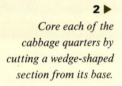

2 ▶

Core each of the cabbage quarters by cutting a wedge-shaped section from its base.

◀ 3

Cut crosswise slices from each quarter to produce strips or shreds.

CUTTING OR SNIPPING HERBS

◀ 1

It's easier to cut herbs such as dill or parsley with scissors than to chop them with a knife.

PEELING A SWEDE

1 ▶

Swedes have a thick skin and a thick coat of wax. Peel off both the wax and skin with a sturdy paring knife.

PEELING GARLIC CLOVES

◀ 1

To crack the skin, place a clove under the flat side of a knife blade (sharp edge away from you); smack blade with the heel of your hand.

STRINGING MANGETOUT

1 ▶

String mangetout peas and sugar snap peas by pinching the tips of the pods, then pulling the strings off both front and back.

PARING CITRUS FRUIT

1 ▶

When peeling citrus fruits for use in recipes, use a paring knife to remove all of the bitter white pith.

GRATING CITRUS RIND

◀ 1

Cover the face of the grater with a sheet of plastic wrap before grating the rind; cleaning up will be much easier.

JUICING CITRUS

1 ▶

You don't need an electrical appliance to squeeze citrus juice. This cheap, practical wooden reamer does the job quickly.

◀ 2

There are also juicers with a strainer top set into a bowl or cup to catch the juice. The container at the bottom is sometimes conveniently marked as a measuring cup.

CORING AND SLICING APPLES

◀ 1

A timesaver when you need apple wedges, a corer-slicer does two jobs at once. Use it on a peeled or an unpeeled apple.

PREPARING FRESH PINEAPPLE

1 ▶

Delicious fresh pineapple is worth the trouble of preparing. To start, twist off the leafy 'crown'.

◀ 2

Stand the pineapple on the work surface and use a chef's knife to slice downward through the rind. Don't cut too deeply or you'll lose a lot of the fruit.

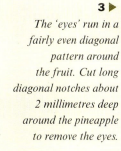

3 ▶

The 'eyes' run in a fairly even diagonal pattern around the fruit. Cut long diagonal notches about 2 millimetres deep around the pineapple to remove the eyes.

PREPARING MANGO

1 ▶

A mango has a large, flat seed in the centre. To avoid it, cut away each 'cheek' of the fruit, leaving the centre piece intact.

◀ 2

It's hard to peel mango flesh; try this method instead. Score the fruit into cubes, cutting to, but not through, the skin.

3 ▶

Push the skin side of the mango slice upward to turn the whole fruit 'inside out'.

◀ 4

Then simply slice the mango cubes off the skin. (Finally, slice the remaining strip of flesh off the pit and cube it as well.)

FREEZING BERRIES

◀ 1

Freeze berries this way to keep them from crushing. Spread the berries in a shallow pan or tray and freeze them rock-hard.

2 ▶

Then pour the frozen berries into freezer bags. In many recipes you can use them without thawing. This method works for freezing any kind of berries.

ADDING CORNFLOUR TO FRUIT SAUCE

◀ 1

For a glossy sauce, stir a mixture of cornflour and cold water into cooked fruit. Simmer, stirring gently.

2 ▶

In a few minutes the juices will be glossy and thick. Remove the sauce from the heat as soon as it thickens since overcooking can 'break' the sauce.

BAKING BREAD

1 ▶

Dissolve yeast in warm water to which a little sugar has been added. If the yeast is properly 'live' the mixture will foam.

◀ 2

To knead dough, push into it with the heel of your hand to stretch it away from you. Fold back the stretched portion, then give the dough a quarter turn. Repeat until the dough is smooth and elastic.

3 ▶

Let the dough rise, covered, in a warm, draft-free spot. When the dough is doubled in size and does not spring back when poked with your fingers, punch it down with your fist.

◀ 4

If making a conventional loaf, shape the dough into a rectangle whose width matches the tin's length, then fold in the sides and place the loaf in the tin seam-side down. Set aside to rise.

TRANSFERRING DOUGH TO PIE DISH

◀ 1

When the pie dough is rolled out to the proper size, roll the dough partway onto the pin, using a light touch.

2 ▶

Carefully place the rolling pin over the pie dish so that the edge of the dough hangs over about 2,5 centimetres. Unroll the dough, then press it gently into the plate.

TOASTING NUTS

◀ 1

Toast nuts in a dry pan over moderate heat, stirring and shaking the pan frequently, for 5 to 7 minutes.

2 ▶

When the nuts are a light golden colour and fragrant, turn them out of the pan immediately, or they will overcook from the pan's retained heat.

MAKING LOW-FAT WHIPPED 'CREAM'

1 ▶

Soften gelatine in water in a heatproof cup. Place the cup in simmering water for about 2 minutes to dissolve the gelatine; cool.

◀ 2

For maximum volume, pre-chill evaporated milk in a large mixing bowl for 30 minutes in the freezer. Then begin beating at medium speed. Beat until the milk is foamy.

3 ▶

Increase the mixer speed to high and beat until the milk holds soft peaks when the beaters are lifted (with mixer turned off). If the recipe requires it, continue beating until stiff peaks form.

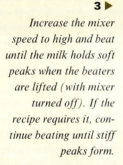

◀ 4

Fold the cooled gelatine mixture into the milk. Then chill the whipped milk in the refrigerator for 15 minutes, or until you can mound it with a spoon.

BEATING EGG WHITES

◀ 1

Have egg whites at room temperature. Use a clean, dry bowl and beaters. Starting at medium-low speed, beat until frothy.

2 ▶

Increase the mixer speed to medium and continue beating until the whites have become foamy and increased in volume.

◀ 3

Continue beating, occasionally tilting the bowl and moving the beaters around to incorporate as much air as possible. Beat until egg whites are stiff, but still look moist and glossy.

MAKING YOGHURT CHEESE IN A COFFEE FILTER

1 ▶

Drain the whey from yoghurt in a coffee filter. In 2 hours the yoghurt will be slightly thickened; in 12 hours it will be quite firm.

DEBONING SALMON FILLETS

1 ▶

Salmon fillets sometimes contain pin-bones. Pull them out with large tweezers or needle-nose pliers.

BAKING FOOD IN PACKETS

◀ 1

Place the food on one side of a sheet of foil. Fold the foil over and crimp the long edges together, leaving a little breathing room.

OPENING AN OYSTER

◀ 1

Oysters are quite tricky to open with a knife. It is quicker and easier to place them in the microwave for 10 seconds, until they open.

2 ▶

When the long side is sealed, fold over the short ends and crimp them, again leaving a little room. This seals in the moisture so that the food will steam in the oven.

DEVEINING PRAWNS

1 ▶

You can devein prawns with a paring knife or scissors, but these shelling and deveining tools, though hard to find, make it easier.

CHECKING LIVE MUSSELS

◀ 1

Check to see if mussels are still alive by rapping them on the counter. Discard any that don't snap shut.

◀ 2

To shell and devein the prawn in one stroke, slip the tool into the back of the shell and slide it toward the tail. The shell should come off in one piece.

DEBEARDING MUSSELS

1 ▶

Before cooking mussels, scrub the shells under running water with a stiff brush and pull out the hairlike 'beards'.

CRUMBING CHICKEN BREASTS

1 ▶

Rinse the chicken breasts and pat dry. Lightly beat egg whites in a shallow bowl, then dip the chicken in the egg.

◀ 2

Shake off excess egg, then dip both sides of each chicken breast in the bread crumbs. Gently shake off any excess crumbs.

ROASTING CHICKEN

1 ▶

Rinse and dry chicken. Remove and discard the pockets of fat from the cavity. Set aside the bag of giblets for use in stocks, if desired.

◀ 2

Place the chicken breast-side down on a rack. The rack lets the fat drain off. Starting the chicken breast-side down keeps the white meat moist (turn the chicken halfway through cooking time).

DEGLAZING A ROASTING PAN

◀ 1

After roasting meat or poultry, add liquid (stock, wine, etc.) to the pan and stir to scrape the brown pieces from the bottom.

2 ▶

Pour the juices into a gravy separator. (Or pour the juices into a deep, narrow bowl and place in the freezer for 15 minutes, then spoon off the congealed fat.)

◀ 3

The gravy separator lets you pour off the juices while leaving the fat behind. To make gravy, pour the pan juices into a saucepan.

4 ▶

Add a mixture of flour and water to the pan juices, then cook, stirring, over medium heat until the gravy is thickened.

1 ▶

A stir-fry requires meat which is cut into uniform strips. Start by cutting the steak in half lengthwise.

◀ 2

Then cut each half crosswise into strips about 2 millimetres thick.

GRILLING AND CARVING STEAK

1 ▶

Lean cuts like steak are best grilled on a nonstick grilling pan. (Other nonstick pans should not go under the griller.)

◀ 2

For truly tender steak, cook it only to medium-rare. Carve it across the grain, on a sharp angle to the surface.

MAKING MEDALLIONS FROM BONE-IN CHOPS

◀ 1

You can make deboned pork medallions from loin pork chops which are 1 to 2 centimetres thick. First, cut away the bone.

2 ▶

Then trim all the fat from the edges of the chop with a paring knife.

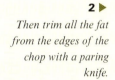

◀ 3

Using a large, sharp knife, carefully halve each pork chop horizontally to make two thin slices.

4 ▶

If the recipe calls for pork schnitzels, place the medallions between sheets of plastic wrap and pound with a meat mallet or small, heavy pan to a 2-millimetre thickness.

Vegetables

Artichokes with Lemon-Herb Yoghurt

Artichokes

Artichokes with Lemon-Herb Yoghurt

PREP: 30 MINUTES / COOK: 25 MINUTES

A whole artichoke is a pleasurably 'slow' food to eat, making it a most convivial appetizer.

- 6 large whole artichokes
- 6 cloves garlic, peeled
- 2,5 ml dried rosemary, crumbled
- 125 ml plain low-fat yoghurt
- 10 ml grated lemon rind
- 60 ml lemon juice
- 5 ml dried tarragon
- 5 ml prepared English mustard
- 0,6 ml salt

1. With a stainless-steel knife, trim the artichoke stems to about 2,5 cm. With your fingers, snap off any discoloured leaves from the bottoms. Cut off 2,5 cm from the tops of the artichokes. (For a nicer presentation, cut off about 1 cm from the tops of all the remaining outer leaves.) Peel the stems.

2. Fill a saucepan large enough to hold a steamer basket and 6 artichokes comfortably with 2,5 cm of water. Add the garlic and rosemary and bring to a boil. Add the steamer basket with the artichokes, cover and steam for 30 minutes (adding water as necessary) or until a heart is tender when pierced with a knife. Set the artichokes upside down to drain. Discard the garlic and rosemary.

3. In a small bowl, combine the yoghurt, lemon rind, lemon juice, tarragon, mustard and salt. Serve the hot steamed artichokes with the dipping sauce. Serves 6.

Per serving: Kilojoules 395; Fibre 8g; Protein 6g; Total Fat 1g; Saturated Fat 0g; Cholesterol 2mg; Sodium 233mg

Autumn Artichoke Stew

PREP: 15 MINUTES / COOK: 30 MINUTES

Artichokes have a short season so tinned artichoke hearts are a handy substitute. They are also a great timesaver.

- 10 ml olive oil
- 1 medium onion, finely chopped
- 2 cloves garlic, finely chopped
- 2 large carrots, halved lengthwise and thinly sliced
- 50 g ham, finely chopped
- 1 tin (400 g) artichoke hearts, drained
- 125 ml dry red wine
- 150 ml chicken stock
- 2,5 ml dried thyme
- 1,25 ml salt
- 60 ml chopped parsley
- 10 ml unsalted butter

1. In a large nonstick frying pan, heat the oil over moderate heat. Add the onion and garlic and sauté for 7 minutes or until the onion is soft. Add the carrots and ham and cook for 4 minutes or until the carrots are crisp-tender.

2. Stir in the artichoke hearts and the wine, bring to a boil and cook for 3 minutes or until the liquid is reduced by half.

3. Add the stock, 150 ml of water, the thyme and salt and return to a boil. Reduce to a simmer and cook, uncovered, for 12 minutes or until the

Pasta Shells & Artichoke Hearts in a Creamy Green Sauce is brightened with thin slivers of crisp red pepper.

artichoke hearts are tender. Add the chopped parsley and butter, stirring to melt the butter. Serves 4.

Per serving: Kilojoules 593; Fibre 6g; Protein 6g; Total Fat 6g; Saturated Fat 2g; Cholesterol 13mg; Sodium 611mg

Pasta Shells & Artichoke Hearts in a Creamy Green Sauce

PREP: 10 MINUTES / COOK: 20 MINUTES

This fibre-rich dinner dish features a light, clean-tasting sauce made from peas. The sauce is enriched with a touch of sour cream.

- **15ml olive oil**
- **4 cloves garlic, finely chopped**
- **1 tin (400g) artichoke hearts, drained**
- **175ml chicken stock**
- **225g medium pasta shells**
- **250ml frozen peas, thawed**
- **15ml lemon juice**
- **2,5ml dried tarragon**
- **2,5ml each salt and black pepper**
- **60ml sour cream**
- **10ml flour**
- **60ml red pepper, cut into thin slivers**

1. In a large frying pan, heat the oil over moderate heat. Add the garlic and sauté for 1 minute. Add the artichoke hearts and cook, stirring, for 1 minute or until well coated. Add the stock and 175ml of water and bring to a boil. Reduce to a simmer, cover and cook for 10 minutes.

2. Meanwhile, in a large pot of boiling water, cook the pasta according to package directions until *al dente*. Drain, reserving 60ml of the pasta cooking liquid.

3. In a food processor, combine the reserved pasta cooking liquid, the peas, lemon juice, tarragon, salt and black pepper and process until smooth. Pour the sauce into the pan with the artichokes and bring to a boil.

4. In a small bowl, whisk together the sour cream and flour. Stir the sour cream mixture into the pan and cook for 1 minute or until the sauce is slightly thickened. Pour over the hot pasta, tossing to combine. Sprinkle with the slivered red pepper. Serves 3.

Per serving: Kilojoules 2023; Fibre 14g; Protein 17g; Total Fat 12g; Saturated Fat 5g; Cholesterol 17mg; Sodium 871mg

Shopping & prep

At the market Globe artichokes are available mainly in summer, but most supermarkets stock tinned artichoke hearts.

Look for Artichokes should be a healthy green colour. Choose meaty-leaved artichokes that are heavy for their size.

Prep Pull off the loose lower leaves; trim stem to about 2,5cm. Slice about 2,5cm off the top of the artichoke.

Trimming the top of the artichoke eliminates some of the sharp, inedible leaf tips. Use a knife or, even easier, a pair of kitchen scissors.

Basic cooking Steam whole artichokes in a steamer basket over boiling water for 20 to 40 minutes or until an inner petal can easily be pulled out. To microwave, rinse but do not dry the artichokes, then wrap individually in plastic wrap and cook on high, allowing 9 to 15 minutes for 4 artichokes. Let stand for 3 minutes, then check if they are cooked as above.

Asparagus

White Asparagus
**PER 180G COOKED
(1 CUP)**

Kilojoules	247
Fibre	3,8 g
Protein	4 g
Total Fat	0,7 g
Saturated Fat	0,1 g
Cholesterol	0 mg
Sodium	trace

NUTRIENTS

**% RDA for people older
than 10 years**

Vitamin C	87 %
Folate	68 %
Vitamin E	68 %
Riboflavin	18 %
Vitamin A	12 %
Thiamin	12 %

Did you know? . . .

Throw out the water after cooking asparagus and you discard nutrients too. So try to include the cooking liquid in the dish.

If stored at room temperature, fresh asparagus will lose as much as half of its vitamin C within two days.

Creamy Asparagus & Sweet Potato Bisque

PREP: 15 MINUTES / COOK: 35 MINUTES

- 700 g asparagus, trimmed and cut into 2,5-cm lengths (trimmings reserved)
- 1 medium sweet potato (225 g), peeled and cut into 1-cm cubes
- 10 ml olive oil
- 1 onion, halved and thinly sliced
- 30 ml flour
- 250 ml chicken stock
- 2,5 ml dried marjoram
- 0,6 to 1,25 ml cayenne pepper
- 2,5 ml salt
- 175 ml low-fat (2%) milk
- 85 g cooked ham, finely diced

1. In a medium saucepan, bring 625 ml of water to a boil. Add 8 of the asparagus tips and cook for 2 minutes to blanch. Remove with a slotted spoon and set aside for garnish.

2. Add the sweet potato to the boiling water and cook for 10 minutes or until tender. Remove with a strainer or slotted spoon. Add the asparagus trimmings, reduce to a simmer, cover and cook for 10 minutes. Reserving the liquid, strain and discard the trimmings. You should have 500 ml of liquid.

3. Meanwhile, in a medium saucepan, heat the oil over moderately low heat. Add the onion and sauté for 7 minutes

or until light golden. Stir in the flour until well coated. Add the reserved cooking liquid, the stock, the remaining asparagus, the marjoram, cayenne and salt and bring to a boil. Reduce to a simmer, cover and cook for 7 minutes or until the asparagus are tender.

4. Transfer the mixture to a food processor and process to a smooth purée. Return the purée to the pot and stir in the milk, ham and sweet potato. Cook for 2 minutes or until heated through. Serve the soup garnished with the reserved asparagus tips. Serves 4.

Per serving: Kilojoules 862; Fibre 5 g; Protein 10 g; Total Fat 7 g; Saturated Fat 1 g; Cholesterol 15 mg; Sodium 989 mg

Linguine with Roasted Asparagus & Pecan Nuts

PREP: 10 MINUTES / COOK: 20 MINUTES

Toasted pecan nuts add a crunchy accent to pasta tossed with tender asparagus and a creamy lemon sauce. Roasting the asparagus intensifies its flavour.

- 900 g asparagus, trimmed and cut into 5-cm lengths
- 15 ml olive oil
- 60 ml pecan nut halves
- 225 g linguine pasta
- 2 cloves garlic, finely chopped
- 45 ml sour cream
- 70 ml chicken stock
- 2,5 ml grated lemon rind
- 2,5 ml salt
- 1,25 ml pepper

1. Preheat the oven to 230°C. Bring a large pot of water to a boil.

2. In a large glass baking dish, toss the asparagus and oil together. Bake for 15 minutes or until the asparagus are lightly browned. In a separate pan, bake the pecan nut halves for 5 minutes or until fragrant and lightly toasted. When cool enough to handle, chop the pecan nuts.

3. Meanwhile, add the pasta to the boiling water and cook according to package directions until *al dente*, adding the garlic during the final 3 minutes of cooking. Drain the pasta and transfer to a large bowl.

4. In a small bowl, combine the sour cream, stock, lemon rind, salt and pepper. Add the sour cream mixture to the pasta, tossing to coat. Add the asparagus (and any juices from the baking dish) and the pecan nuts, tossing gently to combine. Serves 4.

Per serving: Kilojoules 1 641; Fibre 8g; Protein 15g; Total Fat 14g; Saturated Fat 3g; Cholesterol 10mg; Sodium 412mg

Asparagus & Chicken Stir-Fry

PREP: 15 MINUTES / COOK: 10 MINUTES

Stir-fries can feature all sorts of flavours; soya sauce is not essential. Here, the taste of the vegetables themselves predominates, subtly underscored by the lemon rind.

- **15 ml olive oil**
- **6 spring onions, thinly sliced**
- **350 g skinless, boned chicken breasts, cut across the grain into 1-cm-wide pieces**
- **700 g asparagus, trimmed and cut into 5-cm lengths**
- **170 g frozen peas**
- **125 ml chicken stock**
- **2,5 ml grated lemon rind**
- **1,25 ml salt**
- **3 radishes, cut into thin matchsticks**
- **5 ml cornflour blended with 15 ml water**

1. In a large frying pan or wok, heat 10 ml of the oil over moderate heat. Add the spring onions and sauté for 1 minute or until they are wilted. Add the chicken and sauté for 3 minutes or until it is no longer pink.

2. Add the remaining 5 ml oil and the asparagus and sauté for 2 minutes to coat the asparagus.

3. Add the peas, stock, 125 ml water, the lemon rind and salt and bring to a boil. Reduce to a simmer and cook, uncovered, for 2 minutes or until the chicken and asparagus are just cooked through.

4. Stir in the radishes and the cornflour mixture and cook, stirring, for 1 minute or until the sauce is slightly thickened. Serves 4.

Per serving: Kilojoules 888; Fibre 8g; Protein 22g; Total Fat 7g; Saturated Fat 1g; Cholesterol 33mg; Sodium 372mg

Asparagus & Chicken Stir-Fry *teams plump asparagus with tender chicken breast, green peas and radishes.*

At the market Asparagus is available from September to May and is grown mainly in the eastern Free State. Both white and green varieties are sold, the white being more nutritious than the green. Most locally grown asparagus is exported.

Look for Whether fat or skinny, stalks should be full and round, buds tight and unwilted and trimmed ends moist.

Prep Hold each stalk with both hands, close to the base, then bend the stalk until it snaps. The stalk should break where the tough part begins.

Snap off the tough ends of asparagus stalks, discard or use to flavour stock.

Basic cooking Steam whole stalks for 3 to 5 minutes or until the thickest part is tender. To microwave 450 g asparagus, arrange stalks in shallow dish with tips towards the centre. Add 60 ml water, cover and cook on high for 5 to 7 minutes. Let stand, covered, for 5 minutes.

Beetroot

Beetroot
PER 160G COOKED (1 CUP)

Kilojoules	346
Fibre	4,5g
Protein	3g
Total Fat	trace
Saturated Fat	0g
Cholesterol	0mg
Sodium	96mg

NUTRIENTS

% RDA for people older than 10 years	
Vitamin C	8%
Folate	7%

Beetroot Leaves
PER 180G COOKED (1 CUP)

Kilojoules	261
Fibre	5,2g
Protein	4,7g

NUTRIENTS

% RDA for people older than 10 years	
Vitamin A	115%
Vitamin C	75%
Magnesium	41%
Iron	24%
Calcium	17%
Thiamin	15%

Beetroot & Watercress Salad with Walnuts
PREP: 15 MINUTES
COOK: 1 HOUR 15 MINUTES

To save time, microwave the beetroot (see 'Basic cooking') rather than roast them.

- 1 kg fresh beetroot
- 2,5 ml grated orange rind
- 125 ml orange juice
- 15 ml tomato paste
- 15 ml olive oil
- 2,5 ml Dijon mustard
- 2,5 ml salt
- 120 g watercress, large stems trimmed (about 4 cups)
- 60 ml coarsely chopped walnuts

1. Preheat the oven to 230°C. Wrap each beetroot separately in foil. Place on a baking sheet and bake for 1 hour and 15 minutes or until the beetroot are tender.

2. Unwrap the beetroot and when cool enough to handle, using a paper towel to keep your hands from getting stained, slip the beetroot out of their skins. Cut each beetroot into 8 wedges.

3. In a medium bowl, whisk together the orange rind, orange juice, tomato paste, oil, mustard and salt. Add the beetroot, watercress and walnuts, tossing well to combine. Serve at room temperature or chilled. Serves 4.

Per serving: Kilojoules 899; Fibre 7g; Protein 6g; Total Fat 9g; Saturated Fat 1g; Cholesterol 0mg; Sodium 435mg

Chunky Beetroot, Potato & Beef Soup
PREP: 30 MINUTES / COOK: 35 MINUTES

Here's a healthy, hearty version of borscht, the famous eastern European beetroot soup. You can make it ahead of time and reheat it.

- 10 ml olive oil
- 1 medium onion, chopped
- 4 cloves garlic, finely chopped
- 1 kg fresh beetroot, peeled and cut into small cubes
- 350 g potatoes, peeled and cut into small cubes
- 2 medium carrots, thinly sliced
- 60 ml red wine vinegar
- 20 ml sugar
- 5 ml salt
- 1,25 ml pepper
- 350 g trimmed beef sirloin, cut into 5-mm pieces
- 60 ml sour cream

1. In a large saucepan, heat the oil over moderate heat. Add the onion and garlic and sauté for 2 minutes or until the onion is tender.

2. Add the beetroot, potatoes, carrots, vinegar, sugar, salt, pepper and 1 litre of water. Bring to a boil, reduce to a simmer, cover and cook for 30 minutes or until the beetroot and potatoes are tender. Add the beef and cook for 3 minutes or until just cooked through. Serve topped with a spoon of sour cream. Serves 4.

Per serving: Kilojoules 1571; Fibre 8g; Protein 23g; Total Fat 11g; Saturated Fat 6g; Cholesterol 64mg; Sodium 779mg

Chunky Beetroot, Potato & Beef Soup is a welcoming dish on a chilly winter day.

At the market You'll find beetroot in shops all year round.

Look for Look for fresh, tender beetroot with their tops on. The leaves should look fresh and the beetroot should be smooth, firm and unbruised.

Prep Cut off the stems 1 cm from the beetroot (any closer and the colour will bleed as the beetroot cook). Scrub the beetroot gently but thoroughly, being careful not to nick the skin.

Don't cut the stems too close to the beetroot, or the colour will bleed.

Basic cooking Bake whole beetroot in foil at 230°C for 1 to 2 hours (time will depend on the age and size of beetroot). Simmer whole beetroot, covered, in boiling water for 40 minutes to 2 hours. Steam sliced or diced beetroot for 5 to 10 minutes. Microwave 900 g whole beetroot with 60 ml water, covered, for 10 minutes. Cook the nutritious leaves as you would spinach.

Chocolate-Spice Brownies

PREP: 10 MINUTES / COOK: 30 MINUTES

- 375 ml flour
- 7,5 ml baking powder
- 1,25 ml bicarbonate of soda
- 5 ml ground cinnamon
- 1,25 ml grated nutmeg
- 1,25 ml salt
- 125 ml plus 15 ml cocoa powder
- 5 ml vanilla essence
- 300 g cooked, sliced beetroot, drained (not bottled beetroot in vinegar)
- 125 ml low-fat cultured buttermilk
- 125 ml granulated sugar
- 125 ml packed dark brown sugar
- 45 ml vegetable oil
- 3 egg whites
- 100 g chopped walnuts or pecan nuts
- 100 g dark chocolate
- 25 g butter

1. Preheat the oven to 180°C. Spray a 20-cm square baking tin with nonstick cooking spray; set aside.

2. On a sheet of greaseproof paper, combine the flour, baking powder, bicarbonate of soda, cinnamon, nutmeg and salt. In a small bowl, whisk together 125 ml of the cocoa powder, 70 ml of warm water and the vanilla essence. In a food processor, process the beetroot and buttermilk to a smooth purée.

3. In a large bowl, beat the granulated sugar, brown sugar and oil with an electric mixter until combined. Add the egg whites one at a time, beating well after each addition. Beat in the cocoa mixture and the beetroot purée. Fold the flour mixture into the batter. Fold in the chopped nuts.

4. Spoon the batter into the prepared baking tin, smoothing the top. Bake for 30 minutes or until a cake tester inserted in the centre comes out just clean. Cool for 30 minutes in the tin on a rack, then invert onto the rack to cool completely.

5. Meanwhile, melt the chocolate and butter in a small bowl over a pot of simmering water. Spread this icing over the cooled cake, then cut into 16 squares. Makes 16 brownies.

Per brownie: Kilojoules 979; Fibre 2g; Protein 4g; Total Fat 11g; Saturated Fat 3g; Cholesterol 5mg; Sodium 105mg

Broccoli

Nutritional power

Broccoli, both raw and cooked, is a good source of vitamin C. Vitamin C enhances iron absorption, making broccoli an ideal companion for iron-rich meat, poultry or seafood.

PER 150G COOKED (1 CUP)	
Kilojoules	177
Fibre	3,9g
Protein	3g
Total Fat	0,5g
Saturated Fat	0,1g
Cholesterol	0mg
Sodium	6mg

NUTRIENTS	
% RDA for people older than 10 years	
Vitamin C	63%
Vitamin A	8%

Did you know? . . .

Broccoli is not only rich in disease-fighting vitamin C, it also contains phyto-chemicals—including beta carotene, sulphoraphane and indoles—which protect against or slow the growth of some types of cancer.

Broccoli & Barley Soup

PREP: 10 MINUTES / COOK: 45 MINUTES

If you don't have homemade stock, use low-sodium instant chicken stock powder.

15ml olive oil
1 medium onion, finely chopped
3 cloves garlic, finely chopped
2 carrots, thinly sliced
150ml barley
125ml chicken stock
1 tin (410g) tomatoes, chopped
3,5ml salt
2,5ml pepper
2,5ml dried tarragon
240g small broccoli florets

1. In a large saucepan heat the oil over moderate heat. Add the onion and garlic and sauté for 5 minutes or until softened. Add the carrots and sauté for 4 minutes.

2. Add the barley, stirring to coat. Stir in 875ml of water, the stock, tomatoes, salt, pepper and tarragon. Bring to a boil. Reduce to a simmer, cover and cook for 30 minutes or until the barley is tender.

3. Add the broccoli and cook for 5 minutes or until just tender. Serves 4.

Per serving: Kilojoules 942; Fibre 8g; Protein 6g; Total Fat 4g; Saturated Fat 1g; Cholesterol 0mg; Sodium 853mg

Prawns with Broccoli, Tomatoes & Basil

PREP: 20 MINUTES / COOK: 20 MINUTES

The variety of vegetables here gives you a hearty helping of vitamin C; the broccoli, prawns and rice supply plenty of iron.

250ml white rice
3,5ml salt
20ml olive oil
1 medium onion, thinly sliced
3 cloves garlic, finely chopped
500g small broccoli florets
300g cherry tomatoes, halved
125ml chopped fresh basil
70ml chicken stock
450g medium-sized prawns, peeled and deveined
3,5ml cornflour blended with 15ml water

1. In a medium saucepan, bring 560ml of water to a boil. Add the rice and 1,25ml of the salt, reduce to a simmer, cover and cook for 17 minutes or until the rice is tender.

2. Meanwhile, in a large nonstick frying pan, heat 5ml of the oil over moderate heat. Add the onion and garlic and sauté for 2 minutes or until the onion slices are tender.

3. Add the remaining 15ml oil to the frying pan along with the broccoli, stirring to coat. Add the tomatoes, basil,

Prawns with Broccoli, Tomatoes & Basil is perfect for a casual meal with friends.

At the market Fresh broccoli is available all year, but winter is the main season. Pre-cut fresh broccoli is a time-saver, but vegetables lose vitamin C when cut. Flash-frozen broccoli retains high levels of nutrients.

Look for Broccoli tops should be dark green to bluish- or purplish-green. The stalks should be crisp (not rubbery); the bud clusters should be compact, not opened or yellowed.

Prep Cut off broccoli florets of desired size and set aside. If stalks are tough, peel off outer skin before cutting up the stalks for cooking.

To peel, catch edge of skin between thumb and knife blade and pull upward.

Basic cooking Steam broccoli florets for 5 to 8 minutes (stalks a bit longer). To microwave 450g broccoli stalks, arrange spoke-fashion, add 60ml water, cover and cook on high for 6 to 10 minutes. Let stand for 3 minutes.

stock and the remaining salt and cook, stirring frequently, for 3 minutes or until the tomatoes begin to soften. Add the prawns and 70ml of hot water and cook for 3 minutes or until the prawns are just cooked through and the broccoli is crisp-tender.

4. Bring to a boil, add the cornflour mixture and cook, stirring, for 1 minute or until the sauce is slightly thickened. Spoon over the rice and serve hot. Serves 4.

Per serving: Kilojoules 1 600; Fibre 6g; Protein 28g; Total Fat 7g; Saturated Fat 1g; Cholesterol 171mg; Sodium 760mg

Chicken, Broccoli & Pasta Casserole

PREP: 10 MINUTES / COOK: 40 MINUTES

Here's comfort food without the fat. We've used lean, skinless chicken breast, low-fat milk and just 29 grams of Cheddar cheese per serving.

225g medium pasta shells
875ml low-fat (2%) milk
70ml flour
3,5ml salt
1,25ml cayenne pepper
500g chopped broccoli
115g grated Cheddar cheese

4 skinless, boned chicken breasts (about 140g each)
2,5ml dried rosemary, crumbled

1. Preheat the oven to 190°C. In a large pot of boiling water, cook the pasta according to package directions until *al dente*. Drain the pasta well and then transfer to a 33 x 23 x 5-cm baking dish. Steam the broccoli pieces for 5 minutes or until they are just crisp-tender.

2. In a medium saucepan, whisk the milk into the flour. Stir in 2,5ml of the salt and the cayenne. Bring to a boil over moderate heat and cook, stirring constantly, for 5 minutes or until slightly thickened. Add the broccoli and Cheddar and cook, stirring, for 1 minute or until the cheese is melted.

3. Pour the broccoli-cheese mixture over the pasta in the baking dish. Place the chicken on top and sprinkle with the rosemary and the remaining salt. Cover with foil and bake for 25 minutes or until the chicken is cooked through. Serves 4.

Per serving: Kilojoules 2 642; Fibre 7g; Protein 52g; Total Fat 18g; Saturated Fat 7g; Cholesterol 100mg; Sodium 720mg

VEGETABLES ■ 51

Italian Beef & Broccoli Sauté

A wealth of vege-tables—tomatoes, peppers, onion and garlic—rounds out this family-pleasing main dish.

Did you know? . . .

Cooked broccoli offers even more benefits than raw. Cooking the vegetable increases the indole content by freeing a crucial enzyme.

Broccoli contains dithi-olthiones, which trigger the formation of enzymes that may stop carcinogens from damaging DNA.

Broccoli is a rich source of lutein and zeaxanthin, two carotenoids. According to a Harvard University study, these substances may protect against macular degeneration, the leading cause of irreversible blindness in adults over 65. Lutein also seems to offer lung cancer protection.

There may be broccoli sprouts in your future: scientists have bred sprouts (like alfalfa sprouts) with 30 to 50 times the concentration of cancer-fighting phytochemicals found in ordinary broccoli.

Italian Beef & Broccoli Sauté

PREP: 25 MINUTES / COOK: 20 MINUTES

- 3 pickled peppadews (mild)
- 350 g trimmed beef sirloin, thinly sliced
- 30 ml balsamic vinegar
- 2 cloves garlic, finely chopped
- 10 ml olive oil
- 1 onion, thinly sliced (red, if available)
- 1 yellow or red pepper, slivered
- 500 g small broccoli florets
- 3,5 ml dried oreganum
- 300 g cherry tomatoes, halved
- 70 ml chopped fresh basil
- 2,5 ml salt

1. Finely chop one of the peppadews. In a medium bowl, combine the chopped peppadew, beef, vinegar and garlic. Let stand for 15 minutes. Meanwhile, dice the remaining peppadews.

2. In a large frying pan, heat the oil over moderate heat. Add the onion and pepper and cook for 5 minutes. Add the broccoli and oreganum, reduce the heat to moderately low, cover and cook, stirring occasionally, for 10 minutes or until the broccoli is crisp-tender.

3. Push the vegetables to one side, increase the heat to moderately high, and add the reserved peppadews and the beef and its marinade. Sauté for 2 minutes. Add the cherry tomatoes, basil and salt and sauté for 2 minutes or until heated through. Serves 4.

Per serving: Kilojoules 985; Fibre 6 g; Protein 24 g; Total Fat 8 g; Saturated Fat 3 g; Cholesterol 51 mg; Sodium 373 mg

Hearty Broccoli, Potato & Chicken Stew

PREP: 20 MINUTES / COOK: 35 MINUTES

- 15 ml olive oil
- 1 large onion, finely chopped
- 3 cloves garlic, finely chopped
- 2 carrots, cut into 2,5-cm lengths
- 350 g potatoes, peeled and cut into small pieces
- 175 ml chicken stock
- 2,5 ml dried tarragon
- 1,25 ml pepper
- 300 g broccoli
- 225 g cooked chicken, diced (leftover roast chicken is ideal)
- 250 ml frozen corn kernels

1. In a large saucepan, heat the oil over moderate heat. Add the onion and garlic and sauté for 7 minutes. Add the carrots and potatoes, stirring to coat.

2. Add the stock, tarragon, pepper and 175 ml of water. Bring to a boil, reduce to a simmer, cover and cook for 17 minutes or until the potatoes and carrots are almost tender.

3. Meanwhile, trim the tough stem ends of the broccoli. Cut the broccoli tops into small florets. Peel the stalks and slice thinly. Add the broccoli to the pan, cover and cook for 5 minutes.

4. Add the chicken and corn kernels and cook for 3 minutes or just until heated through. Serves 4.

Per serving: Kilojoules 1314; Fibre 7g; Protein 28g; Total Fat 9g; Saturated Fat 2g; Cholesterol 50mg; Sodium 345mg

---

Broccoli-Stuffed Potatoes

PREP: 10 MINUTES / COOK: 55 MINUTES

To save time, microwave the potatoes instead of baking them.

4 large (225g) potatoes
250 ml low-fat cottage cheese
60 ml sour cream
1,25 ml salt
2,5 ml dried tarragon
1,25 ml cayenne pepper
300 g chopped broccoli

1. Preheat the oven to 200°C. Pierce the potatoes with a fork and bake for 45 minutes. Leave the oven on.

2. Steam the broccoli for 5 minutes or until soft. In a medium bowl mix the cottage cheese, sour cream, salt, tarragon and cayenne until smooth. Stir in the broccoli.

3. Split each potato open and scrape out most of the flesh with a fork, leaving a 5-mm shell. Stir the potato flesh into the broccoli-cottage cheese mixture. Spoon the mixture back into the potato shells, place on a baking sheet and return to the oven for 10 minutes or until heated through. Serves 4.

Per serving: Kilojoules 770; Fibre 4g; Protein 11g; Total Fat 6g; Saturated Fat 2g; Cholesterol 16mg; Sodium 272mg

Creamy Broccoli Soup Sauté 1 small onion in 10 ml olive oil until tender. Add 300 g broccoli, 375 ml chicken stock, 1,25 ml marjoram or oreganum and a pinch of cayenne. Simmer until broccoli is tender. Purée with 250 ml low-fat (2%) milk. Heat through to serve. Serves 4. *[kJ 396; Fat 6g; Sodium 609mg]*

Broccoli Pizza In a nonstick frying pan, sauté 500 g broccoli florets and 2 cloves finely chopped garlic in 10 ml olive oil until crisp-tender. In a 230°C oven, bake a large frozen pizza until lightly crisped. Top with 250 ml ricotta, 30 ml Parmesan and the broccoli. Sprinkle with 125 ml coarsely chopped roasted red pepper and bake until heated through. Serves 6. *[kJ 1215; Fat 9g; Sodium 406mg]*

Broccoli, Roasted Pepper & Olive Salad In a bowl, combine 45 ml balsamic vinegar, 15 ml olive oil and 10 ml Dijon mustard. Steam 500 g broccoli florets until crisp-tender. Add to bowl along with 250 ml sliced roasted red peppers and 70 ml chopped green olives. Toss. Serves 4. *[kJ 461; Fat 5g; Sodium 116mg]*

Brussels sprouts

Nutritional power

When the US Department of Agriculture tested some common fruits and vegetables for their overall antioxidant power, Brussels sprouts ranked number five.

PER 160G COOKED (1 CUP)	
Kilojoules	240
Fibre	5,8 g
Protein	4 g
Total Fat	0,2 g
Saturated Fat	0 g
Cholesterol	0 mg
Sodium	14 mg

NUTRIENTS	
% RDA for people older than 10 years	
Vitamin C	77%
Biotin	15%
Iron	13%
Magnesium	10%
Vitamin B6	9%
Folate	6%

Did you know? . . .

The slightly bitter taste in Brussels sprouts comes from sinigrin, a natural compound in the plant that helps keep away insects. The substance is not toxic to humans—in fact, it shows promise in combating the early stages of colon cancer.

Warm Winter Salad

PREP: 20 MINUTES / COOK: 15 MINUTES

This substantial first course (or side dish) is a tempting change from the usual light, leafy salads.

225 g small or baby potatoes, quartered
300 g Brussels sprouts, quartered
1 medium red apple, cut into 1-cm pieces
2 stalks celery, thinly sliced
6 spring onions, thinly sliced
125 ml apple juice
70 ml distilled white vinegar
30 ml flour
15 ml Dijon mustard
15 ml prepared white horseradish, drained
5 ml olive oil
2,5 ml caraway seeds
2,5 ml salt

1. In a large pot of boiling water, cook the potatoes for 5 minutes. Add the Brussels sprouts and cook for 5 to 8 minutes or until firm-tender. Drain and place in a salad bowl along with the apple, celery and spring onions.

2. In a small saucepan, whisk together the apple juice, vinegar, flour, mustard, horseradish, oil, caraway seeds and salt. Bring to a simmer, whisking, over moderate heat. Cook for 2 minutes to develop the flavours. Pour the hot dressing over the vegetables, tossing to combine. Serve warm or at room temperature. Serves 4.

Per serving: Kilojoules 596; Fibre 5 g; Protein 4 g; Total Fat 1 g; Saturated Fat 0 g; Cholesterol 0 mg; Sodium 314 mg

Brussels Sprouts & Mushrooms à la Grecque

PREP: 20 MINUTES / COOK: 20 MINUTES

15 ml olive oil
2 medium onions, diced
900 g small button mushrooms, quartered
600 g Brussels sprouts, halved
250 ml chicken stock
2,5 ml dried oreganum
20 ml Dijon mustard
10 ml honey
2,5 ml salt
1,25 ml pepper
10 ml cornflour blended with 30 ml water
30 ml lemon juice

1. In a large nonstick frying pan, heat the oil over moderate heat. Add the onions and sauté for 6 minutes or until softened. Add the mushrooms and sauté for 4 minutes or until beginning to brown.

2. Add the Brussels sprouts, stock, 250 ml of water and the oreganum and bring to a boil. Reduce to a simmer, cover and cook for 8 minutes or until the Brussels sprouts are just tender. Stir in the mustard, honey, salt and pepper.

3. Bring to a simmer, stir in the cornflour mixture and cook, stirring, for 2 minutes or until slightly thickened. Off the heat, stir in the lemon juice. Serve warm or at room temperature. Serves 6.

Per serving: Kilojoules 563; Fibre 7 g; Protein 7 g; Total Fat 3 g; Saturated Fat 0 g; Cholesterol 0 mg; Sodium 580 mg

Sautéed Brussels Sprouts with Chicken & Hazelnuts

PREP: 25 MINUTES / COOK: 25 MINUTES

This meal has a tangy apple-wine sauce.

- 600 g Brussels sprouts, halved
- 100 g hazelnuts
- 20 ml olive oil
- 350 g skinless, boned chicken breasts, cut into 2-cm pieces
- 3,5 ml each dried thyme and tarragon
- 125 ml dry white wine
- 30 ml flour
- 250 ml apple juice
- 5 ml salt
- 2,5 ml pepper
- 30 ml sour cream

1. In a large nonstick frying pan, bring 2,5 cm of water to a boil. Add the Brussels sprouts, cover and cook for 10 minutes or until they are tender at the stem end. Drain. Meanwhile, heat the oven to 180°C and roast the hazelnuts for 10 to 15 minutes, shaking the pan once or twice. Turn onto a clean kitchen towel and rub the nuts until the skins flake off. Chop and set aside.

2. In the same frying pan, heat the oil over moderate heat. Add the chicken and sauté for 3 minutes or until the chicken is browned. Add the thyme and tarragon and cook for 1 minute or until the herbs are fragrant.

3. Add the wine to the pan and bring to a simmer, scraping up any browned bits clinging to the bottom of the pan. Boil for 2 minutes or until the liquid is reduced by half.

4. In a small bowl, whisk together the flour and apple juice. Stir the apple juice mixture into the pan along with the Brussels sprouts, hazelnuts, salt and pepper. Cook for 2 minutes or until heated through and thickened. Off the heat, stir in the sour cream. Serves 4.

Per serving: Kilojoules 1 768; Fibre 7 g; Protein 25 g; Total Fat 25 g; Saturated Fat 4 g; Cholesterol 7 mg; Sodium 649 mg

At the market Brussels sprouts are an autumn and winter vegetable, but you can occasionally find them in spring and summer too. Frozen broccoli is a good substitute for fresh broccoli.

Look for Rich green colour indicates freshness; avoid sprouts that are yellowed or wilted. Pick small, compact sprouts with undamaged leaves.

Prep Trim stems, but not too close to the base of the sprout or the leaves may fall off during cooking. (If you buy sprouts on the stalk, you'll need to cut them off before cooking.)

Slice most of the stem off each sprout, but leave on a bit as a base.

Basic cooking Steam whole Brussels sprouts for 6 to 12 minutes, depending on size. To microwave 450 g sprouts, place in a dish with 60 ml water, cover, and cook 4 to 8 minutes, depending on size. Let stand for 3 minutes.

Warm Winter Salad *Mustard and horseradish lend a bold bite to the creamy dressing.*

Cabbage

Green Cabbage
PER 80G RAW (1 CUP)

Kilojoules	109
Fibre	1,6 g
Protein	1 g
Total Fat	0,1 g
Saturated Fat	0 g
Cholesterol	0 mg
Sodium	23 mg

NUTRIENTS

% RDA for people older than 10 years	
Vitamin C	40%

Red Cabbage
PER 80G RAW (1 CUP)

Kilojoules	118
Fibre	2 g
Protein	1 g
Total Fat	0,1 g
Saturated Fat	0 g
Cholesterol	0 mg
Sodium	13 mg

NUTRIENTS

% RDA for people older than 10 years	
Vitamin C	85%

Old-Fashioned Stuffed Cabbage Rolls

PREP: 40 MINUTES / COOK: 1 HOUR

A meatless filling makes this humble homestyle favourite low in fat and high in fibre.

15 g dried mushrooms
250 ml boiling water
1 small head of green cabbage (500 g)
7,5 ml olive oil
125 ml finely chopped red pepper
2 medium carrots, grated
1 small onion, chopped
3,5 ml dried thyme
1 tin (410 g) tomatoes, chopped, with their juice
125 ml quick-cooking brown rice
2,5 ml salt
30 ml chopped parsley
70 ml grated Gruyère cheese
125 ml chicken stock
5 ml cornflour blended with 15 ml water

1. In a small heatproof bowl, combine the dried mushrooms and the boiling water and let stand for 15 minutes or until the mushrooms have softened. Reserving the soaking liquid, scoop out the dried mushrooms and chop them. Strain the soaking liquid through a coffee filter or a paper towel-lined sieve. Measure out 175 ml and discard any remainder.

2. Meanwhile, bring a large pot of water to a boil. Add the whole head of cabbage and cook for 3 minutes to soften the leaves. Peel back and cut off 4 leaves, being careful not to tear them. Repeat twice more (returning the water to a boil each time) to remove a total of 12 leaves. Chop enough of the remaining cabbage to weigh 120 grams.

3. In a large nonstick frying pan, heat the oil over moderate heat. Add the pepper and chopped cabbage and sauté for 8 minutes. Add the carrots, onion and thyme and sauté for 2 minutes.

4. Add the chopped mushrooms, the reserved soaking liquid, 250 ml of the tomatoes, the brown rice and salt. Bring to a simmer and cook for 20 minutes or until the rice is almost tender. Transfer the mixture to a bowl and stir in 15 ml of the parsley and the cheese; set aside to cool slightly.

5. Spoon 60 ml of the filling into the centre of each leaf. Fold the bottom up and the sides in, then roll up. Place the rolls in a large pan, seam-side down, and add the stock, 125 ml of water, the

Creamy Cabbage & Carrot Soup has a warming touch of ground ginger in the broth.

At the market Widely grown, cabbage is always in good supply and quite inexpensive.

Look for Choose a firm head; the outer leaves should be free of tiny worm holes. The stem should not be woody or split.

Prep Remove and discard loose outer leaves. For shredded or chopped cabbage, halve or quarter the head through the stem, then cut out the core. For quarters, do not core the cabbage. Chinese cabbage is sliced crosswise to shred it; the leaves and stalk of bok choy may be cooked together or the stalks cut off and cooked separately.

Basic cooking Steam shredded cabbage for 5 to 8 minutes, wedges 12 to 20. Microwave 450g cabbage wedges in a dish with 60ml liquid; cook, covered, for 6 to 8 minutes. Cook shredded cabbage the same way for 4 to 6 minutes.

Chinese cabbage (left) and bok choy—newer cabbages on the market.

remaining tomatoes and the remaining 15ml parsley. Bring to a simmer, cover and cook for 20 minutes or until the cabbage is tender.

6. Transfer the rolls to a serving dish. Bring the cooking liquid in the pan to a boil. Stir in the cornflour mixture and cook, stirring, for 1 minute or until slightly thickened. Pour the sauce over the rolls and serve. Serves 4.

Per serving: Kilojoules 866; Fibre 6g; Protein 7g; Total Fat 5g; Saturated Fat 2g; Cholesterol 7mg; Sodium 788mg

Creamy Cabbage & Carrot Soup

PREP: 15 MINUTES / COOK: 40 MINUTES

Make this soup with firm-textured cabbage which will not disintegrate on cooking.

- **15ml olive oil**
- **1 large onion, finely chopped**
- **4 cloves garlic, finely chopped**
- **2 medium carrots, thinly sliced**
- **640g shredded green cabbage (8 cups)**
- **675ml chicken stock**
- **10ml cumin**
- **70ml tomato paste**
- **3,5ml ground ginger**
- **1,25ml each salt and pepper**
- **60ml plain low-fat yoghurt**

1. In a large saucepan heat the oil over moderate heat. Add the onion and garlic and sauté for 7 minutes or until the onion is soft. Add the carrots and sauté for 5 minutes or until the carrots are crisp-tender.

2. Stir in the cabbage, cover and cook, stirring occasionally, for 10 minutes or until the cabbage is wilted.

3. Add the stock, 625ml of water, the cumin, tomato paste, ginger, salt and pepper. Bring to a boil, reduce to a simmer, cover and cook for 15 minutes or until the cabbage is very tender. Top each bowl of soup with 15ml yoghurt. Serves 4.

Per serving: Kilojoules 630; Fibre 5g; Protein 5g; Total Fat 5g; Saturated Fat 1g; Cholesterol 1mg; Sodium 1176mg

Chinese Cabbage

PER 80 G RAW
(1 CUP)

Kilojoules	70
Fibre	1,4 g
Protein	1 g
Total Fat	0,1 g
Saturated Fat	0 g
Cholesterol	0 mg
Sodium	10 mg

NUTRIENTS

% RDA for people older than 10 years	
Vitamin C	91 %
Biotin	5 %
Folate	4 %

Did you know? . . .

Because of its dark green leaves, bok choy is richer in beta carotene than regular green cabbage. The outer darker green leaves of an ordinary cabbage are the most nutritious part of the vegetable.

Over half of the nutrients in cabbage are lost in cooking—microwaving is by far the best method of cooking cabbage as least nutrients are lost in this process.

Colcannon

PREP: 25 MINUTES / COOK: 35 MINUTES

A traditional Irish recipe (also enjoyed in Scotland), colcannon is a simple combination of mashed potatoes and cabbage.

700 g small potatoes
70 ml low-fat (2%) milk
3,5 ml salt
3 slices (50 g) lean, rindless back
   bacon, coarsely chopped
500 ml finely chopped onions
3 cloves garlic, finely chopped
600 g green cabbage chunks
   (2,5 cm)
1,25 ml pepper

1. In a medium pot of boiling water, cook the potatoes for 25 minutes or until tender. When cool enough to handle, peel the potatoes and transfer to a medium bowl. With a potato masher or electric mixer, beat in the milk and 1,25 ml of the salt; set aside.

2. Meanwhile, in a large frying pan, cook the bacon in 60 ml of water over moderate heat for 7 minutes or until the bacon is crisp and has rendered its fat. With a slotted spoon, transfer the bacon to a plate.

3. Add the onions and garlic to the pan and cook, stirring frequently, for 10 minutes or until the onion is golden brown and very tender. Add the cabbage, pepper, the remaining salt and the bacon and cook, stirring frequently, for 15 minutes or until the cabbage is tender but not mushy.

4. Stir in the mashed potatoes and cook, stirring frequently, for 5 minutes or until the potatoes are piping hot. Serves 6.

Per serving: Kilojoules 365; Fibre 4 g; Protein 5 g; Total Fat 2 g; Saturated Fat 1 g; Cholesterol 5 mg; Sodium 437 mg

Stir-Fried Chinese Cabbage with Garlic Sauce

PREP: 15 MINUTES / COOK: 15 MINUTES

The garlic in this sauce is simmered in stock to soften its pungency. Sesame oil gives the sauce a nutlike flavour.

10 ml olive or peanut oil
10 cloves garlic, finely chopped
15 ml chopped fresh ginger
60 ml chicken stock
1 red pepper, cut into 1-cm squares
2 medium carrots, halved lengthwise
   and thinly sliced
300 g 2,5-cm strips of Chinese or
   green cabbage (4 cups)
5 ml sugar
2,5 ml salt
10 ml sesame oil

1. In a large wok, heat the oil over moderately low heat. Add the garlic and ginger and sauté for 1 minute or until slightly softened. Add the stock and 60 ml of water, cover and cook for 7 minutes or until the garlic and ginger are very soft.

2. Add the pepper and carrots and cook for 1 minute. Add the cabbage and toss with the other ingredients until well coated. Sprinkle with the sugar and salt and cook for 4 minutes (6 minutes if using green cabbage) or until the

Three-Cabbage Slaw with Creamy Honey-Mustard Dressing

Three-Cabbage Slaw with Creamy Honey-Mustard Dressing
To boost flavour and nutrition, there are carrots and spring onions in the mix as well.

Did you know? . . .
Cabbage contains iso-thiocyanates which appear to stimulate the production of cancer-fighting enzymes.

cabbage is tender. Drizzle with the sesame oil and serve hot. Serves 4.

Per serving: Kilojoules 376; Fibre 3g; Protein 1g; Total Fat 5g; Saturated Fat 1g; Cholesterol 0mg; Sodium 411mg

Warm Red Cabbage with Pears

PREP: 15 MINUTES / COOK: 10 MINUTES

- **10 ml olive oil**
- **1 small red onion, finely chopped**
- **15 ml finely chopped fresh ginger**
- **2 cloves garlic, finely chopped**
- **450 g shredded red cabbage (6 cups)**
- **2 medium pears, peeled and cut into 1-cm slices**
- **2,5 ml salt**
- **60 ml balsamic vinegar**

1. In a large nonstick frying pan, heat the oil over moderate heat. Add the onion, ginger and garlic and sauté for 5 minutes or until the onion is tender.

2. Add the cabbage, pears and salt and sauté for 5 minutes or until the cabbage is crisp-tender. Sprinkle with the vinegar, cook for 1 minute and serve hot or at room temperature. Serves 4.

Per serving: Kilojoules 543; Fibre 6g; Protein 2g; Total Fat 3g; Saturated Fat 0g; Cholesterol 0mg; Sodium 327mg

Three-Cabbage Slaw with Creamy Honey-Mustard Dressing

PREP: 20 MINUTES / CHILL: 1 HOUR

You can also make this coleslaw with one type of cabbage—an all-Chinese cabbage slaw, for example, is particularly crisp and delicate.

- **60 ml cider vinegar**
- **70 ml low-fat plain yoghurt**
- **30 ml honey**
- **30 ml Dijon mustard**
- **5 ml olive oil**
- **3,5 ml salt**
- **450 g shredded red and green cabbage**
- **180 g shredded Chinese cabbage**
- **4 medium carrots, grated**
- **4 spring onions, thinly sliced**

1. In a large bowl, whisk together the vinegar, yoghurt, honey, mustard, oil and salt.

2. Add the cabbages, carrots and spring onions, tossing to combine. Refrigerate for 1 hour or until chilled. Serves 6.

Per serving: Kilojoules 356; Fibre 4g; Protein 3g; Total Fat 2g; Saturated Fat 0g; Cholesterol 1mg; Sodium 471mg

Red cabbage provides more vitamin C than green. Crinkly Savoy, which has medium-green leaves, has a significant amount of beta carotene.

Buy a whole cabbage, rather than a head that has been halved. When cabbage is cut, it loses vitamin C.

You can avoid the lin gering, sulphurous odour of boiled cab-bage by cooking it quickly in lots of water, in an uncovered pot.

Although plain cabbage is (like most vegeta-bles) virtually fat-free, a 80g (1 cup) serving of mayonnaise-dressed deli coleslaw may con-tain as much as 11 grams of fat.

Carrots

PER 104G RAW (1 CUP)	
Kilojoules	177
Fibre	2,8g
Protein	1g
Total Fat	0,2g
Saturated Fat	0g
Cholesterol	0mg
Sodium	25mg

NUTRIENTS	
% RDA for people older than 10 years	
Vitamin A	563%
Vitamin C	7%

Did you know? . . .

As part of a cancer study in the US, scientists devised a vegetable 'cocktail' packed with disease-fighting ingredients: carrot juice was a main component.

Flavonoids, found in carrots, may inhibit enzymes responsible for the spread of malignant cells. Research indicates that they may also fight heart disease.

Chicken & Carrot Stew

PREP: 20 MINUTES / COOK: 20 MINUTES

15 ml olive oil
4 skinless, boned chicken breasts (500 g total), cut crosswise into quarters
30 ml flour
1 large onion, cut into 2,5-cm pieces
3 cloves garlic, finely chopped
450 g peeled baby carrots
150 ml chicken stock
2,5 ml dried marjoram
2,5 ml salt
1,25 ml ground ginger
1,25 ml pepper

1. In a large nonstick pan, heat the oil over moderate heat. Dredge the chicken in the flour, shaking off the excess. Sauté for 2 minutes per side or until lightly browned. With a slotted spoon, transfer the chicken to a plate.

2. Add the onion and garlic to the pan and sauté for 7 minutes or until the onion is tender. Add the carrots, tossing to coat. Add the stock, 150 ml of water, the marjoram, salt, ginger and pepper and bring to a boil. Reduce to a simmer and cook for 7 minutes or until the carrots are crisp-tender.

3. Add the chicken, cover and cook for 4 minutes or until the chicken and carrots are tender. Serves 4.

Per serving: Kilojoules 929; Fibre 4g; Protein 24g; Total Fat 4g; Saturated Fat 1g; Cholesterol 47mg; Sodium 602mg

Carrot Cake with Cottage Cheese Icing

PREP: 15 MINUTES / COOK: 45 MINUTES

One of the few vegetables suitable for use in a dessert, carrots bring sweetness, moisture and pleasing texture to this popular cake. This recipe is lower in fat than most.

250 ml flour
5 ml bicarbonate of soda
5 ml ground cinnamon
2,5 ml ground ginger
1,25 ml ground cardamom
1,25 ml salt
45 ml peanut or other vegetable oil
125 ml granulated sugar
125 ml packed light brown sugar
1 egg
2 egg whites
225 g grated carrots
60 ml sultanas
30 ml sunflower seeds
250 ml icing sugar
50 g smooth low-fat cottage cheese
50 ml soft butter
15 ml lemon juice

1. Preheat the oven to 180°C. Spray a 20-cm round cake tin with nonstick cooking spray. Line the bottom of the tin with greaseproof paper and spray it with nonstick cooking spray.

2. Sift together the flour, bicarbonate of soda, cinnamon, ginger, cardamom and salt. In a large bowl, beat the oil, granulated sugar and brown sugar with an electric mixer until light and fluffy. Beat in the whole egg, then beat in the

egg whites. Fold in the carrots, sultanas and sunflower seeds. Fold in the flour mixture until just combined.

3. Spoon the batter into the prepared tin. Bake for 30 minutes or until a cake tester inserted in the centre comes out clean. Cool in the tin on a rack for 20 minutes, then invert onto the rack to cool completely.

4. In a food processor pulse the icing sugar once to remove any lumps. Add the cottage cheese, butter and lemon juice and pulse (or beat in a bowl) until smooth. Spread over the cooled cake. Serves 8.

Per serving: Kilojoules 1 682; Fibre 2g; Protein 5g; Total Fat 13g; Saturated Fat 8g; Cholesterol 40mg; Sodium 169mg

Carrot Cake with Cottage Cheese Icing
Sunflower seeds and sultanas increase the nutritional value in this luscious cake.

Carrot-Apricot Muffins with Pecans

Prep: 22 minutes / Cook: 30 minutes

Dried apricots, brimming with beta carotene, potassium, iron and fibre, are a healthy addition to these pecan nut-flecked muffins.

- 60 ml pecan nuts
- 500 ml flour
- 8,5 ml baking powder
- 3,5 ml ground cinnamon
- 1,25 ml salt
- 125 ml unsweetened applesauce
- 60 ml granulated sugar
- 60 ml packed light brown sugar
- 45 ml vegetable oil
- 1 egg
- 1 egg white
- 200 g grated carrots
- 70 ml coarsely chopped dried apricots

1. Preheat the oven to 190° C. Lightly spray a muffin tin consisting of 12 muffin cups with nonstick cooking spray; set the muffin tin aside.

2. In a small baking tin, toast the pecan nuts for 5 minutes or until lightly fragrant. When cool enough to handle, chop coarsely.

3. In a medium bowl, combine the flour, baking powder, cinnamon and salt. In a separate bowl, combine the applesauce, granulated sugar, brown sugar, oil, whole egg and egg white. Stir in the pecan nuts, carrots and apricots.

4. Make a well in the centre of the dry ingredients and stir in the applesauce mixture until just moistened. Spoon into the prepared muffin tins and bake for 30 minutes or until a cake tester inserted in the centre of a muffin comes out clean. Makes 12 muffins.

Per muffin: Kilojoules 751; Fibre 2g; Protein 3g; Total Fat 3g; Saturated Fat 1g; Cholesterol 18mg; Sodium 66mg

At the market Carrots are always in good supply. They're sold 'topped' (minus their leaves) in plastic bags, and in bunches with leaves attached. Baby carrots (trimmed to thumb size) are sold washed and peeled.

Look for Carrot bags often have orange lines printed on them, making the carrots look brighter. Don't be fooled: try to check through a clear section of the bag. The leaves on bunched carrots should be springy and a fresh green.

Prep Peel carrots with a vegetable peeler, then slice, dice or grate as needed.

Carrot slices cut on a long diagonal are pretty and they cook quickly.

Basic cooking Steam sliced carrots (or cook them in a small amount of orange or apple juice) for 3 to 4 minutes. To microwave 450g of sliced carrots, place in a dish, add 30ml water, cover and cook on high for 4 to 6 minutes.

Pork Medallions with Roasted Carrot Purée *The carrots are roasted to concentrate their sweetness, then puréed and seasoned.*

Did you know? . . .
A US Department of Agriculture study suggests that calcium pectate, a type of soluble fibre found in carrots, has a cholesterol-lowering effect.

Raw carrots are a nutritious snack, but you should eat cooked carrots, too: cooking breaks down the vegetable's tough cell walls, releasing more beta carotene. Cooking also brings out carrots' natural sweetness.

Carrots really can be good for your eyes: beta carotene, in its antioxidant capacity, may help prevent cataracts.

If you eat lots of carrots, the palms of your hands (and the soles of your feet) may turn yellow-orange. This is harmless—just an accumulation of carotenoids—and the colour will fade with time . . . and it's no reason to cut down on your carrot intake.

Pork Medallions with Roasted Carrot Purée

PREP: 15 MINUTES / COOK: 35 MINUTES

- **450 g carrots, thinly sliced**
- **3 cloves garlic, peeled**
- **25 ml olive oil**
- **125 ml chicken stock**
- **15 ml tomato paste**
- **2,5 ml salt**
- **0,6 ml cayenne pepper**
- **450 g well-trimmed pork fillet, cut into 8 slices**
- **30 ml flour**
- **30 ml chopped fresh basil**

1. Preheat the oven to 230°C. In a metal baking tin or flat ovenproof dish, toss together the carrots, garlic and 10 ml of the olive oil. Bake, tossing the carrots occasionally, for 25 minutes or until the carrots are tender.

2. Transfer the carrots to a food processor and purée along with the stock, 125 ml of water, the tomato paste, salt and cayenne. Set aside.

3. In a large nonstick pan, heat the remaining 15 ml oil over moderately high heat. Dredge the pork in the flour, shaking off the excess. Sauté for 2 minutes per side or until browned and cooked through. Transfer to a plate.

4. Wipe out the pan, add the carrot purée and bring to a boil. Spoon onto 4 plates, top with the pork and sprinkle with the basil. Serves 4.

Per serving: Kilojoules 1 114; Fibre 4 g; Protein 18 g; Total Fat 11 g; Saturated Fat 3 g; Cholesterol 48 mg; Sodium 560 mg

Moroccan-Style Carrot Salad

PREP: 25 MINUTES / COOK: 5 MINUTES
MARINATE: 1 HOUR

- **450 g carrots, sliced diagonally**
- **1 red pepper, diced**
- **125 ml fresh orange juice**
- **45 ml lemon juice**
- **15 ml honey**
- **10 ml vegetable oil**
- **5 ml ground cumin**
- **5 ml ground coriander**
- **2,5 ml salt**
- **1,25 ml ground ginger**
- **70 ml chopped fresh coriander**
- **70 ml chopped dates**
- **60 ml pitted, chopped black olives**

1. In a steamer or colander set over a pot of boiling water, steam the carrots for 5 minutes. Add the pepper and steam for 1 minute or until the carrots and pepper are crisp-tender.

2. In a serving bowl, whisk together the orange juice, lemon juice, honey, oil, cumin, coriander, salt and ginger. Stir in the fresh coriander, dates and olives.

3. Add the carrots and pepper to the dressing, tossing to coat. Let stand at room temperature for at least 1 hour before serving. Serves 4.

Per serving: Kilojoules 638; Fibre 5g; Protein 2g; Total Fat 4g; Saturated Fat 1g; Cholesterol 0mg; Sodium 418mg

Vegetable Antipasto

PREP: 20 MINUTES / COOK: 15 MINUTES
MARINATE: 4 HOURS

250 ml vegetable or chicken stock
125 ml dry white wine
2,5 ml dried oreganum
0,6 ml crushed red chilli flakes
450 g carrots, diagonally sliced
200 g cauliflower florets
115 g green beans, halved crosswise
125 ml pickled pepperoncini peppers
60 ml white wine vinegar
5 ml olive oil
2,5 ml salt
125 ml cubed (2 cm) mozzarella cheese
125 ml chopped fresh basil

1. In a large frying pan, bring the stock, wine, oreganum and red chilli flakes to a simmer. Add the carrots, cover and cook for 6 minutes. Add the cauliflower and beans, return to a simmer and cook for 8 minutes.

2. Transfer the vegetables and liquid to a medium bowl, stir in the pepperoncini, vinegar, oil and salt. Cover and refrigerate for at least 4 hours or overnight. Just before serving, stir in the mozzarella and basil. Serves 4.

Per serving: Kilojoules 689; Fibre 6g; Protein 7g; Total Fat 7g; Saturated Fat 3g; Cholesterol 14mg; Sodium 794mg

Carrot Slaw In a bowl, combine 60 ml light mayonnaise, 30 ml white vinegar, 5 ml Dijon mustard and 1,25 ml pepper. Add 70 ml sultanas and 450 g carrots, grated; toss to combine. Serves 4. *[kJ 435; Fat 2g; Sodium 198mg]*

Orange-Glazed Carrots Steam 450 g very small, peeled carrots (or pre-peeled baby carrots), until crisp-tender. In a large pan, heat 60 ml orange juice, 30 ml orange marmalade (or apricot jam), 10 ml unsalted butter and 2,5 ml salt. Add the carrots and cook over moderate heat until nicely glazed. Serves 4. *[kJ 394; Fat 2g; Sodium 385mg]*

Creamy Carrot & Mint Soup In a saucepan, combine 300 g thinly sliced carrots, 15 ml rice, 250 ml chicken stock, 250 ml water, 5 ml sugar, 2,5 ml salt and 1,25 ml cayenne pepper. Simmer, covered, for 17 minutes or until the rice is tender. Purée in a food processor along with 250 ml low-fat (2%) milk. Reheat and stir in 70 ml chopped fresh mint. Serves 4. *[kJ 340; Fat 2g; Sodium 732mg]*

Cauliflower

Nutritional power

A good source of vitamin C, cauliflower shares the health benefit of all brassica (cabbage family) vegetables: cancer-fighting phytochemicals.

PER 160G COOKED (1 CUP)	
Kilojoules	150
Fibre	2,9g
Protein	2g
Total Fat	0,2g
Saturated Fat	0g
Cholesterol	0mg
Sodium	10mg

NUTRIENTS	
% RDA for people older than 10 years	
Vitamin C	101%
Pantothenic acid	14%
Biotin	12%

Did you know? . . .

A 100-gram serving of fresh cauliflower contains more vitamin C than the recommended daily intake and only 133 kilojoules.

Cauliflower quickly loses its folacin to the cooking water when boiled. When possible, steam, braise or roast it.

Cauliflower-Onion Relish with Carrots & Peppers

PREP: 15 MINUTES / COOK: 15 MINUTES

A zesty side dish for a braai, this colourful relish is great with grilled chicken breasts or chicken burgers.

250 ml distilled white vinegar
125 ml sugar
30 ml mustard seeds
7 ml turmeric
2,5 ml salt
1 head of cauliflower, cut into florets
2 medium carrots, thinly sliced
1 medium onion (preferably red), chopped
1 red pepper, diced
30 ml prepared English mustard

1. In a large saucepan, bring the vinegar, sugar, mustard seeds, turmeric and salt to a boil over moderate heat.

2. Add the cauliflower, carrots, onion and pepper and return to a boil. Reduce to a simmer, cover and cook for 12 minutes or until the cauliflower is tender. Cool to room temperature, stir in the mustard. Serve warm, at room temperature or chilled. Serves 4.

Per serving: Kilojoules 694; Fibre 4g; Protein 3g; Total Fat 1g; Saturated Fat 0g; Cholesterol 0mg; Sodium 252mg

Roasted Cauliflower with Tomatoes & Garlic

PREP: 10 MINUTES / COOK: 45 MINUTES

Roasting the vegetables intensifies their flavour and helps preserve B vitamins. Squeeze the garlic out of its skin and spread on toasted bread as an accompaniment.

30 ml olive oil
8 cloves garlic, unpeeled
2,5 ml dried rosemary, crumbled
1 medium head of cauliflower, cut into florets
375 ml chopped plum tomatoes (about 4)
2,5 ml salt

1. Preheat the oven to 220°C. In a 33 x 23-cm glass baking dish, combine the oil, garlic and rosemary. Place in the oven and when the oil is hot but not smoking, add the cauliflower. Roast, turning the cauliflower occasionally, for 20 minutes or until lightly browned.

2. Add the tomatoes and salt, tossing well. Roast for 20 minutes or until the tomatoes are piping hot and the cauliflower is tender. Serves 4.

Per serving: Kilojoules 440; Fibre 3g; Protein 4g; Total Fat 8g; Saturated Fat 1g; Cholesterol 0mg; Sodium 311mg

Cauliflower-Onion Relish with Carrots & Peppers dresses up simple meals.

At the market Cauliflower is available all year round.

Look for The florets should be cream or pure white, free of brown or soft spots. The leaves should be crisp and green.

Did you know?... Cauliflower contains sulphur which can cause an unpleasant smell when cooking. Boil quickly with the lid off the pot.

Prep Pull off the leaves and cut off the stem, then cut around the core to free the branched florets. Cut the florets apart, if you wish.

Use a small, sharp knife to cut the cauliflower florets from the stem.

Basic cooking Steam cauliflower florets for 3 to 5 minutes; a whole head, cored, for 15 to 20 minutes. Microwave 450 g cauliflower florets with 60 ml water; cover and cook on high for 4 to 7 minutes; let stand for 3 minutes.

Cauliflower with Devilled Cheese Sauce

PREP: 10 MINUTES / COOK: 10 MINUTES

As homely and rich as old-fashioned macaroni and cheese, this comforting dish has the added benefits of the fibre and phytochemicals from the cauliflower.

375 ml low-fat (2%) milk

45 ml flour

115 g grated medium to sharp Cheddar cheese

30 ml grated Parmesan cheese

2,5 ml Dijon mustard

1,25 ml cayenne pepper

1,25 ml salt

1 medium head of cauliflower, cut into florets

60 ml chopped fresh chives or spring onions

1. In a medium saucepan, whisk the milk into the flour. Bring to a boil over moderate heat, reduce to a simmer and cook, stirring constantly, for 5 minutes or until the sauce is slightly thickened. Remove from the heat. Whisk in the Cheddar cheese, Parmesan cheese, mustard, cayenne pepper and salt, whisking the sauce until smooth.

2. Meanwhile, in a steamer or colander set over a pot of boiling water, steam the cauliflower for 5 minutes or until crisp-tender. Transfer the hot cauliflower to the pan of sauce, stirring to coat. Serve the cauliflower sprinkled with the chives. Serves 4.

Per serving: Kilojoules 902; Fibre 1 g; Protein 13 g; Total Fat 12 g; Saturated Fat 6 g; Cholesterol 42 mg; Sodium 391 mg

Chillies

PER 55G RAW (¼ CUP)	
Kilojoules	133
Fibre	3,1g
Protein	1g
Total Fat	0,2g
Saturated Fat	0g
Cholesterol	0mg
Sodium	1mg

NUTRIENTS

% RDA for people older than 10 years	
Vitamin C	73%

Did you know? . . .

Red chillies contain more than five times the beta carotene of green chillies.

Chillies are a leading source of vitamin C and an excellent source of chromium.

Capsaicin is concentrated in the seeds and ribs; to cool the heat, remove them.

Capsaicin acts as an anticoagulant, thus may help prevent heart attacks.

Thai Chicken Curry

PREP: 20 MINUTES / COOK: 10 MINUTES

Unlike Indian curries, which are primarily seasoned with dried ground spices, Thai curries are flavoured with fresh herbs, fresh chillies and coconut milk.

- 1 tin (250 ml) coconut milk
- 8 spring onions, thinly sliced
- 3 cloves garlic, crushed and peeled
- 45 ml lime or lemon juice
- 30 ml light soya sauce
- 2 fresh large green chilli peppers or red chillies, stemmed
- 15 ml chopped fresh ginger
- 2,5 ml each ground coriander and cumin
- 10 ml olive oil
- 350 g skinless, boned chicken breasts, cut across the grain into 5-mm-wide strips
- 225 g green beans, cut into 2,5-cm lengths
- 3 plum tomatoes, coarsely chopped

1. In a food processor or blender, combine the coconut milk, spring onions, garlic, lime juice, soya sauce, chilli peppers, ginger, coriander, cumin and 250 ml of water and process until smooth; set aside.

2. In a large pan, heat the oil over moderate heat. Add the chicken and green beans and sauté for 3 minutes or until the chicken is lightly browned.

3. Add the tomatoes and spring onion purée to the pan and bring to a boil. Reduce to a simmer, cover and cook for 4 minutes or until the beans are crisp-tender and the chicken is cooked through. Serves 4.

Per serving: Kilojoules 1 192; Fibre 2g; Protein 19g; Total Fat 17g; Saturated Fat 14g; Cholesterol 33mg; Sodium 469mg

Green Chilli Salsa

PREP: 15 MINUTES / COOK: 10 MINUTES

Spoon this snappy sauce over vegetables, use it to top chicken or fish (kingklip is particularly good) or serve with chips.

- 1 medium green pepper, cut lengthwise into flat panels
- 8 large green chilli peppers, seeded and finely chopped
- 125 ml chopped fresh coriander
- 30 ml lime or lemon juice
- 15 ml olive oil
- 2,5 ml each dried oreganum and ground cumin
- 1,25 ml salt

1. Preheat the grill. Place the pepper pieces, skin-side up, on the grill rack and grill 10 centimetres from the heat for 12 minutes or until the skin is blackened. When the peppers are cool enough to handle, peel and dice them.

2. Transfer the peppers to a medium bowl. Add the chilli peppers, fresh coriander, lime juice and oil. Stir in the oreganum, cumin and salt. Makes 500 millilitres.

Per 125ml: Kilojoules 173; Fibre 3g; Protein 1g; Total Fat 4g; Saturated Fat 1g; Cholesterol 0mg; Sodium 152mg

Pepper and Tomato Soup with Chillies

PREP: 10 MINUTES / COOK: 50 MINUTES

- 1 large red pepper, cut into flat panels
- 6 medium tomatoes, cored and halved
- 4 large chillies, halved lengthwise, seeds removed
- 30 ml olive oil
- 2,5 ml crushed coarse sea salt
- 1 large onion, halved and thinly sliced
- 2 cloves garlic, finely chopped
- 500 ml chicken stock
- 500 g sweet potatoes, peeled and cut into small cubes
- 250 ml frozen or fresh corn kernels
- 60 ml coriander leaves, chopped

1. Preheat the oven to 200°C. Place the peppers, tomatoes and chillies in a roasting pan. Brush with 15 ml olive oil and sprinkle with salt. Roast for 30 minutes or until soft and slightly charred. Transfer to a food processor. Add 250 ml boiling water to the pan juices, stir to mix and pour into the food processor. Blend to a chunky consistency.

2. In a saucepan, heat 15 ml oil. Add the onions and garlic and sauté for 2 minutes or until tender. Add the pepper and tomato mixture, sweet potatoes and chicken stock and bring to a boil. Reduce to a simmer, cover and cook for 20 minutes or until the sweet potatoes are tender. Stir in the corn kernels and coriander and cook for 3 minutes or until the corn is heated through. Serves 4.

Per serving: Kilojoules 1 066; Fibre 5 g; Protein 4 g; Total Fat 9 g; Saturated Fat 1 g; Cholesterol 0 mg; Sodium 1 086 mg

Pepper and Tomato Soup with Chillies *contains a rainbow assortment of ingredients.*

At the market Small red and green chillies are freely available, but few supermarkets sell fresh jalapeños—although pickled jalapeños (which contain almost no vitamin C) are sometimes available. Large fairly mild chilli peppers, also called Zambian or Malawian peppers, are also sold.

Look for Fresh chillies should be glossy, colourful, plump and unwrinkled.

Prep The capsaicin in chillies can burn your skin and eyes; wear rubber gloves when handling chillies or wash your hands well with soap and water afterwards. Halve chillies lengthwise and scrape out seeds and ribs with a paring knife; leave some ribs for more heat. A jalapeño can be as mild as a sweet pepper or fiery hot, so before you cook, taste a sliver of the chilli. Add a pinch of chilli flakes to the dish if the chilli is too mild.

Rubber gloves protect you from the burning capsaicin as you scrape out the seeds.

67

Fennel

Nutritional power

Along with its unique flavour, this favourite Italian vegetable offers fibre, vitamin C and potassium, as well as respectable amounts of folate and calcium.

PER 174G RAW (1 CUP)	
Kilojoules	226
Fibre	5,4 g
Protein	2 g
Total Fat	0,3 g
Saturated Fat	0 g
Cholesterol	0 mg
Sodium	90 mg

NUTRIENTS	
% RDA for people older than 10 years	
Vitamin C	34 %
Folate	12 %

Did you know? . . .

Recipes that call for fennel sometimes suggest celery as an alternative, but the nutritional difference is significant. Although they're similar in texture, fennel has considerably more fibre. Fennel also provides more calcium, potassium and vitamin C than celery. And of course, there's that wonderful liquorice-like flavour.

Pork & Fennel Sauté

PREP: 15 MINUTES / COOK: 25 MINUTES

A dish where the vegetables outweigh the meat is likely to be a healthy one. With fennel, onion, garlic and apple, this is a sure winner.

4 bulbs fennel (total 625 g)
450 g well-trimmed pork fillet,
    cut into 8 slices
30 ml flour
20 ml olive oil
1 medium onion, finely chopped
2 cloves garlic, finely chopped
1 medium cooking apple (Granny
    Smith), cut into 5-mm-thick wedges
125 ml chicken stock
2,5 ml salt
1,25 ml pepper
30 ml sour cream

1. Cut off the fennel stalks and fronds. Finely chop 30 ml of the fronds and reserve; discard the stalks. Cut the bulb in half lengthwise and thinly slice crosswise. Set aside.

2. With the heel of your hand, lightly flatten the pieces of pork. On a sheet of greaseproof paper, dredge the pork in the flour, shaking off the excess. In a large nonstick frying pan, heat 15 ml of the oil over moderately high heat. Add the pork and cook for 3 minutes per side or until browned and just cooked through. With a slotted spoon, transfer the pork to a plate.

3. Add the remaining 5 ml olive oil, the onion and garlic to the pan and sauté for 5 minutes or until softened.

Add the sliced fennel and sauté for 5 minutes or until crisp-tender. Add the apple and sauté for 5 minutes or until crisp-tender.

4. Stir in the stock, 125 ml of water, the salt and pepper and bring to a boil. Reduce to a simmer, return the pork to the pan and cook for 1 minute or until cooked through. Spoon the pork and fennel mixture onto 4 plates. Whisk the sour cream and reserved fennel fronds into the sauce, spoon over the pork and serve. Serves 4.

Per serving: Kilojoules 1 304; Fibre 6 g; Protein 20 g; Total Fat 12 g; Saturated Fat 4 g; Cholesterol 54 mg; Sodium 618 mg

Fennel & Potato Hash with Caramelized Onions

PREP: 25 MINUTES / COOK: 40 MINUTES

Served with a salad, this meatless hash will make a small but satisfying meal. For a more substantial dish, add cubed cooked beef or chicken and cook, stirring, until heated through.

450 g potatoes
1 kg (total) fennel bulbs
15 ml olive oil
2 large onions, finely chopped
2 cloves garlic, finely chopped
3,5 ml salt
1,25 ml pepper

1. In a large pot of boiling water, cook the potatoes for 30 minutes or until

At the market Fennel is mainly an autumn and winter vegetable, but is increasingly available all year round. If your supermarket doesn't sell it, try a delicatessen which carries more unusual varieties of fruit and vegetables.

Look for The bulb should be smooth and glossy, not dry or brown. Stalks and fronds, if attached, should be fresh and green. If you have any left over, sliver the fennel and add to salads or serve as a crudité.

Prep Trim and discard stalks; save fronds for garnishing and flavouring. Halve the bulb lengthwise, then slice it crosswise.

Don't discard fennel fronds— they're rich in flavour and vitamin C.

Basic cooking Steam sliced or chopped fennel for 10 to 15 minutes. Braise halved fennel bulbs (or sliced fennel) in a frying pan with just enough boiling liquid to cover; cook for 25 to 40 minutes or until tender.

Fresh Fennel Salad with Lemon *Serve this simple and refreshingly crunchy salad before or alongside a rich main course.*

tender. Drain and when cool enough to handle, peel and slice thinly.

2. Meanwhile, cut off the fennel stalks and fronds. Finely chop 60 ml of the fronds and reserve; discard the stalks. Cut the bulb in half lengthwise and thinly slice crosswise. Set aside.

3. In a large nonstick frying pan, heat the oil over moderate heat. Add the onions and garlic, and sauté for 12 minutes or until the onions are golden brown

4. Add the sliced fennel to the pan and cook, stirring, for 10 minutes or until crisp-tender. Add the potatoes, sprinkle with the salt and pepper and cook, stirring frequently, for 10 minutes or until the potatoes and fennel are tender. Stir in the chopped fennel fronds and serve. Serves 4.

Per serving: Kilojoules 900; Fibre 10g; Protein 5g; Total Fat 4g; Saturated Fat 1g; Cholesterol 0mg; Sodium 563mg

Fresh Fennel Salad with Lemon

PREP: 10 MINUTES

60 ml lemon juice
20 ml olive oil
2,5 ml salt
650 g (total) fennel bulbs
60 ml shaved Parmesan cheese

1. In a medium bowl, whisk together the lemon juice, 30 ml of water, the oil and salt.

2. Cut off the fennel stalks and fronds. Finely chop 60 ml of the fronds and add to the bowl of dressing; discard the stalks. Cut the bulbs in half lengthwise and slice thinly crosswise. Add the fennel to the bowl and toss well to combine. Serve the salad sprinkled with the Parmesan. Serves 4.

Per serving: Kilojoules 523; Fibre 5g; Protein 4g; Total Fat 7g; Saturated Fat 2g; Cholesterol 4mg; Sodium 488mg

Garlic

Chicken Breasts with Roasted Garlic Sauce

PREP: 10 MINUTES / COOK: 1 HOUR

Yes, there are two full heads (not cloves) of garlic in this savoury chicken dish, but roasting mellows and sweetens the garlic.

- 2 heads of garlic (140 g total)
- 4 skinless, boned chicken breasts (about 500 g total)
- 30 ml flour
- 10 ml olive oil
- 125 ml chicken stock
- 1,25 ml dried rosemary, crumbled
- 1,25 ml each salt and pepper
- 2,5 ml grated lemon rind
- 15 ml lemon juice
- 30 ml chopped parsley

1. Preheat the oven to 230°C. Wrap each head of garlic in foil. Bake for 45 minutes or until very soft when squeezed. When cool enough to handle, cut off the stem end from each head of garlic, squeeze the garlic pulp into a small bowl and mash with a fork.

2. Dredge the chicken in the flour, shaking off the excess. In a large non-stick frying pan, heat the oil over moderate heat. Add the chicken and cook for 8 minutes or until lightly browned on both sides.

3. Add the mashed garlic, the stock, 125 ml of water, the rosemary, salt, pepper and lemon rind and bring to a boil. Reduce to a simmer, cover and cook, stirring occasionally, for 4 minutes or until the sauce coats the chicken and the chicken is cooked through. Stir the lemon juice and parsley into the sauce. Serve the chicken topped with the sauce. Serves 4.

Per serving: Kilojoules 859; Fibre 1g; Protein 25g; Total Fat 6g; Saturated Fat 1g; Cholesterol 47mg; Sodium 383mg

White Bean Garlic Dip

PREP: 10 MINUTES / COOK: 5 MINUTES

This velvety and aromatic bean purée is a smart alternative to a dip based on cream cheese or sour cream. Serve it with raw vegetables as crudités.

- 10 cloves garlic
- 2 tins (410 g each) cannellini beans, rinsed and drained
- 30 ml low-fat smooth cottage cheese
- 15 ml lemon juice
- 10 ml sesame oil
- 2,5 ml ground coriander
- 1,25 ml salt
- 60 ml chopped parsley
- 5 ml paprika

1. In a small pot of boiling water, cook the garlic for 3 minutes to blanch. Drain, reserving 30 ml of the cooking liquid. Peel the garlic.

2. In a food processor, combine the garlic, reserved cooking liquid and beans and process to a smooth purée. Add the cottage cheese, lemon juice, sesame oil, coriander and salt and process briefly to blend. Transfer the mixture to a small serving bowl. Serve sprinkled with the parsley and paprika. Makes 500 millilitres.

Per 60 ml: Kilojoules 259; Fibre 5g; Protein 3g; Total Fat 2g; Saturated Fat 0g; Cholesterol 0mg; Sodium 330mg

Creamy Garlic Soup with Herbed Croutons

PREP: 30 MINUTES / COOK: 45 MINUTES

To make the task of peeling three heads of garlic easier, blanch the unpeeled garlic cloves in boiling water for 1 to 2 minutes.

- **3 slices (25 g each) firm-textured white sandwich bread**
- **15 ml olive oil**
- **15 ml grated Parmesan cheese**
- **2,5 ml each dried thyme and sage**
- **375 ml chicken stock**
- **3 heads of garlic (200 g total), peeled**
- **350 g potatoes, peeled and thinly sliced**
- **1,25 ml salt**
- **45 ml mayonnaise**
- **60 ml chopped parsley**

1. Preheat the oven to 190°C. Brush the bread with the oil. Cut the bread into 1-cm squares, then toss with the Parmesan and 1,25 ml each of the thyme and sage. Spread the squares on a baking sheet and bake for 5 minutes or until lightly crisped. To cut down on fat even more, spray the bread with olive oil nonstick cooking spray instead of brushing with the oil.

2. In a medium saucepan, combine the stock, garlic and the remaining thyme and sage. Bring to a a simmer, cover and cook for 25 minutes or until the garlic is very soft.

3. Meanwhile, in another medium saucepan, bring 500 ml of water to a boil. Add the potatoes and cook for 12 minutes or until very tender; drain.

4. Transfer the garlic mixture to a food processor and process to a smooth purée. Return the purée to the pan. Add the potatoes, their cooking liquid and the salt and bring to a boil. Reduce to a simmer, add the mayonnaise and cook, whisking, for 2 minutes or until the soup is slightly thickened. Serve the soup topped with the croutons and sprinkled with the parsley. Serves 4.

Per serving: Kilojoules 1 182; Fibre 3 g; Protein 7 g; Total Fat 11 g; Saturated Fat 2 g; Cholesterol 8 mg; Sodium 887 mg

At the market A kitchen staple, garlic is always in good supply.

Look for Choose a full, plump head of garlic with taut, unbroken outer skin. Avoid heads with shrivelled cloves or green shoots sprouting from the top.

Prep Separate the cloves from the head; avoid piercing the skin on the remaining cloves. To peel, place each clove under the flat side of a broad knife blade; strike the blade with your fist. This will crack and loosen the peel, making it easy to remove.

After roasting, garlic pulp can be squeezed out of the skin—no peeling required.

Basic cooking Blanching whole, unpeeled garlic cloves for just a few minutes tempers the pungent flavour a bit and makes the garlic easier to peel. Roasting a whole head of garlic (elephant garlic is best), wrapped in foil, renders it sweet and spreadable. Roast at 450°C for about 45 minutes.

Chicken Breasts with Roasted Garlic Sauce *Serve with potatoes to mop up the sauce.*

Ginger

PER 15G RAW	
Kilojoules	43
Fibre	0,4 g
Protein	0 g
Total Fat	0,1 g
Saturated Fat	0 g
Cholesterol	0 mg
Sodium	2 mg

Did you know? . . .

For centuries, various forms of ginger have been used to quell nausea. Several studies have investigated this effect and in Germany ginger is approved as a medical treatment for motion sickness and also for heartburn.

Ground ginger contains useful amounts of manganese—which is involved in energy production and helps build strong bones.

Kingklip & Oriental Vegetable Sauté

PREP: 20 MINUTES / COOK: 10 MINUTES

45 ml light soya sauce
20 ml lemon juice
15 ml grated plus 70 ml slivered fresh ginger
450 g kingklip, cut into 2,5-cm pieces,
12,5 ml vegetable oil
650 g Chinese cabbage, sliced (8 cups)
120 g mangetout
8 spring onions, sliced
4 cloves garlic, finely chopped
15 ml rice vinegar
5 ml cornflour blended with 15 ml water
3,5 ml honey
3,5 ml sesame oil

1. In a medium bowl, combine the soya sauce and lemon juice with the grated ginger. Add the kingklip, tossing to coat. Let marinate for 15 minutes.

2. Meanwhile, in a large nonstick frying pan or wok, heat the vegetable oil over moderately high heat. Add the cabbage and sauté for 4 minutes. Stir in the slivered ginger, the mangetout, spring onions and garlic and sauté for 2 minutes. With a slotted spoon, transfer the vegetables to a serving dish.

3. Add the kingklip pieces and their marinade to the pan. Cook for 2 minutes or until the kingklip is just opaque. With a slotted spoon, transfer the kingklip to the serving dish. Add the vinegar, cornflour mixture and honey to the pan and cook, stirring, for 1 minute or until the sauce is slightly thickened. Return the fish and vegetables to the pan to warm through. Stir in the sesame oil and serve. Serves 4.

Per serving: Kilojoules 784; Fibre 4 g; Protein 22 g; Total Fat 5 g; Saturated Fat 1 g; Cholesterol 55 mg; Sodium 749 mg

Homemade Ginger Ale

PREP: 5 MINUTES / COOK: 30 MINUTES

Bottled ginger ale just can't compare to this potent, peppery syrup; there's far more real ginger in this homemade brew. If you let the ginger cool in the liquid in Step 1 instead of straining it right away, you will get a 'hotter' ginger syrup.

175 ml thinly sliced unpeeled fresh ginger
250 ml sugar
3 strips (2 x 1 cm) lemon rind
0,6 ml whole black peppercorns
0,6 ml allspice berries (optional)
soda water

1. In a medium saucepan, bring 500 ml of water and the ginger to a boil over moderate heat. Reduce the heat to low, cover and simmer for 25 minutes. Strain, reserve the liquid and discard the ginger.

2. In the same saucepan, combine the ginger liquid, the sugar, lemon rind, peppercorns and allspice over low heat. Bring to a boil and boil for 2 minutes. Cover the syrup and let stand until cooled to room temperature. Strain the ginger syrup and refrigerate.

3. To serve, pour 60 ml of the syrup into a tall glass. Add 175 ml of cold soda water; add ice if you wish. Serves 8.

Per serving: Kilojoules 403; Fibre 0 g; Protein 0 g; Total Fat 0 g; Saturated Fat 0 g; Cholesterol 0 mg; Sodium 1 mg

At the market You'll find fresh ginger in the vegetable section of most supermarkets, and at greengrocers.

Look for A 'hand' of ginger should be smooth and very firm, with glossy, pinkish-tan skin. Fresh ginger should not look dry or shrivelled.

Prep Cut off a knob or 'finger' of ginger as needed; pare it with a vegetable peeler. Then grate, chop, mince or sliver as needed. To make ginger juice, see below.

To make ginger juice, first grate the desired amount of ginger (a 5-cm piece of ginger will yield about 10 ml juice). To extract the juice, squeeze the grated ginger with your fingers, press it in a tea strainer or wring it in a square of cheesecloth.

Gingerbread Cup Cakes with Ginger Glaze *are homely yet sophisticated party fare.*

Gingerbread Cup Cakes with Ginger Glaze

PREP: 15 MINUTES / COOK: 25 MINUTES

'Triple-gingerbread' we might have said— these cup cakes are made with fresh ginger juice as well as ground ginger and are decorated with crystallized ginger.

- **320 ml flour**
- **15 ml ground ginger**
- **5 ml dry mustard**
- **5 ml bicarbonate of soda**
- **2,5 ml ground cinnamon**
- **1,25 ml salt**
- **0,6 ml ground cloves**
- **125 ml packed dark brown sugar**
- **60 ml molasses**
- **45 ml vegetable oil**
- **2 egg whites**
- **125 ml low-fat cultured buttermilk**
- **1 piece (5 cm) of fresh ginger**
- **125 ml icing sugar**
- **30 ml chopped crystallized ginger (optional)**

1. Preheat the oven to 180°C. Line 12 x 6-cm muffin tins with paper cups; set aside. On a sheet of greaseproof paper, sift the flour, ginger, mustard, bicarbonate of soda, cinnamon, salt and cloves.

2. In a bowl, beat the brown sugar, molasses and oil with an electric mixer until well combined. Beat in the egg whites, one at a time, until well incorporated and light in texture. Alternately fold the flour mixture and the buttermilk into the sugar mixture, beginning and ending with the flour mixture. Spoon into the prepared muffin cups and bake for 20 minutes or until a cake tester inserted in the centre of a cup cake comes out clean. Cool in the pan on a wire rack.

3. Grate the fresh ginger on the fine side of a box grater. Squeeze the ginger to extract the juice and measure out 10 ml. In a small bowl, combine the icing sugar and ginger juice. Spread the tops of the cooled cup cakes with the ginger glaze. Sprinkle with the crystallized ginger. Makes 12 cup cakes.

Per cup cake: Kilojoules 691; Fibre 0g; Protein 2g; Total Fat 4g; Saturated Fat 1g; Cholesterol 1 mg; Sodium 75 mg

Green beans

Green Beans
**PER 150G COOKED
(1 CUP)**

Kilojoules	206
Fibre	4,8g
Protein	2,7g
Total Fat	0,3g
Saturated Fat	0,1g
Cholesterol	0mg
Sodium	6mg

NUTRIENTS

**% RDA for people older
than 10 years**

Vitamin C	13%
Magnesium	12%
Iron	10%
Calcium	6%
Vitamin A	5%

Did you know? . . .

Although most people associate beta carotene with orange vegetables and fruits, the chlorophyll in green vegetables often masks the orange colour. Green beans are a good example of this 'hidden' beta carotene.

Lemony Green Beans

PREP: 15 MINUTES / COOK: 10 MINUTES

Green beans used to be called 'string beans' because their pods had a fibrous string along the sides. The string has been bred out of modern varieties.

- 650g green beans, halved crosswise
- 10ml olive oil
- 3 cloves garlic, finely chopped
- 60ml chicken stock
- 5ml grated lemon rind
- 60ml lemon juice
- 2,5ml salt
- 70ml snipped fresh lemon thyme
  or dill leaves
- 10ml unsalted butter

1. In a steamer or colander set over a pot of boiling water, steam the beans for 6 minutes or until crisp-tender.

2. Meanwhile, in a large nonstick pan, heat the oil over moderately low heat. Add the garlic and cook for 2 minutes or until soft. Add the stock, lemon rind, lemon juice and salt and bring to a boil. Add the beans and cook for 2 minutes or until heated through and well coated. Add the lemon thyme, remove from the heat and stir in the butter until melted. Serves 4.

Per serving: Kilojoules 419; Fibre 5g; Protein 3g; Total Fat 5g; Saturated Fat 2g; Cholesterol 5mg; Sodium 419mg

Green Beans with Onions, Fresh Tomatoes & Basil

PREP: 20 MINUTES / COOK: 15 MINUTES

Serving the beans in their cooking liquid ensures that you get all the available nutrients. You can substitute chopped onions for the pickling onions.

- 15ml olive oil
- 140g small pickling or pearl onions
- 3 cloves garlic, finely chopped
- 650g green beans, halved crosswise
- 2 medium tomatoes, chopped
- 125ml chopped fresh basil
- 30ml balsamic vinegar
- 2,5ml salt

1. In a large nonstick frying pan, heat the oil over moderate heat. Add the onions and sauté for 4 minutes or until lightly browned.

2. Add the garlic, green beans, tomatoes, basil, vinegar and salt and bring to a boil. Reduce to a simmer, partially cover and cook for 9 minutes or until the beans are crisp-tender. Serves 4.

Per serving: Kilojoules 483; Fibre 6g; Protein 4g; Total Fat 4g; Saturated Fat 1g; Cholesterol 0mg; Sodium 316mg

Green Bean and Potato Salad with Smoked Turkey *Green beans are combined with potatoes, cherry tomatoes, black olives and smoked turkey for a filling main dish.*

At the market Fresh beans are almost always available, although the season peaks in the summer.

Look for The beans should snap crisply when you bend them. Choose slender, straight beans with a 'peach fuzz' feel, free of nicks or rusty brown spots. For uniform cooking, choose beans that are of roughly equal size.

Prep Although they don't need to be 'stringed', fresh beans should be topped and tailed—their stem ends and pointed tips removed.

For a more attractive presentation, cut green beans on the diagonal.

Basic cooking Steam green beans, or cook them in a small amount of water, for 3 to 5 minutes; they should remain bright green and crisp-tender. Microwave 450 g green beans with 60 ml liquid on high for 5 to 6 minutes.

Green Bean and Potato Salad with Smoked Turkey

PREP: 15 MINUTES / COOK: 15 MINUTES

This salad is so versatile it can be served at a dinner party or at your next picnic. It is healthy, tasty, colourful and, best of all, contains only 15 millilitres of oil. At the supermarket ask for a piece of pressed turkey breast—it is usually sold thinly shaved.

- 175 ml chicken stock
- 30 ml lemon juice
- 15 ml olive oil
- 15 ml wholegrain mustard
- 500 g baby potatoes
- 250 g green beans, topped and tailed and halved on the diagonal
- 200 g cherry tomatoes, halved
- 125 g black olives, pitted and halved
- 300 g smoked turkey breast, cut into 5-cm matchsticks

1. In a small bowl, make the dressing by combining the chicken stock, lemon juice, olive oil and mustard. Transfer the dressing to a large salad bowl.

2. In a large saucepan of boiling water, cook the baby potatoes for 15 minutes or until tender but not so soft that they fall apart. Drain. Cut in half and transfer to the salad bowl. Set aside.

3. In a steamer or colander set over a saucepan of boiling water, cook the green beans for 4 minutes or until just tender. Drain. Add to the potatoes in the salad bowl.

4. Just before serving, add the cherry tomatoes, olives and matchstick-sized pieces of turkey, tossing well to combine. Serve the salad at room temperature. Serves 4.

Per serving: Kilojoules 1 287; Fibre 7 g; Protein 20 g; Total Fat 9 g; Saturated Fat 1 g; Cholesterol 57 mg; Sodium 1 663 mg

Mushrooms

Pasta with Creamy Mushroom Sauce

PREP: 25 MINUTES / COOK: 25 MINUTES

- 350g fusilli pasta
- 10ml vegetable oil
- 1 medium onion, thinly sliced
- 4 cloves garlic, finely chopped
- 225g fresh oyster mushrooms, trimmed and sliced
- 450g button mushrooms, halved and thinly sliced
- 2,5ml salt
- 30ml flour
- 500ml low-fat (2%) milk
- 2,5ml pepper
- 5ml unsalted butter
- 60ml grated Parmesan cheese

1. In a large pot of boiling water, cook the pasta according to package directions until *al dente*. Drain well and transfer to a large serving bowl.

2. Meanwhile, in a large nonstick frying pan, heat the oil over moderate heat. Add the onion and garlic and sauté for 2 minutes. Add the oyster mushrooms, cover and cook, stirring occasionally, for 5 minutes or until tender.

3. Add the button mushrooms and sprinkle with the salt. Cover and cook, stirring occasionally, for 5 minutes. Increase the heat to high, uncover and cook for 4 minutes or until the liquid has evaporated. Sprinkle with the flour, stirring until absorbed. Gradually add the milk and cook, stirring, for 5 minutes or until the sauce is slightly thickened. Stir in the pepper.

4. Add the sauce, butter and Parmesan to the hot pasta, tossing well to coat. Serves 4.

Per serving: Kilojoules 2 201; Fibre 8g; Protein 23g; Total Fat 10g; Saturated Fat 2g; Cholesterol 16mg; Sodium 496mg

Vegetable-Stuffed Mushrooms

PREP: 20 MINUTES / COOK: 20 MINUTES

- 24 large or 12 extra-large mushrooms, stems removed
- 10ml vegetable oil
- 1 medium onion, finely chopped
- 3 cloves garlic, finely chopped
- 1 medium carrot, grated
- 1 medium red pepper, finely chopped
- 125ml chicken stock
- 2,5ml dried oreganum
- 45ml grated Parmesan cheese
- 30ml chopped parsley

1. Preheat the oven to 200°C. In a medium pot of boiling water, cook the mushroom caps for 2 minutes to blanch. Drain on paper towels.

2. In a large frying pan, heat the oil over moderate heat. Add the onion and garlic and sauté for 5 minutes. Add the carrot and pepper and cook for 4 minutes. Add the stock and oreganum and cook for 4 minutes or until the vegetables are very soft. Remove from the heat; stir in the Parmesan and parsley.

3. Spoon the mixture into the mushroom caps. Place on a baking sheet and bake for 10 minutes or until piping hot. Serves 4.

Per serving: Kilojoules 631; Fibre 7g; Protein 8g; Total Fat 4g; Saturated Fat 1g; Cholesterol 3mg; Sodium 300mg

Fresh & Dried Mushroom Soup

PREP: 20 MINUTES / COOK: 30 MINUTES

Dried porcini have a special flavour, but they can be pricey. Fortunately, only a small amount is needed for this recipe. Any other dried mushrooms sold in supermarkets make an acceptable substitute.

- 20 g dried porcini or other dried mushrooms
- 250 ml boiling water
- 10 ml vegetable oil
- 1 large onion, finely chopped
- 4 cloves garlic, finely chopped
- 225 g fresh oyster mushrooms, trimmed, halved and thinly sliced
- 450 g button mushrooms, thinly sliced
- 60 ml dry sherry or chicken stock
- 375 ml chicken stock
- 1 large tomato, finely chopped
- 5 ml dried tarragon
- 2,5 ml pepper

1. In a small bowl, combine the dried mushrooms and boiling water and let stand for 10 minutes or until softened.

Reserving the liquid, scoop out the dried mushrooms and chop coarsely. Strain the soaking liquid through a coffee filter or a paper towel-lined sieve.

2. In a large saucepan, heat the oil over moderate heat. Add the onion and garlic and sauté for 5 minutes or until the onion has softened. Stir in the dried mushrooms. Add the oyster mushrooms and sauté for 5 minutes or until they are soft. Add the button mushrooms and cook, stirring frequently, for 5 minutes or until they begin to give up liquid.

3. Add the reserved soaking liquid and bring to a boil. Add the sherry and cook for 5 minutes or until reduced by half. Add the stock, 375 ml of water, the tomato, tarragon and pepper. Bring to a boil, reduce to a simmer, cover and cook for 10 minutes or until the soup is richly flavoured. Serves 4.

Per serving: Kilojoules 590; Fibre 6 g; Protein 7 g; Total Fat 4 g; Saturated Fat 1 g; Cholesterol 0 mg; Sodium 611 mg

At the market White mushrooms are in the shops all year round and oyster mushrooms are now appearing regularly as well. If you can't find dried mushrooms at the supermarket, try a delicatessen.

Look for Fresh mushrooms should look clean, plump and moist; pass up those that are dry or darkening. The gills (under the caps) should be tightly closed.

Prep Trim the stem bases of mushrooms. Wipe mushrooms with a damp paper towel or a soft brush, if necessary. Soak dried mushrooms in boiling water to soften, then drain. If using the soaking liquid in the dish, strain it through a coffee filter or paper towel to remove any dirt.

Shiitake stems are too tough to eat. Trim them close to the base of the cap.

Basic cooking Simmer mushrooms in a little stock to give them extra flavour with no added fat. Cook for 3 to 5 minutes.

***Vegetable-Stuffed Mushrooms** make a healthy start for a festive meal.*

Onions

Onions
PER 170G COOKED (1 CUP)

Kilojoules	326
Fibre	2,6g
Protein	2g
Total Fat	0,2g
Saturated Fat	0g
Cholesterol	0mg
Sodium	2,4mg

NUTRIENTS
% RDA for people older than 10 years

Vitamin C	26%
Biotin	24%
Vitamin B6	10%
Iron	6%

Spring Onions
PER 40G RAW (½ CUP)

Kilojoules	54
Fibre	1g
Protein	1g
Total Fat	0,1g
Saturated Fat	0g
Cholesterol	0mg
Sodium	8mg

NUTRIENTS
% RDA for people older than 10 years

Vitamin C	13%

Chicken with Smothered Onions

PREP: 10 MINUTES / COOK: 35 MINUTES

- 20ml vegetable oil
- 450g skinless, boned chicken breasts
- 30ml flour
- 550g onions, halved and thinly sliced
- 2,5ml sugar
- 2,5ml salt
- 70ml chicken stock
- 1,25ml dried rosemary, crumbled
- 1,25ml pepper
- 30ml chopped parsley

1. In a large nonstick frying pan, heat 10ml of the oil over moderate heat. Dredge the chicken in the flour, shaking off the excess. Add the chicken to the pan and cook for 3 minutes per side or until golden brown. Transfer the chicken to a plate and set aside.

2. Add the remaining 10ml oil to the frying pan and heat over moderate heat. Add the sliced onions, sugar and 1,25ml of the salt. Cover and cook, stirring occasionally, for 10 minutes or until very soft. Uncover and cook for 10 minutes or until the onions are golden brown.

3. Add the stock, 70ml of water, the rosemary, pepper and the remaining salt to the pan. Bring to a boil. Reduce to a simmer, return the chicken to the pan, cover and cook for 5 minutes or until the chicken is cooked through. Serve the chicken topped with the onions and parsley. Serves 4.

Per serving: Kilojoules 926; Fibre 2g; Protein 21g; Total Fat 8g; Saturated Fat 2g; Cholesterol 42mg; Sodium 459mg

Spring Onion Pancakes

PREP: 1 HOUR 20 MINUTES
COOK: 15 MINUTES

- 375ml flour
- 3,5ml salt
- 3,5ml sugar
- 2,5ml baking powder
- 175ml boiling water
- 10ml sesame oil
- 8 spring onions, thinly sliced
- 20ml peanut oil

1. In a bowl, combine the flour, salt, sugar and baking powder. Stir in the boiling water until the dough forms a ball. Place on a floured surface and knead for 5 minutes or until smooth. Cover with plastic and let rest for 1 hour.

2. Transfer the dough to a floured surface and knead again until smooth. Roll out to a 28 x 20-cm rectangle. Brush the dough with the sesame oil, sprinkle with the onions and press them into the dough. Roll up the dough jam-roll style, then slice into 4 pieces. Cover and let rest for 10 minutes.

Pasta with Golden Onion Sauce is made with sweet Spanish onions and garlic.

At the market Dry onions are always in good supply. Red onions (Spanish) are available from November to September, but store poorly. Leeks are most abundant in the autumn and winter. Spring onions (actually immature onion plants) are in the shops all year round.

Look for Dry onions should be hard, with crisp, papery skins; pass up any with green shoots. Leeks should be fresh, moist and green.

Prep To peel a dry onion, cut off the stem (not the root) end, and peel downward. Then cut off the root end and slice or chop the onion. Rinse spring onions and cut off the roots. Cut off the dark green tops of leeks, then trim roots, split stems lengthwise and rinse thoroughly: soil is often trapped in the base of the leaves.

3. Preheat the oven to 120°C. Roll out each piece of dough to a 13-cm round. In a small nonstick pan, cook 1 pancake in 5 ml of the peanut oil for 3 minutes per side or until light golden. Transfer to a baking sheet. Repeat with the remaining 15 ml oil and pancakes. Bake for 5 minutes. Serves 4.

Per serving: Kilojoules 1 014; Fibre 1 g; Protein 4 g; Total Fat 8 g; Saturated Fat 1 g; Cholesterol 0 mg; Sodium 424 mg

Pasta with Golden Onion Sauce

PREP: 25 MINUTES / COOK: 35 MINUTES

10 ml vegetable oil
2 onions (Spanish or red, if possible), finely chopped (650 g total)
3 cloves garlic, finely chopped
5 ml sugar
3,5 ml salt
1 medium carrot, quartered lengthwise and thinly sliced
350 g penne rigate pasta
45 ml Marsala or water
175 ml chicken stock
10 ml unsalted butter
60 ml chopped parsley

1. In a large nonstick frying pan, heat the oil over moderate heat. Add the onions and garlic and sprinkle with the sugar and salt. Cover and cook, stirring frequently, for 20 minutes or until the onion is very soft. Stir in the carrot and cook, uncovered, for 7 minutes or until the onions are golden and the carrot is very soft.

2. Meanwhile, in a large pot of boiling water, cook the pasta according to package directions until *al dente*. Reserving 175 ml of the cooking liquid, drain the pasta and transfer to a large serving bowl.

3. Stir the Marsala into the pan and cook for 1 minute or until evaporated. Add the stock and the reserved pasta cooking water and cook, stirring frequently, for 5 minutes or until the liquid is reduced by half.

4. Add the onion sauce, butter and chopped parsley to the hot pasta, tossing well to combine. Serves 4.

Per serving: Kilojoules 1 924; Fibre 6 g; Protein 13 g; Total Fat 7 g; Saturated Fat 2 g; Cholesterol 5 mg; Sodium 737 mg

Splitting the stem of a leek lengthwise is the first step in washing it free of soil.

Double-Onion Pizza *is topped with savoury sautéed onions and garlic and flavoured with Parmesan cheese and sage.*

Leeks
PER 200G COOKED (1 CUP)

Kilojoules	300
Fibre	1,8g
Protein	2g
Total Fat	0,4g
Saturated Fat	0g
Cholesterol	0mg
Sodium	16mg

Did you know? . . .
Saponins, as well as sulphur compounds called allyl sulphides, are cancer-fighting substances found in all onion-family plants—onions, leeks, spring onions and others. Saponins also have a heart-protective effect.

A study of Dutch men and their intake of flavonoids (anti-oxidants found in fresh produce, tea and wine) showed that those who con-sumed the most flavonoids had the lowest heart-disease risk. Onions, apples and tea were the main flavonoid sources in the subjects' diets.

Onion-Orzo Pilaf

PREP: 15 MINUTES / COOK: 35 MINUTES
This recipe uses orzo (a grain-shaped pasta) in place of rice for a pilaf that will dress up a simple meal of grilled chicken or fish.

- 10ml vegetable oil
- 650g onions, finely chopped
- 6 spring onions, thinly sliced
- 2 cloves garlic, finely chopped
- 175ml orzo
- 250ml chicken stock
- 2,5ml each salt and pepper
- 70ml grated Parmesan cheese

1. In a medium-size nonstick sauce-pan, heat the oil over moderate heat. Add the onions, spring onions and gar-lic. Cover and cook, stirring occasional-ly, for 7 minutes or until the onions are soft. Uncover and cook, stirring occa-sionally, for 5 minutes or until golden.

2. Stir in the orzo. Add the stock, 250ml of water, the salt and pepper. Bring to a boil, reduce to a simmer, cover and cook for 20 minutes or until the orzo is tender. Stir in the Parmesan. Serves 6.

Per serving: Kilojoules 549; Fibre 3g; Protein 5g; Total Fat 3g; Saturated Fat 1g; Cholesterol 2mg; Sodium 548mg

Double-Onion Pizza

PREP: 25 MINUTES / COOK: 30 MINUTES

- 20ml olive oil
- 3 red onions (if available), halved and cut into 5-mm-thick slices (450g total)
- 3 yellow onions (450g total), halved and cut into 5-mm-thick slices
- 2 cloves garlic, finely chopped
- 2,5ml sugar
- 1,25ml salt
- 5ml dried sage leaves, crumbled
- 1,25ml pepper
- 1 ready-made pizza base (or make your own)
- 60ml bottled pizza sauce
- 70ml grated Parmesan cheese

1. In a large nonstick pan, heat 10ml of the oil over moderate heat. Add the onions and garlic and sprinkle with the sugar and salt. Cover and cook, stirring occasionally, for 7 minutes or until the onions are soft. Uncover and cook, stirring frequently, for 5 minutes or until golden brown. Stir in the sage and pepper.

2. Preheat the oven to 250°C. When the oven is hot, place the ready-made pizza base onto a baking sheet.

3. Brush the bottled tomato pizza sauce over the pizza and bake on the lowest shelf in the oven for 10 minutes. Spread the onion mixture on top, sprinkle with the Parmesan and bake for 7 minutes or until the pizza is crisp and the onions are piping hot. Serves 6.

Per serving: Kilojoules 1170; Fibre 4g; Protein 9g; Total Fat 6g; Saturated Fat 1g; Cholesterol 3mg; Sodium 583mg

---

Braised Leeks with Tomato, Orange & Olives

PREP: 20 MINUTES / COOK: 25 MINUTES

Leeks are a good source of potassium and folate, while olives, although high in sodium if soaked in brine, provide useful amounts of vitamin E.

- **8 medium leeks (1.3kg total), roots and dark green ends trimmed**
- **15ml olive oil**
- **3 cloves garlic, finely chopped**
- **1 large tomato, diced**
- **125ml fresh orange juice**
- **15ml tomato paste**
- **60ml pitted, coarsely chopped black or green olives**
- **1,25ml salt**

1. With a sharp paring knife, starting 2,5cm above the root end of each leek, make 4 lengthwise cuts. Soak the leeks in several changes of warm water until thoroughly clean. Pat dry.

2. In a large nonstick frying pan, heat the oil over moderate heat. Add the leeks, turning until well coated. Add the garlic and cook for 2 minutes or until tender.

3. Add the tomato, orange juice, tomato paste, olives and salt and bring to a boil. Reduce to a simmer, cover and cook for 10 minutes or until the leeks are fork-tender. Serve warm, at room temperature or chilled. Serves 4.

Per serving: Kilojoules 999; Fibre 5g; Protein 5g; Total Fat 6g; Saturated Fat 1g; Cholesterol 0mg; Sodium 287mg

Onion & Red Pepper Relish In a nonstick pan, sauté 750ml diced (red) onions, 250ml diced red pepper and 2 cloves chopped garlic in 10ml olive oil until tender. Add 60ml red wine vinegar, 15ml tomato paste and 10ml honey. Simmer 2 minutes. Serve chilled. Makes 500ml/ 8 servings. *[kJ 181; Fat 1g; Sodium 24mg]*

Creamy Onion & Spring Onion Soup In a nonstick saucepan, heat 10ml olive oil. Add 750ml diced onions, 6 sliced spring onions and 3 cloves chopped garlic. Sprinkle with 5ml sugar, 2,5ml thyme and 1,25ml salt and sauté until tender. Add 175ml each chicken stock and water and simmer, covered, for 5 minutes. Purée with 250ml low-fat (2%) milk. Heat through to serve. Serves 4. *[kJ 457; Fat 2g; Sodium 611mg]*

Sweet & Sour Pearl Onions In a nonstick pan, bring 125ml distilled white vinegar, 70ml sugar, 2,5ml salt and 1,25ml thyme to a boil. Add 500g pearl onions. Cover and simmer until tender. Uncover and cook until glazed. Stir in 30ml chopped parsley. Serves 4. *[kJ 527; Fat 0g; Sodium 326mg]*

Parsnips

PER 160 G COOKED (1 CUP)	
Kilojoules	584
Fibre	6,4 g
Protein	2 g
Total Fat	0,5 g
Saturated Fat	0,1 g
Cholesterol	0 mg
Sodium	16 mg

NUTRIENTS	
% RDA for people older than 10 years	
Vitamin C	35 %
Folate	23 %
Magnesium	15 %

Did you know? . . .

Try young, tender parsnips raw in salad or slaw. You'll get every bit of their vitamin C.

Some of a parsnip's starch turns to sugar when the vegetable is chilled (making it tastier). However, chilling does not diminish the nutritional value of the vegetable.

Honey-Glazed Parsnips

PREP: 10 MINUTES / COOK: 20 MINUTES

Like carrots, parsnips are right at home in a sweet, satiny sauce. The cooking liquid is reduced to make the glaze, so you don't lose nutrients.

550 g parsnips, peeled and thinly sliced
70 ml honey
30 ml lemon juice
15 ml unsalted butter
2,5 ml salt
1,25 ml pepper
1,25 ml dried rosemary, crumbled
60 ml chopped parsley

1. In a large pan, combine the parsnips, honey, lemon juice, butter, salt, pepper, rosemary and 250 ml of water. Bring to a boil over moderate heat. Cover and cook for 10 minutes or until crisp-tender.

2. Uncover and cook for 10 minutes or until the liquid has evaporated and the parsnips are richly glazed and tender. Stir in the parsley. Serves 4.

Per serving: Kilojoules 754; Fibre 4 g; Protein 2 g; Total Fat 3 g; Saturated Fat 2 g; Cholesterol 8 mg; Sodium 314 mg

Parsnip-Apple Purée

PREP: 20 MINUTES / COOK: 30 MINUTES

Your first taste of this mashed-potato lookalike will be a happy surprise. The apples underscore the parsnips' natural sweetness; onions and garlic lend savoury contrast.

10 ml vegetable oil
1 small onion, thinly sliced
6 cloves garlic, thinly sliced
650 g parsnips, peeled and thinly sliced
2 cooking apples apples, peeled and coarsely chopped
30 ml rice
500 ml low-fat (2%) milk
2,5 ml each salt and pepper

1. In a medium saucepan, heat the oil over moderate heat. Add the onion and garlic and sauté for 7 minutes or until the onion is tender.

2. Add the parsnips, tossing to coat with the oil. Add the apples, rice, milk, salt and pepper. Bring to a boil, reduce to a simmer, cover and cook for 20 minutes or until the rice and parsnips are tender. (Don't worry if the mixture appears curdled.) Transfer to a food processor and process until smooth. Serves 6.

Per serving: Kilojoules 747; Fibre 6 g; Protein 4 g; Total Fat 4 g; Saturated Fat 1 g; Cholesterol 6 mg; Sodium 252 mg

Parsnip Pancakes with Spring Onions

PREP: 20 MINUTES / COOK: 10 MINUTES

Parsnips and carrots complement one another in these delicately crusty pancakes. Take a cue from potato-pancake traditions and serve them with applesauce or sour cream.

450 g parsnips, peeled and grated
1 large carrot, grated
2 spring onions, thinly sliced
1 egg
15 ml flour
2,5 ml baking powder
2,5 ml salt
15 ml vegetable oil

1. Preheat the oven to 130°C. In a steamer or colander set over a pot of boiling water, steam the parsnips and carrot for 5 minutes or until softened, but not mushy. Set aside to cool slightly.

2. Transfer the vegetables to a medium bowl and add the spring onions, egg, flour, baking powder and salt, stirring until well combined.

3. In a large nonstick pan, heat 7,5 ml of the oil over moderate heat. Using a 60-ml measure, spoon 6 pancakes into the pan, using half of the batter. Cook for 2 minutes per side or until golden brown. Transfer the first batch of parsnip pancakes to a large baking tray.

4. Repeat with the remaining batter and 7,5 ml oil. Bake the parsnip pancakes in the oven for 7 minutes or until they are heated through and lightly crisped. Serves 4.

Per serving: Kilojoules 612; Fibre 5g; Protein 3g; Total Fat 5g; Saturated Fat 1g; Cholesterol 53mg; Sodium 333mg

At the market
Parsnips are in best supply from autumn through to early spring, but some markets offer them all year round. Parsnips are not popular in South Africa and availability is limited.

Look for Firm, medium-size, uniformly shaped roots are best. Large parsnips may have a tough, woody core.

Prep Peel parsnips and trim the top and bottom. Cook whole or sliced for faster cooking.

Peel parsnips with a vegetable peeler, just as you would carrots.

Basic cooking Steam sliced parsnips (or cook them in a small amount of liquid) for 5 to 15 minutes. Bake whole parsnips in a little liquid, covered, for 20 to 30 minutes at 180°C. To microwave 450 g of sliced parsnips, place in a dish with 60 ml water. Cover and cook on high for 9 to 11 minutes.

Parsnip Pancakes with Spring Onions *A delightful change from rice or potatoes.*

Peas

Green Peas
PER 170G COOKED (1 CUP)

Kilojoules	619
Fibre	11,2 g
Protein	9 g
Total Fat	1,2 g
Saturated Fat	0 g
Cholesterol	0 mg
Sodium	22 mg

NUTRIENTS

% RDA for people older than 10 years

Vitamin C	37%
Thiamin	24%
Biotin	22%
Folate	19%
Iron	18%
Niacin	15%

Did you know? . . .
Peas contain lutein, a carotenoid that fights macular degeneration, a leading cause of blindness in older people.

Nutritionally, frozen green peas are very close to fresh, except that most of the folate is lost.

Peas & Cheese Salad
PREP: 20 MINUTES / CHILL: 4 HOURS

This is a lower-fat version of a classic layered salad. Make it in a glass bowl to show off the layers.

250 ml plain fat-free yoghurt
70 ml light mayonnaise
3,5 ml grated lemon rind
45 ml lemon juice
120 g shredded iceberg lettuce
650 g frozen peas, thawed
1 large red pepper, diced
1 large yellow pepper, diced
1 large onion (red, if available), diced
100 g grated Cheddar cheese

1. In a small bowl, combine the yoghurt, mayonnaise, lemon rind and lemon juice; set aside.

2. In an 2- to 2,5-litre glass bowl, arrange the remaining ingredients in layers as follows: the lettuce, peas, red and yellow peppers and onion. Pour the yoghurt mixture on top and sprinkle with the cheese. Cover well and refrigerate for at least 4 hours or up to 12 hours.

3. At serving time, toss the salad at the table. Serves 4.

Per serving: Kilojoules 1423; Fibre 12 g; Protein 17 g; Total Fat 15 g; Saturated Fat 6 g; Cholesterol 37 mg; Sodium 354 mg

Penne with Mangetout & Smoked Salmon
PREP: 20 MINUTES / COOK: 15 MINUTES

Cook mangetout quickly to preserve their tempting colour. A brief blanching does the trick and also conserves vitamins.

350 g penne pasta
450 g mangetout, strings removed
70 ml snipped fresh dill
3 spring onions, thinly sliced
175 ml hot chicken stock
45 ml sour cream
15 ml unsalted butter
5 ml grated lemon rind
30 ml lemon juice
2,5 ml salt
115 g smoked salmon, cut into strips

1. In a large pot of boiling water, cook the pasta according to package directions until *al dente*. Add the mangetout to the water during the final 1 minute of cooking; drain.

2. Meanwhile, in a large bowl, combine the dill, spring onions, stock, sour cream, butter, lemon rind, lemon juice and salt. Add the hot pasta and mangetout, tossing well. Add the smoked salmon and toss again. Serves 4.

Per serving: Kilojoules 2055; Fibre 7 g; Protein 20 g; Total Fat 10 g; Saturated Fat 4 g; Cholesterol 30 mg; Sodium 762 mg

Sweet & Sour Prawns with Mangetout

PREP: 40 MINUTES / COOK: 10 MINUTES.

Serve the prawns and vegetables over rice to take advantage of the deliciously tangy sauce. Dried mushrooms are available at some supermarkets and delicatessens.

- 10 g dried mushrooms (porcini or shiitake)
- 250 ml boiling water
- 60 ml tomato sauce
- 30 ml light soya sauce
- 30 ml rice vinegar or cider vinegar
- 10 ml light brown sugar
- 5 ml cornflour
- 2,5 ml ground ginger
- 10 ml vegetable oil
- 2 large carrots, halved lengthwise and thinly sliced
- 2 cloves garlic, finely chopped
- 550 g medium prawns, peeled and deveined
- 350 g mangetout, strings removed, halved crosswise

1. In a small bowl, combine the dried mushrooms and the boiling water and let stand for 10 minutes or until softened. Reserving the soaking liquid, scoop out the dried mushrooms. Rinse, slice thinly and set aside.

2. Strain the mushroom soaking liquid through a coffee filter or a paper towel-lined sieve into a small bowl. Add the tomato sauce, soya sauce, vinegar, brown sugar, cornflour and ginger, whisking to combine.

3. In a large nonstick frying pan, heat the oil over moderately high heat. Add the carrots and garlic and sauté for 3 minutes or until crisp-tender. Add the prawns, mangetout, sliced mushrooms, and 60 ml of water. Cover the frying pan and cook for 5 minutes or until the prawns are just cooked through and the mangetout are crisp-tender. Stir the tomato sauce mixture to recombine and pour into the pan. Cook for 1 minute or until slightly thickened. Serves 4.

Per serving: Kilojoules 968; Fibre 4 g; Protein 27 g; Total Fat 4 g; Saturated Fat 1 g; Cholesterol 219 mg; Sodium 782 mg

At the market Fresh green peas are abundant from August to December. Edible-pod peas such as sugar snaps and mangetout are available all year round, as are frozen peas.

Look for Shop where peas are kept refrigerated (this keeps their sugars from turning to starch). Choose plump, medium-size pods with satiny skins and good green colour.

Prep Crack open green pea pods and push out peas. Pinch tips off mangetout and zip off strings from mangetout and both edges of sugar snap peas.

You need to remove the strings from both sides of sugar snap pea pods.

Basic cooking Cook green peas in a little liquid for 5 to 10 minutes; mangetout and sugar snaps, just 1 to 2 minutes. Or steam mangetout or sugar snaps for 3 to 5 minutes. Microwave 250 ml shelled green peas with 15 ml water. Cook on high for 5 minutes.

__Penne with Mangetout & Smoked Salmon__ partners emerald-green mangetout and luxurious smoked salmon in a creamy lemon-dill sauce.

__Warm Mangetout Salad with Mushrooms & Goat Cheese__ is served slightly warm to enhance its flavours.

Did you know? . . .

Cooked edible-pod peas contain three times as much vitamin C as green peas. If they are eaten raw or just barely cooked, their vitamin C levels are even higher.

Sugar snap peas have a thin, edible pod enclosing good-sized peas; both pod and peas are super-sweet. Because their peas are more fully developed, sugar snaps are somewhat higher in protein than mangetout (the figures given above are an average).

Warm Mangetout Salad with Mushrooms & Goat Cheese

PREP: 15 MINUTES / COOK: 10 MINUTES
MARINATE: 20 MINUTES

10 ml olive oil
225 g mushrooms, thinly sliced
2 cloves garlic, finely chopped
450 g mangetout, strings removed
1 small red pepper, cut into
   2 x 5-mm strips
2,5 ml salt
45 ml rice vinegar
10 ml honey
120 g watercress leaves (about 4 cups)
115 g soft mild goat cheese, crumbled
30 ml pecan nuts, toasted and
   chopped

1. In a large nonstick frying pan, heat 5 ml of the oil over moderately high heat. Add the mushrooms and sauté for 4 minutes or until tender and lightly browned. Add the garlic and cook for 1 minute. Add the mangetout, pepper and salt and sauté for 4 minutes or until crisp-tender.

2. Transfer to a large bowl. Mix vinegar, honey and remaining oil. Pour over the salad and toss to combine.

3. Divide the watercress among 4 salad plates and top with the mangetout mixture. Sprinkle with the goat cheese and pecan nuts. Serves 4.

Per serving: Kilojoules 949; Fibre 6 g; Protein 10 g; Total Fat 11 g; Saturated Fat 5 g; Cholesterol 13 mg; Sodium 428 mg

Sautéed Lamb & Sugar Snaps

PREP: 20 MINUTES / COOK: 15 MINUTES

10 ml vegetable oil
1 small onion, thinly sliced
2 cloves garlic, finely chopped
15 ml finely chopped fresh ginger
1 large red pepper, cut into thin strips
450 g well-trimmed, deboned leg of
   lamb, cut into 2 x 1-cm strips
450 g sugar snap peas, strings
   removed
125 ml chicken stock
60 ml chilli sauce
15 ml light soya sauce
10 ml honey
1,25 ml salt

1. In a large nonstick pan, heat the oil over moderate heat. Add the onion, garlic and ginger and sauté for 3 minutes or until the garlic is tender.

2. Add the pepper and sauté for 2 minutes or until crisp-tender. Add the lamb and sugar snaps and sauté for 4 minutes or until the lamb is just cooked through but still juicy and the peas are crisp-tender.

3. In a small bowl, combine the stock, chilli sauce, soya sauce, honey and salt. Pour into the pan and cook for 1 minute to heat through. Serves 4.

Per serving: Kilojoules 1 350; Fibre 9g; Protein 32g; Total Fat 10g; Saturated Fat 3g; Cholesterol 79mg; Sodium 711mg

Risi e Bisi

PREP: 10 MINUTES / COOK: 40 MINUTES

Risi e bisi simply means 'rice and peas' in Italian. In spring and summer, you can substitute fresh peas for frozen: add the fresh peas along with the rice in Step 2.

- **2 slices bacon (25g), finely chopped**
- **1 small onion, finely chopped**
- **250 ml rice**
- **425 ml chicken stock**
- **5 ml pepper**
- **1,25 ml salt**
- **500 ml frozen peas**
- **60 ml chopped parsley**
- **60 ml grated Parmesan cheese**

1. In a large nonstick saucepan, combine the bacon and 60ml of water over moderate heat. Cook, stirring occasionally, for 5 minutes or until the bacon has rendered its fat. Add the onion and sauté for 7 minutes or until golden brown and tender.

2. Add the rice, stirring to coat. Add the stock, 375ml of water, the pepper and salt and bring to a boil. Reduce to a simmer and cook for 15 minutes, stirring to prevent the rice from sticking to the saucepan. Stir in the peas and parsley, reduce the heat, cover and cook, stirring occasionally, for 10 minutes or until the rice is tender and the peas are heated through. Stir in the Parmesan and butter. Serves 4.

Per serving: Kilojoules 1 297; Fibre 8g; Protein 12g; Total Fat 6g; Saturated Fat 2g; Cholesterol 9mg; Sodium 990mg

Sugar Snaps with Mint Remove strings from 650g sugar snap peas. In a large steamer, cook sugar snaps until crisp-tender. Transfer to large bowl, add 15ml olive oil, 125ml chopped fresh mint and 3,5ml salt. Toss to combine. Serves 4. *[kJ 496; Fat 4g; Sodium 425mg]*

Mangetout & Pepper Salad Remove strings from 650g mangetout. In large steamer, cook mangetout until crisp-tender. In a large bowl, combine 30ml balsamic vinegar, 15ml olive oil, 2,5ml brown sugar and 2,5ml salt. Add mangetout, 1 slivered small onion (red, if available), 1 small slivered yellow pepper and one 230-g tin drained sliced water chestnuts. Toss well. Serves 4. *[kJ 867; Fat 4g; Sodium 307mg]*

Mockamole In a food processor, combine 500g thawed frozen peas, 125ml coriander-leaves, 30ml lime (or lemon) juice, 30ml light mayonnaise, 2,5ml ground coriander and 2,5ml salt. Process until smooth. Transfer to serving bowl and stir in 175ml chopped tomato and 2 sliced spring onions. Serves 4. *[kJ 608; Fat 4g; Sodium 384mg]*

Peppers

Green Pepper
PER 110 G RAW
(1 CUP)

Kilojoules	112
Fibre	2g
Protein	1g
Total Fat	0,1g
Saturated Fat	0g
Cholesterol	0mg
Sodium	6mg

NUTRIENTS

% RDA for people older than 10 years

Vitamin C	141%
Vitamin B6	9%
Vitamin A	5%

Did you know? . . .

The longer a pepper ripens, the sweeter and more healthy it becomes. A red pepper supplies nearly 13 times the beta carotene of a green pepper—and half again as much vitamin C.

Gram for gram, a red pepper contains four times as much vitamin C as an orange.

Roasted Red Peppers

PREP: 10 MINUTES / COOK: 12 MINUTES

Roasting peppers transforms them, rendering them savoury and slightly smoky-tasting. The traditional method of roasting peppers calls for holding a whole pepper directly over a flame and turning it as it chars. Here the process is considerably streamlined.

- 4 large peppers, cut lengthwise into flat panels and seeds removed
- 30 ml balsamic vinegar
- 15 ml olive oil
- 1,25 ml salt
- 1 clove garlic, crushed and peeled

1. Preheat the grill. Place the pepper pieces, skin-side up, on the grill rack and grill 10 centimetres from the heat for 12 minutes or until the skin is blackened. When the peppers are cool enough to handle, peel them and cut into 5-cm-wide strips.

2. In a medium bowl, combine the vinegar, oil and salt. Add the garlic and the peppers, tossing well. Cover and refrigerate for at least 1 hour or up to 3 days. Remove and discard the garlic before serving. Makes 750 millilitres (3 cups).

Per 125 ml (½ cup): Kilojoules 229; Fibre 1g; Protein 1g; Total Fat 3g; Saturated Fat trace; Cholesterol 0mg; Sodium 102mg

Bread Salad with Roasted Peppers

PREP: 15 MINUTES / COOK: 20 MINUTES

If you use an English cucumber, do not peel it as the skin is tender enough to eat.

- 4 roasted red peppers (see at left)
- 750 ml Italian or French bread cubes (3 cups)
- 1 large tomato, diced
- 375 ml diced (1 cm) English cucumber
- 85 g feta cheese, crumbled
- 60 ml black olives (in brine), pitted and coarsely chopped

1. Prepare the roasted red peppers as directed in recipe on left, but omit the salt and garlic.

2. Preheat the oven to 190°C. Spread the bread cubes on a baking sheet and bake, tossing occasionally, for 7 minutes or until lightly crisped, but not browned.

3. In a large salad bowl, combine the peppers and their marinade with the toasted bread, the tomato, cucumber, feta and olives, tossing well. Serve at room temperature or chilled. Serves 4.

Per serving: Kilojoules 1 058; Fibre 4g; Protein 9g; Total Fat 12g; Saturated Fat 4g; Cholesterol 15mg; Sodium 461mg

Tex-Mex Stuffed Peppers

PREP: 15 MINUTES / COOK: 25 MINUTES

- 2 large red peppers
- 2 large green peppers
- 20 ml olive oil
- 3 small onions, thinly sliced
- 3 cloves garlic, finely chopped
- 250 ml rice
- 2,5 ml salt
- 2,5 ml ground cumin
- 0,6 ml cayenne pepper (optional)
- 1 tin (410 g) red kidney beans, rinsed and drained
- 115g mild Cheddar cheese, grated
- 2 plum tomatoes, coarsely chopped

1. Slice off the top 1 cm of each pepper at the stem end and reserve. Remove and discard the ribs and seeds from the inside of the peppers. Discard the stems and finely chop the reserved pepper tops; set aside.

2. In a medium saucepan, heat the oil over moderate heat. Add the onions and garlic and sauté for 2 minutes or until softened. Add the chopped pepper pieces and cook, stirring occasionally, for 4 minutes or until crisp-tender.

3. Add the rice, salt, cumin, cayenne and 560 ml of water. Bring to a boil, reduce to a simmer, cover and cook for 17 minutes or until the rice is tender. Stir in the beans and cheese and cook just until the cheese has melted and the beans are piping hot.

4. Meanwhile, in a large pot of boiling water, cook the peppers for 4 minutes or until softened. Spoon the rice mixture into the drained pepper halves, top with the chopped tomato and serve. Serves 4.

Per serving: Kilojoules 1 961; Fibre 9g; Protein 17g; Total Fat 15g; Saturated Fat 6g; Cholesterol 33mg; Sodium 708mg

At the market Peppers are now available all year round. Green peppers are most common, but red and yellow peppers are also available. Red and yellow peppers can be quite expensive because the seed is imported from Holland and they are grown in hothouse tunnels on a limited scale.

Look for Peppers should be smooth, unblemished and bright in colour. Choose peppers that are heavy for their size: hefty peppers have thick, meaty walls.

Prep If you're slicing or chopping peppers, halve them lengthwise and pull off the stem and cap; pull out the ribs and seeds with your fingers. For roasting, slice the pepper lengthwise into flat panels. Peppers can be roasted and then frozen.

It's easier to peel roasted peppers if you stem them and cut them into relatively flat pieces instead of roasting them whole.

Bread Salad with Roasted Peppers *is a satisfying variation on an Italian classic.*

Red Pepper Relish is
sweet, sour, hot, herby
and vividly colourful.

Red Pepper
PER 110G RAW
(1 CUP)

Kilojoules	145
Fibre	2,2g
Protein	1g
Total Fat	0,2g
Saturated Fat	0g
Cholesterol	0mg
Sodium	2mg

NUTRIENTS

% RDA for people older than 10 years	
Vitamin C	348%
Vitamin A	78%
Vitamin B6	14%

Did you know? . . .

Because of their high vitamin C content, peppers are a good choice to serve with iron-rich foods such as beef. The vitamin C enhances iron absorption.

You can add a lot of nutritional value to a salad (such as tuna, chicken or pasta) by serving it in a 'bowl' made from a seeded pepper.

Peppers belong to the same species as chilli peppers, but sweet peppers lack the tongue-tingling heat of chillies because they do not contain capsaicin.

Pipérade

PREP: 20 MINUTES / COOK: 15 MINUTES

Here's a lightened version of a traditional pepper and scrambled egg dish from the Basque region of France. Extra egg whites stand in for some of the yolks and cottage cheese adds a satisfying richness.

- 15 ml olive oil
- 3 large red peppers, cut into 5-mm-wide strips
- 2 large green peppers, cut into 5-mm-wide strips
- 1 onion, halved and thinly sliced
- 4 cloves garlic, finely chopped
- 3,5 ml salt
- 1 large tomato, finely chopped
- 2 eggs
- 4 egg whites
- 60 ml smooth low-fat cottage cheese
- 15 ml flour
- 2,5 ml black pepper

1. In a large nonstick frying pan, heat the oil over moderate heat. Add the peppers, onion, garlic and 1,25 ml of the salt and sauté for 5 minutes or until the peppers are crisp-tender. Add the tomato and cook, stirring, for 7 minutes or until the liquid has evaporated.

2. Meanwhile, in a food processor, combine the whole eggs, egg whites, cottage cheese, flour, black pepper and the remaining salt and process until smooth.

3. Pour the egg mixture into the frying pan, reduce the heat to low and cook, stirring, for 3 minutes or until set. Serves 4.

Per serving: Kilojoules 797; Fibre 4g; Protein 11g; Total Fat 7g; Saturated Fat 1g; Cholesterol 105mg; Sodium 531mg

Pepper Steak

PREP: 15 MINUTES / COOK: 10 MINUTES

- 15 ml olive oil
- 4 green peppers, cut into thin strips
- 1 onion, halved and thinly sliced
- 4 cloves garlic, finely chopped
- 450 g well-trimmed beef steak, cut into 1-cm-wide strips
- 125 ml chicken stock
- 30 ml dry sherry
- 15 ml light soya sauce
- 10 ml cornflour
- 2,5 ml crushed chilli flakes

1. In a large nonstick frying pan, heat 10 ml of the oil over moderate heat. Add the peppers, onion and garlic and sauté for 5 minutes.

2. Add the remaining 5 ml oil and the beef and sauté for 2 minutes or until no longer pink. In a small bowl, whisk the stock, sherry and soya sauce into the cornflour. Stir in the chilli flakes and 125 ml of water. Pour into the frying pan, bring to a boil and cook, stirring, for 1 minute or until slightly thickened. Serves 4.

Per serving: Kilojoules 1188; Fibre 4 g; Protein 29 g; Total Fat 11 g; Saturated Fat 3 g; Cholesterol 71 mg; Sodium 473 mg

Red Pepper Relish

PREP: 15 MINUTES / COOK: 20 MINUTES
CHILL: 1 HOUR

Serve this lively condiment with grilled chicken or fish and reap the benefits: a 125-ml serving supplies three times the RDA for vitamin C.

125 ml balsamic or red wine vinegar
60 ml firmly packed light brown sugar
4 large red peppers, cut into 1-cm squares
1 large tomato, diced
1 small onion, thinly sliced
2,5 ml salt
0,6 ml cayenne pepper
70 ml chopped fresh basil

1. In a medium saucepan, combine the vinegar and sugar. Bring to a boil over moderate heat, stirring to dissolve the sugar. Add the peppers, tomato, onion, salt and cayenne. Reduce to a simmer, cover and cook for 5 minutes or until the peppers are tender.

2. Reserving the cooking liquid, drain the relish and transfer to a bowl. Return the liquid to the saucepan, bring to a boil and cook for 5 to 10 minutes or until reduced by half. Stir in the basil, pour over the relish and cool at room temperature. Refrigerate for at least 1 hour. Makes 750 millilitres (3 cups).

Per 125 ml (½ cup): Kilojoules 341; Fibre 2 g; Protein 1 g; Total Fat 0 g; Saturated Fat 0 g; Cholesterol 0 mg; Sodium 206 mg

Pepper Soup In a covered saucepan, simmer 3 diced red peppers, 1 diced green pepper, 1 small diced onion, 2 cloves finely chopped garlic, 250 ml chopped tomatoes, 250 ml chicken stock, 5 ml ground coriander and 2,5 ml salt until flavourful. Stir in some chopped parsley. Serves 4. *[kJ 325; Fat 1 g; Sodium 692 mg]*

Pasta with Red Pepper Sauce
In small pan of boiling water, blanch 3 cloves garlic for 2 minutes. In food processor, purée the garlic, 500 ml drained, bottled roasted red peppers, 125 ml chicken stock, 30 ml tomato paste, 15 ml olive oil and 1,25 ml pepper. Cook 350 g fusilli pasta. Toss with pepper purée and sprinkle with 30 ml Parmesan. Serves 4. *[kJ 1630; Fat 6 g; Sodium 393 mg]*

Multi-Pepper Stir-Fry
In a large nonstick wok or frying pan, sauté 2 each sliced red and yellow peppers, 1 sliced green pepper and 2 cloves finely chopped garlic in 15 ml olive oil until crisp-tender. Add 60 ml chopped basil, 30 ml red wine vinegar, 5 ml sugar and 2,5 ml salt and cook for 2 minutes. Serves 4. *[kJ 436; Fat 4 g; Sodium 308 mg]*

Potatoes

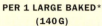

Nutritional power

Potatoes combine energy-giving complex carbohydrates, with plenty of vitamin C, fibre and potassium. They're filling and, if sensibly prepared, low in fat.

PER 1 LARGE BAKED* (140 G)	
Kilojoules	659
Fibre	3,4 g
Protein	3,2 g
Total Fat	0,1 g
Saturated Fat	0 g
Cholesterol	0 mg
Sodium	11 mg

NUTRIENTS	
% RDA for people older than 10 years	
Vitamin C	30 %
Vitamin B6	24 %
Iron	14 %
Pantothenic acid	13 %
Niacin	12 %
Thiamin	11 %

*with skin

Did you know? . . .

Potatoes are an excellent source of vitamin C in a westernized diet, simply because they are eaten regularly.

A baked potato supplies more than twice as much potassium as a banana.

Onion & Potato Pancakes

PREP: 15 MINUTES / COOK: 40 MINUTES

Sautéed onions bring robust flavour to these mashed-potato pancakes.

700 g large potatoes, peeled and thinly sliced
25 ml vegetable oil
2 medium onions, finely chopped
45 ml sour cream
3,5 ml salt
1,25 ml pepper
0,6 ml grated nutmeg
45 ml flour

1. In a pot of boiling water, cook the potatoes for 15 minutes or until tender. Drain and transfer to a large bowl.

2. Meanwhile, in a large nonstick frying pan, heat 5 ml of the oil over moderate heat. Add the onions and sauté for 7 minutes or until golden brown and tender.

3. Add the sour cream, salt, pepper and nutmeg to the bowl with the potatoes and mash with a potato masher. Stir in the sautéed onions. Using a 70-ml measure, shape into 8 cakes.

4. In a 30-cm nonstick pan, heat 10 ml of the oil over moderate heat. Dredge the cakes in the flour, shaking off the excess. Sauté 4 of the cakes for 3 minutes per side or until golden brown and crusty. Repeat with the remaining oil and 4 potato cakes. Serves 4.

Per serving: Kilojoules 1037; Fibre 3g; Protein 4g; Total Fat 9g; Saturated Fat 3g; Cholesterol 10mg; Sodium 435mg

Potato Salad with Mustard Dressing

PREP: 20 MINUTES / COOK: 30 MINUTES

900 g potatoes (preferably red), peeled and cut into 1-cm pieces
15 ml olive oil
1 large onion, chopped
1 red pepper, cut into 1-cm squares
1 green pepper, cut into 1-cm squares
250 ml chicken stock
45 ml distilled white vinegar
15 ml Dijon mustard
2,5 ml salt
60 g shaved smoked turkey or ham

1. In a large pot of boiling water, cook the potatoes for 15 minutes or until tender. Drain well. Be careful not to overcook them.

2. Meanwhile, in a large frying pan, heat the oil over moderate heat. Add

Mixed Potato Chowder Three kinds of potatoes go into this satisfying stew.

At the market Potatoes are in good supply all year round. Look for new (Nicola), baking (Fianna), red-skin (Lady Rozetta) and all-purpose potatoes.

Look for Well-shaped potatoes, free of sprouts and blemishes, are best. Avoid those with green skin, cracks or wrinkles.

Prep Scrub potatoes under running water; use a vegetable brush if necessary.

A potato masher will leave some texture in mashed potatoes. A food processor can turn them gluey.

Basic cooking When boiling potatoes, start them in boiling water to preserve vitamin C. Whole small potatoes take 10 to 15 minutes, larger potatoes 20 to 40 minutes, depending on size. Boil sliced potatoes for 15 to 20 minutes. Before baking or microwaving, pierce whole potatoes in several places. Oven-bake for 45 to 60 minutes at 190°C. Microwave 4 baking potatoes on high for 13 to 15 minutes.

---

the onion and peppers and sauté for 5 minutes or until the peppers are crisp-tender. Transfer the vegetables to a large serving bowl.

3. Whisk the stock, vinegar, mustard and salt into the bowl. Add the potato pieces and turkey (or ham), tossing until well combined. Serve warm or chilled. Serves 6.

Per serving: Kilojoules 715; Fibre 3g; Protein 5g; Total Fat 3g; Saturated Fat 1g; Cholesterol 8mg; Sodium 677mg

---

Mixed Potato Chowder

PREP: 20 MINUTES / COOK: 40 MINUTES

The red and sweet potatoes will hold their shape, but the ordinary potatoes will fall apart as they simmer, thickening the broth.

- **10 ml vegetable oil**
- **1 medium onion, finely chopped**
- **3 cloves garlic, finely chopped**
- **450 g potatoes, peeled and thinly sliced**
- **350 g red potatoes, cut into 1-cm pieces (red potatoes are essential in this recipe)**
- **225 g sweet potatoes, peeled and cut into 1-cm pieces**
- **250 ml chicken stock**
- **3,5 ml salt**
- **2,5 ml dried sage**
- **250 ml low-fat (2%) milk**
- **150 ml frozen corn kernels**
- **125 ml chopped parsley**

1. In a medium saucepan, heat the oil over moderate heat. Add the onion and garlic and sauté for 7 minutes or until the onion is soft.

2. Add the ordinary potatoes, red potatoes and sweet potatoes, stirring to coat. Add the stock, 500 ml of water, the salt and sage and bring to a boil. Reduce to a simmer, cover and cook for 25 minutes or until the red potatoes and sweet potatoes are tender and the ordinary potatoes are soft and creamy.

3. Stir in the milk and corn kernels and simmer for 4 minutes or until the corn kernels are heated through. Stir in the parsley. Serves 4.

Per serving: Kilojoules 1135; Fibre 5g; Protein 7g; Total Fat 4g; Saturated Fat 1g; Cholesterol 4mg; Sodium 843mg

Potato Torte *Made of thin layers of potatoes, this savoury 'cake' is actually very easy to prepare.*

Did you know? . . .

Starting potatoes to cook in cold water increases the loss of vitamin C and may cause the potatoes to discolour. Instead, add the potatoes to already-boiling water, or place them in a pot and pour boiling water over them.

Greenish skin—or sprouts—on a potato signal elevated levels of solanine, a bitter-tasting compound that is a natural component of this vegetable. Bruising or improper storage encourages solanine to develop. It's best to discard any potatoes that have a greenish tinge or more than one or two sprouts. It would take a lot of solanine to make you ill, but it's preferable to avoid it.

Plain potatoes are virtually fat-free, but 55 grams of commercial potato chips (crisps) pack about 20 grams of fat.

Potato Torte

PREP: 10 MINUTES / COOK: 50 MINUTES

- 25 ml olive oil
- 900 g baking potatoes, peeled and very thinly sliced
- 3,5 ml each salt and pepper
- 60 ml grated Parmesan cheese
- 1 small onion, thinly sliced
- 45 ml chopped fresh parsley

1. Preheat the oven to 230°C. Brush a 23-cm ovenproof pie dish with 5 ml of the oil. Cover the bottom with an over-lapping layer of potatoes, using one-quarter of the total. Sprinkle with 5 ml of the oil, 1,25 ml each of the salt and pepper, 15 ml of the Parmesan cheese, one-third of the onion and 15 ml of the parsley.

2. Repeat for 2 more layers. Top with a final layer of potatoes and the remaining 5 ml oil and 15 ml Parmesan cheese. Cover with heavy foil or a lid and bake in the lower third of the oven for 50 minutes or until the potatoes are crusty on the bottom (lift gently with a spatula to check) and soft and tender throughout.

3. Cool in the dish for 5 minutes before loosening the bottom and sides with a small spatula and inverting onto a platter. Serves 4.

Per serving: Kilojoules 1 031; Fibre 3g; Protein 6g; Total Fat 8g; Saturated Fat 2g; Cholesterol 4mg; Sodium 530mg

Scalloped Potatoes with Roast Chicken

PREP: 20 MINUTES / COOK: 1 HOUR

The aroma of this casserole as it bakes ensures that nobody will be late for dinner. Serve it with a big green salad.

- 1 clove garlic, peeled and halved
- 1 kg potatoes, peeled and thinly sliced
- 60 g diced roast chicken (use left-over roast chicken)
- 60 ml plus 30 ml grated Parmesan cheese
- 45 ml flour
- 2,5 ml each salt and pepper
- 250 ml chicken stock
- 60 ml sour cream

1. Preheat the oven to 200°C. Rub a 23-cm square glass or ceramic baking dish with the garlic; discard the garlic.

2. Dividing evenly, make alternating layers of potatoes, roast chicken, 60 ml of the Parmesan cheese, the flour, salt and pepper.

3. In a medium bowl, whisk together the stock and sour cream. Pour the mixture over the potatoes. Sprinkle the top with the remaining 30 ml Parmesan, cover with foil and bake for 45 minutes. Uncover and bake for 15 minutes or until the potatoes are tender. Serves 4.

Per serving: Kilojoules 1 218; Fibre 3 g; Protein 12 g; Total Fat 8 g; Saturated Fat 4 g; Cholesterol 32 mg; Sodium 855 mg

Curried Cauliflower & Potato Stew

PREP: 15 MINUTES / COOK: 35 MINUTES
Indian spices enliven this unusual stew.

- 10 ml olive oil
- 1 small onion, thinly sliced
- 30 ml chopped fresh ginger
- 1 kg potatoes, peeled and cut into 2,5-cm pieces
- 1 head of cauliflower, cut into florets
- 15 ml curry powder
- 5 ml each ground coriander and cumin
- 2,5 ml salt
- 250 ml tinned tomatoes, chopped
- 70 ml plain low-fat yoghurt
- 10 ml flour

1. In a large nonstick pan, heat the oil over moderate heat. Add the onion and ginger and sauté for 2 minutes or until the onion is tender. Add the potatoes, cauliflower, curry powder, coriander, cumin and salt, stirring to combine. Add 375 ml of water and bring to a boil. Reduce to a simmer, cover and cook for 15 minutes or until the potatoes are not quite tender.

2. Add the tomatoes, cover and cook for 10 minutes or until the potatoes and cauliflower are tender. In a small bowl, combine the yoghurt and flour. Whisk the yoghurt mixture into the pan and cook for 1 minute or until slightly thickened. Serves 4.

Per serving: Kilojoules 1 019; Fibre 6 g; Protein 6 g; Total Fat 3 g; Saturated Fat 1 g; Cholesterol 1 mg; Sodium 430 mg

Garlic-Cheddar Mashed Potatoes

In a saucepan of boiling water, cook 1 kg peeled, thinly sliced baking potatoes and 6 peeled cloves garlic until tender. Drain and mash with 70 ml low-fat buttermilk, 175 ml grated Cheddar, 3,5 ml salt and 2,5 ml paprika. Serves 6.
[kJ 604; Fat 3 g; Sodium 333 mg]

Cajun Oven Fries

Preheat oven to 220°C. Thinly slice 1 kg unpeeled baking potatoes lengthwise. In a large bowl, combine 30 ml vegetable oil, 10 ml chilli powder, 2,5 ml thyme, 2,5 ml black pepper and 1,25 ml cayenne. Add potatoes, tossing to coat. Place on 2 baking trays and bake for 30 to 45 minutes or until browned and crisp. Serves 4.
[kJ 1090; Fat 8 g; Sodium 10 mg]

Deli-Style Potato

Salad In large bowl, combine 70 ml plain fat-free yoghurt, 60 ml light mayonnaise, 60 ml chicken stock, 45 ml red wine vinegar, 1 medium onion, chopped, 2,5 ml salt and 2,5 ml pepper. In large pot of boiling water, cook 1 kg quartered small red potatoes until tender. Drain. Add to bowl and toss. Serves 4.
[kJ 1127; Fat 6 g; Sodium 555 mg]

Crisp Potato Skins with Creamy Mashed Potato Stuffing *rolls two favourites into one delicious side dish.*

Did you know? . . .

'Baking' potatoes in a microwave is a healthy way to cook them and a great timesaver too. But be sure to pierce the potatoes in several places with a fork or knife before microwaving, or the potatoes may explode.

It's a good idea to eat baked potatoes skin and all. Some of the nutrients (such as iron, phosphorus and potassium) are concentrated in or just under the skin. You'll also get more dietary fibre by eating the skin.

To flavour potatoes without adding fat, toss a few garlic cloves, onion slices or dried herbs into the cooking water.

Potatoes and onions shouldn't be stored together. A gas given off by the onions will speed up the spoilage of potatoes (and vice versa).

Spice Cake with Brown Sugar Icing

PREP: 25 MINUTES / COOK: 45 MINUTES

280 g baking potatoes, peeled and thinly sliced
500 ml flour
5 ml ground cinnamon
3,5 ml ground ginger
3,5 ml baking powder
2,5 ml bicarbonate of soda
1,25 m salt
0,6 ml each ground cloves and allspice
70 ml vegetable oil
375 ml granulated sugar
1 egg
2 egg whites
225 g smooth low-fat cottage cheese, at room temperature
60 ml firmly packed light brown sugar
5 ml vanilla essence
125 ml apricot jam

1. Preheat the oven to 180°C. Spray a 23-cm springform tin with nonstick cooking spray. Line the bottom with a circle of greaseproof paper and spray with nonstick cooking spray. Dust with flour, shaking off the excess.

2. In a large pot of boiling water, cook the potatoes for 12 minutes or until tender. Drain well. Mash with a potato masher; set aside.

3. On a sheet of greaseproof paper, sift the flour, cinnamon, ginger, baking powder, bicarbonate of soda, salt, cloves and allspice. In a large bowl beat the oil and granulated sugar with an electric mixer until well blended. Add the whole egg and egg whites, one at a time, beating well after each addition. Beat in the potatoes. Fold in the flour mixture.

4. Scrape the batter into the prepared tin, smoothing the top. Bake for 45 minutes or until a cake tester inserted in the centre comes out just clean. Cool for 15 minutes in the tin on a rack, then invert onto the rack to cool completely. With a long serrated knife, cut the cake into 2 horizontal layers and place the bottom layer on a cake plate.

5. In a medium bowl cream the cottage cheese with the brown sugar and vanilla essence with an electric mixer. In a small saucepan, melt the jam over low heat. Spread the bottom layer with the jam. Top with the second layer and spread the icing over the top and sides of the cake. Serves 10.

Per serving: Kilojoules 1 670; Fibre; 1g; Protein 6g; Total Fat 9g; Saturated Fat 1g; Cholesterol 22mg; Sodium 128mg

Crisp Potato Skins with Creamy Mashed Potato Stuffing

PREP: 15 MINUTES
COOK: 1 HOUR 10 MINUTES

4 large (225g each) baking potatoes
10ml vegetable oil
60ml grated Parmesan cheese
125ml low-fat (2%) milk
45ml smooth low-fat cottage cheese
3,5ml salt
1,25ml pepper
0,6ml grated nutmeg
20ml sour cream
4 spring onions, thinly sliced

1. Preheat the oven to 230°C. Prick the potatoes in several places with a fork and bake for 1 hour or until firm-tender. Leave the oven on.

2. Halve the potatoes lengthwise and scoop out the flesh, leaving 5mm of flesh on the skin. Brush the insides of the potato skins with the oil and sprinkle with 30ml of the Parmesan cheese. Place the skins, cut-sides up, on a baking tray and bake for 5 minutes or until they are crisp and golden. Leave the oven on.

3. Meanwhile, in a medium bowl, mash the potato flesh with the milk, cottage cheese, salt, pepper, nutmeg and the remaining 30ml Parmesan cheese.

4. Spoon the mashed potato mixture into the crisped potato skins, return to the oven and bake for 5 minutes or until piping hot. Top the potatoes with the sour cream and sprinkle with the spring onions. Serves 4.

Per serving: Kilojoules 1 025; Fibre 3g; Protein 7g; Total Fat 6g; Saturated Fat 2g; Cholesterol 9mg; Sodium 549mg

Hash Browns Cook 650g potatoes in boiling water; peel and dice. In a frying pan, sauté 1 large chopped onion, 1 large chopped green pepper and 1 clove chopped garlic in 15ml olive oil. Add potatoes to pan with 3,5ml salt and 2,5ml pepper; cook until browned. Serves 4. *[kJ 789; Fat 4g; Sodium 431mg]*

Potato-Cheese Soup In a saucepan, combine 500ml chicken stock, 500ml water, 3 cloves garlic and 1 large sliced onion. Bring to boil, add 650g peeled and sliced potatoes and cook until tender. Partially mash with potato masher. Stir in 250ml grated Cheddar until melted. Serve garnished with 60ml chopped spring onion. Serves 4. *[kJ 1038; Fat 7g; Sodium 878mg]*

Roasted New Potatoes Preheat the oven to 220°C. Pour 30ml vegetable oil into 23 x 33-cm roasting tin. Add 4 cloves garlic and 2,5ml rosemary. Heat 5 minutes in the oven. Add 900g quartered small red potatoes; cook, tossing occasionally, for 50 minutes or until done. Sprinkle with 2,5ml salt. Serves 4. *[kJ 1009; Fat 8g; Sodium 306mg]*

Pumpkin & Squash

Pumpkin (Boerpampoen)

PER 210 G COOKED (1 CUP)

Kilojoules	193
Fibre	3,4 g
Protein	1 g
Total Fat	0,2 g
Saturated Fat	0,1 g
Cholesterol	0 mg
Sodium	4 mg

NUTRIENTS

% RDA for people older than 10 years

Vitamin A	56 %
Vitamin C	18 %

Did you know? . . .

Pumpkin purée is nearly as nutritious as raw pumpkin. However watch out for extra kilojoules if sugar is added.

Very large pumpkins do not make good eating. Large 'field' pumpkins are stringy and dry. For cooking, choose smaller pumpkins.

Pumpkin-Date Muffins with Almonds

PREP: 20 MINUTES / COOK: 35 MINUTES

The dates and almonds account for a good portion of the dietary fibre in these tender, lightly sweet muffins.

- 250 ml cooked pumpkin purée
- 375 ml flour
- 70 ml packed light brown sugar
- 10 ml baking powder
- 2,5 ml bicarbonate of soda
- 1,25 ml salt
- 125 ml chopped dates
- 60 ml chopped almonds
- 2 eggs, lightly beaten
- 125 ml low-fat cultured buttermilk
- 125 ml sour cream

1. Make the pumpkin purée by steaming 5-cm pieces of pumpkin until soft. Mash with a potato masher.

2. Preheat the oven to 180°C. Line 12 x 6-cm muffin tins with paper cups (or use nonstick cooking spray). In a large bowl, stir together the flour, brown sugar, baking powder, bicarbonate of soda and salt. Stir in the dates and almonds.

3. In a medium bowl, combine the pumpkin, eggs, buttermilk and sour cream. Make a well in the centre of the dry ingredients and pour in the pumpkin mixture. Stir just until combined.

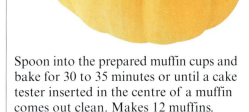

Spoon into the prepared muffin cups and bake for 30 to 35 minutes or until a cake tester inserted in the centre of a muffin comes out clean. Makes 12 muffins.

Per muffin: Kilojoules 645; Fibre 2 g; Protein 4 g; Total Fat 6 g; Saturated Fat 2 g; Cholesterol 45 mg; Sodium 204 mg

Fresh Pumpkin Stew with Chickpeas

PREP: 25 MINUTES / COOK: 35 MINUTES

This tasty combination of pumpkin, potatoes, tomatoes and chickpeas is thickened with peanut butter—a West African technique.

- 15 ml olive oil
- 1 large onion, finely chopped
- 3 cloves garlic, finely chopped
- 1 kg fresh pumpkin or butternut squash, peeled and cut into 2,5-cm pieces
- 350 g small potatoes (red, if available), halved
- 250 ml chicken stock

1 tin (410 g) tomatoes, chopped and peeled with their juice

3,5 ml each dried oreganum and salt

1 tin (425 g) chickpeas, rinsed and drained

30 ml creamy peanut butter

1. In a nonstick large saucepan, heat the oil over moderate heat. Add the onion and garlic and sauté for 5 minutes or until the onion is soft.

2. Add the pumpkin and potatoes, stirring to coat. Add the stock, tomatoes and their juice, oreganum and salt. Bring to a boil, reduce to a simmer, cover and cook for 20 minutes.

3. Add the chickpeas, stir in the peanut butter and cook for 10 minutes or until the pumpkin and potatoes are tender. Serves 4.

Per serving: Kilojoules 1 424; Fibre 10 g; Protein 12 g; Total Fat 10 g; Saturated Fat 2 g; Cholesterol 0 mg; Sodium 1 316 mg

Pumpkin-Date Muffins with Almonds *make a tempting breakfast or snack; they freeze beautifully if well wrapped.*

Pumpkin Cheesecake

Prep: 20 minutes / Cook: 2 hours
Chill: 4 hours

85 g ginger biscuits (about 12 biscuits)

15 ml vegetable oil

175 ml plus 15 ml sugar

675 g smooth low-fat cottage cheese (1 tub weighs 250 g)

425 g cooked pumpkin purée (see opposite page)

2 eggs

4 egg whites

125 ml plain low-fat yoghurt

5 ml vanilla essence

1,25 ml salt

1. Preheat the oven to 150°C. Spray a 23-cm springform tin with nonstick cooking spray.

2. In a food processor, combine the ginger biscuits, oil and 15 ml of the sugar. Process until the crumbs are evenly moistened. Press the crumb mixture into the bottom of the prepared tin; set aside.

3. In a medium bowl, beat the cottage cheese and the remaining 175 ml sugar with an electric mixer until well combined. Beat in the pumpkin purée until well combined. Beat in the whole eggs and egg whites, one at a time, beating well after each addition. Beat in the yoghurt, vanilla essence and salt until blended.

4. Pour the batter into the prepared crust and bake for 1 hour and 30 minutes or until set. Turn the oven off and let the cake stand in the oven for 30 minutes; then cool on a wire rack and refrigerate for 4 hours or until well chilled. Serves 12.

Per serving: Kilojoules 558; Fibre 1 g; Protein 3 g; Total Fat 3 g; Saturated Fat 1 g; Cholesterol 38 mg; Sodium 111 mg

At the market You can buy varieties of pumpkin and squash all year round.

Look for The rind should be dry and clean, with a dull, almost velvety-looking finish and clear, uniform colour.

Prep If you only need a slice, use a heavy chef's knife to split it (notch the rind first to give the blade a secure hold). If necessary, use a mallet to tap the knife through the squash

If the rind is not too tough, 'rock' the knife through it.

Basic cooking Bake squash halves or quarters in a foil-lined pan at 200°C for 40 to 45 minutes. Steam peeled pieces for 15 to 20 minutes. Because of its thick skin, squash may explode if microwaved whole. Instead, microwave halves or quarters, covered, for 7 to 10 minutes.

Chicken Stew with Butternut Squash
Butternut takes the place of potatoes in this hearty stew.

Butternut Squash
PER 210G COOKED (1 CUP)

Kilojoules	494
Fibre	4g
Protein	3g
Total Fat	0,2g
Saturated Fat	0g
Cholesterol	0mg
Sodium	4mg

NUTRIENTS

% RDA for people older than 10 years	
Vitamin A	87%
Vitamin E	28%
Niacin	16%
Vitamin C	14%
Biotin	13%
Vitamin B6	9%
Folate	4%

Did you know? . . .

Pumpkins which have been stored for several months have a higher beta carotene content than freshly-picked pumpkins. In South Africa it is quite a common sight in the countryside to see stored pumpkins on the roofs of farm out-buildings.

Pumpkin rarely causes allergies and is easily digested—hence its popularity as a baby food.

Chicken Stew with Butternut Squash

PREP: 25 MINUTES / COOK: 35 MINUTES

An appealing autumn supper with its bright orange colour.

15ml vegetable oil
550g skinless, boned chicken breasts, cut into 2,5-cm pieces
45ml flour
1 large onion, cut into 1-cm pieces
4 cloves garlic, slivered
1 large butternut squash (1kg), peeled and cut into 2,5-cm pieces
500ml tinned chopped tomatoes
250ml chicken stock
125ml apple juice
30ml tomato paste
2,5ml each dried sage and salt
1,25ml pepper

1. In a large nonstick casserole dish or heavy-bottomed saucepan, heat 7,5ml of the oil over moderate heat. Dredge the chicken in the flour, shaking off the excess. Add half of the chicken to the casserole dish and sauté for 3 minutes or until lightly browned on both sides. Transfer the chicken to a plate. Repeat with the remaining chicken and 7,5ml oil.

2. Add the onion and garlic to the casserole and sauté for 7 minutes or until the onion is soft. Add the butternut squash, stirring to coat. Add the chopped tomatoes, stock, apple juice, tomato paste, sage, salt and pepper and bring to a boil. Once it is boiling, reduce to a simmer, cover and cook for 7 minutes.

3. Return the chicken to the pan, bring to a simmer, cover and cook for 10 minutes or until the chicken is cooked through and the squash is tender. Serves 4.

Per serving: Kilojoules 1438; Fibre 5g; Protein 29g; Total Fat 7g; Saturated Fat 1g; Cholesterol 51mg; Sodium 993mg

Butternut Squash Tea Bread

PREP: 15 MINUTES
COOK: 1 HOUR 30 MINUTES

Maize meal adds a lovely texture to this not-too-sweet bread. For best results, don't overmix after adding the dry ingredients.

1 small butternut squash (650 g),
  halved lengthwise and seeded
310 ml flour
125 ml yellow maize meal (mealie
  meal)
5 ml baking powder
3,5 ml cinnamon
2,5 ml each ground ginger, bicarbonate
  of soda and salt
1,25 ml pepper
125 ml packed light brown sugar
60 ml vegetable oil
1 egg
2 egg whites

1. Preheat the oven to 200°C. Spray a 22 x 12,5 x 7,5-cm loaf tin with non-stick cooking spray; set aside. Place the squash, cut-sides down, in a small baking tin. Add 125 ml water, cover and bake for 30 minutes or until the squash is tender. When cool enough to handle, scoop the flesh into a bowl and mash with a fork. Measure out 310 ml (save any remainder for another use). Reduce the oven temperature to 180°C.

2. In a medium bowl, stir together the flour, maize meal, baking powder, cinnamon, ginger, bicarbonate of soda, salt and pepper; set aside.

3. In another medium bowl, beat together the brown sugar and oil with an electric mixer until well combined. Add the whole egg and egg whites, one at a time, beating well after each addition. Beat in the 310 ml mashed squash. Fold in the dry ingredients.

4. Spoon the batter into the prepared tin and bake for 1 hour or until a cake tester inserted in the centre comes out clean. Serves 12.

Per serving: Kilojoules 707; Fibre 1 g; Protein 3 g; Total Fat 6 g; Saturated Fat 1 g; Cholesterol 18 mg; Sodium 116 mg

Pumpkin-Cheese Soup

In a saucepan, sauté 1 small onion and 2 cloves garlic in 10 ml oil until tender. Add 425 g cooled pumpkin purée, 375 ml low-fat (2%) milk, 3,5 ml salt and 2,5 ml pepper. Boil 1 minute. Add 250 ml grated Cheddar and stir until melted. Serves 4. *[kJ 699; Fat 10 g; Sodium 579 mg]*

Sweet Spiced Pumpkin Butter

In a heavy-bottomed saucepan, combine 425 g pumpkin purée, 150 ml packed light brown sugar, 70 ml granulated sugar, 60 ml orange juice, 5 ml ground ginger and 3,5 ml cinnamon. Cook over moderate heat, stirring, for 25 minutes or until thick enough to spread like jam. Keep refrigerated. Makes 500 ml/16 servings. *[kJ 205; Fat 0 g; Sodium 3 mg]*

Apricot-Maple Gem Squash

Halve and seed four large ripe gem squash. Place cut-sides down in baking pan, add 70 ml water, cover with foil and bake for 25 minutes at 200°C. Drain. Turn cut-sides up. Stir together 60 ml apricot jam and 30 ml maple syrup. Spoon into squash. Bake for 35 minutes or until tender. Serves 4. *[kJ 445; Fat 0 g; Sodium 26 mg]*

Salad greens

Cos Lettuce

PER 120G RAW (2 CUPS)	
Kilojoules	71
Fibre	2,0 g
Protein	2 g
Total Fat	0,2 g
Saturated Fat	0 g
Cholesterol	0 mg
Sodium	10 mg

NUTRIENTS

% RDA for people older than 10 years	
Vitamin C	48%
Folate	40%
Vitamin A	39%
Iron	9%

Iceberg Lettuce

PER 120G RAW (2 CUPS)	
Kilojoules	80
Fibre	1,3 g
Protein	1 g
Total Fat	0,3 g
Saturated Fat	0 g
Cholesterol	0 mg
Sodium	10 mg

NUTRIENTS

% RDA for people older than 10 years	
Vitamin C	6%
Folate	6%
Iron	4%
Vitamin A	2%

Tossed Salad with Pears, Pecan Nuts & Blue Cheese

PREP: 20 MINUTES

An elegant starter for a dinner party, this salad combines three salad greens plus chives for lots of beta carotene.

2 medium pears, halved, cored and sliced lengthwise
175 ml low-fat cultured buttermilk
30 ml blue cheese, crumbled
15 ml white wine vinegar
2,5 ml salt
0,6 ml pepper
30 ml snipped fresh chives
240 g torn butter lettuce (4 cups)
360 g torn red leaf or other looseleaf lettuce (6 cups)
70 g watercress leaves (2 cups)
225 g thinly sliced cucumber half-rounds (1,5 cups)
45 ml chopped toasted pecan nuts

1. In a small bowl, toss the pears with 30 ml of the buttermilk. In another small bowl, whisk together the remaining 145 ml buttermilk, the blue cheese, vinegar, salt and pepper. Stir in the chives.

2. In a large bowl, toss together the butter and red leaf lettuces, the watercress and cucumber. Arrange the greens on plates and top with the sliced pears and toasted pecan nuts. Drizzle with some of the dressing and serve the remainder alongside. Serves 6.

Per serving: Kilojoules 459; Fibre 4g; Protein 3g; Total Fat 4g; Saturated Fat 1g; Cholesterol 4mg; Sodium 292mg

Greek-Style Lettuce Salad with Lemon & Coriander

PREP: 10 MINUTES

Sturdy but sweet, cos stands up to zesty dressings and robust ingredients, such as the feta cheese in this salad.

60 ml lemon juice
15 ml olive oil
1,25 ml salt
360 g shredded cos lettuce (6 cups)
125 ml chopped fresh coriander leaves
6 spring onions, thinly sliced
115 g feta cheese, crumbled

1. In a large bowl, whisk together the lemon juice, oil and salt.

2. Add the lettuce, coriander and spring onions, tossing well. Add the feta and toss again. Serves 4.

Per serving: Kilojoules 620; Fibre 2g; Protein 7g; Total Fat 12g; Saturated Fat 5g; Cholesterol 20mg; Sodium 458mg

Cos Salad with Avocado & Oranges

PREP: 15 MINUTES

The oranges and avocado team up to bestow a good portion of potassium on this sun-bright salad.

2 medium oranges
30 ml lemon juice
10 ml extra-virgin olive oil
5 ml Dijon mustard
1,25 ml salt
360 g shredded cos lettuce (6 cups)
4 spring onions, thinly sliced
125 ml diced avocado

1. With a paring knife, remove the skin and white pith from the oranges. Working over a large salad bowl to catch the juices, cut between the membranes to release the orange sections; set aside.

2. Add the lemon juice, oil, mustard and salt to the orange juice in the bowl, whisking to blend. Add the lettuce and spring onions, tossing well. Add the avocado and toss gently to combine. Serves 4.

Per serving: Kilojoules 592; Fibre 5g; Protein 3g; Total Fat 8g; Saturated Fat 1g; Cholesterol 0mg; Sodium 197mg

At the market Most salad greens are sold all year round and more varieties are being added constantly. Salad greens also also sold pre-washed and bagged.

Look for It's easy to tell when salad greens are fresh: they're crisp, unbrowned and moist, but not wet.

Prep Don't wash or tear salad greens until shortly before you use them; this helps conserve their vitamin C. Rinse greens lightly but thoroughly in cool water, then shake or spin them dry. Blot any excess moisture with a kitchen towel. Tear greens rather than cut them; contact with a steel knife causes the leaves to brown. The tough lower stems of watercress should be trimmed off. Some recipes call for watercress leaves, but this can easily include the more tender upper stems.

Tossed Salad with Pears, Pecan Nuts & Blue Cheese *is more than a bowl of greens.*

Remove the toughest, lower portions of watercress stems and use the rest of the sprigs.

Wilted Greens with Bacon Dressing

PREP: 20 MINUTES / COOK: 10 MINUTES

Lean bacon adds great smoky flavour to this salad—but with considerably less fat than regular bacon. For a bit of crunch and extra health benefits, we've added radishes, a cruciferous vegetable with the cancer-fighting potential of all members of this family.

30 ml flour
15 ml light brown sugar
5 ml dry mustard
1,25 ml salt
70 ml cider vinegar
15 ml vegetable oil
60 g lean, rindless, back bacon, diced
15 ml sour cream
480 g torn cos lettuce (8 cups)
70 g watercress leaves (2 cups)
125 ml thinly sliced radishes
225 g cooked chicken breast, cut into
    2 x 5-mm matchsticks

1. In a small bowl, combine the flour, brown sugar, mustard and salt. Add the vinegar and 150 ml of water and whisk until blended.

2. In a small saucepan, heat the oil over moderate heat. Add the bacon and cook for 3 minutes or until lightly browned.

3. Remove from the heat and stir in the flour mixture. Return to the heat and cook, stirring, for 5 minutes or until thickened. Remove from the heat and stir in the sour cream.

4. In a salad bowl, toss together the cos, watercress, and radishes. Pour the hot dressing over the salad, tossing to coat. Top with the chicken and serve warm. Serves 4.

Per serving: Kilojoules 919; Fibre 3 g; Protein 22 g; Total Fat 9 g; Saturated Fat 2 g; Cholesterol 45 mg; Sodium 406 mg

Rocket Salad with Spicy Vinaigrette

PREP: 25 MINUTES

125 ml fresh orange juice
30 ml red wine vinegar
10 ml mild green pepper sauce
5 ml olive oil
2,5 ml salt
1,25 ml sugar
0,6 ml pepper
160 g rocket leaves (8 cups)
120 g torn cos lettuce (2 cups)
140 g yellow and/or red cherry
    tomatoes, halved
1 medium orange, peeled and sliced
    into half-rounds
6 oil-cured black olives, slivered
1 small pickling onion, thinly sliced

1. In a small bowl, whisk together the orange juice, vinegar, green pepper sauce, oil, salt, sugar and pepper.

2. In a salad bowl, combine the rocket, lettuce, tomatoes, orange, olives and onion. Add the dressing, tossing to coat well. Serves 4.

Per serving: Kilojoules 378; Fibre 5 g; Protein 3 g; Total Fat 3 g; Saturated Fat 0 g; Cholesterol 0 mg; Sodium 385 mg

Rocket Salad with Spicy Vinaigrette *features the tang of citrus and the piquancy of hot pepper sauce.*

Did you know? . . .
Rocket and watercress are both cruciferous vegetables, relatives of cabbage and broccoli. Vegetables in this family contain cancer-fighting nitrogen compounds called indoles.

Tuna Salad with Mixed Greens, Roasted Peppers & Potatoes

PREP: 25 MINUTES / COOK: 30 MINUTES

Inspired by the Provençal classic, salade niçoise, this great summer supper dish is made with a nutrition-packed variety of vegetables. Use tuna packed in brine. You can also garnish the salad with ripe tomato wedges.

- **2 medium red peppers, cut lengthwise into flat panels**
- **2 cloves garlic, peeled**
- **450 g small potatoes (red, if possible), quartered**
- **1 medium onion (red, if possible), halved and thinly sliced**
- **70 g chicken stock**
- **45 ml red wine vinegar**
- **30 ml light mayonnaise**
- **1,25 ml salt**
- **2 bags (120 g each) mixed salad leaves**
- **2 tins (185 g each) water-packed white tuna chunks, drained**

1. Preheat the grill. Place the pepper pieces, skin-side up, on a baking tray. Grill the peppers 10 centimetres from the heat for 10 minutes, or until the skin is blackened. When the peppers are cool enough to handle, peel them and cut into 5-cm-wide strips.

2. In a large pot of boiling water, cook the garlic for 3 minutes to blanch. Remove with a slotted spoon. Add the potatoes and cook for 12 minutes or until firm-tender. Meanwhile, place the onion in a small bowl and cover with iced water. Let stand at room temperature while the potatoes cook.

3. In a large bowl, whisk together the stock, vinegar, mayonnaise and salt. Mash the garlic and add to the bowl. Drain the potatoes and onion and add them to the bowl along with the peppers and lettuce. Toss well. Divide the vegetable mixture among 4 plates and top with the tuna. Serves 4.

Per serving: Kilojoules 1020; Fibre 4g; Protein 23g; Total Fat 3g; Saturated Fat 1g; Cholesterol 33mg; Sodium 602mg

A colourful salad mixture called *mesclun* is sold in many supermarkets. An authentic *mesclun* consists of young, tender leaves of a variety of lettuces and herbs. Torn leaves of more mature greens are sometimes sold as *mesclun,* but they'll be less nutritious. Tearing causes the leaves to lose water-soluble nutrients, including vitamin C.

Other greens to consider when making salads are chicory and curly endive—both members of the same family. Curly endive, with its dark green leaves, is the more nutritious of the two.

Spinach

Nutritional power

A real powerhouse, spinach is loaded with beta carotene, folate, vitamin C and the phytochemical lutein, which helps keep your eyes healthy.

Small-leaved Spinach
PER 80G RAW (2 CUPS)

Kilojoules	100
Fibre	2,2g
Protein	2,3g
Total Fat	0,3g
Saturated Fat	0g
Cholesterol	0mg
Sodium	63mg

NUTRIENTS

% RDA for people older than 10 years

Vitamin A	67%
Folate	39%
Vitamin C	37%
Magnesium	21%
Iron	15%

Did you know? . . .

Spinach contains iron and calcium, but oxalic acid inhibits the body's absorption of these minerals.

Swiss chard, the larger leaved spinach, is higher in iron and calcium than the smaller leaved type.

Spinach Lasagne with Dill & Mint

PREP: 20 MINUTES / COOK: 55 MINUTES

- 280g lasagne noodles
- 20ml olive oil
- 1 medium onion, chopped
- 2 cloves garlic, finely chopped
- 600g frozen chopped spinach, thawed and squeezed dry
- 5ml grated lemon rind
- 425g ricotta cheese
- 450g smooth low-fat cottage cheese
- 60ml plus 30ml grated Parmesan cheese
- 2 eggs
- 150ml snipped fresh dill
- 60ml chopped fresh mint
- 5ml salt
- 3,5ml pepper

1. Preheat the oven to 180°C. In a large saucepan of boiling water, cook the lasagne noodles according to package directions until *al dente*. Drain well.

2. Meanwhile, in a large nonstick frying pan, heat 10ml of the oil over moderate heat. Add the onion and garlic and sauté for 2 minutes or until the onion is soft. Add the spinach and lemon rind and cook for 4 minutes or until the spinach is heated through. Transfer to a large bowl. Stir in the ricotta cheese, cottage cheese, 60ml of the Parmesan, the eggs, dill, mint, salt and pepper.

3. Line the bottom of a 23 x 33-cm baking dish with a layer of lasagne noodles. Spoon one-third of the spinach mixture over and top with another layer of noodles. Make 2 more layers with the remaining spinach and noodles, ending with noodles. Cover with foil and bake for 30 minutes. Uncover, brush with the remaining 10ml oil and sprinkle with the remaining 30ml Parmesan. Bake for 15 minutes or until the lasagne is piping hot and just set. Serves 6.

Per serving: Kilojoules 1984; Fibre 5g; Protein 29g; Total Fat 20g; Saturated Fat 8g; Cholesterol 114mg; Sodium 784mg

Sautéed Spinach & Red Peppers

PREP: 15 MINUTES / COOK: 15 MINUTES

- 10ml olive oil
- 1 small onion, finely chopped
- 3 cloves garlic, finely chopped
- 1 large red pepper, cut into 1-cm squares
- 320g fresh spinach leaves (large or small-leaved), shredded (8 cups)
- 1,25ml salt
- 0,6ml sugar

1. In a large nonstick frying pan, heat the oil over moderate heat. Add the onion and garlic and sauté for 5 minutes. Add the pepper and sauté for 3 minutes or until crisp-tender.

2. Add the spinach, sprinkle with the salt and sugar and cook, turning, for 4 minutes or until the spinach is wilted. Serves 4.

Per serving: Kilojoules 272; Fibre 3g; Protein 3g; Total Fat 3g; Saturated Fat 0g; Cholesterol 0mg; Sodium 217mg

Wilted Spinach Salad with Garlic Croutons

PREP: 15 MINUTES / COOK: 15 MINUTES

- 115g Italian bread, cut into 1-cm slices
- 1 clove garlic, peeled and halved
- 30ml olive oil
- 1 large onion (red, if available), cut into 1-cm pieces
- 225g mushrooms, thinly sliced
- 1kg spinach, torn into bite-size pieces
- 150ml chicken stock
- 125ml balsamic vinegar
- 10ml light brown sugar
- 1,25ml salt
- 3,5ml cornflour blended with 15ml water

1. Preheat the oven to 190°C. Place the bread on a baking tray and bake for 5 minutes or until golden brown and crisp. Rub the toast lightly with the cut garlic (discard the garlic). Cut the toast into cubes.

2. Meanwhile, in a large nonstick pan, heat 10ml of the oil over moderate heat. Add the onion and sauté for 4 minutes or until crisp-tender. Add the mushrooms and cook, stirring occasionally, for 4 minutes or until the mushrooms are softened. Transfer to a large bowl. Add the spinach and toast cubes, tossing to combine.

3. Add the remaining 20ml oil to the pan along with the stock, vinegar, brown sugar and salt. Bring to a rolling boil and cook for 1 minute. Stir in the cornflour mixture and cook, stirring, for 1 minute or until slightly thickened. Pour the hot dressing over the spinach mixture and toss. Serve immediately. Serves 4.

Per serving: Kilojoules 1 111; Fibre 9g; Protein 13g; Total Fat 10g; Saturated Fat 1g; Cholesterol 0mg; Sodium 746mg

At the market Curly-leaved spinach is sold either in bunches or in bags and is always available. This spinach, called Swiss chard spinach, is a member of the beet-root family. True spinach is difficult to grow in hot conditions.

Look for Choose spinach with crisp but tender leaves and slender stems. Avoid wilted or yellowed spinach. Bagged spinach should feel springy when you squeeze the bag.

Prep Wash spinach carefully (even if labelled 'prewashed'), as it is often sandy. Strip the coarse stems from curly-leaf spinach; the stems of flat-leaf spinach can be left on, but they should be trimmed.

Be sure to squeeze excess liquid out of frozen spinach after thawing it.

Basic cooking Cook damp, washed spinach in a covered pan (or steam it over boiling water) for 3 to 5 minutes. Microwave 225g spinach for 2 to 3 minutes on high.

Spinach Lasagne with Dill & Mint *features a flavour innovation: fresh dill and mint.*

Sweet potatoes

Yellow-flesh Sweet Potato (Borrie Patat)

PER 325G BAKED (WITH SKIN) (1 LARGE)

Kilojoules	1450
Fibre	9,8g
Protein	6g
Total Fat	0,3g
Saturated Fat	0g
Cholesterol	0mg
Sodium	33mg

NUTRIENTS

% RDA for people older than 10 years

Vitamin A	886%
Vitamin C	135%
Vitamin B6	39%
Pantothenic acid	35%
Riboflavin	26%
Magnesium	22%
Folate	19%
Niacin	11%

Did you know? . . .

One cup (250ml) of mashed yellow-flesh sweet potato sup-plies eight times the RDA of vitamin A for a person older than 10 years.

Moroccan Lamb & Sweet Potato Stew

PREP: 20 MINUTES
COOK: 1 HOUR 15 MINUTES

This subtly spiced stew was inspired by a North African dish called a tagine. Couscous is a traditional accompaniment for a tagine and is freely available, although the stew can also be served over rice.

10 ml olive oil
450 g well-trimmed boned lamb shoulder, cut into 1-cm pieces
1 large onion, finely chopped
3 cloves garlic, finely chopped
5 ml ground coriander
3,5 ml paprika
3,5 ml salt
2,5 ml pepper
30 ml tomato paste
650 g sweet potatoes, peeled and cut into 2,5cm pieces
125 ml pitted prunes, coarsely chopped

1. Preheat the oven to 180°C. In a nonstick pan, heat the oil over moder-ately high heat. Add the lamb and sauté for 4 minutes or until lightly browned. With a slotted spoon, transfer the lamb to a plate. Add the onion and garlic to the pan and sauté for 7 minutes or until the onion is tender.

2. Return the lamb to the pan. Add the coriander, paprika, salt and pepper, stirring to coat. Add the tomato paste mixed with 250ml of water and bring to a boil. Transfer to an ovenproof casserole dish and place in the oven. Bake for 30 minutes.

3. Add the sweet potatoes, prunes and 70ml of water. Re-cover and bake for 30 minutes or until the lamb and sweet potatoes are tender. Serves 4.

Per serving: Kilojoules 1581; Fibre 5g; Protein 27g; Total Fat 9g; Saturated Fat 3g; Cholesterol 79mg; Sodium 526mg

Sweet Potato & Apple Bake

PREP: 20 MINUTES / COOK: 45 MINUTES

Apples make a substantial nutritional contribution to a sweet-potato casserole.

15 ml unsalted butter
1 medium onion, finely chopped
900 g sweet potatoes, peeled and thinly sliced
2 medium cooking apples, cut into 1-cm-thick wedges
45 ml sugar
30 ml lemon juice
175 ml chicken stock
2,5 ml salt
1,25 ml pepper

1. Preheat the oven to 230°C. In a very large nonstick frying pan, heat the butter over moderate heat. Add the onion and sauté for 5 minutes or until tender.

2. Add the sweet potatoes, apples, 30ml of the sugar and the lemon juice and cook until the sugar has melted. Add the stock, salt and pepper and bring to a boil.

3. Transfer the mixture to a 18 x 28-cm glass baking dish. Cover with foil and

Sweet Potato & Apple Bake *goes beautifully with roast chicken, turkey or pork.*

At the market Sweet potatoes are in best supply in the autumn and early winter, but they can usually be bought all year long.

Look for Choose smooth, hard sweet potatoes with intact skins; avoid those with nicks, soft spots or bruises. Potatoes that are heavy for their size will be good and moist.

Prep Scrub the potatoes gently, being careful not to nick the skin.

Basic cooking To bake, pierce with a fork in several places, then bake for 45 to 60 minutes. Boil whole, unpeeled potatoes for 20 to 40 minutes, sliced potatoes for 10 to 20 minutes. Pierce whole potatoes before microwaving, then cook on high for 15 to 20 minutes (for 4 potatoes). Remove potatoes from microwave, wrap or cover and let stand for 3 minutes.

The yellow-flesh sweet potato (borrie patat) has a higher nutrional content than the white-flesh sweet potato.

bake for 25 minutes or until the sweet potatoes are tender. Uncover, sprinkle with the remaining 15 ml sugar and bake for 10 minutes or until lightly browned. Serves 4.

Per serving: Kilojoules 1201; Fibre 7 g; Protein 3 g; Total Fat 3 g; Saturated Fat 2 g; Cholesterol 8 mg; Sodium 607 mg

Thai Sweet Potato & Chicken Salad

PREP: 15 MINUTES / COOK: 30 MINUTES

Many Thai dishes incorporate a peanut butter sauce, its richness 'cut' with hot pepper and lime juice. The use of several different herbs is also typical of Thai cuisine.

- **900 g sweet potatoes, peeled and cut into 1-cm cubes**
- **2 cloves garlic, peeled**
- **450 g skinless, boned chicken breasts**
- **45 ml peanut butter**
- **30 ml lime or lemon juice**
- **3,5 ml salt**
- **2,5 ml hot red chilli sauce**
- **125 ml chopped fresh basil**
- **60 ml chopped fresh mint**
- **450 g tomatoes, cut into 1-cm-thick wedges**

1. In a large steamer or colander set over a pot of boiling water, steam the sweet potatoes for 30 minutes or until they are fork-tender.

2. Meanwhile, in a small frying pan, bring 375 ml of water to a boil over moderate heat. Add the garlic and cook for 3 minutes or until softened. Remove the garlic from the pan with a slotted spoon; when cool enough to handle, finely chop the garlic.

3. Add the chicken to the pan, reduce to a simmer, cover and cook for 10 minutes or until the chicken is just cooked through. Turn the chicken over midway. Reserving the cooking liquid, transfer the chicken to a plate. When cool enough to handle, cut across the grain into 1-cm-thick slices.

4. In a large bowl, combine the peanut butter, lime juice, salt and hot chilli sauce. Whisk in the garlic, 175 ml of the reserved cooking liquid, the basil and mint. Add the chicken, sweet potatoes and tomatoes, tossing to combine. Serve at room temperature or chilled. Serves 4.

Per serving: Kilojoules 1450; Fibre 6 g; Protein 26 g; Total Fat 8 g; Saturated Fat 6 g; Cholesterol 42 mg; Sodium 527 mg

Layered Chocolate-Sweet Potato Cake *has a healthy amount of beta carotene concealed in every slice.*

Did you know? . . .
Their scrumptious flavour and lush texture are misleading: Gram for gram, sweet potatoes have no more kilojoules than white potatoes.

Researchers studying carotenoids at the US Beltsville Human Nutrition Research Centre experimented on themselves by eating a high-carotenoid lunch every day for three weeks. They chose sweet potatoes as their beta-carotene source; eating just 150 grams per day raised their plasma levels of beta carotene by more than 100 per cent.

Studies have shown that high doses of beta carotene *supplements* may be harmful to smokers, but there's no evidence that a diet rich in sweet potatoes and other natural beta-carotene sources can be anything other than beneficial.

Layered Chocolate-Sweet Potato Cake

PREP: 30 MINUTES / COOK: 30 MINUTES

Here's a healthy treat—a low-fat chocolate cake packed with beta carotene.

- **500 ml flour**
- **3,5 ml bicarbonate of soda**
- **3,5 ml ground cinnamon**
- **1,25 ml salt**
- **350 g yellow-flesh sweet potatoes, peeled and thinly sliced**
- **60 ml vegetable oil**
- **175 ml granulated sugar**
- **175 ml packed light brown sugar**
- **2 eggs**
- **3 egg whites**
- **85 g dark chocolate, melted**
- **7,5 ml vanilla essence**
- **125 ml low-fat, cultured buttermilk**
- **450 g smooth low-fat cottage cheese**
- **250 ml icing sugar**
- **60 ml cocoa powder**
- **125 ml apricot jam**

1. Preheat the oven to 180°C. Spray two 20-cm round cake tins with non-stick cooking spray; set aside. In a medium bowl, stir together the flour, bicarbonate of soda, cinnamon and salt.

2. In a large steamer, cook the sweet potatoes for 20 minutes or until very tender. Transfer to a bowl and mash.

3. In a large bowl, beat the oil, granulated sugar and brown sugar with an electric mixer until well combined. Beat in the whole eggs and egg whites, one at a time, beating well after each addition. Beat in the chocolate, vanilla essence and mashed potato. Alternately fold in the flour mixture and buttermilk, beginning and ending with the flour mixture.

4. Divide the batter evenly between the prepared tins. Bake for 30 minutes or until a cake tester inserted in the centre comes out clean. Cool for 10 minutes in the tins on a wire rack, then turn out onto the rack to cool completely.

5. Meanwhile, in a medium bowl cream the cottage cheese, the icing sugar and cocoa together in an electric mixer.

6. Place one layer on a cake plate. Spread the layer with the apricot jam. Top with the second layer and ice the top and sides with the cottage cheese icing. Serves 16.

Per serving: Kilojoules 1 295; Fibre 1g; Protein 7g; Total Fat 8g; Saturated Fat 2g; Cholesterol 28mg; Sodium 125mg

Stir-Fried Sweet Potatoes

PREP: 30 MINUTES / COOK: 20 MINUTES

- 900 g sweet potatoes, peeled and thinly sliced
- 12,5 ml sesame oil
- 12,5 ml vegetable oil
- 3 cloves garlic, finely chopped
- 4 spring onions, finely chopped
- 15 ml crushed fresh ginger
- 3,5 ml sesame seeds
- 3,5 ml salt

1. In a large steamer, cook the sweet potatoes for 12 minutes or until tender.

2. Meanwhile, in a large frying pan, heat the sesame oil and vegetable oil over moderate heat. Add the garlic, spring onions and ginger and sauté for 2 minutes or until the onions are tender.

3. Add the sweet potatoes to the pan, tossing until well coated and cooked through. Sprinkle with the sesame seeds and salt. Serves 4.

Per serving: Kilojoules 875; Fibre 4g; Protein 2g; Total Fat 7g; Saturated Fat 1g; Cholesterol 0mg; Sodium 446mg

Sugar-Glazed Sweet Potatoes

PREP: 15 MINUTES / COOK: 25 MINUTES

- 900 g sweet potatoes, peeled and thinly sliced
- 20 ml unsalted butter
- 60 ml firmly packed dark brown sugar
- 60 ml lime or lemon juice
- 3,5 ml salt
- 2,5 ml ground ginger

1. In a large steamer, cook the sweet potatoes for 12 minutes or until tender.

2. In a large pan, melt the butter over moderate heat. Add the sugar and lime or lemon juice and bring to a boil. Add the sweet potatoes, salt and ginger and cook for 10 minutes or until the sweet potatoes are well glazed. Serves 4.

Per serving: Kilojoules 1 041; Fibre 4g; Protein 2g; Total Fat 4g; Saturated Fat 2g; Cholesterol 11mg; Sodium 469mg

Twice-Baked Sweet Potatoes Bake four 225-g sweet potatoes at 220°C for 45 minutes or until firm-tender. Scoop out flesh, leaving 5-mm shell. Mash flesh with 60 ml Parmesan, 15 ml butter, 5 ml salt and 1,25 ml pepper. Spoon into shells and bake 20 minutes or until shell is crispy. Serves 4. *[kJ 944; Fat 5g; Sodium 763 mg]*

Spiced Sweet Potato Soup Peel and thinly slice 650 g sweet potatoes. Combine in a saucepan with 425 ml chicken stock, 250 ml water, 5 ml ground coriander 1,25 ml red chilli flakes, 2,5 ml sugar and 2,5 ml salt. Simmer, covered, until tender. Purée in food processor. Stir in 30 ml lime or lemon juice. Serves 4. *[kJ 518; Fat 1g; Sodium 965 mg]*

Oven-Roasted Sweet Potatoes & Garlic In a large baking tin, combine 30 ml olive oil, 8 cloves garlic (unpeeled) and 2,5 ml rosemary. Heat in 220°C oven for 5 minutes. Add 900 g peeled, thinly sliced sweet potatoes. Bake, turning occasionally, for 40 minutes or until tender. Sprinkle with 2,5 ml salt. Serves 4. *[kJ 1004; Fat 8g; Sodium 178 mg]*

Tomatoes

PER 200G RAW (1 CUP)	
Kilojoules	182
Fibre	2,2g
Protein	2g
Total Fat	0,4g
Saturated Fat	0,1g
Cholesterol	0mg
Sodium	10mg

NUTRIENTS	
% RDA for people older than 10 years	
Vitamin C	67%
Vitamin A	10%
Folate	9%

Did you know? . . .
Tomatoes in all their forms—fresh, tinned, dried and as juice or pasta sauce—are loaded with lycopene. A large study done in 1995 revealed that men who ate lots of tomato products had a greatly reduced risk of prostate cancer; the researchers theorized that the lycopene might be the protective factor.

Three-Tomato Marinara Sauce

PREP: 15 MINUTES / COOK: 40 MINUTES

This makes a big batch of sauce—enough for 20 servings. When the sauce is done, ladle it into 500-ml freezer containers, cool to room temperature and refrigerate or freeze.

125ml sun-dried tomatoes (not oil-packed)
30ml olive oil
2 large onions, finely chopped
8 cloves garlic, finely chopped
2,5 litres tinned tomatoes, chopped with their juice
45ml tomato paste
7,5ml salt
2,5ml sugar

1. In a small bowl, soak the sun-dried tomatoes in boiling water to cover. Let stand for 15 minutes or until softened. Drain and chop finely.

2. Meanwhile, in a large saucepan, heat the oil over low heat. Add the onions and garlic and sauté for 15 minutes or until the onions are very soft.

3. Add the sun-dried tomatoes, the tinned tomatoes and their juice, the tomato paste, salt and sugar. Bring to a boil, reduce to a simmer, cover and cook for 20 minutes or until the sauce is richly flavoured and slightly thickened. Makes 2,5 litres.

Per 125ml serving: Kilojoules 224; Fibre 2g; Protein 1g; Total Fat 2g; Saturated Fat 0g; Cholesterol 0mg; Sodium 511mg

Tomato Bruschetta

PREP: 20 MINUTES / COOK: 10 MINUTES

This delightful Italian appetizer makes brilliant use of fresh tomatoes. Plum tomatoes are less juicy than other types, so the topping won't 'wilt' the bread.

24 slices (1-cm thick) Italian bread (350g total)
3 cloves garlic, peeled and halved
30ml olive oil
675g plum tomatoes, coarsely chopped
70ml chopped fresh basil
15ml tomato pesto (or paste)
3,5ml salt
2,5ml grated orange rind
1,25ml pepper

1. Preheat the oven to 200°C. Rub the bread with one of the halved garlic cloves. Discard the garlic. Brush the bread with 15ml of the oil and bake for 7 minutes or until golden brown and crisp.

2. In a small pan of boiling water, cook the 2 remaining garlic cloves for 3 minutes to blanch. Chop finely.

3. In a medium bowl, combine the chopped garlic, tomatoes, basil, tomato pesto, salt, orange rind, pepper and the remaining 15ml oil. Spoon on top of the toasted garlic bread. Serves 4.

Per serving: Kilojoules 1320; Fibre 5g; Protein 9g; Total Fat 9g; Saturated Fat 1g; Cholesterol 0mg; Sodium 860mg

Seafood Chowder

PREP: 25 MINUTES / COOK: 30 MINUTES

This style of chowder, made with tomatoes, has a distinct nutritional advantage over cream-based chowder: it's lower in fat and is high in lycopene.

- **1 medium onion, finely chopped**
- **125 ml dry white wine or chicken stock**
- **12 fresh mussels, well scrubbed (use frozen mussels or tinned mussels in brine, if fresh mussels are not available)**
- **350 g potatoes, peeled and cut into 1-cm cubes**
- **1 red pepper, cut into 1-cm squares**
- **1 stalk celery, cut into 5-mm dice**
- **750 ml tinned tomatoes, chopped with their juice**
- **250 ml chicken stock**
- **2,5 ml dried thyme**
- **2,5 ml salt**
- **450 g hake fillets, cut into 1-cm cubes**

1. In a saucepan, combine the onion, wine and mussels. Bring to a boil over moderate heat, cover and cook for 5 minutes or until the mussels have opened. Remove the mussels from the saucepan (discard any that have not opened). Remove the mussel meat from the shells and discard the shells.

2. Add the potatoes, pepper, celery, and 250 ml of water to the saucepan and bring to a boil. Reduce to a simmer, cover and cook for 5 minutes. Add the tomatoes and their juice, the stock, thyme and salt and return to a boil. Reduce the heat to a simmer, cover and cook for 15 minutes or until the potatoes are tender.

3. Add the hake to the saucepan, cover and cook for 5 minutes or until the fish is almost cooked through. Return the mussels to the saucepan and cook just until heated through.
Serves 4.

Per serving: Kilojoules 1 219; Fibre 4g; Protein 29g; Total Fat 3g; Saturated Fat 1g; Cholesterol 72 mg; Sodium 1 448 mg

At the market Tomatoes now come in a variety of colours and sizes, from the small cherry tomato to the huge Beefsteak variety. Flavours also vary from sweet to acidic to almost tasteless. Generally tomatoes are available all year round, especially since the advent of growing tunnels. Do shop where the tomatoes are kept at room temperature (not chilled).

Look for Choose tomatoes that are heavy for their size, evenly coloured and unblemished. Even if unripe, they should be more pink than green.

Prep If the tomatoes are not fully ripe, keep them in a paper bag at room temperature for a few days. Don't store tomatoes in the refrigerator unless they're threatening to spoil.

Seafood Chowder boasts mussels and cubes of hake in a tomato broth.

Dry-packed sun-dried tomatoes need to be soaked in boiling water to soften them before chopping.

113

Gazpacho

PREP: 30 MINUTES / CHILL: 2 HOURS

To make gazpacho in a food processor, chop one vegetable at a time, using quick on-and-off pulses so that the vegetables are very coarsely chopped, not puréed. Add each vegetable in turn to a large bowl, then stir in the remaining ingredients.

900 g tomatoes, coarsely chopped
1 red pepper, cut into 5-mm dice
1 green pepper, cut into 5-mm dice
1 small onion (red, if available), finely chopped
1 stalk celery, cut into 5-mm dice
60 ml red wine vinegar
3,5 ml salt
2,5 ml ground coriander
2,5 ml hot red chilli sauce

1. In a large bowl, combine the chopped tomatoes, peppers, onion, celery, vinegar, salt, coriander and hot chilli sauce.

2. Refrigerate the gazpacho for 2 hours or until well chilled. Ladle into soup bowls. Serves 4.

Per serving: Kilojoules 330; Fibre 4g; Protein 3g; Total Fat 1g; Saturated Fat 0g; Cholesterol 0mg; Sodium 437mg

Stir-Fried Beef with Cherry Tomatoes

PREP: 20 MINUTES / COOK: 15 MINUTES

15 ml cornflour
15 ml light soya sauce
2,5 ml ground ginger
5 ml sugar
450 g beef schnitzel, cut into thin strips
15 ml vegetable oil
6 spring onions, cut into 2,5-cm lengths
3 cloves garlic, finely chopped
175 g mangetout, strings removed
560 g cherry tomatoes, halved

1. In a medium bowl, combine the cornflour, soya sauce, ginger and 2,5 ml of the sugar. Add the beef, tossing well to coat.

2. In a large nonstick pan, heat 7,5 ml of the oil over moderately high heat. Add half of the beef and sauté for 2 minutes or until no longer pink. With a slotted spoon, transfer the beef to a plate. Repeat with the remaining 7,5 ml oil and the remaining beef.

3. Add the spring onions and garlic to the pan and sauté for 1 minute or until the spring onions are crisp-tender. Add the mangetout, tomatoes and the remaining 2,5 ml sugar and cook for 2 minutes or until the tomatoes just

Stir-Fried Beef with Cherry Tomatoes
Hot, juicy tomatoes liven up this beef and vegetable dish.

begin to collapse. Return the beef to the pan and cook until heated through. Serves 4.

Per serving: Kilojoules 1 092; Fibre 4g; Protein 25g; Total Fat 11g; Saturated Fat 4g; Cholesterol 65mg; Sodium 289mg

Chicken Cacciatore

PREP: 15 MINUTES / COOK: 40 MINUTES

You can make this a day ahead and reheat it: it will taste even better the second day.

- **4 skinless, bone-in chicken breasts (900g total)**
- **45ml flour**
- **15ml olive oil**
- **1 small onion (red, if available), finely chopped**
- **4 cloves garlic, finely chopped**
- **1 red pepper, cut into 1cm squares**
- **225g small mushrooms, quartered**
- **450g tomatoes, finely chopped**
- **60ml chicken stock**
- **3,5ml salt**
- **2,5ml dried rosemary, crumbled**
- **2,5ml black pepper**

1. Dredge the chicken in the flour, shaking off the excess. In a large nonstick frying pan, heat the oil over moderate heat. Add the chicken and cook for 3 minutes on each side or until golden brown. Transfer the chicken to a plate.

2. Reduce the heat to moderately low, add the onion and garlic and sauté for 7 minutes or until the onion is tender. Add the pepper and cook for 4 minutes or until crisp-tender. Add the mushrooms and cook, stirring, for 3 minutes or until softened.

3. Add the tomatoes, stock, salt, rosemary and black pepper and bring to a boil. Return the chicken to the frying pan, reduce the heat to a simmer, cover and cook, turning the chicken over midway, for 20 minutes or until the chicken is cooked through. Serves 4.

Per serving: Kilojoules 1 337; Fibre 4g; Protein 43g; Total Fat 9g; Saturated Fat 2g; Cholesterol 84mg; Sodium 592mg

Caprese Salad In medium bowl, combine 560g halved cherry tomatoes, 115g mozzarella cheese cut into 1-cm cubes, 70ml slivered green olives, 70ml chopped fresh basil, 30ml balsamic vinegar, 15ml olive oil and 2,5ml salt. Toss. Serves 4. *[kJ 675; Fat 12g; Sodium 530mg]*

Baked Herbed Tomatoes Slice off and discard top quarter of four large (250g) tomatoes. Scoop out and discard the seeds. In a small bowl, mix 125ml chopped parsley, 60ml sliced spring onion, 60ml seasoned dried bread crumbs and 15ml olive oil. Spoon into tomatoes. Bake at 200°C for 20 to 30 minutes or until piping hot. Serves 4. *[kJ 385; Fat 4g; Sodium 224mg]*

Fresh Tomato Salsa In a bowl, combine 450g chopped tomatoes, 4 sliced spring onions, 125ml chopped coriander, 2 finely chopped jalapeño peppers (fresh or pickled), 30ml red wine vinegar, 2,5ml each ground coriander and cumin and 1,25ml salt. Makes 750ml/use 125ml per serving. *[kJ 83; Fat 0g; Sodium 105mg]*

Turnips

White Turnip

PER 180G COOKED (1 CUP)	
Kilojoules	178
Fibre	3,6 g
Protein	1 g
Total Fat	0,1 g
Saturated Fat	0 g
Cholesterol	0 mg
Sodium	90 mg

NUTRIENTS

% RDA for people older than 10 years

Vitamin C	36 %

Swede

PER 180G COOKED (1 CUP)	
Kilojoules	293
Fibre	3,2 g
Protein	2 g
Total Fat	0,4 g
Saturated Fat	0,1 g
Cholesterol	0 mg
Sodium	36 mg

NUTRIENTS

% RDA for people older than 10 years

Vitamin C	56 %
Magnesium	14 %
Vitamin A	13 %
Thiamin	11 %
Vitamin B	9 %
Calcium	7 %

Mashed Swedes with Carrots & Potatoes

PREP: 15 MINUTES / COOK: 35 MINUTES

- 800 g swedes peeled, quartered and thinly sliced
- 225 g potatoes, peeled and thinly sliced
- 225 g carrots, thinly sliced
- 5 cloves garlic, peeled
- 1 bay leaf
- 3,5 ml salt
- 2,5 ml dried thyme
- 1,25 ml pepper
- 15 ml olive oil
- 60 ml grated Parmesan cheese

1. In a large saucepan, combine the swedes, potatoes, carrots, garlic, bay leaf, 1,25 ml of the salt, the thyme, pepper and 1 litre of water. Bring to a boil over moderate heat, reduce to a simmer, cover and cook for 30 minutes or until tender. Reserving 125 ml of the cooking liquid, drain the vegetables and garlic. Remove and discard the bay leaf.

2. With a potato masher, mash the vegetables and garlic along with the reserved cooking liquid and the oil. Stir in the Parmesan and the remaining salt. Serves 4.

Per serving: Kilojoules 793; Fibre 6 g; Protein 6 g; Total Fat 6 g; Saturated Fat 2 g; Cholesterol 4 mg; Sodium 863 mg

Pan-Roasted Turnips with Garlic

PREP: 10 MINUTES / COOK: 35 MINUTES

Crusty and golden, these pan-roasted turnips are every bit as tasty as roast potatoes.

- 900 g white turnips, peeled and cut into 1-cm-thick wedges
- 15 ml olive oil
- 5 cloves garlic, peeled and halved
- 15 ml sugar
- 125 ml chicken stock
- 2,5 ml each crumbled dried rosemary and salt
- 60 ml chopped parsley

1. In a steamer or colander set over a pot of boiling water, steam the turnips for 10 minutes or until crisp-tender.

2. In a large nonstick pan, heat the oil over low heat. Add the garlic and cook, turning it as it colours, for 2 minutes or until light golden. Add the turnips and sugar and cook for 7 minutes or until the turnips are golden.

3. Add the stock, rosemary and salt and bring to a boil. Cook for 10 minutes or until the liquid has evaporated and the turnips are tender. Add the parsley, tossing to combine. Serves 4.

Per serving: Kilojoules 505; Fibre 4 g; Protein 2 g; Total Fat 4 g; Saturated Fat 1 g; Cholesterol 0 mg; Sodium 642 mg

At the market Turnips and swedes are winter vegetables, but you'll find them in the market all year round.

Look for Choose smooth, firm, heavy turnips on the small side (large ones may be woody). If the green tops are attached, they should look fresh. Choose clean, firm swedes which feel heavy for their size.

Swedes, also known as rutabagas, are not often seen in supermarkets.

Prep Cut off and reserve turnip greens, which can be prepared like other cooking greens. Using a vegetable peeler, peel turnips very thinly; remove the hard skin from swedes with a sturdy paring knife.

Basic cooking Steam sliced turnips for about 15 minutes; sliced swedes will take 25 to 35 minutes. Microwave 450 g cubed turnips or swedes with 45 ml water, covered, for 7 to 9 minutes.

Mashed Swedes with Carrots & Potatoes *Serve this mellow golden vegetable blend instead of mashed potatoes; it's perfect with poultry, pork or beef.*

Braised Pork with Turnips

PREP: 20 MINUTES / COOK: 25 MINUTES

When braising, brown the meat and vegetables, then cook them, covered, in a small amount of liquid; the cooking liquid becomes a sauce. This conserves all the flavour and a substantial amount of the nutrients.

- **15 ml cornflour**
- **15 ml light soya sauce**
- **2,5 ml sugar**
- **22,5 ml vegetable oil**
- **450 g well-trimmed pork fillet, cut into 1-cm pieces**
- **900 g white turnips, peeled and cut into 1-cm-thick wedges**
- **6 cloves garlic, finely chopped**
- **320 ml chicken stock**
- **2,5 ml dried rosemary, crumbled**
- **1,25 ml each salt and pepper**

1. In a medium bowl, combine the cornflour, soya sauce and sugar. Add the pork, tossing until well coated.

2. In a large nonstick pan, heat 7,5 ml of the oil over moderately high heat. Add half of the pork and cook for 3 minutes or until lightly browned. Transfer the pork to a plate. Repeat with another 7,5 ml oil and the remaining pork.

3. Add the turnips and the remaining 7,5 ml oil to the pan and cook, stirring frequently, for 4 minutes or until lightly browned. Add the garlic and cook for 1 minute.

4. Add the stock, rosemary, salt and pepper and bring to a boil. Reduce to a simmer, cover and cook for 10 minutes or until the turnips are tender. Add the pork to the pan and cook for 2 minutes or until just cooked through. Serves 4.

Per serving: Kilojoules 1 032; Fibre 4g; Protein 22g; Total Fat 12g; Saturated Fat 3g; Cholesterol 54 mg; Sodium 1 042 mg

Dairy & Eggs

Crème Caramel

Milk

Nutritional power

Milk is our main calcium source. Some fresh milk is also enriched with vitamin D which enhances calcium absorption.

Low-Fat (2%) Milk	
PER 250 ML (1 CUP)	
Kilojoules	**535**
Fibre	**0 g**
Protein	**8 g**
Total Fat	**5 g**
Saturated Fat	**3,2 g**
Cholesterol	**18 mg**
Sodium	**115 mg**
NUTRIENTS	
% RDA for people older than 10 years	
Vitamin B12	**100 %**
Calcium	**25 %**
Riboflavin	**25 %**
Pantothenic acid	**13 %**
Magnesium	**10 %**
Vitamin A	**8 %**

Did you know? . . .
A US study called DASH—Dietary Approaches to Stop Hypertension—found that a diet rich in fruits, vegetables and low-fat dairy products could substantially reduce blood pressure.

Creamy Espresso Milkshake

PREP: 5 MINUTES / COOK: 5 MINUTES

For a really thick shake, place the milk in the freezer for about 10 minutes before blending. A 450-millilitre glass would contain 46% of the RDA of calcium for a person older than 10 years of age.

- 60 ml sugar
- 30 ml instant espresso powder
- 5 ml cocoa powder
- 1 litre ice-cold low-fat (2%) milk
- 8 ice cubes
- 2,5 ml vanilla essence

1. In a small saucepan, combine the sugar, espresso powder, cocoa powder and 60 ml of water. Bring to a boil over low heat. Remove from the heat; set aside to cool to room temperature.

2. Pour half of the espresso mixture into a blender. Add 500 ml of the milk, 4 of the ice cubes and 1,25 ml of the vanilla essence and blend until thick and foamy. Pour into 2 tall (450-ml) glasses. Repeat with the remaining espresso mixture, milk, ice and vanilla essence. Serves 4.

Per serving: Kilojoules 731; Fibre 0g; Protein 8g; Total Fat 5g; Saturated Fat 0g; Cholesterol 18mg; Sodium 119mg

Butterscotch Pudding

PREP: 10 MINUTES / COOK: 10 MINUTES

Although packaged pudding mixes are temptingly convenient, they usually contain artificial colours and flavours. But with just six ingredients (and in only 20 minutes), you can produce a delicious, all-natural dessert.

- 20 ml unsalted butter
- 175 ml packed dark brown sugar
- 700 g low-fat evaporated milk
- 70 ml flour
- 1,25 ml salt
- 7,5 ml vanilla essence

1. In a medium-size heavy-bottomed saucepan, melt the butter over moderate heat. Add 125 ml of the brown sugar and cook, stirring, until well blended. Gradually stir in all but 125 ml of the evaporated milk, bring to a boil and stir until the brown sugar has melted.

2. In a small bowl, whisk together the flour and the remaining sugar. Stir in the remaining 125 ml evaporated milk until blended. Gradually whisk some of the hot milk mixture into the flour mixture, then whisk the flour mixture back into the saucepan. Whisk in the salt. Bring to a boil and cook for 5 minutes or until no floury taste remains and the pudding is thick.

3. Remove the pudding from the heat. Cool to room temperature and stir in the vanilla essence. Spoon into 4 dessert bowls, cover and chill until serving time. Serves 4.

Per serving: Kilojoules 1 614; Fibre 0g; Protein 14g; Total Fat 10g; Saturated Fat 7g; Cholesterol 207mg; Sodium 355mg

---

White Borscht

PREP: 15 MINUTES / COOK: 10 MINUTES
CHILL: 3 HOURS

A cool purée that includes potatoes, cucumber, onion, radishes and walnuts.

350g small potatoes (red, if available), thinly sliced
750ml low-fat cultured buttermilk
1 large cucumber, peeled, seeded and thinly sliced
1 small (red) onion, thinly sliced
70ml walnuts
3,5ml salt
2,5ml pepper
175ml thinly sliced radishes, cut into thin matchsticks
60ml snipped fresh dill

1. In a medium pot of boiling water, cook the potatoes for 10 minutes or until tender. Drain well and set aside to cool to room temperature.

2. Meanwhile, in a food processor, combine 500ml of the buttermilk, the cucumber, onion, walnuts, salt and pepper. Process until well blended.

3. Transfer the mixture to a large bowl and whisk in the remaining 250ml buttermilk. Add the potatoes, radishes and dill. Cover and refrigerate for 3 hours or until well chilled. Serves 4.

Per serving: Kilojoules 929; Fibre 3g; Protein 9g; Total Fat 8g; Saturated Fat 2g; Cholesterol 8mg; Sodium 632mg

White Borscht *Tangy buttermilk is the perfect foil for potatoes, dill and crisp radishes.*

At the market Low-fat (2%) milk has about half the fat of whole milk. Milk also comes in fat-free (skim) form. Our recipes call for low-fat buttermilk, which has a 1% fat content.

Look for Studies suggest that milk in translucent plastic jugs loses riboflavin and vitamin D when exposed to fluorescent light, so buy milk in cardboard cartons if you can.

Basic cooking When a recipe says to 'scald' milk, bring it nearly to the boiling point. Heat the milk over low heat just until small bubbles begin to form around the edge.

To make fresh cheese (page 122), curdle milk with lemon juice, pour off the whey and compress the drained curds with a weight (here, a tin placed in a saucepan). The firmed cheese will cut cleanly.

Low-Fat Buttermilk

PER 250 ML (1 CUP)	
Kilojoules	423
Fibre	0 g
Protein	8 g
Total Fat	2,2 g
Saturated Fat	1,4 g
Cholesterol	10 mg
Sodium	263 mg

NUTRIENTS

% RDA for people older than 10 years	
Calcium	24%
Riboflavin	23%
Magnesium	9%

Low-Fat Evaporated Milk

PER 125 ML (½ CUP)	
Kilojoules	563
Fibre	0 g
Protein	9 g
Total Fat	4,4 g
Saturated Fat	2,6 g
Cholesterol	36 mg
Sodium	175 mg

NUTRIENTS

% RDA for people older than 10 years	
Riboflavin	32%
Calcium	28%
Magnesium	13%
Vitamin A	8%

Did you know? . . .
To appreciate the advantage of low-fat evaporated milk, compare it with cream. A half cup (125 ml) of heavy cream has 46 g fat and 171 mg cholesterol.

Curried Spinach & Fresh Cheese

PREP: 15 MINUTES / DRAIN: 2 HOURS
COOK: 30 MINUTES

This cheese (called 'panir' in India) is also served with other curry-sauced vegetables such as potatoes, green beans or peas.

2 litres low-fat (2%) milk
70 ml lemon juice
20 ml vegetable oil
1 medium onion, finely chopped
4 cloves garlic, finely chopped
5 ml ground coriander
3,5 ml turmeric
1,25 ml salt
280 g frozen chopped spinach, thawed and squeezed dry
250 ml chicken stock
30 ml tomato paste
10 ml mild green pepper sauce (jalapeño)

1. In a large saucepan, bring the milk to a boil over moderate heat. Remove from the heat and stir in the lemon juice. Let stand until the curds and whey separate. Line a sieve with a double layer of cheesecloth. Place the sieve in the sink and pour in the curdled milk, draining off the whey. Place the sieve over a bowl and let stand for 20 minutes. Tie the cheesecloth up and gently squeeze to remove any remaining liquid. Flatten the cheese into a disc, place a weight on top (see photo, page 125) and let stand at room temperature for 2 hours or until firm enough to cut.

2. In a large nonstick frying pan, heat 10 ml of the oil over moderate heat. Add the onion and garlic and sauté for 7 minutes or until tender. Add the coriander, turmeric and salt, stirring to combine. Add the spinach, stock, tomato paste and mild pepper sauce and bring to a boil. Reduce to a simmer, cover and cook for 5 minutes or until the spinach is flavourful. Transfer the

mixture to a bowl and wipe out the frying pan.

3. Cut the cheese into 1-cm pieces. Add the remaining 10 ml oil to the pan and heat over moderate heat. Add the cheese and cook, stirring frequently, for 4 minutes or until lightly browned and crusty on all sides. Gently stir in the spinach mixture and cook for 4 minutes or until heated through. Serves 4.

Per serving: Kilojoules 1 473; Fibre 2 g; Protein 20 g; Total Fat 16 g; Saturated Fat 1 g; Cholesterol 35 mg; Sodium 815 mg

Orange Buttermilk Sherbet

PREP: 10 MINUTES / COOK: 5 MINUTES
FREEZE: 1 TO 4 HOURS

A noteworthy dessert with emphatic orange flavour and 213 mg calcium per serving.

150 ml sugar
70 ml orange blossom honey (or corn syrup, if available))
6 strips (7,5 x 1 cm) orange rind
0,6 ml salt
1 litre low-fat cultured buttermilk
350 ml frozen orange juice concentrate (unsweetened)

1. In a medium saucepan, combine the sugar, honey, orange rind, salt and 125 ml of water. Bring to a boil over moderate heat and cook for 2 minutes. Cool to room temperature. Discard the orange rind.

2. In a medium bowl, combine the buttermilk, orange juice concentrate and sugar syrup. Transfer to the canister of an ice cream machine and freeze according to the manufacturer's directions. Alternatively, to still-freeze, pour into a shallow 23 x 33 x 5-cm tin and freeze for 2 to 3 hours or until almost frozen. Cut into pieces and process in a

Curried Spinach & Fresh Cheese *This Indian dish features fresh cheese made from low-fat milk, combined with spinach and lively seasonings.*

food processor until smooth. Serve immediately. Serves 6.

Per serving: Kilojoules 1 200; Fibre 1 g; Protein 7 g; Total Fat 2 g; Saturated Fat 1 g; Cholesterol 7 mg; Sodium 217 mg

Chocolate Latte Cotto

PREP: 15 MINUTES / COOK: 10 MINUTES
CHILL: 4 HOURS

This 'latte cotto' (cooked milk) is a lightened version of the Italian classic 'panna cotta' (cooked cream). It's a chilled chocolate pudding made in individual cups.

45 ml cocoa powder
10 g (1 envelope) unflavoured gelatine
750 ml low-fat (2%) milk
125 ml packed light brown sugar
25 g milk chocolate, coarsely chopped
0,6 ml grated nutmeg

1. In a small bowl, combine the cocoa powder and 45 ml of water, stirring until the cocoa is moistened. In a separate bowl, sprinkle the gelatine over 250 ml of the milk and let stand for 5 minutes or until softened.

2. Meanwhile, in a medium saucepan, combine the remaining 500 ml milk, the brown sugar, milk chocolate and nutmeg. Bring to a simmer and cook just until the chocolate has melted. Remove from the heat and stir in the cocoa mixture.

3. Stir in the softened gelatine and warm over low heat until gelatine is fully dissolved. Divide the mixture among six 175-ml custard cups and cool to room temperature. Refrigerate for at least 4 hours or until set and well chilled. Serves 6.

Per serving: Kilojoules 652; Fibre 0 g; Protein 5 g; Total Fat 4 g; Saturated Fat 1 g; Cholesterol 10 mg; Sodium 91 mg

Yoghurt

Low-Fat Yoghurt
PER 250 ML (1 CUP)

Kilojoules	635
Fibre	0g
Protein	11g
Total Fat	4,8g
Saturated Fat	2,9g
Cholesterol	20mg
Sodium	165mg

NUTRIENTS

% RDA for people older than 10 years	
Vitamin B12	125%
Calcium	31%
Riboflavin	30%
Zinc	14%

Fat-Free Yoghurt
PER 250 ML (1 CUP)

Kilojoules	583
Fibre	0g
Protein	14g
Total Fat	0,5g
Saturated Fat	0,3g
Cholesterol	5mg
Sodium	190mg

NUTRIENTS

% RDA for people older than 10 years	
Vitamin B12	150%
Calcium	41%
Riboflavin	34%
Zinc	16%

Fruit-Topped Yoghurt Cheese Tart

PREP: 25 MINUTES / CHILL: 1 HOUR
COOK: 40 MINUTES

This splendid dessert is rich in vitamin C, thanks to the kiwifruit and strawberries.

250 ml flour
15 ml plus 70 ml sugar
1,25 ml salt
60 ml unsalted butter, cut up
30 ml sour cream or crème fraîche
500 ml Yoghurt Cheese (at right)
3,5 ml vanilla essence
300 g strawberries, halved (2 cups)
2 kiwifruit, peeled and thinly sliced
60 ml smooth apricot jam

1. In a large bowl, combine the flour, 15 ml of the sugar and the salt. With a pastry blender or two knives, cut in the butter until the mixture resembles coarse crumbs. In a small bowl, combine the sour cream and 15 ml of iced water. Stir into the flour mixture until just combined. Flatten the dough into a disc, wrap in plastic wrap and refrigerate for at least 1 hour.

2. Preheat the oven to 180°C. On a lightly floured surface, roll the dough out to a 33-cm round. Fit into a 23-cm tart tin with a removable bottom. With a fork, prick the bottom of the tart shell in several places. Line with foil and weigh down with rice or dried beans. Bake for 20 minutes or until the crust is beginning to set. Remove the beans or rice and foil and bake for 15 minutes or until the crust is cooked through. Transfer the shell to a wire rack to cool completely.

3. In a medium bowl, combine the Yoghurt Cheese, the remaining 70 ml sugar and the vanilla. Spread in the bottom of the baked and cooled shell. Arrange the strawberries and kiwi slices in concentric circles on top of the tart.

4. In a small saucepan, melt the jam over low heat. Brush the jam over the fruit. Let cool until set. Serves 8.

Per serving: Kilojoules 1 149; Fibre 2g; Protein 7g; Total Fat 10g; Saturated Fat 6g; Cholesterol 30mg; Sodium 162mg

Fruity Yoghurt Parfait

PREP: 1 HOUR 15 MINUTES

1 litre plain low-fat yoghurt
240 g ricotta cheese
60 ml plus 30 ml sugar
2,5 ml almond or vanilla essence
600 g mixed fruit, such as sliced peaches, cubed bananas and strawberries
20 ml chopped toasted almonds

1. Place the yoghurt in a cheesecloth- or paper towel-lined sieve set over a bowl and drain at room temperature for 1 hour.

2. In a food processor, process the ricotta and all the sugar for 1 minute or until very smooth. Transfer to a medium bowl and stir in the drained yoghurt and almond essence.

3. Dividing evenly, spoon one-third of the yoghurt mixture into each of 6 parfait glasses. Divide half the fruit among the glasses. Spoon in another one-third of the yoghurt mixture; top with the remaining fruit. Spoon the remaining yoghurt mixture on top and sprinkle with the toasted almonds. Serves 6.

Per serving: Kilojoules 1 197; Fibre 2g; Protein 13g; Total Fat 10g; Saturated Fat 5g; Cholesterol 34mg; Sodium 147mg

Yoghurt Cheese

PREP: 5 MINUTES / DRAIN: 12 HOURS

Draining the whey from plain yoghurt produces nutritious, creamy yoghurt cheese, which can stand in for cream cheese, sour cream or even mayonnaise. Offer one of the variations as a spread for savoury biscuits or toast, or as a dip with vegetable sticks or sliced fruit.

1 litre plain low-fat yoghurt

Line a fine-mesh sieve with dampened cheesecloth. Spoon the yoghurt into the sieve and set it over a bowl. Place in the refrigerator and let stand overnight. Makes about 500 millilitres.

Per 60ml: Kilojoules 318; Fibre 0g; Protein 5g; Total Fat 2g; Saturated Fat 1g; Cholesterol 10mg; Sodium 83mg

SPRING ONION-PEPPER YOGHURT CHEESE
In a small frying pan, heat 10ml vegetable oil over moderate heat. Add 4 thinly sliced spring onions and 2 diced red peppers and cook, stirring occasionally, for 4 minutes or until tender. Cool, then stir into the Yoghurt Cheese. Cover and refrigerate. Serve chilled. Makes about 625 millilitres.

GARLIC-DILL YOGHURT CHEESE
In a small pot of boiling water, cook 8 cloves of garlic for 3 minutes to blanch. Mash with the flat side of a knife. Stir the garlic and 150ml snipped fresh dill into the Yoghurt Cheese. Cover and refrigerate. Serve chilled. Makes about 500 millilitres.

RASPBERRY YOGHURT CHEESE
To make the sugar syrup, dissolve 45ml of sugar in 45ml of water in a small saucepan. Bring to the boil, then cool. In a food processor, process 700g frozen raspberries and the sugar syrup, until smooth. Stir into the Yoghurt Cheese. Cover and refrigerate. Serve chilled. Strawberries may also be used. Makes about 625 millilitres.

At the market Most supermarkets offer a wide variety of yoghurts. Health-food stores may yield variations such as organic or goat's-milk yoghurt.

Look for For maximum health benefits, choose a carton with the words 'active yoghurt cultures' or 'live AB cultures' on it. 'Live' yoghurt is thought to restore essential intestinal bacteria which may be damaged by a course of antibiotics. All yoghurts are 'live' whether they stipulate this or not.

Prep If shop-bought yoghurt is slightly sep-arated, stir the liquid (whey) back in, as the whey contains nutri-ents, including calcium.

To make yoghurt cheese, drain yoghurt in a sieve lined with dampened cheesecloth or paper towels or through a coffee filter.

Basic cooking Yoghurt used in cooked dishes will curdle if subjected to high heat. Combin-ing the yoghurt with flour before adding it will help, but keep the heat moderate.

Fruit-Topped Yoghurt Cheese Tart *A pretty pattern of fruit tops a vanilla-scented filling.*

Pear-Yoghurt Cake with Yoghurt Topping

A crowning glory for any meal, this upside-down cake is served with sweet, lemony yoghurt 'cream'.

The bacteria used to culture yoghurt—either *Lactobacillus bulgaricus* or *Streptococcus thermophilus*—are good for your digestive system. They help you digest the milk protein in the yoghurt and there is good evidence that they help maintain a healthy balance of 'friendly' bacteria in your intestines.

The 'fruit' in shop-bought yoghurt is usually jam or preserves—more sugar than fruit. Nutritionally speaking, you're better off stirring your favourite fresh or dried fruit into plain yoghurt. A touch of vanilla or almond essence will enhance the flavour of the fruit.

Pear-Yoghurt Cake with Yoghurt Topping

PREP: 20 MINUTES
COOK: 1 HOUR 5 MINUTES

455 ml sugar
70 ml plus 15 ml unsalted butter
15 ml lemon juice
900 g pears, peeled, cored and
   quartered
625 ml flour
7,5 ml baking powder
2,5 ml bicarbonate of soda
1,25 ml salt
1 egg
2 egg whites
7,5 ml grated lemon rind
810 ml plain low-fat yoghurt

1. Preheat the oven to 180°C. In a 25-cm nonstick ovenproof baking tin, combine 60 ml of the sugar, 15 ml of the butter and the lemon juice. Cook over moderate heat for 5 minutes or until the sugar has melted and is beginning to brown. Remove from the heat and cover the bottom of the baking tin with the pears, arranging them spoke fashion, with the narrow ends of the pears toward the centre. Set the baking tin aside.

2. In a medium bowl, sift together the flour, baking powder, bicarbonate of soda and salt; set aside.

3. In a large bowl, cream the remaining 70 ml butter with 370 ml of the sugar with an electric mixer. Beat in the whole egg and egg whites, one at a time, beating well after each addition. Beat in 5 ml of the lemon rind. Alternately fold in the flour mixture and 310 ml of the yoghurt, beginning and ending with the flour mixture. Spoon the batter over the pears. Bake for 1 hour and 5 minutes or until a cake tester inserted in the centre of the cake portion comes out clean.

4. Meanwhile, place the remaining 500 ml yoghurt in a fine-mesh sieve set over a bowl; drain at room temperature while the cake bakes. Just before serving, stir in the remaining 30 ml sugar and 2,5 ml lemon rind.

5. Cool the cake in the baking tin on a rack for 5 minutes. Cover the tin with a heatproof plate, then invert the tin and plate together. Leave the tin upside down until the pears release, then carefully remove the baking tin. Serve warm or at room temperature with the sweetened yoghurt topping. Serves 12.

Per serving: Kilojoules 1 435; Fibre 2g; Protein 6g; Total Fat 8g; Saturated Fat 4g; Cholesterol 38mg; Sodium 109mg

Tandoori-Style Chicken

PREP: 25 MINUTES / MARINATE: 2 HOURS / COOK: 20 MINUTES

3 cloves garlic, peeled and crushed
5 ml paprika
3,5 ml each salt, ground cumin and coriander
2,5 ml ground cinnamon
1,25 ml pepper
500 ml plain low-fat yoghurt
900 g skinless, bone-in chicken breasts
1 small onion (red, if available), finely chopped
1 cucumber, seeded and diced
125 ml chopped fresh coriander

1. In a shallow glass or ceramic baking dish, combine the garlic, paprika, salt, cumin, coriander, cinnamon and pepper. Stir in 250 ml of the yoghurt until well blended. With a sharp knife, make several slashes in the flesh of the chicken, cutting almost to the bone. Place the chicken, cut-sides down, in the yoghurt mixture. Cover and refrigerate for at least 2 hours or overnight, turning the chicken several times.

2. Preheat the oven to 230°C. Lift the chicken from its marinade and place on a grill; discard any leftover marinade. Bake the chicken for 20 minutes or until cooked through but still juicy.

3. Meanwhile, in a medium bowl, combine the onion, cucumber, fresh coriander and the remaining 250 ml yoghurt. Serve the chicken with the yoghurt mixture on the side. Serves 4.

Per serving: Kilojoules 1 219; Fibre 0g; Protein 45g; Total Fat 7g; Saturated Fat 3g; Cholesterol 94mg; Sodium 574mg

Tropical Smoothie In a blender, combine 250 ml plain low-fat yoghurt, 175 ml mango pieces, 125 ml banana slices, 15 ml lime or lemon juice, 10 ml sugar and 4 ice cubes. Blend until smooth and thick. Garnish with a mint sprig and slices of mango and lime (or lemon). Serves 2. *[kJ 716; Fat 3g; Sodium 84mg]*

Green Goddess Salad Dressing In food a processor, combine 500 ml plain fat-free yoghurt, 125 ml packed parsley leaves, 10 ml anchovy paste, 15 ml lemon juice, 10 ml dried tarragon, 2,5 ml salt and 1 small garlic clove; process until smooth. Makes 500 ml. Use 125 ml dressing and 360 g (6 cups) mixed greens to serve 4. *[Per 30-ml serving: kJ 88; Fat 1g; Sodium 101mg]*

Two-Berry Yoghurt Frozen Suckers In a food processor, process 175 g strawberries, 60 ml raspberry coulis (or sieved raspberry jam) and 30 ml honey until smooth. Add 500 ml plain low-fat yoghurt; process to combine. Freeze in frozen sucker moulds. Serves 6. *[kJ 389; Fat 2g; Sodium 57mg]*

Fresh cheeses

Ricotta Cheese
PER 120 G (½ CUP)

Kilojoules	869
Fibre	0 g
Protein	14 g
Total Fat	15,6 g
Saturated Fat	10 g
Cholesterol	61 mg
Sodium	101 mg

NUTRIENTS

% RDA for people older than 10 years

Calcium	21 %
Vitamin A	20 %
Riboflavin	15 %

Low-Fat Cottage Cheese
PER 120 G (½ CUP)

Kilojoules	443
Fibre	0 g
Protein	13 g
Total Fat	4,8 g
Saturated Fat	0,1 g
Cholesterol	6 mg
Sodium	193 mg

NUTRIENTS

% RDA for people older than 10 years

Vitamin B12	84 %
Riboflavin	16 %
Calcium	12 %

Liptauer Cheese
PREP: 10 MINUTES / CHILL: 1 HOUR

Serve this Hungarian specialty with toasted rye bread or whole-grain biscuits.

- 225 g low-fat cream cheese
- 115 g smooth fat-free cottage cheese
- 30 ml low-fat (2%) milk
- 70 ml finely chopped onion (red, if available)
- 4 anchovies, rinsed and mashed, or 10 ml anchovy paste
- 30 ml capers, rinsed and drained
- 3,5 ml grated lemon rind

1. In a bowl, with an electric mixer, beat together both the cheeses and the milk. Fold in the onion, anchovies, capers and lemon rind.

2. Line a small (500- to 625-ml) bowl with plastic wrap, leaving a 5-cm overhang and spoon the cheese mixture into it, smoothing the top. Fold the plastic wrap over and refrigerate for 1 hour or until well chilled and firm. Unmould onto a serving plate and remove the plastic wrap. Makes 425 millilitres.

Per 60 ml: Kilojoules 462; Fibre 0 g; Protein 7 g; Total Fat 8 g; Saturated Fat 5 g; Cholesterol 37 mg; Sodium 385 mg

Fettuccine Alfredo with Green Noodles
PREP: 10 MINUTES / COOK: 15 MINUTES

- 350 g spinach fettuccine
- 15 ml unsalted butter
- 250 ml low-fat (2%) milk
- 30 ml flour
- 115 g smooth low-fat cream cheese
- 70 ml grated Parmesan cheese
- 2,5 ml salt
- 2,5 ml pepper

1. In a large pot of boiling water, cook the pasta according to package directions until *al dente*. Reserving 125 ml of the cooking liquid, drain the pasta and transfer to a large bowl. Add the butter, tossing well to coat.

2. Meanwhile, in a medium saucepan, whisk the milk into the flour until well combined. Whisk over low heat for 3 minutes or until slightly thickened. Whisk in the cream cheese, Parmesan, salt, pepper and reserved pasta cooking liquid. Pour the sauce over the pasta, tossing well to coat. Serves 4.

Per serving: Kilojoules 1 793; Fibre 6 g; Protein 18 g; Total Fat 14 g; Saturated Fat 7 g; Cholesterol 49 mg; Sodium 533 mg

Coeur à la Crème

PREP: 10 MINUTES
DRAIN: 4 TO 6 HOURS

This French 'cream heart' is traditionally made in a special heart-shaped mould, but as these are difficult to find in South Africa, a cheesecloth-lined sieve will work as well.

225 g smooth low-fat cream cheese
225 g smooth fat-free cottage cheese
225 g smooth low-fat cottage cheese
150 ml icing sugar
2,5 ml vanilla essence
300 g strawberries
30 ml honey
15 ml lime or lemon juice

1. In a food processor, combine the cream cheese and cottage cheeses and process until smooth. Add the sugar and vanilla and pulse until combined.

2. Line a heart-shaped ceramic coeur à la crème mould (or a 1- to 1,5-litre sieve set over a bowl) with a double layer of dampened cheesecloth. Spoon the cream cheese mixture into the mould, wrap the cheesecloth over and place the mould on a plate to drain. Refrigerate 4 to 6 hours or overnight.

3. Before serving, combine the strawberries, honey and lime juice in a food processor or blender. Process until smooth. At serving time, unwrap the cheesecloth mould and invert the mould onto a large plate. Remove the mould and peel off the cheesecloth. Serve with the strawberry sauce. Serves 6.

Per serving: Kilojoules 1 132; Fibre 1 g; Protein 12 g; Total Fat 11 g; Saturated Fat 6 g; Cholesterol 45 mg; Sodium 326 mg

Coeur à la Crème *Berry sauce is the ideal accompaniment for this charming dessert.*

At the market

Cream cheese is available in full-fat and low-fat versions, while cottage cheese can be either full-fat, low-fat or fat-free. The fat content of ricotta is relatively low at 13%. The high moisture content of ricotta means that it is low in kilojoules, but still higher than full-fat cottage cheese.

Prep Some recipes call for cottage cheese and ricotta to be drained before you use them. Draining a 'creamed' cottage cheese will also help remove some of the fat. To drain, place the cheese in a fine-mesh sieve and shake it gently to drain off some of the liquid.

Mix together 250 ml low-fat plain yoghurt and 250 ml fat-free smooth cottage cheese and you will have a salad dressing which is low in fat (0,5 g total fat in a 50 ml portion) and low in kilojoules (129 kJ in a 50 ml portion). A 50 ml portion will provide 0,5 g of fat compared to 16 g in an equivalent amount of reduced-fat salad dressing. Season the dressing to taste and add chopped herbs or a few drops of chilli sauce for extra flavour.

129

Lemon-Lime
Cheesecake

PREP: 20 MINUTES
COOK: 1 HOUR 5 MINUTES

If you don't tell, no one will know that this fabulous cake is made with low-fat cheeses.

85g plain sweet biscuits (vanilla wafers, if available)
30ml unsalted butter, melted
360g smooth low-fat cottage cheese
225g low-fat cream cheese
225g smooth fat-free cottage cheese
250ml plus 15ml sugar
2 eggs
4 egg whites
30ml flour
7,5ml grated lemon rind
7,5ml grated lime rind
15ml lemon juice
15ml lime juice
1,25ml salt
125ml sour cream

1. Preheat the oven to 180°C. In a food processor, process the biscuits until finely ground. Add the butter and pulse until moistened. Spoon the mixture into a 23-cm springform tin, patting it into the bottom. Bake for 10 minutes or until lightly browned; set aside. Leave the oven on.

2. In a food processor (you can use the same bowl), blend the cottage cheeses until combined.

3. In a medium bowl, beat the cream cheese and 250ml of the sugar with an electric mixer until light and fluffy. Beat in the whole eggs and egg whites, one at a time, beating well after each addition. Beat in the puréed cottage cheeses, the flour, lemon rind, lime rind, lemon juice, lime juice and salt until well blended. Pour the batter into the prepared tin and bake for 50 minutes or until the centre is set and the top is golden.

4. Meanwhile, in a small bowl, combine the sour cream and the remaining 15ml sugar. Spread over the top of the hot cake and bake for 5 minutes. Remove from the oven to a wire rack to cool. Refrigerate until serving time. Serves 12.

Per serving: Kilojoules 1045; Fibre 0g; Protein 10g; Total Fat 12g; Saturated Fat 6g; Cholesterol 75mg; Sodium 284mg

Cannoli Pudding
with Chocolate &
Roasted Almonds

PREP: 10 MINUTES / COOK: 10 MINUTES
CHILL: 2 HOURS

40g tapioca
50g unsalted slivered almonds
125ml sugar
0,6ml salt
500ml low-fat (2%) milk
250g smooth low-fat cottage cheese
5ml vanilla essence
125ml milk chocolate, chopped

1. Soak the tapioca in cold water for 30 minutes. Drain. In a frying pan dry-roast the almond slivers until golden brown. Set aside.

2. In a saucepan, mix the sugar, salt, tapioca and milk. Cook over moderate heat, stirring constantly. Reduce to a simmer and cook, stirring frequently for 5 minutes or until the tapioca is tender.

3. Remove from the heat and stir in the cottage cheese. Let cool to room temperature, then stir in the vanilla. Fold in the chocolate pieces and almonds. Spoon into 6 serving bowls, cover and refrigerate for 2 hours or until well chilled. Serves 6.

Per serving: Kilojoules 1193; Fibre 1g; Protein 10g; Total Fat 12g; Saturated Fat 3g; Cholesterol 12mg; Sodium 171mg

Lemon-Lime Cheesecake *A topping of sweetened sour cream crowns this elegant cake.*

Did you know? . . .

Sodium content can vary among different brands of cottage cheese. New labelling legislation will make it easy to distinguish between brands.

Sweet Noodle Kugel with Apricots

PREP: 10 MINUTES / COOK: 30 MINUTES

In Eastern Europe, noodles are used in desserts as well as main dishes. This old-fashioned noodle-cheese pudding, studded with apricots and sprinkled with cinnamon-sugar, is a pleasing way to round out a family dinner.

225 g wide egg noodles
360 g smooth low-fat cottage cheese
125 ml low-fat (2%) milk
30 ml unsalted butter, melted
1 egg
2 egg whites
70 ml plus 15 ml sugar
60 ml frozen orange juice concentrate, thawed
2,5 ml vanilla essence
1,25 ml salt
125 ml dried apricots, chopped
1,25 ml ground cinnamon

1. Preheat the oven to 180°C. Butter a 18 x 28-cm baking dish; set aside. In a large saucepan of boiling water, cook the noodles according to the directions on the package until *al dente*. Drain well.

2. Meanwhile, combine the cottage cheese, milk, butter, whole egg, egg whites, 70 ml of the sugar, the orange juice concentrate, vanilla essence and salt in a food processor. Process to a smooth purée. Transfer the purée to a large bowl and add the drained noodles and the apricots, tossing well to combine. Spoon the noodle mixture into the prepared baking dish.

3. In a small bowl, combine the remaining 15 ml sugar and the cinnamon. Sprinkle over the top of the noodle mixture.

4. Bake, uncovered, for 30 minutes or until the kugel is set and the top is slightly crusty. Serve warm, at room temperature or lightly chilled. Serves 8.

Per serving: Kilojoules 1 036; Fibre 2 g; Protein 11 g; Total Fat 7 g; Saturated Fat 2 g; Cholesterol 62 mg; Sodium 175 mg

A 125 ml serving of low-fat cottage cheese supplies about 13 g of protein—about one-quarter of an adult's daily protein requirement. And the protein in cottage cheese is as high in quality as that found in meat or fish.

Ricotta cheese, also an excellent protein source, has an additional advantage over meat: ricotta supplies 207 mg of calcium per 100 g, while meat contains negligible amounts of this important mineral.

Goat & Feta

Goat Cheese (Soft)

PER 30 G

Kilojoules	333
Fibre	0 g
Protein	6 g
Total Fat	6,3 g
Saturated Fat	4,4 g
Cholesterol	14 mg
Sodium	110 mg

NUTRIENTS

% RDA for people older than 10 years

Riboflavin	7 %
Calcium	4 %

Feta Cheese

PER 30 G

Kilojoules	406
Fibre	0 g
Protein	5 g
Total Fat	8,3 g
Saturated Fat	5,2 g
Cholesterol	21 mg
Sodium	310 mg

NUTRIENTS

% RDA for people older than 10 years

Calcium	10 %
Riboflavin	5 %

Crustless Mini-Quiches with Broccoli & Feta

PREP: 15 MINUTES / COOK: 35 MINUTES

Cheese, milk and broccoli make this a calcium-rich main dish. Serve the tartlets with a green salad and whole-grain bread.

- 5 ml olive oil
- 4 spring onions, thinly sliced
- 2 cloves garlic, finely chopped
- 280 g frozen chopped broccoli, thawed and squeezed dry, or fresh broccoli
- 70 ml smooth low-fat cottage cheese
- 150 ml low-fat (2%) milk
- 2 eggs
- 3 egg whites
- 45 ml flour
- 2,5 ml pepper
- 175 g feta cheese or mild goat cheese

1. Preheat the oven to 180°C. Spray four 225-ml custard cups or ramekins with nonstick cooking spray; set aside. If using fresh broccoli, steam for 5 to 8 minutes. In a medium nonstick pan, heat the oil over moderate heat. Add the spring onions and garlic and sauté for 1 minute or until the garlic is tender. Stir in the broccoli and cook for 1 minute.

2. In a food processor, process the cottage cheese until smooth. Add the milk, whole eggs, egg whites, flour and pepper and process until well combined. Transfer the custard to a large bowl. Add the broccoli mixture and crumble in the feta cheese, stirring to combine. Spoon into the prepared cups, place on a baking sheet and bake for 30 minutes or until the mini-quiches are puffy and set. Serves 4.

Per serving: Kilojoules 1 165; Fibre 2g; Protein 19g; Total Fat 18g; Saturated Fat 9g; Cholesterol 139mg; Sodium 583mg

Creamy Polenta with Cheese

PREP: 10 MINUTES / COOK: 20 MINUTES

A staple food in Northern Italy, polenta is simply maize-meal mush. Our hearty polenta side dish is enlivened with tangy cheese.

- 250 ml yellow maize meal (sold as polenta)
- 375 ml low-fat (2%) milk
- 1,25 ml salt
- 0,6 ml cayenne pepper
- 175 g feta cheese or mild goat cheese

1. In a small bowl, stir the maize meal and 250 ml of the milk together until blended and smooth.

2. In a medium-size heavy-bottomed saucepan, bring 375 ml of water, the

Composed Salad with Grilled Goat Cheese A sophisticated salad-and-sandwich meal.

Goat cheese often has a covering—a traditional covering for certain French goat cheeses is a fine layer of ash (left). Other coatings include such ingredients as dried herbs or crushed peppercorns (right).

remaining 125 ml milk, the salt and cayenne to a simmer over low heat. Stirring constantly, gradually pour in the maize meal-milk mixture. Cook over low heat, stirring constantly, for 10 minutes or until thick and creamy.

3. Crumble in the feta and cook, stirring, for 3 to 4 minutes or until the cheese is melted. Serves 4.

Per serving: Kilojoules 1 295; Fibre 1 g; Protein 14 g; Total Fat 15 g; Saturated Fat 8 g; Cholesterol 37 mg; Sodium 648 mg

Composed Salad with Grilled Goat Cheese

PREP: 20 MINUTES / COOK: 15 MINUTES

Roasted pattipan squashes and peppers bring rich flavour to this contemporary classic.

60 ml chicken stock
1 clove garlic, finely chopped
150 g pattipans, thinly sliced
1 large red pepper, cut lengthwise into flat panels
1 large green pepper, cut lengthwise into flat panels
12 slices (5 x 6 cm) Italian bread
225 g mild goat cheese, cut into 12 slices
45 ml red wine vinegar

15 ml olive oil
5 ml Dijon mustard
2,5 ml light brown sugar
1,25 ml salt
480 g torn cos lettuce (8 cups)

1. Preheat the grill. In a small bowl, combine the stock and garlic. Add the pattipans, tossing to coat. Place the pattipans under the grill. Place the pepper pieces, skin-side up, under the grill. Grill the vegetables 15 centimetres from the heat for 10 minutes or until the pattipans are tender and the pepper skin is blackened. Leave the grill on. When the peppers are cool enough to handle, peel them and cut into 2,5-cm-wide strips.

2. Top each slice of bread with the cheese and grill for 1 minute or until the cheese is slightly melted and the bread is toasted.

3. In a small bowl, whisk together the vinegar, oil, mustard, brown sugar and salt. Place the lettuce on 4 plates and arrange the peppers and pattipans on top. Drizzle the dressing over the salads and place 3 cheese toasts on each. Serves 4.

Per serving: Kilojoules 1 321; Fibre 5 g; Protein 17 g; Total Fat 17 g; Saturated Fat 9 g; Cholesterol 26 mg; Sodium 670 mg

Look for The flavour of goat cheese (also known as chevres) ranges from gently tangy to sharply pungent; choose a cheese that suits your taste. Locally available goat cheese comes in plain, garlic and parsley and sweet red pepper flavours. A mild flavour is best for these recipes. Apart from plain feta, other feta flavours such as black pepper and herb are also available.

Prep Remove the rind from goat cheese (which usually comes in the form of a log) if necessary. Feta should be rinsed under cold running water and drained well.

Provolone & Mozzarella

Provolone
PER 30 G

Kilojoules	441
Fibre	0 g
Protein	8 g
Total Fat	8 g
Saturated Fat	5,1 g
Cholesterol	21 mg
Sodium	263 mg

NUTRIENTS

% RDA for people older than 10 years

Calcium	21 %

Mozzarella
PER 30 G

Kilojoules	350
Fibre	0 g
Protein	5,8 g
Total Fat	6,5 g
Saturated Fat	3,9 g
Cholesterol	23 mg
Sodium	112 mg

NUTRIENTS

% RDA for people older than 10 years

Phosphorus	14 %
Calcium	13 %
Vitamin A	9 %

Mozzarella Salad with Balsamic Dressing

PREP: 10 MINUTES / COOK: 10 MINUTES
MARINATE: 1 HOUR

What a luxurious way to get your calcium! Mozzarella, basil and tomatoes are the ideal taste combination.

- 2 large red peppers, cut lengthwise into flat panels
- 3 cloves garlic, peeled
- 60 ml balsamic vinegar
- 15 ml olive oil, preferably extra-virgin
- 5 ml light brown sugar
- 2,5 ml salt
- 1,25 ml black pepper
- 60 ml chopped fresh basil
- 1 small onion (red, if available), halved and thinly sliced
- 225 g mozzarella cheese, cut into 16 slices
- 450 g tomatoes, cut into 16 slices

1. Preheat the grill. Place the pepper pieces, skin-side up, on a grill rack and grill 10 centimetres from the heat for 10 minutes or until the skin is blackened. When the peppers are cool enough to handle, peel them and cut into 1-cm-wide strips.

2. Meanwhile, in a small pan of boiling water, cook the garlic for 3 minutes to blanch. Drain, chop finely and transfer to a large bowl. Whisk in the vinegar, oil, brown sugar, salt and black pepper. Add the peppers, basil and onion, tossing well. Cover and refrigerate for 1 hour. Arrange the cheese and tomatoes on a platter and spoon the pepper mixture on top. Serves 4.

Per serving: Kilojoules 1 036; Fibre 3g; Protein 13g; Total Fat 16g; Saturated Fat 8g; Cholesterol 44mg; Sodium 520mg

Italian-Style Enchiladas with Provolone

PREP: 20 MINUTES / COOK: 45 MINUTES

Here's a favourite Mexican dish restyled with Italian seasonings. Thanks to the bounty of vegetables, these enchiladas are rich in beta carotene and vitamin C. Both corn and wheat tortillas, along with other Mexican foods, are available in supermarkets countrywide.

- 5 ml olive oil
- 1 small onion, finely chopped
- 2 cloves garlic, finely chopped
- 1 red pepper, cut into 1-cm squares
- 2 baby marrows, halved lengthwise and thinly sliced
- 70 ml chicken stock
- 500 ml tinned chopped tomatoes
- 125 ml chopped fresh basil
- 1,25 ml crushed red chilli flakes
- 8 corn tortillas (47 g each)
- 225 ml strained, crushed tomatoes
- 175 g provolone cheese, grated

1. Preheat the oven to 190°C. Spray a 18 x 28-cm baking tin with nonstick cooking spray.

2. In a large nonstick frying pan, heat the oil over moderate heat. Add the onion and garlic and sauté for 5 minutes. Add the pepper, baby marrow and stock. Reduce to a simmer, cover and cook for 3 minutes or until the baby marrow is firm-tender. Stir in the chopped tomatoes, basil and red chilli flakes and bring to a boil. Reduce to a simmer, cover and cook for 7 minutes or until the vegetable mixture is flavourful.

3. Place the tortillas on a baking sheet, cover with foil and bake in the oven for 5 minutes or until just hot. Spoon one-third of the vegetable mixture over the warmed tortillas. Top with half the cheese. Stir the tomato sauce into the remaining vegetable mixture. Spoon half of the remaining vegetable mixture into the bottom of the prepared baking tin. Roll the tortillas up and place them, seam-side down, in the tin. Top with the remaining vegetable mixture.

4. Cover the tin with foil and bake for 15 minutes. Uncover, sprinkle the

Mushroom-Pepper Pizza *Quick and easy to prepare with a ready-made pizza base.*

remaining cheese on top and bake for 5 minutes or until the cheese has melted and the enchiladas are hot. Serves 4.

Per serving: Kilojoules 2 253; Fibre 7 g; Protein 21 g; Total Fat 22 g; Saturated Fat 12 g; Cholesterol 30 mg; Sodium 1 397 mg

---

Mushroom-Pepper Pizza

PREP: 20 MINUTES / RISE: 25 MINUTES
COOK: 30 MINUTES

- 5 ml olive oil
- 1 large red pepper, thinly sliced
- 1 large green pepper, thinly sliced
- 225 g mushrooms, thinly sliced
- 2,5 ml dried oreganum
- 1,25 ml salt
- 1 large ready-made pizza base
- 250 ml bottled tomato pizza sauce
- 0,6 ml ground cinnamon
- 225 g mozzarella cheese, thinly sliced

1. In a large nonstick frying pan, heat the oil over moderate heat. Add the peppers and sauté for 5 minutes or until crisp-tender. Add the mushrooms, oreganum and salt and cook for 4 minutes or until the mushroom liquid has evaporated. Set aside.

2. Preheat the oven to 230°C. Spray a 30-cm pizza pan or large baking sheet with nonstick cooking spray. Place the pizza base on the baking sheet and bake for 5 minutes.

3. In a small bowl, combine the pizza sauce and the ground cinnamon. Spoon over the pizza. Top with the pepper mixture and the mozzarella cheese. Bake for 15 minutes or until the cheese has melted and the crust is browned. Serves 6.

Per serving: Kilojoules 1 403; Fibre 5 g; Protein 15 g; Total Fat 10 g; Saturated Fat 5 g; Cholesterol 29 mg; Sodium 815 mg

At the market Mozzarella is widely available, as is provolone. Mozzarella has become synonymous with pizzas. Freshly made mozzarella has a deliciously delicate, milky flavour. It should have no holes and should feel soft and elastic. Provolone is similar to mozzarella, but has a much firmer texture and stronger yellow colour. It is mild when young but the flavour sharpens as the cheese ages. It is usually smoked.

Smoked mozzarella has a rich, tangy taste.

Prep These cheeses are easier to grate or slice if well chilled.

Basic cooking Unlike factory mozzarella, fresh mozzarella softens and melts (rather than turning stringy) when heated. But like other cheeses, any type of mozzarella or provolone will turn rubbery if cooked too long or at too high a temperature.

Mild Cheddar

Mild and Mature Cheddar

PER 30G

Kilojoules	**494**
Fibre	**0g**
Protein	**7g**
Total Fat	**9,7g**
Saturated Fat	**5,5g**
Cholesterol	**35mg**
Sodium	**146mg**

NUTRIENTS

% RDA for people older than 10 years

Calcium	**20%**
Vitamin A	**15%**
Riboflavin	**7%**

Did you know? . . .

Forty grams of Cheddar cheese supplies as much calcium as 250 millilitres of low-fat milk.

Although Cheddar cheese is high in saturated fat, it also provides high quality protein, calcium and B-vitamins.

Cheesy Rice Bake

PREP: 10 MINUTES / COOK: 40 MINUTES

This baked rice-and-cheese dish makes a fine meatless main course. Serve it with a salad of sliced tomatoes. For a more substantial main dish, add 225 grams of cubed cooked chicken in Step 2.

5 ml vegetable oil
1 small onion, finely chopped
3 cloves garlic, finely chopped
1 red pepper, diced
250 ml rice
310 ml chicken stock
250 ml low-fat (2%) milk
2,5 ml salt
0,6 ml black pepper
175 g mild Cheddar, grated
70 ml chopped parsley or fresh
   coriander

1. Preheat the oven to 180°C. In a nonstick flameproof casserole, heat the oil over moderate heat. Add the onion and garlic and sauté for 5 minutes or until the onion is soft. Add the pepper and cook, stirring frequently, for 4 minutes or until firm-tender.

2. Stir in the rice. Add the stock, milk, salt and black pepper and bring to a boil. Stir in the cheese, cover tightly, and place in the oven for 25 minutes or until the rice is tender. Stir in the parsley and serve. Serves 4.

Per serving: Kilojoules 1 706; Fibre 1g; Protein 17g; Total Fat 17g; Saturated Fat 8g; Cholesterol 55mg; Sodium 1 019mg

Mashed Potatoes with Chilli and Cheese

PREP: 10 MINUTES / COOK: 20 MINUTES

Highly preferable to potatoes whipped with butter and cream, this super side dish includes disease-fighting garlic, tomatoes and chilli powder as well as plenty of calcium.

900 g potatoes, peeled and thinly sliced
60 ml sun-dried tomato halves (not oil-
   packed), cut into quarters
2 cloves garlic, peeled
3,5 to 5 ml chilli powder
2,5 ml salt
175 g mild Cheddar cheese, sliced

1. In a large pot of boiling water, cook the potatoes, sun-dried tomatoes and garlic for 15 minutes or until the potatoes are tender. Reserving 70 ml of the cooking liquid, drain and transfer the potatoes, sun-dried tomatoes and garlic to a large bowl.

2. Add the reserved cooking liquid, the chilli powder and salt to the bowl. With a potato masher or fork, mash the potatoes until well combined.

3. Add the Cheddar and mash for 3 to 4 minutes or until the cheese is melted. Serves 6.

Per serving: Kilojoules 954; Fibre 2g; Protein 10g; Total Fat 10g; Saturated Fat 5g; Cholesterol 34mg; Sodium 394mg

Chicken & Cheese Tostadas

PREP: 15 MINUTES / COOK: 15 MINUTES

A tostada is an open-faced 'sandwich' based on a crisp fried tortilla; baking the tortillas makes for a lighter tostada. The chillies in the topping supply cancer-fighting capsaicin. Both bottled peperoncini and jalapeños are available at large supermarkets.

- 10 ml vegetable oil
- 1 small onion, thinly sliced
- 2 cloves garlic, finely chopped
- 280 g skinless, boned chicken breasts, cut into 1-cm pieces
- 250 ml frozen corn kernels, thawed
- 115 g bottled peperoncini, chopped
- 125 ml chopped fresh coriander
- 1 pickled jalapeño, halved, seeded and finely chopped
- 30 ml lime or lemon juice
- 8 corn tortillas (47 g each)
- 175 g mild Cheddar cheese, diced

1. In a large nonstick frying pan, heat the oil over moderate heat. Add the onion and garlic and sauté for 2 minutes or until the onion is tender. Add the chicken and sauté for 5 minutes or until just cooked through. Transfer to a large bowl. Add the corn kernels, peperoncini, coriander, jalapeño and lime juice, tossing to combine.

2. Meanwhile, preheat the oven to 200°C. Place the tortillas on a baking sheet and bake for 2 minutes.

3. Sprinkle half of the cheese over the tortillas. Top with the chicken mixture and the remaining cheese. Bake for 5 minutes or until the cheese is melted and bubbling. Serves 4.

Per serving: Kilojoules 2 680; Fibre 6 g; Protein 32 g; Total Fat 28 g; Saturated Fat 13 g; Cholesterol 76 mg; Sodium 877 mg

At the market Mild Cheddar cheese does not have a sharp flavour and has a light straw colour. Mild Cheddar is usually not older than two months and, as the flavour intensifies with age, some supermarkets note the age of the Cheddar on the package.

The flavour of some Cheddar cheeses is enhanced with the addition of ingredients such as crushed pepper or garlic.

Prep Mild Cheddar can be quite soft, so to grate it more easily keep it refrigerated until ready for use. Keep all exposed surfaces covered with plastic wrap to prevent hardening. Cheddar which is to be eaten after a meal should be left out of the refrigerator for a least an hour beforehand. Slice with a hot knife to prevent sticking and crumbling.

Cheesy Rice Bake *is an easy oven main dish with the rich flavour of cheese.*

Mature Cheddar & Gruyère

Gruyère
PER 30G

Kilojoules	518
Fibre	0g
Protein	9g
Total Fat	9,7g
Saturated Fat	5,7g
Cholesterol	26mg
Sodium	101mg

NUTRIENTS

% RDA for people older than 10 years	
Calcium	25%

Parmesan
PER 30G

Kilojoules	564
Fibre	0g
Protein	12g
Total Fat	9g
Saturated Fat	5,7g
Cholesterol	24mg
Sodium	559mg

NUTRIENTS

% RDA for people older than 10 years	
Calcium	34%

Did you know? . . .

Cheese—especially Cheddar cheese—is reputed to be an impressive cavity fighter.

Chicken Cheddar Chowder

PREP: 20 MINUTES / COOK: 20 MINUTES

You can enjoy Cheddar's robust bite in many dishes, but it's best if the other ingredients are low in fat. Here, skinless chicken breast, vegetables and low-fat milk do the trick.

- 375ml chicken stock
- 350g potatoes (red, if available), cut into 1-cm pieces
- 1 large carrot, thinly sliced
- 1 green pepper, cut into 1-cm squares
- 5ml paprika
- 2,5ml black pepper
- 1,25ml salt
- 350g skinless, boned chicken breasts, cut into 2,5-cm pieces
- 125ml low-fat (2%) milk
- 30ml flour
- 175g mature Cheddar cheese, grated

1. In a large saucepan, bring the stock and 675ml of water to a boil over moderate heat. Add the potatoes, carrot, pepper, paprika, black pepper and salt. Reduce to a simmer, cover and cook for 10 minutes or until the potatoes are firm-tender. Add the chicken and cook for 5 minutes or until it is cooked through.

2. In a small bowl, whisk the milk into the flour until smooth. Whisk the milk mixture into the soup and simmer for 3 minutes or until the soup is slightly thickened. Remove from the heat and stir in the cheese until melted. Serves 4.

Per serving: Kilojoules 1576; Fibre 3g; Protein 30g; Total Fat 18g; Saturated Fat 11g; Cholesterol 85mg; Sodium 990mg

Dijon Cheese Tart

PREP: 1 HOUR 25 MINUTES
COOK: 1 HOUR 10 MINUTES

Serve this calcium-rich tart with a crisp mixed green salad. or a fresh tomato salsa.

- 250ml flour
- 2,5ml sugar
- 1,25ml salt
- 1,25ml cayenne pepper
- 55g low-fat cream cheese
- 30ml unsalted butter, cut up
- 30ml sour cream
- 250ml low-fat (2%) milk
- 1 egg
- 3 egg whites
- 15ml Dijon mustard
- 175g Gruyère or other Swiss-style cheese, grated

1. In a large bowl, combine the flour, sugar, salt and cayenne. With a pastry blender or two knives, cut in the cream cheese and butter until the mixture resembles coarse crumbs. In a small bowl, combine the sour cream and 15ml of iced water. Stir into the flour mixture until just combined. Flatten into a disc, wrap in plastic wrap and refrigerate for at least 1 hour or overnight.

2. Preheat the oven to 180°C. On a lightly floured surface, roll the dough out to a 33-cm round. Fit into a 23-cm tart tin with a removable bottom. With a fork, prick the bottom of the shell in several places. Line with

Cheddar-Potato Bread is tasty with meals or as the base for a chicken or ham sandwich.

foil and weigh down with dried beans or rice. Bake for 20 minutes or until the crust is beginning to set. Remove the beans (or rice) and foil and bake for 15 minutes or until the crust is cooked through. Leave the oven on.

3. In a medium bowl, whisk together the milk, whole egg, egg whites and mustard. Stir in the Gruyère. Place the tart tin on a baking sheet with sides. Pour the cheese mixture into the crust and bake for 35 minutes or until puffed and golden brown. Serve warm or at room temperature. Serves 8.

Per serving: Kilojoules 972; Fibre 0g; Protein 12g; Total Fat 14g; Saturated Fat 8g; Cholesterol 73mg; Sodium 263mg

Cheddar-Potato Bread

PREP: 15 MINUTES / RISE: 1 HOUR
COOK: 35 MINUTES

An unusual savoury bread which is quick to make if you use instant dry yeast.

280g potatoes (1 or 2 medium), peeled and thinly sliced
2 cloves garlic, peeled
30ml olive oil
875ml flour
10g (1 envelope) instant dry yeast
5ml sugar
6,25ml salt
1,25ml cayenne pepper
225g grated medium-sharp Cheddar cheese

1. In a medium pot of boiling water, cook the potato and garlic for 15 minutes or until the potato is tender. Reserving 310ml of the liquid, drain the potatoes and garlic and transfer to a large bowl. Add the oil and mash with a potato masher until smooth.

2. Add the flour, salt, yeast, sugar and cayenne to the potatoes, stirring until well combined. Stir in the 310ml reserved cooking liquid. Stir in the Cheddar.

3. Turn the dough out onto a lightly floured surface and knead for 5 minutes or until smooth and elastic. Spray a large bowl with nonstick cooking spray; add the dough, turning to coat. Cover and let rise in a warm draft-free spot for 45 minutes or until doubled in bulk.

4. Preheat the oven to 200°C. Spray two 22 x 12-cm loaf tins with nonstick cooking spray. Punch the dough down, divide in half, form each portion into a loaf shape and place in the prepared tins. Cover and let rise in a warm draft-free spot for 15 minutes.

5. Bake for 30 to 35 minutes or until the loaves have browned. Makes 2 loaves or 16 servings.

Per serving: Kilojoules 1233; Fibre 2g; Protein 8g; Total Fat 7g; Saturated Fat 3g; Cholesterol 16mg; Sodium 252mg

At the market You'll find 'basic' mature Cheddar and Gruyère in every supermarket. Delicatessens will offer more options. Parmesan, which is used throughout the book, should be bought in a piece and grated at home, rather than as a packet of pregrated cheese.

Cheddar is also made without yellow colouring.

Look for Mature Cheddar (6 months old) is hard and has a deep yellow colour and sharp flavour. It should have no cracks on the surface. If not prepackaged, it should have a red wax rind. Gruyère is a Swiss-style cheese (another example is Emmentaler). It is a hard cheese, pale yellow in colour with a light brown rind. It melts beautifully, hence its popularity for fondues.

Basic cooking Grated and added to hot food, these cheeses will melt quickly and smoothly. When subjected to high or prolonged heat, they will turn tough and rubbery.

Eggs

Nutritional power

The protein content is high and the price is right—eggs are a nutrition bargain. You also get riboflavin, folate, iron, B vitamins, phosphorus and vitamin E.

PER 1 LARGE (50 G)

Kilojoules	308
Fibre	0 g
Protein	6 g
Total Fat	5,2 g
Saturated Fat	1,5 g
Cholesterol	210 mg
Sodium	63 mg

NUTRIENTS

% RDA for people older than 10 years

Vitamin E	17%

Did you know? . . .

New methods of analysis have shown eggs to be lower in cholesterol than previously thought. At any rate, saturated fat in the diet has a much greater effect on blood cholesterol, and an egg contains less than 2 mg of saturated fat.

All of an egg's fat and cholesterol is in the yolk, but so is the lion's share of the B vitamins and minerals.

Asparagus & Red Pepper Frittata

PREP: 10 MINUTES / COOK: 20 MINUTES

- 225 g asparagus, trimmed and cut into 1-cm lengths
- 1 red pepper, cut into 1-cm squares
- 3 eggs
- 4 egg whites
- 10 ml flour
- 125 ml grated Parmesan cheese
- 2,5 ml salt
- 1,25 ml black pepper
- 10 ml olive oil
- 5 ml unsalted butter

1. In a medium pot of boiling water, cook the asparagus and pepper for 2 minutes to blanch; drain well.

2. In a medium bowl, whisk together the whole eggs and egg whites. Whisk in the flour until well combined. Whisk in the Parmesan, salt and black pepper. Stir in the asparagus and pepper.

3. In a 25-cm cast-iron or other oven-proof pan, heat the oil and butter over low heat until the butter has melted. Pour in the egg mixture and cook without stirring for 15 minutes or until the eggs are set around the edges and almost set in the centre. Meanwhile, preheat the grill.

4. Grill the frittata 15 centimetres from the heat for 1 to 2 minutes or until the top is just set. Cut into wedges and serve hot, warm, at room temperature or chilled. Serves 4.

Per serving: Kilojoules 780; Fibre 2 g; Protein 14 g; Total Fat 11 g; Saturated Fat 4 g; Cholesterol 170 mg; Sodium 598 mg

Souffléed Omelette with Apple Topping

PREP: 10 MINUTES / COOK: 10 MINUTES

- 3 egg yolks
- 45 ml flour
- 125 ml low-fat (2%) milk
- 15 ml sugar
- 5 ml grated lemon rind
- 1,25 ml salt
- 6 egg whites
- 15 ml unsalted butter
- 45 ml apple juice (or frozen apple juice concentrate)
- 15 ml lemon juice
- 2 large Granny Smith apples, peeled and cut into thin wedges

1. Preheat the oven to 200°C. In a large bowl, whisk together the egg yolks, flour, milk, sugar, lemon rind and salt. In a separate bowl, whisk the egg whites until stiff peaks form. Gently fold the whites into the yolk mixture.

2. In a deep, 25-cm ovenproof pan, melt the butter over moderate heat. Pour in the egg mixture, place in the oven and bake for 10 minutes or until set, puffed and lightly browned.

3. Meanwhile, in a medium pan, bring the apple juice and lemon juice to a boil over moderate heat. Add the apples and cook, tossing occasionally, for 4 minutes or until the apples are tender. Top the hot souffléed omelette with the apples. Serves 4.

Per serving: Kilojoules 925; Fibre 3 g; Protein 9 g; Total Fat 8 g; Saturated Fat 3 g; Cholesterol 196 mg; Sodium 236 mg

Crème Caramel

PREP: 15 MINUTES / COOK: 50 MINUTES

Since the orange rind is used only for flavouring, cut it off the orange in broad strips.

175 ml plus 150 ml sugar
500 ml low-fat (2%) milk
250 ml low-fat evaporated milk
6 strips of orange rind
1,25 ml salt
4 eggs
2 egg whites
2,5 ml vanilla essence

1. In a small saucepan, combine 175 ml of the sugar and 125 ml of water. Bring to a boil over moderately high heat and cook, without stirring, for 5 minutes or until amber-coloured. Pour the caramel into eight 175-ml custard cups, tilting them to cover the bottom and partway up the sides. Place the cups in a roasting pan and set aside.

2. In a medium saucepan, combine the milk, evaporated milk, 70 ml of the sugar, the orange rind and salt. Bring to a simmer over moderate heat. Remove from the heat, cover and let stand for 30 minutes at room temperature. Discard the orange rind.

3. Preheat the oven to 170°C. In a large bowl, whisk together the whole eggs, egg whites, vanilla and the remaining 80 ml sugar until well combined. Strain the milk mixture into the egg mixture and whisk to combine.

4. Pour the custard into the prepared custard cups. Pour boiling water into the roasting pan to come halfway up the sides of the cups. Bake for 45 minutes or until a knife inserted in the centre of a custard comes out clean.

5. Remove the cups from the water bath and cool on a rack. When cool, refrigerate until ready to serve. Run a knife around the outside edge of the custard cups and invert the crème caramel onto dessert plates. Serves 8.

Per serving: Kilojoules 968; Fibre 0g; Protein 8g; Total Fat 5g; Saturated Fat 2g; Cholesterol 118mg; Sodium 189mg

At the market Shops offer Small, Medium, Large, Extra-large and Jumbo eggs. Most published recipes—including ours—use Large eggs.

Look for All eggboxes should be dated. Open the box to see if the shells are intact. Eggs absorb odours so keep the eggs in the insulating eggbox in the refrigerator—not in the egg containers on the door as the constant change in temperature will affect the eggs.

Prep The easiest way to separate eggs is to use an egg separator (see below). Or you can crack the egg into your (clean) hand, letting the white run between your fingers.

An egg separator is a useful tool.

Basic cooking To avoid salmonella, it's best to cook eggs thoroughly. Cook soft-boiled eggs for at least 3½ minutes, scrambled eggs, omelettes and fried eggs past the runny stage.

Asparagus & Red Pepper Frittata *A typically quick, easy egg dish with Italian flair.*

Grains & Pasta

Kasha Varnishkes with Caramelized Onions

Pasta

Enriched Pasta
PER 150G COOKED (1 CUP)

Kilojoules	885
Fibre	2,4g
Protein	7g
Total Fat	1,1g
Saturated Fat	0,2g
Cholesterol	0mg
Sodium	2mg

NUTRIENTS

% RDA for people older than 10 years

Iron	22%
Riboflavin	19%
Thiamin	19%
Vitamin B6	17%
Folate	17%

Egg Noodles
PER 150G COOKED (1 CUP)

Kilojoules	833
Fibre	3,3g
Protein	7,2g
Total Fat	2,3g
Saturated Fat	0,5g
Cholesterol	50mg
Sodium	11mg

Fettuccine alla Giardiniera

PREP: 20 MINUTES / COOK: 25 MINUTES

'Gardener's-style' pasta with a light sauce.

- 200g small cauliflower florets (2 cups)
- 160g small broccoli florets (2 cups)
- 280g spinach fettuccine
- 15ml olive oil
- 1 onion (red, if available), diced
- 3 cloves garlic, finely chopped
- 225g mushrooms, thinly sliced
- 3,5ml salt
- 2,5ml dried rosemary, crumbled
- 1 large tomato, cut into 1-cm-thick wedges
- 15ml flour
- 375ml low-fat (2%) milk
- 70ml grated Parmesan cheese
- 60ml chopped parsley

1. In a large pot of boiling water, cook the cauliflower and broccoli for 2 minutes to blanch. With a slotted spoon, transfer the vegetables to a plate.

2. Add the fettuccine to the boiling water and cook according to package directions until *al dente*. Drain and transfer to a large serving bowl.

3. Meanwhile, in a large nonstick pan, heat 10ml of the oil over moderate heat. Add the onion and garlic and sauté for 5 minutes or until tender. Add the mushrooms and sauté for 3 minutes or until softened.

4. Add the remaining 5ml oil to the pan. Return the cauliflower and broccoli to the pan, sprinkle with the salt and rosemary and sauté for 1 minute or until the vegetables are heated through. Add the tomato and cook for 3 minutes or until softened.

5. Sprinkle the flour over the vegetables, stirring to coat. Add the milk and bring to a boil. Reduce to a simmer and cook, stirring, for 3 minutes or until slightly thickened. Stir in the Parmesan and parsley. Add to the hot pasta, tossing until combined. Serves 4.

Per serving: Kilojoules 1 783; Fibre 9g; Protein 19g; Total Fat 11g; Saturated Fat 3g; Cholesterol 72mg; Sodium 626mg

Linguine with Creamy Garlic-Mint Sauce

PREP: 15 MINUTES / COOK: 15 MINUTES

- 125ml fresh mint leaves
- 350g linguine pasta
- 8 cloves garlic, finely chopped
- 425ml chicken stock
- 20ml flour
- 60ml low-fat cream cheese
- 3,5ml salt
- 125ml sour cream

1. Bring a large pot of water to a boil for the pasta. Place the mint in a strainer and place the strainer in the boiling water for 10 seconds to blanch the mint. Drain the mint well, transfer to a food processor and process until smooth.

2. Return the water to a boil, add the linguine and cook according to package directions until *al dente*. Drain and transfer to a large serving bowl.

3. Meanwhile, in a large frying pan, cook the garlic in 175 ml of the stock over low heat for 5 minutes or until the garlic is very soft. Whisk in the flour and stir until well combined. Add the remaining 250 ml stock, the mint purée, the cream cheese and salt and cook, stirring, for 4 minutes or until the sauce is slightly thickened and no floury taste remains. Remove from the heat and stir in the sour cream. Add to the hot pasta, tossing well. Serves 4.

Per serving: Kilojoules 1 917; Fibre 4 g; Protein 14 g; Total Fat 14 g; Saturated Fat 7 g; Cholesterol 44 mg; Sodium 1 126 mg

Baked Macaroni with Vegetables & Cheese

PREP: 20 MINUTES / COOK: 40 MINUTES

280 g elbow macaroni
10 ml olive oil
250 g pattipans or baby marrows, halved lengthwise and thinly sliced
4 spring onions, thinly sliced
1 roasted red pepper, diced
3 cloves garlic, finely chopped
45 ml flour
675 ml low-fat (2%) milk
3,5 ml salt
115 g grated sharp Cheddar cheese
60 ml grated Parmesan cheese

1. In a large pot of boiling water, cook the pasta according to package directions until *al dente*. Drain and transfer to a large bowl. Preheat the oven to 200°C.

2. Meanwhile, in a large nonstick pan, heat the oil over moderate heat. Add the pattipans (or baby marrows), spring onions, roasted pepper and garlic to the pan and sauté for 5 minutes or until the pattipans are crisp-tender. Add the flour and stir until well combined. Gradually add the milk, stirring until combined. Stir in the salt and cook, stirring, for 5 minutes or until the sauce is slightly thickened and no floury taste remains.

3. Add the white sauce to the pasta along with the Cheddar, tossing until well coated. Transfer to a 18 x 28-cm baking dish, sprinkle with the Parmesan and bake for 25 minutes or until crusty and piping hot. Serves 4.

Per serving: Kilojoules 2 295; Fibre 3 g; Protein 25 g; Total Fat 18 g; Saturated Fat 7 g; Cholesterol 49 mg; Sodium 745 mg

At the market There are hundreds of different pasta shapes, but all dried pastas (except egg noodles) are very similar in nutritional value. Some pastas have been enriched with vitamins B1, B2, B6, folate and iron.

Pastas coloured with vegetable extracts (these are spinach and tomato) add colour to your favourite pasta dishes, but offer little or no nutritional advantage over regular pasta.

Look for For the best texture, choose a brand of pasta made from pure semolina.

Basic cooking Cook pasta in plenty of boiling water to keep it from sticking together. Add the pasta all at once, stir briefly and return the water to a boil. Time the cooking from the second boil. Test the pasta for doneness a little sooner than the package directions recommend (overcooking ruins pasta) and drain it immediately when it is firm-tender (*al dente*) to the bite.

Baked Macaroni with Vegetables & Cheese increases the nutrition in a classic dish.

Spaghetti Bolognese
Even a creamy meat sauce can be healthy when made with lean beef and low-fat milk.

Did you know? . .
Pasta with tomato sauce is not just a tradition, it's a smart nutritional choice. The tomatoes' vitamin C helps your body absorb the pasta's iron.

People used to think that pasta was fattening, but only the sauce can make it a high-fat dish. One cup (150 g) of plain cooked pasta contains about 1 g fat.

Mushroom-Stuffed Lasagne Rolls

PREP: 30 MINUTES / COOK: 40 MINUTES
A new twist—literally—on a pasta classic.

450 g mushrooms, trimmed
280 g lasagne noodles
10 ml olive oil
1 small onion, finely chopped
3 cloves garlic, finely chopped
2,5 ml salt
1,25 ml dried sage
1,25 ml pepper
250 ml ricotta cheese
2 egg whites
375 ml chicken stock
375 ml low-fat (2%) milk
45 ml flour
60 ml grated Parmesan cheese

1. Preheat the oven to 190°C. Spray a 23 x 33-cm glass baking dish with nonstick cooking spray; set aside. In a food processor or by hand, chop the mushrooms coarsely.

2. In a large pot of boiling water, cook the lasagne noodles according to package directions until *al dente*; drain.

3. Meanwhile, in a large nonstick pan, heat the oil over moderate heat. Add the onion and garlic and sauté for 5 minutes or until the onion is tender. Add the mushrooms, 1,25 ml of the salt, the sage and pepper and sauté for 7 minutes or until the mushrooms are tender and their liquid has evaporated. Transfer the mushroom mixture to a medium bowl and stir in the ricotta cheese and egg whites.

4. Lay the lasagne noodles on a work surface. Spread 60 ml of the mushroom mixture over each noodle and roll up. Place the rolls, seam-sides down, in the prepared baking dish.

5. In a medium saucepan, whisk the stock and milk into the flour. Stir in the remaining 1,25 ml salt and bring to a boil over moderate heat. Reduce to a simmer and cook, stirring constantly, for 5 minutes or until the sauce is slightly thickened. Pour the sauce over the lasagne rolls and sprinkle with the Parmesan. Bake, uncovered, for 25 minutes or until the filling is piping hot and the sauce is bubbling. Serves 4.

Per serving: Kilojoules 2 253; Fibre 6 g; Protein 46 g; Total Fat 16 g; Saturated Fat 7 g; Cholesterol 43 mg; Sodium 1 105 mg

Spaghetti Bolognese

Prep: 15 minutes / Cook: 30 minutes

Italians call this type of sauce a 'ragù'.

10 g dried porcini or other dried mushrooms
175 ml boiling water
55 g bacon, coarsely chopped (2 thick slices)
1 medium onion, finely chopped
1 large carrot, finely chopped
1 stalk celery, finely chopped
225 g extra-lean ground beef
175 g strained, crushed tomatoes
125 ml dry red wine
2,5 ml each salt and pepper
310 ml low-fat (2%) milk
350 g spaghetti

1. In a small heatproof bowl, combine the dried mushrooms and the boiling water and let stand for 10 minutes or until softened. Reserving the soaking liquid, scoop out the mushrooms, rinse and chop finely. Strain the soaking liquid through a coffee filter or a paper towel-lined sieve.

2. In a large pan, combine the bacon and 30 ml of water over low heat. Cook for 4 minutes or until the bacon has rendered its fat but is not crisp. Add the onion, carrot and celery and cook for 5 minutes or until the onion is soft.

3. Crumble in the beef and add the reserved soaking liquid, chopped mushrooms, tomato sauce, wine, salt and pepper. Bring to a boil, reduce to a simmer and cook for 5 minutes or until the liquid has almost evaporated. Add half of the milk and cook until it has been absorbed. Add the remaining milk and simmer for 12 minutes or until the sauce is thick and richly flavoured.

4. Meanwhile, in a large pot of boiling water, cook the pasta according to package directions until *al dente*. Drain and toss with the sauce. Serves 4.

Per serving: Kilojoules 2 315; Fibre 5 g; Protein 30 g; Total Fat 12 g; Saturated Fat 4 g; Cholesterol 49 mg; Sodium 545 mg

Pasta-Tuna Salad

In a bowl, combine 125 ml plain low-fat yoghurt, 60 ml light mayonnaise, 60 ml snipped fresh dill, 30 ml lemon juice and 1,25 ml salt. Add 2 x 185 g tins tuna in brine, drained, and 120 g thawed frozen peas. Cook 280 g penne, drain, add to bowl and toss. Serves 4. *[kJ 1872; Fat 9 g; Sodium 1248 mg]*

Moroccan Couscous

Bring 310 ml water, 250 ml chicken stock, 15 ml vegetable oil, 7,5 ml grated lemon rind and 2,5 ml salt to a boil. Add 280 g couscous, remove from heat, cover and let stand 5 minutes. Fluff the couscous with a fork; add 600 g rinsed, cooked (2 tins) chickpeas and 160 g raisins. Toss. Serves 4. *[kJ 2515; Fat 9 g; Sodium 700 mg]*

Bow-Ties with Mozzarella & Fresh Tomatoes

Cook 350 g bow-tie pasta. Drain. Meanwhile, in large pan, bring 250 ml tinned strained, crushed tomato to a boil. Add 250 ml chopped fresh tomatoes, 60 ml chopped fresh basil and 2,5 ml each sugar and salt. Transfer to bowl, add hot pasta and 175 g diced mozzarella. Serves 4. *[kJ 1951; Fat 11 g; Sodium 472 mg]*

Pasta with Pesto

These ruffled pasta shapes—modelled after Italian radiators—are uniquely suited to creamy sauces such as this basil-garlic purée. Fusilli (spiral)pasta is also suitable.

Did you know? . . .

Egg noodles (and some fresh pastas) contain more cholesterol than regular pasta. A cup (150 g) of cooked egg noodles has about 50 mg cholesterol.

Did you know? . . .

The most nutritious pastas are made from semolina, a coarse flour ground from durum wheat. Durum is a hard grain which has a higher protein content.

Enriched pasta loses considerable riboflavin when exposed to light. So choose pasta packed in cardboard boxes rather than in clear plastic bags. At home, store pasta in an opaque container rather than a glass jar.

Whole-wheat pasta has much more fibre than semolina pasta. It also has about 14 per cent more kilojoules and 10 per cent more protein.

Pasta with Butternut Squash Sauce

PREP: 10 MINUTES / COOK: 55 MINUTES

- **1 butternut squash (900 g), halved lengthwise and seeded**
- **350 g fusilli or rotelle pasta**
- **10 ml olive oil**
- **2 cloves garlic, finely chopped**
- **70 ml almonds**
- **70 ml grated Parmesan cheese**
- **30 ml sugar**
- **10 ml English mustard**
- **3,5 ml each dried sage and salt**
- **2,5 ml pepper**

1. Preheat the oven to 200°C. Place the squash, cut-sides down, in a small baking tin. Add 125 ml water, cover and bake for 45 minutes or until the squash is tender. When cool enough to handle, scoop the flesh into a food processor.

2. Meanwhile, in a large pot of boiling water, cook the pasta according to package directions until *al dente*. Reserving 150 ml of the pasta cooking water, drain the pasta and transfer to a large bowl.

3. In a small nonstick pan, heat the oil over low heat. Add the garlic and cook for 2 minutes or until softened.

4. Transfer the garlic to the food processor along with the reserved pasta cooking water, the almonds, Parmesan, sugar, mustard, sage, salt and pepper. Process until smooth and add to the pasta, tossing to coat. Serves 4.

Per serving: Kilojoules 2 251; Fibre 7 g; Protein 18 g; Total Fat 11 g; Saturated Fat 2 g; Cholesterol 5 mg; Sodium 616 mg

Pasta with Pesto

PREP: 15 MINUTES / COOK: 15 MINUTES

- **3 cloves garlic, peeled**
- **350 g radiatore pasta (or use fusilli or spiral pasta)**
- **60 g fresh basil leaves (2 packed cups)**
- **90 ml chicken or vegetable stock**
- **15 ml olive oil**
- **15 ml low-fat cream cheese**
- **2,5 ml salt**
- **1,25 ml pepper**
- **125 ml grated Parmesan cheese**

1. In a large pot of boiling water, cook the garlic for 2 minutes to blanch. With a slotted spoon, transfer the garlic to a food processor.

2. Bring the water to a boil, add the pasta and cook according to package directions until *al dente*. Drain and transfer to a large bowl.

3. Meanwhile, add the basil, stock, oil, cream cheese, salt and pepper to the garlic and process to a smooth purée. Add the Parmesan and process briefly just to combine. Add to the hot pasta, tossing well. Serves 4.

Per serving: Kilojoules 1 739; Fibre 4 g; Protein 16 g; Total Fat 10 g; Saturated Fat 3 g; Cholesterol 9 mg; Sodium 661 mg

Angel Hair with Asparagus & Lemon Cream Sauce

PREP: 15 MINUTES / COOK: 15 MINUTES

    350 g angel hair pasta
    450 g asparagus, trimmed and thinly
        sliced on the diagonal
    250 ml chicken stock
    20 ml flour
    12,5 ml grated lemon rind
    3,5 ml salt
    1,25 ml each dried marjoram and
        pepper
    125 ml sour cream

1. In a large pot of boiling water, cook the pasta according to package directions until *al dente*. Add the asparagus for the last 1 minute of cooking. Drain; transfer to a large serving bowl.

2. Meanwhile, in a large nonstick pan, combine the stock with 60 ml of water; whisk in the flour and bring to a boil over moderate heat. Whisk in the lemon rind, salt, marjoram and pepper. Reduce to a simmer and cook, stirring frequently, for 3 minutes or until slightly thickened. Remove the sauce from the heat and whisk in the sour cream.

3. Add the lemon cream sauce to the hot pasta and asparagus, tossing well to combine. Serves 4.

Per serving: Kilojoules 1 860; Fibre 7 g; Protein 15 g; Total Fat 11 g; Saturated Fat 5 g; Cholesterol 28 mg; Sodium 815 mg

Mexican Confetti Orzo In a large bowl, toss together 1 large diced red pepper, 1 tin rinsed red kidney beans, 250 ml frozen thawed corn kernels, 15 ml olive oil, 3,5 ml salt and 1,25 ml cayenne pepper. Cook 280 g orzo pasta, drain, add to bowl and toss. Serves 4. *[kJ 1759; Fat 6 g; Sodium 674 mg]*

Chinese Chicken-Noodle Soup Bring 500 ml chicken stock, 750 ml water, 10 ml soya sauce, 15 ml sesame oil and 15 ml rice vinegar to a boil. Add 225 g diced chicken breast and cook 2 minutes. Add 175 g fresh linguine, 60 g watercress leaves and 1 finely chopped spring onion and cook for 2 minutes or until pasta is done. Serves 4. *[kJ 1089; Fat 6 g; Sodium 926 mg]*

Tortellini with Zesty Tomato Sauce In a large nonstick pan, sauté 1 diced onion and 3 finely chopped cloves garlic in 10 ml olive oil until tender. Add 410-g tin stewed tomatoes, 250 g strained crushed tomatoes, 2,5 ml salt and 1,25 ml red chilli flakes. Simmer 10 minutes. Meanwhile, cook 500 g ready-made spinach and ricotta tortellini. Toss with sauce. Serves 4. *[kJ 1725; Fat 10 g; Sodium 668 mg]*

Bulgur

PER 190G COOKED (1 CUP)	
Kilojoules	659
Fibre	9 g
Protein	6 g
Total Fat	0,5 g
Saturated Fat	0,1 g
Cholesterol	0 mg
Sodium	10 mg

NUTRIENTS	
% RDA for people older than 10 years	
Magnesium	20 %
Iron	13 %
Niacin	11 %
Folate	9 %
Vitamin B6	8 %
Thiamin	8 %

Did you know? . . .

Bulgur also contains manganese which helps to prevent osteoporosis.

A small percentage of the fibre-rich bran is removed from bulgur during processing, but plenty remains: 375 ml cooked bulgur supplies 36 per cent of your daily fibre requirement.

Mushroom-Bulgur Pilaf

Prep: 15 minutes / Cook: 30 minutes

Bulgur has a delicate nutlike flavour and cooks far more quickly than brown rice.

15 ml olive oil
1 small onion, finely chopped
2 cloves garlic, finely chopped
1 medium carrot, thinly sliced
1 stalk celery, thinly sliced
225 g mushrooms, thinly sliced
250 ml coarse bulgur
375 ml chicken stock
1,25 ml crumbled dried rosemary
1,25 ml salt
1,25 ml pepper

1. Preheat the oven to 180°C. In a flameproof casserole, heat the oil over moderate heat. Add the onion and garlic and sauté for 2 minutes or until the onion is soft. Stir in the carrot and celery and sauté for 4 minutes or until the carrot is crisp-tender. Add the mushrooms and sauté for 3 minutes or until the mushrooms are softened.

2. Stir in the bulgur, stock, 250 ml of water, the rosemary, salt and pepper and bring to a boil. Cover and bake for 20 minutes or until the bulgur is tender and the liquid has been absorbed. Serves 4.

Per serving: Kilojoules 829; Fibre 9g; Protein 7g; Total Fat 5g; Saturated Fat 1g; Cholesterol 0mg; Sodium 740mg

Mexican-Style Tabbouleh

Prep: 15 minutes / Soak: 1 hour Stand: 1 hour

Tabbouleh, a refreshing grain salad, is Middle Eastern in origin. We've adapted the recipe with corn kernels, pepper, fresh coriander and other Mexican seasonings.

250 ml fine or coarse bulgur
750 ml boiling water
60 ml lime or lemon juice
15 ml olive oil
3,5 ml salt
2,5 ml cumin
1,25 ml dried oreganum
0,6 ml allspice
280 g cherry tomatoes, halved
250 ml frozen corn kernels, thawed
1 large green pepper, diced
6 spring onions, thinly sliced
125 ml chopped coriander or parsley

1. In a large bowl, combine the bulgur and boiling water. Let stand 1 hour at room temperature. Drain and squeeze the bulgur dry.

2. Meanwhile, in a large bowl, whisk together the lime juice, oil, salt, cumin, oreganum and allspice. Stir in the tomatoes, corn kernels, pepper, spring onions and coriander. Add the drained bulgur and toss to combine. Let stand for at least 1 hour. Serve chilled or at room temperature. Serves 4.

Per serving: Kilojoules 1 034; Fibre 10g; Protein 7g; Total Fat 5g; Saturated Fat 1g; Cholesterol 0mg; Sodium 444mg

Bean & Bulgur Chilli

PREP: 15 MINUTES / COOK: 40 MINUTES

One of the smartest meatless-chilli tricks is using bulgur in place of minced beef—the texture is distinctly meaty. And this spicy chilli is remarkably low in fat.

15 ml olive oil
1 large onion, finely chopped
3 cloves garlic, finely chopped
1 large red pepper, diced
1 large chilli, seeded and finely chopped
250 ml coarse bulgur
1 tin (410 g) tomatoes, chopped with their juice
5 ml mild chilli powder
5 ml ground coriander
3,5 ml salt
1 tin (410 g) speckled sugar beans, rinsed and drained

1. In a flameproof casserole, heat the oil over moderate heat. Add the onion and garlic and sauté for 7 minutes or until the onion is tender. Add the pepper and fresh chilli and cook for 5 minutes or until the pepper is tender.

2. Stir in the bulgur, tomatoes, chilli powder, coriander, salt and 500 ml of water and bring to a boil. Reduce to a simmer, cover and cook for 15 minutes or until most of the water has evaporated.

3. Stir in the beans and cook, uncovered, for 10 minutes or until the beans are heated through and the flavours have blended. Serves 4.

Per serving: Kilojoules 1 230; Fibre 14 g; Protein 10 g; Total Fat 5 g; Saturated Fat 1 g; Cholesterol 0 mg; Sodium 656 mg

At the market Bulgur (which is sometimes spelled 'bulghur') is a form of cracked wheat. The cracked wheat is parboiled and dried and some of the bran is removed. Although bulgur comes in three granulations: coarse, medium and fine, only the medium is easily obtainable in South Africa. Bulgur can be found in the 'health-food' section of the supermarket or at health-food shops.

Basic cooking To cook bulgur by steeping, use a 1-to-3 ratio of bulgur to water. For 250 ml dry bulgur, place the grain in a heatproof bowl or a saucepan; add 750 ml boiling water and let stand for 1 hour. Drain off any excess liquid and squeeze the bulgur dry.

After steeping bulgur, pour off any water which remains and then squeeze the bulgur with your hands until it's quite dry, transferring the bulgur to a clean bowl as you work.

***Mexican-Style Tabbouleh** is a light and tempting main dish for warm-weather dining.*

151

Wheat

Whole-Wheat Flour

PER 80G (½ CUP)	
Kilojoules	1136
Fibre	10,1g
Protein	11g
Total Fat	1,5g
Saturated Fat	0,3g
Cholesterol	0mg
Sodium	4mg

NUTRIENTS	
% RDA for people older than 10 years	
Magnesium	37%
Niacin	28%
Thiamin	26%
Zinc	16%

Wheat Germ

PER 40G (½ CUP)	
Kilojoules	639
Fibre	5,2g
Protein	11,6g
Total Fat	4,3g
Saturated Fat	0,9g
Cholesterol	0mg
Sodium	2mg

NUTRIENTS	
% RDA for people older than 10 years	
Vitamin E	60%
Thiamin	48%
Magnesium	43%

Mushroom Roll-Ups

PREP: 30 MINUTES / CHILL: 1 HOUR
COOK: 35 MINUTES

A rich-tasting yet healthy appetizer.

220 ml whole-wheat flour
60 ml all-purpose flour
3,5 ml salt
2,5 ml dried rosemary, crumbled
1,25 ml bicarbonate of soda
45 ml unsalted butter
45 ml honey
1 whole egg plus 1 egg white
125 ml chicken stock
2 spring onions, thinly sliced
3 cloves garlic, finely chopped
225 g button mushrooms, finely chopped
225 g fresh oyster mushrooms, trimmed and coarsely chopped
70 ml ricotta cheese

1. In a small bowl, combine both flours, 2,5 ml of the salt, 1,25 ml of the rosemary and the bicarbonate of soda. In a medium bowl, cream the butter and honey. Beat in the whole egg. Stir in the dry ingredients until the mixture forms a dough. Divide in half, flatten into rectangles, wrap in plastic wrap and refrigerate for at least 1 hour.

2. Meanwhile, in a large pan, heat the stock over moderately low heat. Add the spring onions and garlic and cook for 4 minutes. Add both mushrooms, the remaining salt and rosemary and cook, stirring, for 9 minutes or until the mushrooms are dry. Transfer to a bowl to cool slightly. Stir in the ricotta and egg white.

3. Preheat the oven to 180°C. Spray a baking sheet with nonstick cooking spray. On a floured surface, roll one piece of dough out to a 18 x 28-cm rectangle. Spoon half of the mushroom mixture down the centre, leaving a 5-cm border on each long side and a 1-cm border at each short end. Fold the ends over the filling, then fold in the sides; pinch together to seal. Place seam-side down on the baking sheet. Repeat with the remaining dough and filling. Bake for 35 minutes. Cut each roll into 6 slices. Serves 6.

Per serving: Kilojoules 1019; Fibre 5g; Protein 8g; Total Fat 9g; Saturated Fat 5g; Cholesterol 57mg; Sodium 444mg

Crunchy Dessert Topping

PREP: 5 MINUTES / COOK: 25 MINUTES

This crisp, toasty topping is low in fat and kilojoules.

125 ml packed dark brown sugar
10 ml lemon juice
375 ml toasted wheat germ
15 ml vegetable oil
60 ml chopped pecan nuts

1. In a large pan, combine the brown sugar and lemon juice. Cook over low heat, stirring frequently, for 2 minutes or until the sugar has melted. Stir in the wheat germ and oil and cook, stirring frequently, for 9 minutes or until richly browned.

2. Stir in the pecan nuts and cook for 1 minute. Cool to room temperature,

Crunchy Dessert Topping adds a sweet and crunchy fillip to frozen yoghurt and sorbet.

transfer to an airtight container, and store at room temperature for up to 3 days. Freeze for longer storage. Makes 250 millilitres/16 servings.

Per serving: Kilojoules 304; Fibre 1g; Protein 2g; Total Fat 3g; Saturated Fat 0g; Cholesterol 0mg; Sodium 2mg

Banana Bran Muffins

PREP. 15 MINUTES / COOK: 35 MINUTES
COOL: 10 MINUTES

Tops as a fibre source, wheat bran has other nutritional benefits as well. It's a good source of niacin, iron, potassium and magnesium. This recipe calls for more bran than flour—a healthy switch from the usual formula.

375 ml wheat bran
125 ml whole-wheat flour
7,5 ml bicarbonate of soda
2,5 ml salt
60 ml vegetable oil
60 ml packed light brown sugar
1 egg
1 egg white
250 ml low-fat cultured buttermilk
1 large banana, diced
125 ml grape-nuts cereal

1. Preheat the oven to 200°C. Spray a 12-cup muffin tin with nonstick cooking spray. On a baking sheet with sides, bake the bran for 15 minutes or until lightly toasted. Leave the oven on.

2. In a medium bowl, stir together the toasted bran, the flour, bicarbonate of soda and salt. In another medium bowl, beat the oil and sugar with an electric mixer until well combined. Add the egg and egg white, one at a time, beating well after each addition. Alternately fold the flour mixture and the buttermilk into the egg mixture, beginning and ending with the flour mixture. Fold in the banana and cereal.

3. Spoon the batter into the prepared muffin cups and bake for 20 minutes or until a cake tester inserted in the centre of a muffin comes out clean. Cool for 10 minutes in the tin on a rack, then transfer to the rack to cool completely. Serve warm or at room temperature. Makes 12 muffins.

Per muffin: Kilojoules 540; Fibre 4g; Protein 4g; Total Fat 6g; Saturated Fat 1g; Cholesterol 18mg; Sodium 151mg

At the market Most whole-wheat flour in the supermarket is ground with steel rollers or hammers, so its texture is quite fine. Stone-ground flour, found in health-food shops, has a coarser texture. Wheat germ comes plain, toasted, sweetened and in flavours (to eat as a cereal). Wheat bran (the outer layers of the wheat grain) is obtainable from supermarkets and health-food shops. Whole-wheat flour, wheat germ and wheat bran should be bought in small quantities and kept in tightly covered containers in the refrigerator or freezer.

You can increase your fibre intake by substituting wheat bran for some of the flour in your favourite muffin recipes. You may need to add a little extra liquid, as bran absorbs more liquid than flour does.

Barley

PER 104 G RAW (½ CUP)	
Kilojoules	1532
Fibre	16 g
Protein	10 g
Total Fat	1,2 g
Saturated Fat	0,3 g
Cholesterol	0 mg
Sodium	9 mg

NUTRIENTS	
% RDA for people older than 10 years	
Magnesium	27%
Niacin	27%
Iron	19%
Zinc	15%
Thiamin	14%
Vitamin B6	14%
Riboflavin	7%

Did you know? . . .
Barley contains the same kind of soluble fibre found in oats. One study divided subjects into two groups: one group got daily servings of oats, while the other got barley. The cholesterol levels in both groups dropped about 5 per cent.

Summery Barley-Vegetable Salad

PREP: 20 MINUTES / COOK: 35 MINUTES

Lemon juice and mint make this a super-cool supper. Let the salad stand a while before serving so the grain can absorb the dressing.

375 ml pearl barley
3,5 ml salt
15 ml olive oil
1 large yellow or red pepper, cut into 1-cm squares
1 large baby marrow, cut into 1-cm pieces
3 cloves garlic, finely chopped
70 ml chopped fresh mint
60 ml lemon juice
225 g plum tomatoes, cut into thin wedges
1 cucumber, peeled, seeded and cut into 5-mm-thick slices
2,5 ml black pepper
175 g feta cheese or mild goat cheese, crumbled

1. In a large saucepan, bring 750 ml of water to a boil. Add the barley and 1,25 ml of the salt and cook for 30 minutes or until tender. Drain well.

2. Meanwhile, in a large nonstick pan, heat 10 ml of the oil over moderate heat. Add the pepper, baby marrow, garlic and the remaining salt. Cook, stirring frequently, for 5 minutes or until the pepper is crisp-tender.

3. In a large bowl, whisk together the mint, lemon juice and the remaining 5 ml oil. Add the barley, sautéed vegetables, the tomatoes, cucumber and black pepper, tossing to combine. Add the feta cheese and toss gently. Serve at room temperature or lightly chilled. Serves 4.

Per serving: Kilojoules 2028; Fibre 14 g; Protein 17 g; Total Fat 17 g; Saturated Fat 8 g; Cholesterol 31 mg; Sodium 887 mg

Old-Fashioned Mushroom-Barley Soup

PREP: 20 MINUTES / COOK: 1 HOUR

A mixture of shiitake and button mushrooms would add a special depth of flavour. However, you can make the soup with button mushrooms alone as shiitake mushrooms are difficult to find in the shops.

10 ml olive oil
1 medium onion, finely chopped
2 cloves garlic, finely chopped
2 medium carrots, halved lengthwise and thinly sliced
450 g button mushrooms, sliced
125 ml pearl barley
250 ml chicken stock
250 ml tomato purèe
3,5 ml ground ginger
3,5 ml salt
2,5 ml pepper

1. In a large saucepan, heat the oil over moderate heat. Add the onion and garlic and sauté for 5 minutes or until tender. Add the carrots and cook, stirring frequently, for 4 minutes or until crisp-tender. Add the sliced button mushrooms and cook, stirring frequently, for 5 minutes or until tender.

2. Stir in the barley, stock, 500 ml of water, the tomato purèe, ginger, salt and pepper. Bring to a boil, reduce to a simmer, cover and cook for 45 minutes or until the barley is tender. Serves 4.

Per serving: Kilojoules 882; Fibre 9g; Protein 7g; Total Fat 3g; Saturated Fat 1g; Cholesterol 0mg; Sodium 834mg

Spiced Barley & Corn Kernels

PREP: 15 MINUTES / COOK: 55 MINUTES

You might guess by the flavourings—fresh ginger, coriander and garlic—that this dish has Indian roots. The technique of creating a seasoning paste, which is then sautéed, is also distinctly Indian. The blender whirls up the seasoning paste in seconds.

1 small onion, thinly sliced
125 ml packed fresh coriander or
    flat-leaf parsley sprigs
30 ml chopped fresh ginger
3 cloves garlic, peeled
15 ml olive oil

1 large green pepper, diced
250 ml pearl barley
250 ml chicken stock
1 tin (410 g) tinned tomatoes,
    chopped with their juice
2,5 ml ground coriander
2,5 ml salt
310 ml frozen corn kernels, thawed

1. In a blender, combine the onion, fresh coriander, ginger, garlic and 45 ml of water and purée.

2. In a large saucepan, heat the oil over moderate heat. Add the pepper and sauté for 4 minutes or until crisp-tender. Add the onion purée and sauté for 2 minutes. Add the barley, stirring to coat.

3. Add the stock, 125 ml of water, the tomatoes, ground coriander and salt and bring to a boil. Reduce to a simmer, cover and cook for 45 minutes or until the barley is tender. Remove from the heat and stir in the corn kernels. Serves 4.

Per serving: Kilojoules 1 381; Fibre 12g; Protein 9g; Total Fat 5g; Saturated Fat 1g; Cholesterol 0mg; Sodium 906mg

At the market Pearl (or pearled) barley is the most common type; it has been milled several times to remove the hull completely, leaving the grain pearly and smooth. Hulled barley retains its complete bran layer, while pot, or Scotch, barley has about half the bran left on the grain. Both Scotch and hulled barley take longer to cook than pearl barley and have to be purchased from health-food shops.

Barley flakes are rolled and flattened barley grains. Slightly thicker than rolled oats, they are used in baking and in cereals, especially muesli.

Basic cooking For pearl barley, use three times as much water as grain. Stir the barley into boiling water, cover and simmer until tender—about 50 minutes.

Old-Fashioned Mushroom-Barley Soup brims with vegetables in a smooth tomato broth.

Buckwheat

Nutritional power

It's used as a grain, but buckwheat is actually the fruit of a rhubarb-like plant. Like true grains, buckwheat offers some B vitamins and iron.

Roasted Buckwheat Groats
PER 43G RAW
(¼ CUP)

Kilojoules	623
Fibre	4,4 g
Protein	5 g
Total Fat	1,2 g
Saturated Fat	0,3 g
Cholesterol	0 mg
Sodium	5 mg

NUTRIENTS

% RDA for people older than 10 years

Magnesium	32%
Niacin	12%

Buckwheat Flour
PER 30G
(¼ CUP)

Kilojoules	421
Fibre	3,0 g
Protein	4 g
Total Fat	0,9 g
Saturated Fat	0,2 g
Cholesterol	0 mg
Sodium	3 mg

NUTRIENTS

% RDA for people older than 10 years

Magnesium	25%

Chicken & Soba Noodle Salad

PREP: 20 MINUTES / COOK: 15 MINUTES

Japanese soba noodles are chewy and robustly flavourful. Soba noodles can be purchased from health-food shops or Eastern delicatessens.

175 ml chicken stock
2 cloves garlic, finely chopped
2,5 ml ground ginger
1,25 ml crushed red chilli flakes
350 g skinless, boned chicken breasts
280 g soba noodles (buckwheat noodles)
225 g green beans, halved lengthwise
2 carrots, cut into 5-cm matchsticks
30 ml dark brown sugar
15 ml light soya sauce
15 ml peanut or other vegetable oil
140 g finely shredded cabbage (2 cups)

1. In a large pan, bring the stock, garlic, ginger and red chilli flakes to a boil over moderate heat. Reduce to a simmer, add the chicken, cover and cook, turning the chicken over once, for 10 minutes or until the chicken is cooked through. Reserving the cooking liquid, transfer the chicken to a plate. When cool enough to handle, shred the chicken.

2. Meanwhile, in a large pot of boiling water, cook the noodles according to package directions until *al dente*. Add the green beans and carrots for the last 1 minute of cooking time; drain.

3. In a large bowl, whisk together the brown sugar, soya sauce, oil and the reserved chicken cooking liquid. Add the shredded chicken, noodles, green beans, carrots and cabbage, tossing to combine. Serve at room temperature or chilled. Serves 4.

Per serving: Kilojoules 1854; Fibre 6g; Protein 27g; Total Fat 7g; Saturated Fat 2g; Cholesterol 33mg; Sodium 529mg

Kasha Varnishkes with Caramelized Onions

PREP: 15 MINUTES / COOK: 50 MINUTES

This savoury buckwheat-and-noodle combination is an old-fashioned dish. Kasha is available from health-food shops where it might also be sold as 'groats'.

15 ml vegetable oil
560 g thinly sliced onions (4 cups)
5 ml sugar
5 ml salt
250 ml kasha (buckwheat groats)
250 ml chicken stock
1,25 ml dried sage
1,25 ml pepper
280 g bow-tie pasta

1. In a large nonstick pan, heat the oil over moderate heat. Add the onions, sugar and 1,25 ml of the salt and cook, stirring occasionally, for 25 minutes or until the onions are golden brown and caramelized.

2. Meanwhile, stir the kasha into another large (ungreased) nonstick

Chicken & Soba Noodle Salad is tossed with a tangy Asian-style dressing.

frying pan and cook over moderate heat until the kasha is lightly toasted.

3. In a medium saucepan, bring the stock and 250 ml of water to a boil. Add the stock mixture to the kasha along with the sage, pepper and the remaining salt and cook, stirring occasionally, for 20 minutes or until the kasha is tender but not mushy.

4. Meanwhile, in a large pot of boiling water, cook the pasta according to package directions until *al dente*. Drain and add to the kasha along with the onions. Cook until heated through. Serves 4.

Per serving: Kilojoules 2144; Fibre 9g; Protein 15g; Total Fat 7g; Saturated Fat 1g; Cholesterol 0mg; Sodium 1009mg

Buckwheat Pancakes

PREP: 10 MINUTES / COOK: 10 MINUTES

- 250 ml low-fat cultured buttermilk
- 1 egg yolk
- 30 ml vegetable oil
- 2 egg whites
- 175 ml buckwheat flour
- 60 ml all-purpose flour (cake flour can be used)
- 15 ml light brown sugar
- 5 ml baking powder
- 2,5 ml each bicarbonate of soda and salt
- 60 ml honey

1. In a small bowl, combine the buttermilk, egg yolk and oil. In a separate bowl, beat the egg whites until stiff peaks form.

2. Preheat the oven to 130°C. In a medium bowl, combine the buckwheat flour, all-purpose flour, brown sugar, baking powder, bicarbonate of soda and salt. Stir the buttermilk mixture into the flour mixture. Fold in the egg whites.

3. Spray a large nonstick pan with nonstick cooking spray and heat over moderate heat. Spoon the batter, a scant 60 ml at a time, into the pan. Cook for 2 minutes or until the pancakes are bubbly on one side, then turn them over and cook for 1 minute or until cooked through. Place on a baking sheet and keep warm in the oven while you prepare the remaining pancakes, re-spraying the pan with cooking spray (off the heat) for each batch.

4. Serve the pancakes drizzled with the honey. Serves 4.

Per serving: Kilojoules 1313; Fibre 3g; Protein 9g; Total Fat 11g; Saturated Fat 2g; Cholesterol 64mg; Sodium 391mg

At the market Packaged buckwheat groats are usually labelled 'kasha', which is a Russian term for roasted hulled buckwheat. In South Africa only medium granulation is usually available, although unshelled buckwheat kernels can be bought at health-food shops. Buckwheat flour is made in light, medium and dark versions. The dark flour has the highest fibre content. Dried soba noodles are sold in some supermarkets and in Eastern speciality shops. They can be kept for many months.

Soba noodles may be made from buckwheat flour alone or from a combination of buckwheat and wheat flours.

Basic cooking Old-fashioned kasha recipes have you stir a whole egg into kasha before toasting it in a pan. You can reduce cholesterol by toasting the kasha with egg white instead or toasting it in a dry pan. Stir constantly, though, as kasha can burn quickly.

Maize Meal

Nutritional power

Whole maize meal is a good source of B vitamins and iron. Some brands of sifted maize meal are enriched with riboflavin, niacin and iron.

Sifted Maize Meal (not enriched)

PER 65G RAW (½ CUP)

Kilojoules	**1018**
Fibre	**3,0 g**
Protein	**6 g**
Total Fat	**2,3 g**
Saturated Fat	**0,4 g**
Cholesterol	**0 mg**
Sodium	**5 mg**

NUTRIENTS

% RDA for people older than 10 years

Magnesium	**20 %**
Thiamin	**18 %**
Iron	**6 %**
Zinc	**6 %**
Niacin	**4 %**

Did you know? . . .

The colour of maize meal is determined by the type of mealie used to make it. The only nutritional difference between the two types is that yellow maize meal contains minute amounts of beta carotene, alpha-carotene, lutein and zeaxanthin—disease-fighting carotenoids.

Mushroom-Topped Polenta

PREP: 15 MINUTES / COOK: 40 MINUTES

Polenta, an Italian-style maize meal, would be suitable for this recipe.

- **175 ml yellow maize meal (or use polenta, a form of maize meal)**
- **5 ml salt**
- **15 ml olive oil**
- **1 medium onion, finely chopped**
- **4 cloves garlic, finely chopped**
- **1 medium carrot, finely chopped**
- **225 g mushrooms, thinly sliced**
- **1 tin (410 g) tomatoes, chopped with their juice**
- **125 ml dried rosemary, crumbled**
- **0,6 ml crushed red chilli flakes**
- **45 ml grated Parmesan cheese**

1. Preheat the oven to 190°C. Spray a 20-cm square glass baking dish with nonstick cooking spray.

2. In a medium bowl, combine the maize meal (or polenta) and 250 ml of cold water. In a large saucepan, bring 375 ml of water to a boil. Reduce to a simmer, add 2,5 ml of the salt and the maize-meal mixture. Cook, stirring constantly, for 5 minutes or until the mixture is thick and cooked through. Spoon the maize-meal mixture into the prepared baking dish and set aside.

3. In a large nonstick pan, heat the oil over moderate heat. Add the onion and garlic and sauté for 5 minutes or until the onion is tender. Add the carrot and cook for 4 minutes or until tender. Add the mushrooms and cook, stirring occasionally, for 4 minutes or until tender. Add the tomatoes, rosemary, red chilli flakes and the remaining 2,5 ml salt and bring to a boil. Reduce to a simmer, cover and cook for 5 minutes or until the flavours have blended.

4. Pour the mushroom mixture over the maize meal. Sprinkle with the Parmesan and bake for 15 minutes or until piping hot. Serves 4.

Per serving: Kilojoules 804; Fibre 4g; Protein 6g; Total Fat 6g; Saturated Fat 1g; Cholesterol 3mg; Sodium 905mg

Lemon Poppy Seed Tea Bread

PREP: 10 MINUTES / COOK: 1 HOUR

- **30 ml poppyseeds**
- **60 ml vegetable oil**
- **30 ml unsalted butter**
- **250 ml sugar**
- **1 egg**
- **2 egg whites**
- **15 ml grated lemon rind**
- **5 ml bicarbonate of soda**
- **250 ml plain low-fat yoghurt**
- **250 ml yellow maize meal (or use polenta, a form of maize meal)**
- **250 ml flour**

1. Preheat the oven to 180°C. Place the poppyseeds in a small baking tin and bake for 5 minutes or until lightly toasted and crunchy. Spray a 22 x 12-cm loaf tin with nonstick cooking spray.

2. In a medium bowl, blend the oil, butter and sugar with an electric mixer. Add the whole egg and egg whites, one at a time, beating well after each addition. Beat in the lemon rind.

3. In a small bowl, stir the bicarbonate of soda into the yoghurt. Stir together the maize meal and flour. Alternately fold the maize-meal mixture and the yoghurt mixture into the egg mixture, beginning and ending with the maize-meal mixture. Fold in the poppyseeds.

4. Spoon the batter into the prepared tin and bake for 55 minutes or until a cake tester inserted in the centre comes out clean. Cool for 10 minutes in the tin on a rack, then turn out onto the rack to cool completely. Serves 12.

Per serving: Kilojoules 933; Fibre 1g; Protein 4g; Total Fat 8g; Saturated Fat 2g; Cholesterol 24mg; Sodium 134mg

Lemon Poppy Seed Tea Bread *The maize meal gives it a distinctive texture.*

Maize-Meal Muffins with Fennel & Bacon

PREP: 10 MINUTES / COOK: 30 MINUTES

Serve these hearty muffins warm to accompany tomato soup.

- **85g lean, rindless back bacon, coarsely chopped**
- **vegetable oil (optional)**
- **60ml packed light brown sugar**
- **1 egg**
- **250ml yellow maize meal (preferably in the form of polenta)**
- **250ml flour**
- **15ml baking powder**
- **7,5ml fennel seeds**
- **2,5ml salt**
- **250ml low-fat (2%) milk**
- **125ml sultanas**

1. In a small pan, cook the bacon over low heat for 5 minutes or until it has rendered its fat. Drain the bacon on paper towels. Pour the bacon fat into a measuring cup. Add enough vegetable oil to make it up to 60ml.

2. Preheat the oven to 200°C. Spray a 12-cup muffin tin with nonstick cooking spray. In a medium bowl, beat the bacon fat and brown sugar with an electric mixer until well combined. Add the egg and beat until well combined.

3. In a small bowl, stir together the maize meal, flour, baking powder, fennel seeds and salt. Alternately fold the maize-meal mixture and the milk into the egg mixture, beginning and ending with the maize-meal mixture. Fold in the sultanas and bacon.

4. Spoon the batter into the prepared muffin cups and bake for 25 minutes or until a cake tester inserted in the centre of a muffin comes out clean. Cool for 10 minutes in the tin, then transfer the muffins to a rack to cool completely. Makes 12 muffins.

Per muffin: Kilojoules 600; Fibre 1g; Protein 4g; Total Fat 2g; Saturated Fat 2g; Cholesterol 22mg; Sodium 208mg

At the market Maize meal (or mealie meal) can be bought in several forms. Whole maize meal (straight-run) includes both the bran and germ; stone-ground meal retains some of both components. (Both of these types of maize meal should be kept in a tightly covered container in the refrigerator or freezer, as the oil in the germ can become rancid fairly quickly.) Sifted meal lacks both the germ and bran, but has a longer shelf life and some brands are enriched with vitamin B2, niacin and iron to compensate for some of the lost nutrients. It is available as super (most refined), special and sifted (roughest). Polenta is an Italian form of maize meal which has either fine or coarse granulation.

White maize meal is available both unsifted (also known as 'braaipap') and sifted. The unsifted meal has nearly double the amount of fibre than the sifted meal.

Oats

Nutritional power

High in protein and rich in iron and B vitamins, oats are also a renowned source of a type of soluble fibre that helps to lower blood cholesterol.

PER 55G RAW (½ CUP)	
Kilojoules	966
Fibre	5,6 g
Protein	6 g
Total Fat	5,7 g
Saturated Fat	1,0 g
Cholesterol	0 mg
Sodium	7 mg

NUTRIENTS	
% RDA for people older than 10 years	
Thiamin	30 %
Magnesium	28 %
Iron	17 %
Zinc	12 %
Pantothenic acid	12 %
Biotin	11 %
Vitamin E	9 %

Did you know? . . .

Although many foods contain soluble fibre, oats (like barley) contain beta glucans, a type of fibre particularly effective in lowering cholesterol.

Granola Macaroons

PREP: 15 MINUTES / COOK: 25 MINUTES

Mix up your own granola rather than using commercial cereal, which can have up to 5 grams of fat per 25 grams.

210 g rolled oats
125 ml chopped dried apples or raisins
70 ml sliced almonds (28 g)
125 ml granulated sugar
60 ml packed light brown sugar
1,25 ml salt
3 egg whites
5 ml vanilla essence

1. Preheat the oven to 180°C. Spray 2 baking sheets with nonstick cooking spray; set aside. Place the oats in a small baking tin and toast, stirring them occasionally, for 7 minutes or until lightly golden. Transfer to a large bowl and cool to room temperature.

2. Add the apples, almonds, granulated sugar, brown sugar and salt, stirring to combine. Add the egg whites and vanilla and mix until well combined.

3. With moistened hands, roll walnut-size pieces of dough into rounds and place them 2,5 cm apart on the prepared baking sheets. Flatten slightly and bake for 18 minutes or until golden brown and slightly firm, but not hard. Cool the macaroons for 5 minutes on the baking sheets, then transfer to a wire rack to cool completely. Makes 36 macaroons.

Per macaroon: Kilojoules 223; Fibre 1g; Protein 1g; Total Fat 1g; Saturated Fat 0g; Cholesterol 0mg; Sodium 22mg

Cream of Oats Brûlée

PREP: 5 MINUTES / COOK: 10 MINUTES

Here is oatmeal's elegant cousin. Because the oats are finely ground in a food processor, the texture of this hot cereal is smooth and creamy. As a delicious finishing touch, the cream of oats is topped with brown sugar and butter and grilled.

210 g rolled oats
350 ml low-fat evaporated milk
425 ml low-fat (2%) milk
45 ml granulated sugar
2,5 ml each salt and ground cinnamon
125 ml raisins
20 ml light brown sugar
10 ml unsalted butter

1. In a food processor, pulse the oats on and off until finely ground. In a medium saucepan, bring the evaporated milk, low-fat milk, granulated sugar, salt and cinnamon to a boil over moderate heat. Reduce to a simmer, stir in the oats and cook, stirring occasionally, for 5 minutes or until the cereal is thick and creamy. Remove from the heat and stir in the raisins.

2. Preheat the grill. Transfer the oatmeal to a 20-cm square heat-resistant dish. Sprinkle the top of the cereal with the brown sugar and dot with the butter. Grill 15 centimetres from the heat for 2 minutes or until the sugar is melted. Cool slightly and serve. Serves 4.

Per serving: Kilojoules 2100; Fibre 6g; Protein 16g; Total Fat 13g; Saturated Fat 4g; Cholesterol 38mg; Sodium 474mg

Granola Macaroons *With the goodness of oats, these make deliciously sensible snacks.*

At the market Oats come in many forms. In addition to the familiar old-fashioned 'rolled' oats (which are whole oat kernels, rolled flat), you can buy quick-cooking and instant oats as well as steel-cut oats, which have been thinly sliced but not rolled. Whole oat groats, which can be cooked like rice, are sold in health-food stores.

Quick-cooking oats, which have been sliced before rolling, can be substituted for old-fashioned oats in many recipes. However, the finished product may have less textural 'character'.

Double-Oat Batter Bread

PREP: 15 MINUTES / RISE: 1 HOUR 30 MINUTES / COOK: 1 HOUR

These satisfying loaves are made with a combination of oat 'flour' (you grind it in a food processor) and regular flour. Because oats have no gluten, they require some added flour to enable the dough to rise.

- 125 ml pecan nuts
- 440 g rolled oats
- 10 g (1 envelope) instant dry yeast
- 310 ml lukewarm water
  (40° to 46°C)
- 5 ml sugar
- 675 ml flour
- 70 ml molasses
- 15 ml vegetable oil
- 10 ml salt

1. Preheat the oven to 180°C. Place the pecan nuts in a small baking tin and bake for 7 minutes or until crisp and fragrant. When the pecan nuts are cool enough to handle, chop coarsely.

2. At the same time, on a baking sheet, toast the oats, stirring occasionally, for 7 minutes or until lightly browned, crisp and fragrant. (Turn the oven off.) Place 220 g of the oats in a food processor and process until the consistency of flour.

3. In a large bowl, combine the instant yeast, sugar, lukewarm water, flour, molasses, oil and salt. Stir in the oat 'flour', remaining rolled oats and pecan nuts. With a wooden spoon, stir well for 3 minutes. Cover with plastic wrap and let stand in a warm draft-free spot for 1 hour or until doubled in bulk.

4. Spray two 22 x 12-cm loaf tins with nonstick cooking spray. Punch the dough down and transfer to the prepared tins. Cover with plastic wrap and let stand in a warm draft-free spot for 30 minutes or until doubled in bulk.

5. Preheat the oven to 180°C. Bake the bread for 1 hour or until golden brown and crusty. Cool for 10 minutes in the tins on a rack, then transfer to the rack to cool completely. Makes 2 loaves/16 servings.

Per serving: Kilojoules 984; Fibre 4 g; Protein 5 g; Total Fat 7 g; Saturated Fat 1 g; Cholesterol 0 mg; Sodium 309 mg

Basic cooking For basic oatmeal, stir 125 ml old-fashioned or quick-cooking oats into 250 ml boiling water in a small saucepan. Simmer old-fashioned oats for 5 minutes; cook quick-cooking oats for 1 minute, then cover and let stand for a few minutes, until the oatmeal is the desired consistency.

Rice

Nutritional power

Half the world's people rely on rice as their staple starch. Rice offers B vitamins and minerals; its protein features a good balance of amino acids.

White Rice

PER 130 G COOKED (1 CUP)

Kilojoules	701
Fibre	0,5 g
Protein	4 g
Total Fat	0,4 g
Saturated Fat	0,1 g
Cholesterol	0 mg
Sodium	3 mg

NUTRIENTS

% RDA for people older than 10 years

Iron	7 %
Magnesium	6 %
Niacin	3 %

Brown Rice

PER 140 G COOKED (1 CUP)

Kilojoules	789
Fibre	2,4 g
Protein	4 g
Total Fat	1,3 g
Saturated Fat	0,3 g
Cholesterol	0 mg
Sodium	7 mg

NUTRIENTS

% RDA for people older than 10 years

Magnesium	20 %
Niacin	12 %
Thiamin	10 %

Pork Fried Rice

PREP: 10 MINUTES / COOK: 20 MINUTES

Here's how to turn leftover rice into a hearty main dish. You'll get the best results if the rice is cool; if you cook a fresh pot of rice for this dish, spread it out on a platter and quick-chill it in the freezer.

15 ml cornflour
10 ml light soya sauce
350 g well-trimmed pork fillet, cut into 1-cm wide strips
15 ml vegetable oil
1 large red pepper, cut into 1-cm squares
1 large carrot, thinly sliced
3 spring onions, thinly sliced
15 ml finely chopped fresh ginger
2 cloves garlic, finely chopped
3,5 ml salt
240 g Chinese cabbage, cut into 1 x 5-cm strips (about 3 cups)
550 g cooked brown or white rice
30 ml rice vinegar
5 ml sesame oil

1. In a medium bowl, combine the cornflour and soya sauce. Add the pork and toss well. In a large nonstick pan or wok, heat the oil over moderately high heat. Add the pork and stir-fry for 5 minutes or until lightly browned. With a slotted spoon, transfer the pork to a plate.

2. Add the pepper, carrot, spring onion, ginger, garlic and salt and stir-fry for 3 minutes or until the carrot is crisp-tender. Add the Chinese cabbage and stir-fry for 2 minutes or until the cabbage is crisp-tender.

3. Add the rice and cook, stirring, for 5 minutes or until the rice is lightly browned. Return the pork to the pan and cook for 2 minutes or until heated through. Add the vinegar and sesame oil, tossing to combine. Serves 4.

Per serving: Kilojoules 1 532; Fibre 5 g; Protein 19 g; Total Fat 10 g; Saturated Fat 2 g; Cholesterol 41 mg; Sodium 1 902 mg

Baked Chicken & Rice

PREP: 15 MINUTES / COOK: 40 MINUTES

15 ml olive oil
1 kg skinless, bone-in chicken thighs (about 8 thighs)
1 medium onion, finely chopped
4 cloves garlic, finely chopped
450 g mushrooms, quartered
175 g rice
310 ml chicken stock
2,5 ml crumbled dried rosemary
2,5 ml salt
1,25 ml pepper
150 g frozen peas

1. Preheat the oven to 180°C. In a large pan, heat the oil over moderate heat. Add the chicken and cook for 4 minutes or until lightly browned on both sides. Remove and set aside.

2. Add the onion and garlic to the pan and cook, stirring occasionally, for 5 minutes or until soft. Add the mushrooms and cook for 3 minutes. Add the rice, stirring to coat. Add the stock, 375 ml of water, the rosemary, salt and pepper and bring to a boil. Stir in the peas.

3. Pour the rice mixture into a 23 x 33-cm glass baking dish. Place the chicken on top, cover with foil and bake for 25 to 30 minutes or until the chicken is cooked through and the rice is tender. Serves 4.

Per serving: Kilojoules 2187; Fibre 6g; Protein 43g; Total Fat 19g; Saturated Fat 4g; Cholesterol 119mg; Sodium 894mg

Indian Biryani

PREP: 10 MINUTES / COOK: 30 MINUTES

Basmati is an aromatic rice grown in India and Pakistan. It is now widely available in supermarkets.

15ml vegetable oil
2,5ml each cinnamon, ground cardamom and turmeric
1 pinch of ground cloves
1 medium onion, finely chopped
140g basmati rice, well rinsed
30ml plain low-fat yoghurt
3,5ml salt
125ml sultanas
60ml coarsely chopped pistachio nuts

1. Preheat the oven to 180°C. In a small flameproof casserole, heat the oil over moderate heat. Add the cinnamon, cardamom, turmeric and cloves and cook for 30 seconds or until the spices are fragrant. Add the onion and sauté for 7 minutes or until tender.

2. Stir in the rice, yoghurt, 675ml of water and the salt and bring to a boil. Cover and bake for 25 minutes or until the rice is tender. Stir in the sultanas and pistachio nuts. Serves 4.

Per serving: Kilojoules 1148; Fibre 2g; Protein 5g; Total Fat 8g; Saturated Fat 1g; Cholesterol 1mg; Sodium 434mg

At the market In addition to long-grain brown and white rice, try medium- and short-grain types such as Arborio (see photo below), which cook up softer and stickier. Quick-cooking rice is precooked and many varieties and flavours are sold in supermarkets. Fragrant rices, such as basmati and jasmine, have a delicately sweet, nutlike aroma and flavour. Enriched American rice is suitable for creole-type dishes and has the advantage of additional nutritional value.

Plump and pearly grains of Italian Arborio rice are used to make traditional creamy risottos.

Basic cooking Add the rice to boiling water (use about twice as much water as rice), cover, and cook for 15 to 20 minutes (white rice) or 40 minutes (brown). You can add more boiling water if the water is absorbed before the rice is done, but be quick about re-covering the pot.

Pork Fried Rice This favourite Chinese-restaurant dish makes an appealing centrepiece for an informal supper. A bounty of colourful vegetables rounds out the dish.

Sweet Rice Cakes

Surprise the family with a novel dessert. Plump little rice patties served with a sweet yoghurt sauce.

Did you know? . . .

It's not necessary or desirable to wash domestic packaged rice before or after you cook it; doing so will rinse away vitamins and minerals.

Several studies have shown rice bran to lower blood cholesterol. It's believed that the oil found in the rice germ (which ends up in the bran when rice is milled) is the key component. Brown rice includes some of the germ, but pure rice bran is a far more concentrated source. You can sprinkle rice bran over your breakfast cereal or add it to baked goods.

Soaking brown rice overnight can cut cooking time in half. The key to conserving the B vitamins is to soak the rice in the measured amount of cold water and then to cook the rice in the same water.

Sweet Rice Cakes

PREP: 15 MINUTES / COOK: 10 MINUTES

These tender rice patties are dotted with fruit and pine nuts. You can make them with white rice or brown, plain or aromatic.

250 ml plain low-fat yoghurt
150 ml low-fat (2%) milk
70 ml plus 15 ml sugar
30 ml plus 125 ml flour
390 g cooked rice
125 ml mixed dried fruit, chopped
30 ml pine nuts, toasted
5 ml vanilla essence
1,25 ml salt
20 ml vegetable oil
10 ml unsalted butter

1. Place the yoghurt in a fine-meshed sieve and let drain while you prepare the rice patties.

2. In a medium saucepan, whisk the milk and 70 ml of the sugar into 30 ml of the flour and cook over moderate heat, stirring, until combined. Transfer to a medium bowl and stir in the rice, fruit, pine nuts, vanilla and salt. Shape into 8 patties.

3. Dredge the patties in the remaining 125 ml flour, shaking off the excess. In a large nonstick pan, heat the oil and butter over moderate heat until the butter has melted. Add the patties and cook for 3 minutes per side or until the rice cakes are golden brown and heated through.

4. Stir the remaining 15 ml sugar into the yoghurt and serve with the rice cakes. Serves 4.

Per serving: Kilojoules 1855; Fibre 2g; Protein 9g; Total Fat 11g; Saturated Fat 3g; Cholesterol 13mg; Sodium 214mg

Rice Bread

PREP: 10 MINUTES / COOK: 20 MINUTES

This is traditionally made with white rice, but brown rice is fine. Serve the bread fresh and hot with preserves.

250 ml flour
30 ml white or yellow maize meal (Italian polenta would be suitable)
2,5 ml each salt, baking powder and bicarbonate of soda
140 g cooked white or brown rice
125 ml low-fat cultured buttermilk
60 ml sour cream
1 egg, lightly beaten

1. Preheat the oven to 220°C. Spray a 20-cm cast-iron pan or metal cake tin with nonstick cooking spray and place in the oven to preheat.

2. In a small bowl, stir together the flour, maize meal, salt, baking powder and bicarbonate of soda. In a medium bowl, mash the rice with a potato masher until almost smooth. Stir in the buttermilk, sour cream and egg until well combined. Fold in the flour mixture.

3. Pour the batter into the hot pan and bake for 20 minutes or until lightly golden and a cake tester inserted in the centre comes out clean. Serves 4.

Per serving: Kilojoules 988; Fibre 4g; Protein 7g; Total Fat 6g; Saturated Fat 3g; Cholesterol 66mg; Sodium 357mg

---

Raisin-Almond Rice Pudding

PREP: 10 MINUTES / COOK: 40 MINUTES
CHILL: 2 HOURS

The raisins in this creamy rice pudding can be substituted with cherries when in season.

- **165g rice**
- **2,5ml salt**
- **350ml low-fat evaporated milk**
- **70ml packed light brown sugar**
- **2,5ml grated orange rind**
- **125ml low-fat (2%) milk**
- **2,5ml vanilla essence**
- **0,6ml almond essence**
- **125ml dried seedless raisins**
- **60ml slivered almonds, toasted**

1. In a medium saucepan, bring 560ml of water to a boil. Add the rice and salt, reduce to a simmer, cover and cook for 17 minutes or until the rice is tender.

2. Add the evaporated milk, brown sugar and orange rind; cover and cook for 10 minutes. Uncover and cook, stirring frequently, for 10 minutes or until the rice is very creamy and most of the liquid has been absorbed.

3. Stir in the milk, vanilla essence and almond essence and remove from the heat. Cool to room temperature, stir in the raisins and almonds and refrigerate for 2 hours or until chilled. Serves 4.

Per serving: Kilojoules 1 741; Fibre 2g; Protein 13g; Total Fat 8g; Saturated Fat 2g; Cholesterol 28mg; Sodium 448mg

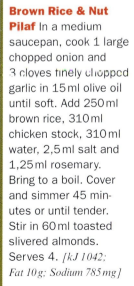

Green Rice In a medium saucepan, sauté 1 small sliced onion and 2 cloves finely chopped garlic in 15ml olive oil until tender. Add 250ml rice, 560ml water and 2,5ml salt and cook until tender. Stir in 125ml chopped fresh coriander or parsley. Serves 4. *[kJ 871; Fat 4g; Sodium 306mg]*

Rice Frittata In a 23-cm grill-proof pan, heat 15ml olive oil over moderately low heat. In large bowl, combine 500ml cooked rice, 4 egg whites, 3 eggs, 70ml grated Parmesan cheese, 2,5ml salt and 1,25ml pepper. Pour into pan and sprinkle with 70ml diced roasted red pepper. Cook until bottom is set. Grill for 2 to 3 minutes to brown top. Serves 4. *[kJ 912; Fat 10g; Sodium 505mg]*

Brown Rice & Nut Pilaf In a medium saucepan, cook 1 large chopped onion and 3 cloves finely chopped garlic in 15ml olive oil until soft. Add 250ml brown rice, 310ml chicken stock, 310ml water, 2,5ml salt and 1,25ml rosemary. Bring to a boil. Cover and simmer 45 minutes or until tender. Stir in 60ml toasted slivered almonds. Serves 4. *[kJ 1042; Fat 10g; Sodium 785mg]*

Wild rice

PER 130G COOKED (1 CUP)	
Kilojoules	550
Fibre	3,0 g
Protein	5 g
Total Fat	0,4 g
Saturated Fat	0,1 g
Cholesterol	0 mg
Sodium	4 mg

NUTRIENTS	
% RDA for people older than 10 years	
Magnesium	14 %
Zinc	12 %
Niacin	9 %
Vitamin B6	9 %
Folate	8 %

Did you know? . . .

Wild rice is a good source of zinc, which might be called the 'food-lover's mineral', because it keeps your sense of taste working properly. In addition, some studies have shown that zinc (in the form of lozenges) helps fight the common cold.

Wild Rice-Brown Rice Pilaf

PREP: 5 MINUTES / COOK: 55 MINUTES

Wild rice is relatively expensive (although the fact that it quadruples in volume when cooked is a saving grace). Wild rice is often cooked along with white or brown rice to make this luxury ingredient go further.

10 ml vegetable oil
1 large onion, finely chopped
175 ml wild rice (about 115 g)
125 ml brown rice
475 ml chicken stock
2,5 ml dried sage
1,25 ml each salt and pepper
60 ml grated Parmesan cheese
130 g frozen peas, thawed
60 ml chopped cashew nuts

1. In a medium saucepan, heat the oil over moderate heat. Add the onion and sauté for 5 minutes or until crisp-tender. Add the wild rice and brown rice, stirring to combine. Stir in the stock, 500 ml of water, the sage, salt and pepper. Bring to a boil, reduce to a simmer, cover, and cook for 45 minutes or until the rice is tender.

2. Stir in the Parmesan, peas and cashew nuts. Serves 6.

Per serving: Kilojoules 904; Fibre 4g; Protein 8g; Total Fat 5g; Saturated Fat 2g; Cholesterol 3mg; Sodium 659mg

Wild Rice & Pecan Nut Stuffing

PREP: 10 MINUTES / COOK: 1 HOUR

This sophisticated 'stuffing', cooked in a casserole in the oven, is a dressy accompaniment to any kind of poultry. The pecan nuts and water chestnuts are added at the last minute so that they keep their crunch.

10 ml vegetable oil
1 large onion, finely chopped
3 cloves garlic, finely chopped
1 large carrot, halved lengthwise and thinly sliced
1 stalk celery, halved lengthwise and thinly sliced
250 ml wild rice (145 g)
250 ml chicken stock
3,5 ml salt
2,5 ml each crumbled dried rosemary and pepper
1 tin (230 g) water chestnuts, sliced and drained
70 ml chopped pecan nuts

1. Preheat the oven to 180°C. In a flameproof casserole, heat the oil over moderate heat. Add the onion and garlic and sauté for 5 minutes or until soft. Add the carrot and celery and sauté for 4 minutes or until the carrot is crisp-tender.

2. Stir in the wild rice, stock, 500 ml of water, the salt, rosemary and pepper.

Bring to a boil. Cover, transfer to the oven and bake for 50 minutes or until the wild rice is tender. Stir in the water chestnuts and pecan nuts. Serves 6.

Per serving: Kilojoules 914; Fibre 4g; Protein 6g; Total Fat 6g; Saturated Fat 1g; Cholesterol 0mg; Sodium 545mg

Wild Rice Salad

PREP: 10 MINUTES / COOK: 45 MINUTES

A Granny Smith apple is just one option here; feel free to use any other firm, crisp apple, such as Braeburn, Fuji, Royal Gala or Topred.

250 ml wild rice (145 g)
2,5 ml each dried thyme and salt
45 ml wine vinegar or cider vinegar
15 ml olive oil
10 ml Dijon mustard
175 g smoked turkey or chicken, cut into 1-cm cubes
320 g chopped plum tomatoes (2 cups)
1 Granny Smith apple, cut into 1-cm pieces
1 cucumber, peeled, halved lengthwise, seeded and cut into 5-mm-thick slices

1. Bring 750 ml of water to a boil. Add the wild rice, thyme and 1,25 ml of the salt. Reduce to a simmer, cover and cook for 45 minutes or until the wild rice is tender. Drain well.

2. Meanwhile, in a large bowl, whisk together the vinegar, oil, mustard and the remaining 1,25 ml salt. Add the wild rice, tossing to coat. Add the turkey (or chicken), tomatoes, apple and cucumber and toss again. Serve at room temperature or chilled. Serves 4.

Per serving: Kilojoules 1 167; Fibre 5g; Protein 16g; Total Fat 5g; Saturated Fat 1g; Cholesterol 33mg; Sodium 962mg

At the market Wild rice is sold at most supermarkets; it is also available at delicatessens and health-food shops. Because it is expensive, it is usually sold in small quantities.

Prep Unlike most packaged rice, wild rice must be thoroughly rinsed before cooking to eliminate any chaff or debris that may remain after the rice is hulled. (Wild rice is not milled like regular rice.)

Place wild rice in a colander or strainer and rinse it under running water until the water runs clear.

Basic cooking Use a 1-to-3 ratio of rice to water. For 145 g (1 cup) of raw rice (which will yield about 520 g (4 cups) cooked), bring 750 ml (3 cups) of water to a boil. Stir in the rice, reduce the heat and simmer, covered, for 45 minutes or until the rice is tender and most of the water has been absorbed.

Wild Rice Salad *Half portions of this salad could be served as a first course.*

Legumes, Nuts & Seeds

Split Pea & Green Pea Soup

Beans

Speckled Sugar Beans
PER 200G COOKED (1 CUP)

Kilojoules	1170
Fibre	16,4 g
Protein	14 g
Total Fat	1 g
Saturated Fat	0,2 g
Cholesterol	0 mg
Sodium	28 mg

NUTRIENTS
% RDA for people older than 10 years

Folate	70%
Magnesium	37%
Iron	30%
Thiamin	17%
Vitamin B6	16%
Zinc	14%
Niacin	8%

Did you know? . . .
Beans provide substantial amounts of insoluble fibre (helps prevent colon cancer) and soluble fibre (helps lower blood cholesterol, thereby helping to prevent heart disease and stroke).

Bean & Cheese Burritos

PREP: 10 MINUTES / COOK: 20 MINUTES

Some of the beans are mashed to give the filling a thick, meaty texture.

- 8 corn tortillas (20-cm diameter)
- 10 ml vegetable oil
- 1 small onion, thinly sliced
- 2 cloves garlic, finely chopped
- 1 green chilli pepper (or pickled jalapeño pepper), seeded and finely chopped
- 600 g cooked red kidney beans
- 5 ml ground coriander
- 1,25 ml salt
- 125 ml chopped fresh coriander or parsley
- 115 g grated mild Cheddar
- 60 ml sour cream
- 125 ml mild or medium bottled salsa (or chilli salsa—page 66)

1. Preheat the oven to 180°C. Wrap the tortillas in foil and bake until heated through, but not crisp.

2. Meanwhile, in a large nonstick pan, heat the oil over moderate heat. Add the onion, garlic and chilli and sauté for 2 minutes or until the onion is soft. Stir in the beans, coriander, salt and 60 ml of water and bring to a boil. Reduce to a simmer, cover and cook for 5 minutes or until the flavours have blended and the beans are hot. With a potato masher or the back of a spoon, mash about half of the beans. Stir in the fresh coriander.

3. Spoon the bean mixture down the centre of each tortilla. Sprinkle the cheese over the beans and roll up. Place, seam-side down, on a baking sheet and bake for 3 minutes or until heated through. Serve the burritos topped with the sour cream and salsa. Serves 4.

Per serving: Kilojoules 2 787; Fibre 15 g; Protein 26 g; Total Fat 25 g; Saturated Fat 9 g; Cholesterol 46 mg; Sodium 1 122 mg

Pork & Bean Stew

PREP: 20 MINUTES / COOK: 20 MINUTES

This stew is not highly spiced, but you can add chilli powder (or hotter chillies) if you wish. Warm bread is the ideal accompaniment for this low-fat, high-protein stew.

- 15 ml vegetable oil
- 225 g well-trimmed pork fillet, cut into 1-cm pieces
- 30 ml flour
- 1 large onion, finely chopped
- 3 cloves garlic, finely chopped
- 1 large green pepper, cut into 1-cm squares
- 1 tin (410 g) tomatoes, chopped with their juice
- 2 large mild green chillies, chopped
- 7,5 ml mild paprika
- 2,5 ml each dried oreganum and salt
- 600 g cooked red kidney beans
- 15 ml lime or lemon juice

1. In a large nonstick pan, heat the oil over moderately high heat. Dust the pork with the flour, shaking off the excess. Add to the pan and sauté for 2 minutes or until lightly browned. With a slotted spoon, transfer the pork to a plate.

At the market Dried and tinned beans are widely available. Supermarkets carry all the basic varieties. For a wider selection, check a health-food shop.

Prep Before cooking dried beans, spread them out and pick through them, removing any dirt or damaged beans; then rinse the beans in cold water. Drain and rinse tinned beans to remove excess sodium.

Basic cooking Soaking dried beans shortens their cooking time: Place beans in a large pot and add cold water to cover. Let stand 8 to 12 hours. (For a quicker soak, bring the water slowly to a boil and simmer the beans 2 minutes. Cover the pot, remove from the heat and let stand 1 to 2 hours.) After soaking, drain the beans, add fresh water to cover, bring to a boil and simmer about 1 hour or until tender.

Soak beans in a large pot— they double in volume when soaked. Place the beans in the pot, then add water to cover by 5 centimetres.

2. Add the onion and garlic to the pan and sauté for 5 minutes or until soft. Add the pepper and sauté for 4 minutes or until soft.

3. Add 60 ml of water, the tomatoes, green chillies, paprika, oreganum and salt and bring to a boil. Reduce to a simmer, return the pork to the pan; add the beans, cover and cook for 7 minutes or until the pork is tender. Stir in the lime juice. Serves 4.

Per serving: Kilojoules 1 370; Fibre 13g; Protein 21g; Total Fat 7g; Saturated Fat 2g; Cholesterol 27mg; Sodium 545mg

Vegetarian Burgers *You can 'hold the beef' and still serve up a hearty, juicy burger.*

Vegetarian Burgers
PREP: 15 MINUTES / COOK: 15 MINUTES

The original veggie burger was a high-fat patty made from nuts and cheese. These bean-based burgers are much healthier.

- **2 cloves garlic, peeled**
- **600 g cooked sugar beans**
- **30 ml light mayonnaise**
- **15 ml chilli sauce**
- **10 ml lime or lemon juice**
- **30 ml plain dry bread crumbs**
- **1 small onion, finely chopped**
- **2,5 ml pepper**
- **1,25 ml salt**
- **30 ml flour**
- **20 ml vegetable oil**
- **4 hamburger rolls, toasted**
- **4 cos lettuce leaves**
- **4 slices each of tomato and onion**

1. In a small pan of boiling water, cook the garlic for 4 minutes to soften. In a large bowl, mash the garlic, beans, mayonnaise, chilli sauce and lime juice with a potato masher or fork. Stir in the bread crumbs, onion, pepper and salt. Shape into 4 patties.

2. Dredge the patties in the flour, shaking off the excess. In a large nonstick pan, heat the oil over moderate heat. Sauté the patties for 3 minutes per side or until browned and crisp on the outside and heated through.

3. Place the burgers on hamburger rolls and top each with lettuce, tomato and onion. Serves 4.

Per serving: Kilojoules 2 048; Fibre 16g; Protein 18g; Total Fat 10g; Saturated Fat 1g; Cholesterol 3mg; Sodium 756mg

Red Kidney Beans

PER 200 G COOKED (1 CUP)

Kilojoules	1038
Fibre	19 g
Protein	18 g
Total Fat	0,2 g
Saturated Fat	0 g
Cholesterol	0 mg
Sodium	8 mg

NUTRIENTS

% RDA for people older than 10 years

Iron	43 %
Folate	37 %
Magnesium	32 %
Thiamin	18 %
Zinc	11 %
Vitamin B6	10 %

White Kidney Beans

PER 200 G COOKED (1 CUP)

Kilojoules	964
Fibre	14,4 g
Protein	16 g
Total Fat	0,8 g
Saturated Fat	0,2 g
Cholesterol	0 mg
Sodium	4 mg

NUTRIENTS

% RDA for people older than 10 years

Folate	42 %
Iron	34 %
Magnesium	29 %
Thiamin	23 %
Vitamin B6	16 %
Pantothenic acid	14 %
Zinc	13 %

Pasta e Fagioli

PREP: 15 MINUTES / COOK: 40 MINUTES

The Italian name of this nourishing soup simply means 'pasta and beans'.

- 15 ml olive oil
- 1 medium onion, diced
- 1 medium carrot, halved lengthwise and cut into 5-mm-thick slices
- 1 large red pepper, cut into 1-cm squares
- 3 cloves garlic, finely chopped
- 1 tin (410 g) tomatoes, chopped with their juice
- 125 ml chopped fresh basil
- 2,5 ml salt
- 1,25 ml black pepper
- 600 g cooked red kidney beans
- 375 ml chicken stock
- 115 g wagon wheel or bow-tie pasta
- 85 g cooked chicken, cut into 5-mm pieces
- 125 ml grated Parmesan cheese

1. In a medium saucepan, heat the oil over moderate heat. Add the onion, carrot, pepper and garlic and sauté for 7 minutes or until the onion is soft. Stir in the tomatoes, basil, salt and black pepper and cook for 5 minutes or until some of the tomato liquid has evaporated.

2. Stir in the beans, stock and 750 ml of water. Bring to a boil, reduce to a simmer, cover and cook for 15 minutes or until the beans are beginning to break up and thicken the liquid. With the back of a spoon, mash one-quarter of the beans against the side of the saucepan.

3. Return to a boil, add the pasta and chicken; cook, uncovered, for 10 minutes or until the pasta is *al dente*. Serve topped with Parmesan. Serves 4.

Per serving: Kilojoules 1807; Fibre 14 g; Protein 27 g; Total Fat 10 g; Saturated Fat 3 g; Cholesterol 22 mg; Sodium 1 316 mg

Sweet Bean Pie

PREP: 20 MINUTES / CHILL: 1 HOUR
COOK: 1 HOUR 15 MINUTES

A pie made out of beans might seem odd, but this variation on an African-American recipe makes clever use of chickpeas, which are puréed with evaporated milk, a whole egg, egg whites and honey to make a smooth custard.

- 250 ml flour
- 15 ml plus 175 ml sugar
- 2,5 ml salt
- 30 ml unsalted butter, cut up
- 30 ml solid vegetable shortening
- 45 ml sour cream
- 15 ml iced water
- 2 x 425 g tins chickpeas, drained
- 175 ml low-fat evaporated milk
- 1 egg
- 2 egg whites
- 30 ml honey
- 7,5 ml vanilla essence
- 5 ml ground cinnamon
- 0,6 ml ground nutmeg

1. In a large bowl, combine the flour, 15 ml of the sugar and 1,25 ml of the salt. With a pastry blender or two knives, cut in the butter and shortening until the mixture resembles coarse crumbs. In a small bowl, combine the sour cream and 15 ml of iced water; stir into the flour mixture until just combined. Flatten the dough into a disc, wrap in plastic wrap and refrigerate for at least 1 hour.

2. Preheat the oven to 180°C. On a lightly floured surface, roll the dough out to a 33-cm round. Fit into a 23-cm pie dish which is quite deep and form a high fluted edge. Lightly prick the bottom of the shell with a fork and line with foil. Fill the foil with dried beans. Place on a baking sheet and bake for 20 minutes. Remove the foil and beans and bake the pie shell for 5 minutes or until lightly golden around the edges.

Pasta e Fagioli
Sautéing the vegetables adds extra flavour to this old-fashioned soup.

Did you know? . . .
To improve the digestibility of beans which are cooked from scratch, discard the soaking water and cook the beans in fresh water.

3. In a blender or food processor, combine the chickpeas, evaporated milk, whole egg, egg whites, honey, vanilla essence, cinnamon, nutmeg and the remaining 1,25 ml salt and 175 ml sugar. Process until smooth. Pour into the prepared shell. Place on the baking sheet and bake for 50 minutes or until set. Serve warm or at room temperature. Serves 12.

Per serving: Kilojoules 979; Fibre 3g; Protein 7g; Total Fat 7g; Saturated Fat 3g; Cholesterol 31 mg; Sodium 343 mg

Molasses Baked Beans

PREP: 10 MINUTES
COOK: 1 HOUR 45 MINUTES

The generous quantity of tomatoes in this recipe adds lycopene, a disease-fighting phytochemical, to the already rich nutritional bounty of white kidney beans.

90 g rindless back bacon, chopped
1 small onion, finely chopped
2 cloves garlic, finely chopped
1 tin (410 g) tomatoes, chopped with their juice
225 ml crushed strained tomato sauce (passata)
60 ml molasses

15 ml cider vinegar
15 ml dark brown sugar
10 ml English mustard
3,5 ml ground ginger
2,5 ml salt
600 g cooked white kidney beans

1. Preheat the oven to 180°C. In a medium ovenproof saucepan, cook the bacon over low heat for 5 minutes or until it has rendered its fat. Add the onion and garlic and sauté for 5 minutes or until soft. Add the tinned tomatoes, tomato sauce, molasses, vinegar, brown sugar, mustard, ginger and salt. Bring to a boil and cook for 5 minutes.

2. Add the beans, cover and transfer to the oven. Bake for 1½ hours or until the beans are richly flavoured, well coated and the cooking liquid is thick. Serves 6.

Per serving: Kilojoules 958; Fibre 9g; Protein 11g; Total Fat 5g; Saturated Fat 2g; Cholesterol 7 mg; Sodium 541 mg

Nutrition researchers at Potchefstroom University have been treating patients with high blood fats very successfully with a diet of legumes. As part of the background low-fat, high fibre diet, they have shown that one daily portion of cooked beans (from 100 to 250 grams, depending on energy requirements) significantly reduces total and LDL-cholesterol. The high bean diet is also successful in controlling blood glucose and reducing insulin or other medication used in diabetic patients.

Cassoulet is a hearty French casserole made with white beans, chicken and sausage.

Tinned Baked Beans
PER 270 G (1 CUP)

Kilojoules	1048
Fibre	20,8 g
Protein	13 g
Total Fat	1,4 g
Saturated Fat	0,3 g
Cholesterol	0 mg
Sodium	1072 mg

NUTRIENTS

% RDA for people older than 10 years

Magnesium	29 %
Thiamin	29 %
Zinc	25 %
Vitamin B6	18 %
Vitamin E	16 %
Folate	16 %
Calcium	11 %
Riboflavin	10 %

Chickpeas
PER 170 G COOKED (1 CUP)

Kilojoules	1166
Fibre	11,2 g
Protein	15 g
Total Fat	4,4 g
Saturated Fat	0,5 g
Cholesterol	0 mg
Sodium	12 mg

NUTRIENTS

% RDA for people older than 10 years

Folate	73 %
Iron	35 %
Magnesium	27 %
Zinc	17 %
Thiamin	15 %
Vitamin B6	12 %
Calcium	7 %

Hummus

PREP: 10 MINUTES / COOK: 10 MINUTES

Serve this Middle Eastern dip with pita wedges or raw vegetable sticks.

- 4 cloves garlic, peeled
- 500 g tinned chickpeas, rinsed and drained
- 70 ml plain low-fat yoghurt
- 30 ml sour cream
- 15 ml lemon juice
- 15 ml sesame oil
- 2,5 ml salt
- 2,5 ml ground coriander
- 0,6 ml each cayenne pepper and allspice
- 60 ml chopped parsley or fresh coriander (optional)
- 5 ml paprika (optional)

1. In a small pot of boiling water, cook the garlic for 2 minutes to blanch. Drain and transfer to a food processor.

2. Add the chickpeas, yoghurt, sour cream, lemon juice, sesame oil, salt, coriander, cayenne and allspice to the processor and purée. Transfer to a serving bowl and sprinkle with the parsley and paprika. Makes 500 millilitres.

Per 60 ml: Kilojoules 561; Fibre 4g; Protein 6g; Total Fat 5g; Saturated Fat 1g; Cholesterol 4mg; Sodium 162mg

Chickpeas & Greens Soup with Carrots

PREP: 10 MINUTES / COOK: 15 MINUTES

For more variations, try less-common Swiss chard or kale instead of the vegetables called for; or try a different bean such as white kidney beans (cannellini).

- 175 ml chicken stock
- 2 medium carrots, quartered lengthwise and thinly sliced
- 3 cloves garlic, finely chopped
- 2,5 ml dried sage
- 1,25 ml pepper
- 400 g cooked chickpeas or red kidney beans
- 120 g torn spinach and/or watercress leaves (3 cups)

1. In a large saucepan, bring the stock to a boil over moderate heat. Add the carrots, garlic, sage and pepper and cook for 5 minutes or until the carrots are tender. Add 175 ml of water and the chickpeas and return to a boil. Reduce to a simmer, cover and cook for 7 minutes or until the soup is flavourful and the chickpeas are piping hot.

2. Stir in the vegetables and cook for 1 minute or until just wilted. Serves 4.

Per serving: Kilojoules 790; Fibre 8g; Protein 10g; Total Fat 3g; Saturated Fat 0g; Cholesterol 0mg; Sodium 304mg

Cassoulet

PREP: 15 MINUTES
REFRIGERATE: 1 HOUR
COOK: 50 MINUTES

This French country dish traditionally takes several days to make and requires 20 or more different ingredients. We've composed a greatly simplified cassoulet for today's cook.

350 g skinless, boned chicken thighs
4 cloves garlic, finely chopped
2,5 ml each dried thyme and salt
1,25 ml pepper
10 ml olive oil
1 small onion, finely chopped
2 medium carrots, halved lengthwise and thinly sliced
1 tin (410 g) tomatoes, chopped with their juice
600 g cooked white kidney beans (cannellini)
175 g smoked garlic sausage, thinly sliced
45 ml plain dry bread crumbs

1. In a large bowl, toss the chicken with the garlic, thyme, salt and pepper. Cover and refrigerate for at least 1 hour.

2. In a small flameproof casserole, heat the oil over moderate heat. Add the chicken and cook for 4 minutes or until the chicken is very lightly browned on both sides. Transfer the chicken to a plate.

3. Preheat the oven to 200°C. Meanwhile, add the onion and carrots to the pan and sauté for 7 minutes or until the onion is soft. Add the tomatoes and their juice, the beans and sausage. Bring to a boil, reduce to a simmer and return the chicken to the pan. Cover, transfer to the oven and bake for 20 minutes or until the chicken is cooked through.

4. Sprinkle the bread crumbs on top, drizzle with 45 ml of the cooking liquid to moisten the crumbs and bake for 20 minutes or until the crumbs are golden. Serves 4.

Per serving: Kilojoules 2046; Fibre 13g; Protein 32g; Total Fat 22g; Saturated Fat 7g; Cholesterol 74mg; Sodium 995mg

Tuscan White Bean & Tuna Salad In a large bowl, toss together 1 tin rinsed and drained white kidney beans, two 185-g tins drained water-packed tuna, 1 medium diced (red) onion, 60 ml light mayonnaise, 15 ml lemon juice and 2,5 ml sage. Sprinkle with chopped parsley. Serves 4. *[kJ 949; Fat 6g; Sodium 1078mg]*

Bean Soup In a saucepan, sauté 1 large diced green pepper, 1 small sliced onion, and 3 cloves finely chopped garlic in 10 ml oil until soft. Add 410-g tin rinsed and drained red kidney beans, 375 ml chicken stock and 5 ml each ground coriander and cumin. Simmer 5 minutes. Purée half the beans; reheat soup. Top with 30 ml sour cream and 60 ml diced tomato. Serves 4. *[kJ 542; Fat 5g; Sodium 817mg]*

Refried Beans In large pan, sauté 1 small diced onion and 1 medium diced carrot in 15 ml olive oil over moderate heat until soft. Add two 410-g tins rinsed and drained sugar beans, 10 ml tomato paste, 60 ml water, 1,25 ml dried oreganum, 1,25 ml salt and 0,6 ml cayenne pepper. Cook, stirring and breaking up half of the beans. Serves 4. *[kJ 936; Fat 4g; Sodium 527mg]*

Lentils

Country Ham & Lentil Salad

PREP: 25 MINUTES / COOK: 25 MINUTES

200 g lentils
3 cloves garlic, finely chopped
2,5 ml salt
2,5 ml black pepper
1,25 ml dried sage
350 g potatoes (red, if available), cut into 1-cm cubes
70 ml red wine vinegar
20 ml Dijon mustard
10 ml olive oil
175 g smoked ham, cut into 1-cm cubes
2 stalks celery, halved lengthwise and thinly sliced
1 large red pepper, cut into 1-cm squares
125 ml snipped fresh dill

1. In a medium saucepan of boiling water, cook the lentils, garlic, 1,25 ml each of the salt and black pepper and the sage for 20 minutes or until the lentils are tender; drain any liquid remaining. Meanwhile, in a separate pot of boiling water, cook the potatoes for 7 minutes or until tender. Drain.

2. As the potatoes cook, in a large bowl, whisk together the vinegar, mustard, oil and the remaining 1,25 ml each salt and black pepper.

3. Add the hot lentils, potatoes, ham, celery, pepper and dill, tossing to combine. Serve warm, at room temperature or chilled. Serves 4.

Per serving: Kilojoules 1 538; Fibre 13 g; Protein 23 g; Total Fat 8 g; Saturated Fat 2 g; Cholesterol 25 mg; Sodium 1 038 mg

Lentil, Pear & Goat Cheese Salad

PREP: 15 MINUTES / COOK: 20 MINUTES

While the lentils cook, you can toast the pecan nuts for 8 to 10 minutes for extra flavour.

300 g lentils
3,5 ml salt
2,5 ml pepper
60 ml lime or lemon juice
30 ml honey
2,5 ml ground ginger
2 medium pears, cut into 1-cm pieces
1 bunch watercress, large stems trimmed (2 cups)
115 g soft mild goat or feta cheese, crumbled
30 ml coarsely chopped pecan nuts

1. In a medium saucepan of boiling water, cook the lentils with 1,25 ml each of the salt and pepper for 20 to 25 minutes or until the lentils are tender. Drain.

2. Meanwhile, in a medium bowl, whisk together the lime juice, honey, ginger, the remaining salt and 1,25 ml pepper. Add the lentils and cool to room temperature.

3. Add the pears and watercress, tossing to combine. Serve the salads sprinkled with the goat cheese and chopped pecan nuts. Serves 4.

Per serving: Kilojoules 1 975; Fibre 19 g; Protein 26 g; Total Fat 9 g; Saturated Fat 4 g; Cholesterol 13 mg; Sodium 550 mg

Hearty Chicken & Lentil Stew

PREP: 20 MINUTES / COOK: 1 HOUR

Even though the lentils simmer for about 45 minutes, they won't turn mushy, because the acid in the tomatoes slows the rate at which the lentils cook.

15 ml olive oil

450 g large skinless, boned chicken thighs, quartered

1 medium onion, finely chopped

1 large yellow or red pepper, diced

4 cloves garlic, finely chopped

150 g lentils

310 ml chicken stock

175 ml tinned tomatoes, chopped with their juice

5 ml ground coriander

5 ml ground ginger

2,5 ml salt

280 g potatoes (red, if available), cut into 1-cm pieces

1. In a large nonstick pan, heat the oil over moderate heat. Add the chicken and cook for 6 minutes or until browned on both sides. With a slotted spoon, transfer the chicken to a plate.

2. Add the onion, pepper and garlic to the pan and cook for 5 minutes or until soft. Add the lentils, stock, 125 ml of water, the tomatoes, coriander, ginger and salt and bring to a boil. Reduce to a simmer, cover and cook for 20 minutes or until the lentils are just barely tender.

3. Return the chicken to the pan and add the potatoes. Return to a boil, reduce to a simmer, cover and cook for 25 minutes or until the chicken is cooked through and the potatoes are tender. Serves 4.

Per serving: Kilojoules 1 636; Fibre 11 g; Protein 30 g; Total Fat 11 g; Saturated Fat 2 g; Cholesterol 55 mg; Sodium 920 mg

At the market Brown and red lentils are a supermarket staple. For other varieties, such as green lentils, try a delicatessen, health-food shop or specialist Indian food shop. All Indian lentils (called 'dals'), including red lentils, have been hulled, so they cook more quickly than whole lentils.

Because red lentils are hulled, they cook quickly. However, they have less fibre than whole lentils.

Prep Unlike dried beans, lentils do not need to be soaked before cooking. They should, however, be picked over and rinsed to remove any debris.

Basic cooking Lentils can be cooked in water or stock. Use three times as much liquid as lentils. Combine the lentils and liquid in a pot and bring to a boil. Cover, reduce the heat and simmer until the lentils are tender but still hold their shape— 20 to 25 minutes for brown lentils, 12 to 15 minutes for red lentils.

Lentil, Pear & Goat Cheese Salad *Lentils are the foil for tart greens and tangy cheese.*

Ditalini with Lentils & Sausage *Sweet Italian sausage, redolent of garlic and fennel, combines beautifully with earthy lentils and pasta.*

Did you know? . . .

Lentils contain protease inhibitors, a class of compounds that interfere with certain types of enzymatic action and thus may help fight cancer.

Lentils are a top non-meat source of the disease-fighting B vitamin, folate.

A 200 g serving of lentils provides one-third of an adult's daily requirement for copper, a mineral that may help lower blood cholesterol.

The iron in lentils is more easily absorbed by the body if you cook or serve the lentils with a food rich in vitamin C, such as tomatoes, peppers, cabbage, broccoli or citrus juice.

Lentils supply a lot of the vital nutrient folate. There is increasing evidence that folate may reduce the risk of heart disease and colon cancer.

Baked Lentil & Mushroom Stuffing

PREP: 15 MINUTES / COOK: 40 MINUTES

10 ml vegetable oil
1 medium onion, finely chopped
3 cloves garlic, finely chopped
450 g mushrooms, quartered
200 g lentils
250 ml chicken stock
2,5 ml each dried sage, salt and pepper
70 ml chopped walnuts

1. Preheat the oven to 180°C. In small ovenproof saucepan, heat the oil over moderate heat. Add the onion and garlic and sauté for 5 minutes or until the onion is soft. Add the mushrooms and sauté for 5 minutes or until beginning to soften.

2. Add the lentils, stock, 125 ml of water, the sage, salt and pepper. Bring to a boil. Cover, transfer to the oven and bake for 30 minutes or until the lentils are tender. Remove from the oven and stir in the walnuts. Serves 4.

Per serving: Kilojoules 1 334; Fibre 14 g; Protein 18 g; Total Fat 10 g; Saturated Fat 1 g; Cholesterol 0 mg; Sodium 806 mg

Ditalini with Lentils & Sausage

PREP: 20 MINUTES / COOK: 40 MINUTES

Ditalini are small pasta tubes named for their resemblance to thimbles. If you can't find them, elbow macaroni will also work well in this dish.

350 g chicken sausage, casings removed
1 large onion, finely chopped
3 cloves garlic, finely chopped
1 large carrot, quartered lengthwise and thinly sliced
1 large tomato, finely chopped
175 ml chicken stock
200 g lentils
280 g ditalini, tubetti or elbow macaroni
70 ml chopped fresh basil

1. Crumble the chicken sausage into a large nonstick pan. Add 125 ml of water and cook over moderately high heat for 5 minutes or until the sausage has rendered its fat. With a slotted spoon, transfer the sausage to a plate.

2. Add the onion and garlic to the pan and sauté for 5 minutes or until soft. Add the carrot and sauté for 4 minutes or until soft. Stir in the tomato, stock and 320 ml of water and bring to a boil. Add the lentils, reduce to a simmer, cover and cook for 25 minutes or until the lentils are tender.

3. Meanwhile, in a large pot of boiling water, cook the pasta according to package directions until *al dente*. Drain and transfer to a large bowl.

4. Return the sausage to the pan, cover and cook, stirring occasionally, for 5 minutes or until heated through. Add the lentil-sausage mixture to the pasta along with the basil, tossing to combine. Serves 4.

Per serving: Kilojoules 2 543; Fibre 15 g; Protein 38 g; Total Fat 10 g; Saturated Fat 2 g; Cholesterol 48 mg; Sodium 780 mg

Curried Lentil Dip

PREP: 10 MINUTES / COOK: 25 MINUTES

You could use any kind of lentils here; just cook them until they're tender enough to make a smooth purée. And although we call for a Granny Smith apple, you could use any other green, tart apple.

210 g lentils
15 ml vegetable oil
1 Granny Smith apple, peeled and thinly sliced
1 small onion, diced
2 cloves garlic, finely chopped
10 ml curry powder
70 ml chicken stock
3,5 ml salt

1. In a medium saucepan of boiling water, cook the lentils for 25 minutes or until tender. Drain the lentils and transfer to a food processor or blender.

2. Meanwhile, in a medium nonstick pan, heat the oil over moderate heat. Add the apple, onion, garlic and curry powder and sauté for 10 minutes or until the apple, onion and garlic are very tender.

3. Add the sautéed apple-onion mixture to the lentils in the food processor. Add the stock and salt and process to a smooth purée. Serve at room temperature or chilled. Makes 750 millilitres.

Per 60 ml: Kilojoules 345; Fibre 4 g; Protein 5 g; Total Fat 1 g; Saturated Fat 0 g; Cholesterol 0 mg; Sodium 180 mg

Cream of Red Lentil Soup In a saucepan, combine 675 ml water, 200 g red lentils, 2 chopped red peppers, 3 sliced garlic cloves, 3,5 ml each salt and cumin and 0,6 ml cayenne; cook until lentils are soft. Purée with 125 ml low-fat evaporated milk. Top with diced red pepper. Serves 4. *[kJ 975; Fat 2 g; Sodium 472 mg]*

Warm Lentil & Tomato Salad Bring 750 ml water to a boil. Add 200 g lentils, 1 medium diced carrot, 3,5 ml dried thyme, 2,5 ml salt and 2,5 ml pepper. Cover and simmer 25 minutes or until tender. Drain and toss with 45 ml red wine vinegar, 15 ml olive oil, 10 ml Dijon mustard, 400 g diced plum tomatoes and 30 ml sliced spring onions. Serves 4. *[kJ 1027; Fat 5 g; Sodium 392 mg]*

Lentils & Peas In a medium saucepan, sauté 1 medium diced onion and 3 finely chopped garlic cloves in 15 ml oil. Add 200 g lentils, 500 ml water, 3,5 ml salt, 2,5 ml crumbled dried rosemary and 1,25 ml pepper. Bring to a boil, reduce to a simmer, cover and cook 25 minutes or until tender. Add 180 g frozen peas and cook until hot. Serves 4. *[kJ 1102; Fat 4 g; Sodium 437 mg]*

Split peas

Nutritional power

An abundant source of fibre and protein, split peas also supply good amounts of minerals, including potassium and the disease-fighting B-vitamin, folate.

PER 170G COOKED (1 CUP)	
Kilojoules	840
Fibre	10g
Protein	14g
Total Fat	0,7g
Saturated Fat	0,1g
Cholesterol	0mg
Sodium	3mg

NUTRIENTS

% RDA for people older than 10 years	
Folate	28%
Thiamin	23%
Magnesium	20%
Iron	16%
Zinc	11%

Did you know? . . .

A 170g serving of cooked split peas supplies more fibre than three slices of whole-wheat bread.

Split peas are a good dietary choice for diabetics, as their complex carbohydrates (starches) are metabolized relatively slowly into glucose (blood sugar).

Mexican Split Pea Salsa

PREP: 20 MINUTES / COOK: 35 MINUTES

Something like a salsa and a bit like guacamole, this nicely spiced appetizer is the perfect mate for oven-baked tortilla chips or warm tortilla triangles.

315g split peas
3 cloves garlic, finely chopped
60ml fresh mint sprigs
3,5ml salt
15ml vegetable oil
3,5ml ground coriander
2,5ml ground cumin
0,6ml cayenne pepper
70ml lime or lemon juice
125ml chopped fresh coriander
1 large tomato, diced

1. In a medium pot of boiling water, combine the split peas, garlic, mint and 1,25ml of the salt. Reduce to a simmer and cook, stirring occasionally, for 30 minutes or until the split peas are tender. Drain; discard the mint.

2. Meanwhile, in a small pan, heat the oil over low heat. Add the coriander, cumin and cayenne and cook for 30 seconds or until fragrant.

3. Transfer the spiced oil to a medium bowl and whisk in the lime juice and the remaining 2,5ml salt. Add the hot split peas, the coriander and tomato, tossing well. Serve warm, at room temperature or chilled. Makes 1,5 litres.

Per 60ml: Kilojoules 221; Fibre 2g; Protein 3g; Total Fat 1g; Saturated Fat 0g; Cholesterol 0mg; Sodium 73mg

Split Pea & Green Pea Soup

PREP: 15 MINUTES / COOK: 35 MINUTES

When fresh peas are in season, you can substitute them for the frozen peas in this recipe. Add them to the soup about 5 minutes earlier than you would add the frozen peas— you only want to soften them slightly.

10ml vegetable oil
1 medium onion, thinly sliced
3 cloves garlic, finely chopped
260g split peas
60g shredded iceberg lettuce (1 cup)
70ml fresh mint leaves
3,5ml salt
1,25ml dried marjoram
210g frozen green peas
350ml low-fat evaporated milk

1. In a large saucepan, heat the oil over moderate heat. Add the onion and garlic and sauté for 2 minutes or until the onion is tender. Add 750ml of water, the split peas, lettuce, mint, salt and marjoram and bring to a boil. Reduce to a simmer, cover and cook for 25 minutes. Stir in the green peas and cook for 5 minutes or until the split peas are tender.

2. Transfer the mixture to a food processor, add the evaporated milk and

At the market Green split peas are the most popular variety of split pea in South Africa and are widely available. Yellow split peas are preferred for certain European dishes and are sold in many supermarkets.

Yellow split peas have a more robust flavour than the green peas.

Prep Split peas do not require presoaking, but they should be picked over and rinsed before cooking.

Basic cooking Use four times as much water as peas. For 125 ml of raw split peas, place the peas in a pot with 500 ml water and bring to a boil. Cover the pot, reduce the heat so that the water simmers and cook for about 30 minutes or until the peas are tender.

Mexican Split Pea Salsa is fragrant with fresh mint and coriander.

purée. Return the soup to the saucepan and cook for 3 minutes or until heated through. Serves 4.

Per serving: Kilojoules 1 656; Fibre 17 g; Protein 26 g; Total Fat 7 g; Saturated Fat 2 g; Cholesterol 25 mg; Sodium 262 mg

Pasta with Creamy Green Sauce

PREP: 15 MINUTES / COOK: 40 MINUTES

Although this dish is meatless, it provides plenty of protein, thanks to the split peas, pasta, low-fat milk and cream cheese.

- **10 ml olive oil**
- **4 cloves garlic, peeled**
- **210 g split peas**
- **250 ml chicken stock**
- **2,5 ml each crumbled dried rosemary, salt and sugar**
- **280 g medium pasta shells**
- **125 ml cooked chopped spinach**
- **250 ml low-fat evaporated milk**
- **45 ml low-fat cream cheese**
- **60 ml grated Parmesan cheese**

1. In a medium saucepan, heat the oil over low heat. Add the garlic and cook for 4 minutes or until the oil is fragrant. Add the split peas, stock, 125 ml of water, the rosemary, salt and sugar. Bring to a boil over moderate heat. Reduce to a simmer, cover and cook for 30 minutes or until the split peas are tender.

2. Meanwhile, in a large pot of boiling water, cook the pasta according to package directions until *al dente*. Drain the pasta well and transfer to a large bowl.

3. Transfer the split-pea mixture to a food processor along with the spinach, evaporated milk and cream cheese and purée. Return the sauce to the saucepan and cook for 3 minutes or until heated through and creamy. Add the sauce to the pasta along with the Parmesan, tossing to combine. Serves 4.

Per serving: Kilojoules 2 460; Fibre 12 g; Protein 30 g; Total Fat 11 g; Saturated Fat 4 g; Cholesterol 35 mg; Sodium 922 mg

Tofu

Nutritional power

This versatile food is remarkably nutritious, supplying complete protein and important minerals. It also contains the cancer-fighting substance genistein.

Tofu
PER 100 G

Kilojoules	456
Fibre	4 g
Protein	11 g
Total Fat	6,5 g
Saturated Fat	1,4 g
Cholesterol	0 mg
Sodium	100 mg

NUTRIENTS

% RDA for people older than 10 years

Iron	39 %
Magnesium	34 %
Calcium	9 %

Did you know? . . .

Asian peoples, who eat soya products on a daily basis, have lower cancer rates than other populations. Genistein, a phytochemical found in soya beans (and tofu), is one likely reason for this. Genistein is currently being studied in the United States as a potential anticancer medicine.

Spicy Tofu with Pork

PREP: 15 MINUTES / COOK: 10 MINUTES

When people replace some of the meat in their diet with soya products such as tofu, their cholesterol levels drop significantly. Tofu is relatively high in fat, but its saturated fat content is very low.

- 175 g lean pork, cut into pieces
- 45 ml light soya sauce
- 12,5 ml red hot pepper sauce
- 7,5 ml sugar
- 15 ml vegetable oil
- 1 small onion, chopped
- 45 ml finely chopped fresh ginger
- 6 cloves garlic, finely chopped
- 175 ml chicken stock
- 675 g tofu (silken, if available), cut into 2,5 x 1-cm pieces
- 10 ml cornflour blended with 30 ml water
- 7,5 ml sesame oil

1. In a food processor, process the pork, 22 ml of the soya sauce, the hot pepper sauce and the sugar until the pork is finely ground.

2. In a large nonstick pan, heat the vegetable oil over moderately high heat. Add the pork and cook for 30 seconds, breaking up any clumps. Add the onion, ginger and garlic and stir-fry for 2 minutes or until the garlic is tender.

3. Add the stock, tofu and the remaining soya sauce and cook, stirring gently, for 2 minutes or until the tofu is heated through. Bring to a boil, stir in the cornflour and water mixture and cook, stirring gently, for 1 minute or until slightly thickened. Stir in the sesame oil and serve. Serves 4.

Per serving: Kilojoules 1 398; Fibre 7 g; Protein 28 g; Total Fat 19 g; Saturated Fat 4 g; Cholesterol 21 mg; Sodium 1 096 mg

Hearty Vegetarian Lasagne

PREP: 15 MINUTES / COOK: 45 MINUTES

Tofu, which also contains the minerals manganese and copper, is a well-kept secret in this delicious and satisfying pasta bake.

- 150 g lasagne sheets (6 sheets)
- 10 ml olive oil
- 1 large onion, finely chopped
- 3 cloves garlic, finely chopped
- 225 g mushrooms, thinly sliced
- 500 g cooked chopped spinach, (frozen spinach, thawed and squeezed dry can also be used)
- 7,5 ml grated lemon rind
- 7,5 ml salt
- 2,5 ml pepper
- 450 g tofu (silken, if available)
- 125 ml smooth low-fat cottage cheese
- 125 ml ricotta cheese
- 125 ml grated Parmesan cheese
- 225 ml strained crushed tomatoes
- 60 ml tomato paste
- 1 egg
- 2 egg whites

1. Preheat the oven to 180°C. In a large pot of boiling water, cook the lasagne sheets according to package directions until *al dente*. Drain.

2. Meanwhile, in a large nonstick pan, heat the oil over moderate heat. Add the onion and garlic and sauté for 5 minutes or until soft. Add the mushrooms and sauté for 4 minutes or until they begin to give up their juices. Add the spinach and cook, stirring, until no liquid remains. Transfer to a medium bowl and add the lemon rind, 3,5 ml of the salt and 1,25 ml of the pepper. Toss well.

3. In a food processor, combine the tofu, cottage cheese, ricotta, 90 ml of the Parmesan, the strained crushed tomatoes, tomato paste, whole egg, egg whites, the remaining salt and remaining 1,25 ml pepper and process to a smooth purée.

4. Spray a 18 x 28-cm glass baking dish with nonstick cooking spray. Line the bottom with 2 of the lasagne sheets. Spoon half of the spinach mixture and one-third of the tofu mixture over the lasagna. Make another layer of sheets, the remaining spinach mixture and another one-third of the tofu mixture. Top with the remaining lasagne sheets and the remaining tofu mixture. Sprinkle the remaining 35 ml Parmesan on top. Bake for 30 minutes or until hot. Serves 6.

Per serving: Kilojoules 1 498; Fibre 8 g; Protein 25 g; Total Fat 14 g; Saturated Fat 5 g; Cholesterol 53 mg; Sodium 963 mg

Stir-Fried Vegetables with Tofu *Tofu has a miraculous ability to absorb flavours. Here, it tastes of soya sauce, ginger and garlic.*

Stir-Fried Vegetables with Tofu

PREP: 15 MINUTES / MARINATE: 1 HOUR
COOK: 10 MINUTES

Very firm tofu has compressed edges; a block of it resembles a little sofa pillow. If you can't find this type (check the health-food shops), firm up regular (not silken) tofu as shown at right.

- 45 ml light soya sauce
- 20 ml dark brown sugar
- 5 ml ground ginger
- 1,25 ml salt
- 450 g very firm tofu, halved horizontally
- 175 ml chicken stock
- 11 ml cornflour
- 15 ml vegetable oil
- 1 large red pepper, cut into 1-cm squares
- 175 g green beans, cut into 2,5-cm lengths
- 2 medium carrots, thinly sliced
- 4 cloves garlic, finely chopped
- 2 spring onions, thinly sliced

1. In a shallow pan, combine the soya sauce, brown sugar, ginger and salt. Add the tofu, cut-side down and set aside to marinate for 1 hour. Reserving the marinade, remove the tofu and cut into 2,5 x 1-cm pieces. Stir the stock and cornflour into the reserved marinade.

2. In a large nonstick pan, heat the oil over moderate heat. Add the pepper, green beans, carrots, garlic and onion and sauté for 5 minutes or until the pepper is crisp-tender. Stir the stock mixture well and pour into the pan. Add the tofu and bring the mixture to a boil. Reduce to a gentle boil and cook for 4 minutes or until the sauce is slightly thickened and the tofu is heated through. Serves 4.

Per serving: Kilojoules 892; Fibre 8 g; Protein 15 g; Total Fat 11 g; Saturated Fat 2 g; Cholesterol 0 mg; Sodium 1 184 mg

At the market Tofu is sold loose (displayed in tubs of water), but it's best to buy it in sealed packages (tofu, like meat, is susceptible to bacterial contamination). Some packaged tofu must be refrigerated before opening, while silken tofu is available in aseptic packages and can be stored at room temperature.

Look for Choose tofu according to how you plan to use it. Delicate 'silken' tofu can be simmered briefly, but it works best when puréed, in a shake, sauce or dip. Regular and extra-firm tofu can be sliced, cubed or crumbled.

Prep Pressing tofu renders it denser, drier and easier to slice. To press regular tofu, wrap, weight and drain it as shown below for 30 minutes.

Cut the tofu in half horizontally, then sandwich it between several layers of paper towels. Place the tofu on a board, weight it and prop it at a slant near the sink to drain.

Soya Milk

PER 250 ML (1 CUP)	
Kilojoules	373
Fibre	3,2 g
Protein	7 g
Total Fat	4,7 g
Saturated Fat	0,5 g
Cholesterol	0 mg
Sodium	30 mg

NUTRIENTS	
% RDA for people older than 10 years	
Thiamin	29 %
Magnesium	16 %
Riboflavin	11 %

Did you know? . . .

Soya milk builds bones. In a university study, postmenopausal women given calcium-fortified soya milk gained significantly more bone density than women given protein and calcium in the form of milk powder.

Because it's made from a legume, soya milk, unlike dairy milk, contains fibre.

Piña Colada Pudding

PREP: 35 MINUTES / COOK: 10 MINUTES
CHILL: 1 HOUR 20 MINUTES

Cooking the soya milk with coconut creates a 'coconut milk' which is low in saturated fat.

750 ml unflavoured soya milk
125 ml sugar
60 ml dessicated coconut
0,6 ml salt
10 g unflavoured gelatine
250 ml tinned juice-packed crushed pineapple, well drained
2,5 ml almond essence

1. In a small saucepan, bring 675 ml of the soya milk, the sugar, coconut and salt to a boil over moderate heat. Remove from the heat, cover and let stand for 30 minutes at room temperature. Strain into a medium bowl, pushing on the solids to extract as much liquid as possible.

2. In a heatproof measuring cup, sprinkle the gelatine over the remaining soya milk. Let stand for 5 minutes to soften. Place the cup in a small saucepan of simmering water and heat for 2 minutes or until the gelatine is dissolved.

3. Stir the gelatine mixture into the soya-milk mixture. Set the bowl in a larger bowl of ice and water and let stand, stirring occasionally, for 20 minutes or until the mixture begins to set. Fold in the pineapple and almond essence. Spoon the mixture into 4 dessert bowls, cover and chill for 1 hour or until set. Serves 4.

Per serving: Kilojoules 988; Fibre 4 g; Protein 6 g; Total Fat 7 g; Saturated Fat 3 g; Cholesterol 0 mg; Sodium 85 mg

Banana-Chocolate Shake

PREP: 5 MINUTES

A terrific snack, this ultra-thick shake is also a fine dessert; serve with crisp wafer biscuits.

45 ml light brown sugar
30 ml cocoa powder
425 ml unflavoured soya milk
225 g bananas, peeled and thickly sliced (2 large)
30 ml chocolate syrup
5 ml vanilla essence
4 ice cubes

1. In a small bowl, combine the brown sugar and cocoa. Add 125 ml of the soya milk and stir until well moistened and smooth.

2. Transfer the mixture to a blender along with the the remaining 375 ml soya milk, the banana, chocolate syrup, vanilla and ice cubes. Process until smooth, thick and creamy. Serves 2.

Per serving: Kilojoules 1 318; Fibre 6 g; Protein 9 g; Total Fat 9 g; Saturated Fat 2 g; Cholesterol 0 mg; Sodium 196 mg

At the market Soya milk is sold in health food stores and some supermarkets.

Look for Buy unflavoured soya milk for these recipes.

Prep To make your own soya milk for drinking (it's too thin for use in these recipes): Soak 250 ml soya beans in 500 ml cold water for 2 days, covered and refrigerated. Drain. Process beans in a blender until paste-like; add 250 ml water and process until creamy. Add 250 ml water and blend. Strain through several thicknesses of fine cheesecloth into a large saucepan. Bring to a simmer and cook, stirring, for 5 to 10 minutes. Cool; refrigerate in a covered container for up to 5 days.

Soaked, dried soya beans (top) are puréed (bottom) to make soya milk.

__Thai Chicken Stew__ This fast, fresh main dish can be on the table in less than an hour.

Thai Chicken Stew

PREP: 25 MINUTES / COOK: 20 MINUTES

Thai cooking demands a careful balance of tastes and textures. Here a creamy sauce, based on soya milk and peanut butter, is sparked with garlic, fresh ginger and lime juice as well as fresh basil and fresh coriander. Large supermarkets now sell fragrant jasmine rice which is the perfect accompaniment for this stew.

10 ml vegetable oil
1 large red pepper, cut into
**   1-cm squares**
2 cloves garlic, finely chopped
15 ml finely chopped fresh ginger
350 g potatoes, peeled and cut into
**   1-cm pieces**
250 ml chicken stock
450 g skinless, boned chicken breasts,
**   cut into 2,5 cm pieces**
500 ml unflavoured soya milk
70 ml chopped fresh basil
60 ml chopped fresh coriander
30 ml lime or lemon juice
30 ml light soya sauce
15 ml peanut butter
10 ml dark brown sugar

1. In a large nonstick frying pan, heat the oil over moderate heat. Add the pepper, garlic and ginger and sauté for 4 minutes or until the pepper is crisp-tender. Add the potatoes and stock and bring to a boil. Reduce to a simmer, cover and cook for 7 minutes or until the potatoes are firm-tender

2. Add the chicken, soya milk, basil, fresh coriander, lime juice, soya sauce, peanut butter and brown sugar to the pan and bring to a boil. Reduce to a simmer, cover and cook for 5 minutes or until the chicken and potatoes are cooked through. Serves 4.

Per serving: Kilojoules 1 222; Fibre 4 g; Protein 27 g; Total Fat 10 g; Saturated Fat 2 g; Cholesterol 42 mg; Sodium 878 mg

Almonds & Walnuts

Almonds
PER 30 G

Kilojoules	735
Fibre	3,3 g
Protein	6 g
Total Fat	16 g
Saturated Fat	1,5 g
Cholesterol	0 mg
Sodium	3 mg

NUTRIENTS
% RDA for people older than 10 years

Vitamin E	61 %
Magnesium	29 %
Riboflavin	13 %

Walnuts
PER 30 G

Kilojoules	806
Fibre	1,4 g
Protein	4 g
Total Fat	19 g
Saturated Fat	1,7 g
Cholesterol	0 mg
Sodium	3 mg

NUTRIENTS
% RDA for people older than 10 years

Magnesium	17 %
Thiamin	8 %
Vitamin E	8 %

Walnut Bread

PREP: 15 MINUTES
RISE: 2 HOURS 15 MINUTES
COOK: 30 MINUTES

- 10 g active dry yeast
- 30 ml honey
- 310 ml warm water
- 125 ml fat-free milk powder
- 30 ml olive oil
- 925 ml flour (3¾ cups)
- 420 g walnuts, coarsely chopped (3 cups)
- 10 ml salt
- 30 ml full-cream milk

1. In a bowl, sprinkle the yeast over 60 ml of the warm water. Add the honey and let stand for 5 minutes or until dissolved. Stir in the milk powder, oil and the remaining 250 ml of warm water.

2. In a food processor, combine 250 ml of the flour and 140 g of the walnuts and process until smooth. Stir the flour-nut mixture into the yeast mixture along with the remaining 675 ml flour and the salt. Turn out onto a lightly floured surface and knead for 5 minutes or until smooth and elastic. Spray a large bowl with nonstick cooking spray, add the dough and turn to coat. Cover with plastic wrap and let rise in a warm, draft-free spot for 1½ hours or until doubled in bulk.

3. Punch the dough down, transfer to a lightly floured work surface, and flatten. Place 140 g of the walnuts on the dough and fold them in. Continue kneading and adding the remaining 140 g nuts, pushing them into the dough as they pop out. Divide the dough in half, shape into balls and flatten slightly. Place on 2 baking sheets, cover with plastic wrap and let rise in a warm, draft-free spot for 45 minutes or until almost doubled in bulk.

4. Preheat the oven to 190°C. Brush the loaves with the milk; then, with a small paring knife, make 2 slashes in the top of each loaf. Bake for 30 minutes or until the bottoms of the loaves sound hollow when tapped and the tops are richly browned. Cool on a wire rack. Makes 2 loaves/24 servings.

Per serving: Kilojoules 854; Fibre 1 g; Protein 5 g; Total Fat 12 g; Saturated Fat 1 g; Cholesterol 1 mg; Sodium 215 mg

Almond Brittle

PREP: 10 MINUTES / COOK: 15 MINUTES

- 170 g whole natural almonds, coarsely chopped (1 cup)
- 70 ml slivered almonds
- 45 ml sesame seeds
- 175 ml sugar
- 125 ml honey
- 5 ml vanilla essence
- 1,25 ml bicarbonate of soda
- 15 ml unsalted butter
- 250 ml air-popped popcorn (1 cup)

1. Preheat the oven to 180°C. Toast the chopped and slivered almonds for 5 minutes or until golden brown. In a separate pan, toast the sesame seeds for 5 minutes or until lightly browned. Spray a large baking sheet with nonstick cooking spray and set aside.

2. In a medium saucepan, combine the sugar, honey and 70 ml of water. Cook over moderately high heat, stirring until the sugar has dissolved. Continue to cook, without stirring, for 7 minutes or until the sugar mixture reaches 144°C on a sugar thermometer.

3. Immediately remove from the heat and stir in the vanilla, bicarbonate of soda and butter. Working as quickly as possible, add the almonds, sesame seeds and popcorn, stirring to coat. Quickly transfer to the prepared tin and use an oiled metal spatula to spread the brittle as flat as possible before it begins to harden. Cool to room temperature, then break the brittle into bite-size pieces. Makes 500 grams.

Per 50 g: Kilojoules 1 086; Fibre 2 g; Protein 5 g; Total Fat 14 g; Saturated Fat 2 g; Cholesterol 3 mg; Sodium 35 mg

Almond Brittle *This old-fashioned sweet is made with sesame seeds as well as almonds.*

Chinese Walnut Chicken

PREP: 20 MINUTES / COOK: 20 MINUTES

The walnuts are coated in a sweet, crunchy glaze, then added to stir-fried chicken and vegetables.

- **30 ml vegetable oil**
- **37 ml sugar**
- **140 g walnut halves (1 cup)**
- **1 large red pepper, cut into 1-cm squares**
- **4 spring onions, cut into 1-cm lengths**
- **2 cloves garlic, finely chopped**
- **15 ml finely chopped fresh ginger**
- **450 g skinless, boned chicken breasts, cut into 2,5-cm pieces**
- **250 ml chicken stock**
- **15 ml soya sauce**
- **5 ml sesame oil**
- **7,5 ml cornflour**

1. In a medium pan, heat 5 ml of the vegetable oil over moderate heat. Add 30 ml of the sugar, stirring to combine. Add the walnuts and cook, stirring constantly, for 7 minutes or until the walnuts are nicely coated and lightly crisped; set aside.

2. In a large nonstick pan, heat the remaining 10 ml vegetable oil over moderately high heat. Add the pepper and sauté for 2 minutes or until crisp-tender. Add the spring onions, garlic and ginger and cook for 2 minutes. Add the chicken and sauté for 4 minutes or until no longer pink.

3. In a small bowl, whisk the stock, soya sauce, sesame oil and the remaining 3,5 ml sugar into the cornflour. Add to the pan, bring to a boil and cook for 3 minutes or until the sauce is slightly thickened and the chicken is cooked through. Stir in the walnuts. Serves 4.

Per serving: Kilojoules 1 907; Fibre 2 g; Protein 26 g; Total Fat 33 g; Saturated Fat 4 g; Cholesterol 42 mg; Sodium 631 mg

At the market
Almonds and walnuts are sold both in the shell and shelled. Whole shelled almonds are sold natural, blanched or roasted; they also come slivered or sliced. Shelled walnuts are sold whole, in large pieces or chopped.

Top row: whole almonds, blanched and natural. Bottom row: sliced natural and slivered blanched almonds.

Look for When buying nuts in the shell, look for clean, uncracked shells. When buying shelled nuts in bulk, check for a pleasant smell; if left too long, nuts will turn rancid.

Basic cooking Toasting almonds and walnuts brings out their flavour. Toast them in a heavy, ungreased pan on the stovetop (or in a shallow baking tin in the oven) for 5 to 7 minutes, shaking the pan frequently; as soon as the nuts are lightly browned turn them out of the pan or they will overcook from the heat retained by the pan.

Walnut-Crusted Hake *Present this savoury baked fish on a bed of steamed vegetables—perhaps a toss of baby marrow, pattipans and carrots.*

Did you know? . . .
Although walnuts and almonds are high in fat, most of it is unsaturated. Almonds are rich in monounsaturates; walnuts are highly polyunsaturated.

Research subjects who ate nuts frequently lowered their risk of heart disease.

A major study of Seventh-Day Adventists (who are vegetarians) revealed that those who ate walnuts, almonds and peanuts almost every day increased their life expectancy and greatly reduced their risk of heart disease.

Almonds are the most nutritious nuts, providing more calcium and iron than other nuts. They also supply more dietary fibre than any other nut.

Storing nuts in the freezer, in a tightly closed container, will help keep them from turning rancid.

Gram for gram, walnuts contain more potassium than bananas.

Walnut-Crusted Hake

PREP: 10 MINUTES / COOK: 15 MINUTES

Light mayonnaise is the basis for the sauce, which puffs lightly as it bakes. Ordinary mayonnaise can be substituted, but the fat content will be much higher.

- 45 ml light mayonnaise
- 2,5 ml grated lemon rind
- 5 ml lemon juice
- 1,25 ml each salt and pepper
- 4 hake fillets (175 g each), skinned
- 70 g walnut halves
- 30 ml grated Parmesan cheese

1. Preheat the oven to 180°C. Spray a large baking sheet with nonstick cooking spray; set aside.

2. In a small bowl, combine the mayonnaise, lemon rind, lemon juice, salt and pepper. Place the fillets, skinned-side down, on the prepared baking sheet. Spread the mayonnaise mixture over the fish.

3. In a food processor, process the walnuts and Parmesan until finely ground (but not pasty). Sprinkle the nut mixture over the fish, patting it on.

Bake for 15 minutes or until the nuts are lightly browned and the fish is just cooked through. Serves 4.

Per serving: Kilojoules 1 255; Fibre 1 g; Protein 32 g; Total Fat 17 g; Saturated Fat 2 g; Cholesterol 42 mg; Sodium 440 mg

Pasta with Almond-Basil Pesto

PREP: 10 MINUTES / COOK: 15 MINUTES

Almonds make a healthier (and cheaper) pesto than the more traditional pine nuts.

- 4 cloves garlic, peeled
- 280 g fusilli, radiatore or wagon wheel pasta
- 60 g basil leaves (2 cups packed)
- 70 ml chicken stock
- 50 g whole natural almonds, toasted
- 70 ml grated Parmesan cheese
- 2,5 ml salt

1. In a large pot of boiling water, cook the garlic for 4 minutes to blanch. Scoop out with a slotted spoon and transfer to a food processor.

2. Add the pasta to the boiling water and cook according to package directions until *al dente*. Drain.

3. Meanwhile, to the garlic in the food processor, add the basil, stock and almonds and purée. Transfer to a large bowl and stir in the Parmesan and salt. Add the hot pasta to the bowl, tossing to combine. Serves 4.

Per serving: Kilojoules 1504; Fibre 4g; Protein 14g; Total Fat 10g; Saturated Fat 2g; Cholesterol 5mg; Sodium 527mg

Chocolate-Almond Bars

PREP: 10 MINUTES / COOK: 15 MINUTES

A good amount of nutrition-packed almonds, rather than butter, makes these bars rich.

  375ml flaked almonds
     plus 30 almond flakes for garnish
  125ml sugar
  45ml cocoa powder
  1,25ml salt
  1 egg white
  5ml vanilla essence
  70ml red raspberry jam or coulis

1. Preheat the oven to 180°C. Spray a large baking sheet with nonstick cooking spray.

2. In a food processor, combine the 375ml almonds, the sugar, cocoa and salt and process until finely ground. Add the egg white and vanilla essence and process until the mixture forms a very stiff dough.

3. Transfer the dough to the prepared baking sheet. With moistened hands, shape the dough into a log 48cm long and 2cm in diameter. With moistened fingers, make an indentation down the centre of the log. Bake for 15 minutes or until set.

4. Meanwhile, in a small saucepan, melt the jam (or coulis) over low heat. Spoon the hot jam into the indentation in the log. Transfer to a wire rack to cool completely. When cool, slice cross-wise into 30 strips (about 1-cm wide). Place an almond flake on top of the jam in each bar. Makes 30 almond bars.

Per almond bar: Kilojoules 211; Fibre 1g; Protein 1g; Total Fat 3g; Saturated Fat 0g; Cholesterol 0mg; Sodium 27mg

Green Beans Amandine In a large pot of boiling water, cook 450g green beans until crisp-tender; drain. In large pan, heat 10ml olive oil and 10ml unsalted butter until melted. Add 40g slivered almonds, tossing to coat. Add beans and 1,25ml salt and cook until heated through. Serves 4. *[kJ 596; Fat 10g; Sodium 157mg]*

Chicken Salad with Almond Dressing In a food processor, purée 30g whole almonds, 60ml light mayonnaise, 30ml lemon juice and 2,5ml salt. Transfer to large bowl. Add 500ml diced cooked chicken, 2 sliced celery stalks and 250ml (1 cup) halved seedless grapes; toss to coat. Serve on a bed of lettuce and garnish with sliced almonds. Serves 4. *[kJ 1188; Fat 12g; Sodium 496mg]*

Spiced Walnuts In a large heavy pan, heat 15ml oil over moderate heat. Add 280g walnut halves, tossing to coat. Add 45ml sugar, 2,5ml salt and 2,5ml cayenne pepper and cook, stirring constantly, for 8 minutes or until nuts are well coated and sugar has caramelized. Serve hot or at room temperature. Serves 12. *[kJ 721; Fat 16g; Sodium 103mg]*

Peanuts

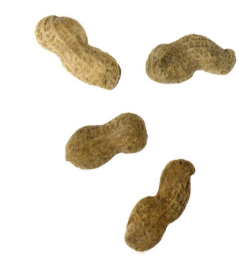

PER 30G DRY-ROASTED	
Kilojoules	729
Fibre	2,6g
Protein	8g
Total Fat	15g
Saturated Fat	2,1g
Cholesterol	0mg
Sodium	2mg

NUTRIENTS	
% RDA for people older than 10 years	
Niacin	24%
Vitamin E	21%
Magnesium	19%
Folate	9%

Did you know? . . .

It has recently been discovered that peanuts, like red wine, contain an antioxidant called resveratrol—which has been associated with a lowered risk of heart disease. The red skin of the peanut (which most people usually discard) has a higher concentration of resveratrol than the nut itself.

Peanut Butter Blondies

PREP: 15 MINUTES / COOK: 25 MINUTES

Prune purée takes the place of most of the shortening in this recipe.

250 ml flour
2,5 ml each baking powder and bicarbonate of soda
1,25 ml salt
70 ml pitted prunes
60 ml hot water
70 ml crunchy peanut butter
30 ml peanut or other vegetable oil
150 ml packed light brown sugar
30 ml honey
1 egg
5 ml vanilla essence

1. Preheat oven to 180°C. Spray a 23-cm square baking tin with nonstick cooking spray; set aside. In a small bowl, whisk together the flour, baking powder, bicarbonate of soda and salt. In a food processor, process the prunes and hot water until smooth.

2. In a medium bowl, beat the peanut butter, oil and brown sugar with an electric mixer until creamy. Beat in the prune purée and honey until well combined. Beat in the egg and vanilla essence until well combined. Fold in the flour mixture.

3. Spoon the batter into the prepared tin. Bake for 25 minutes or until a cake tester inserted in the centre comes out clean. Cool the cake in the tin on a rack. Cut into 16 squares. Makes 16.

Per blondie: Kilojoules 500; Fibre 1g; Protein 2g; Total Fat 4g; Saturated Fat 1g; Cholesterol 13mg; Sodium 127mg

Banana, Apple & Peanut Salad

PREP: 15 MINUTES

You can make the dressing ahead of time, but don't mix the salad too far in advance or the bananas will get mushy and the peanuts will lose their crunch.

70 ml honey
2,5 ml grated lemon rind
45 ml lemon juice
1,25 ml salt
1,25 ml ground ginger
0,6 ml grated nutmeg
450 g bananas, cut into 1-cm-thick slices
450 g apples, cut into 1-cm pieces
100 g dry-roasted peanuts, coarsely chopped

1. In a large bowl, whisk together the honey, lemon rind, lemon juice, salt, ginger and nutmeg.

2. Add the bananas, apples and peanuts, tossing to combine. Serves 4.

Per serving: Kilojoules 1673; Fibre 7g; Protein 8g; Total Fat 13g; Saturated Fat 2g; Cholesterol 0mg; Sodium 159mg

Chicken Satay with Peanut Sauce *Spicy chicken with a rich sauce and a cooling relish.*

Chicken Satay with Peanut Sauce

PREP: 25 MINUTES / COOK: 10 MINUTES

A savoury peanut sauce is the traditional accompaniment for this Indonesian specialty. Garnish the dish with additional crushed peanuts and coriander sprigs.

45 ml rice vinegar
10 ml sesame oil
10 ml sugar
0,6 ml crushed red chilli flakes
2 large cucumbers, peeled, seeded, and cut into 5-mm dice
1 small red pepper, diced
450 g skinless, boned chicken breasts, cut into 2,5-cm pieces
2,5 ml each ground coriander, salt and black pepper
2 cloves garlic, peeled
80 g dry-roasted peanuts
70 ml packed fresh coriander sprigs
125 ml chicken stock
30 ml lime or lemon juice

1. In a medium bowl, whisk together the vinegar, sesame oil, 5 ml of the sugar and the red chilli flakes. Add the cucumbers and red pepper, tossing to combine. Refrigerate until serving time.

2. Preheat the grill. In a medium bowl, toss the chicken with the coriander, salt and black pepper; set aside.

3. In a small pot of boiling water, cook the garlic for 4 minutes to blanch. Transfer to a food processor along with the peanuts, fresh coriander, stock, lime juice and the remaining 5 ml sugar. Purée.

4. Thread the chicken onto eight 20-cm skewers. Grill 15 centimetres from the heat, turning the skewers once, for 5 minutes or until cooked through. Serve 2 skewers of chicken per person, with the peanut sauce and cucumber salad alongside. Serves 4.

Per serving: Kilojoules 1123; Fibre 3g; Protein 26g; Total Fat 15g; Saturated Fat 2g; Cholesterol 42mg; Sodium 531mg

At the market The ever-popular peanut is available in the shell or shelled, unroasted, oil-roasted or dry-roasted. The most commonly produced peanut in South Africa is the common Natal peanut. Giant peanuts are imported from China, India and the United States.

Instead of oil-roasted peanuts, which are very high in fat, use either unroasted peanuts (above) or dry-roasted peanuts for these recipes.

Look for If you're buying peanuts in the shell, choose nuts with clean, uncracked shells. If you're buying shelled peanuts in bulk, sniff them to be sure they're not rancid.

Prep You can toast shelled peanuts—on the stovetop in a heavy, ungreased pan or in a 180°C oven in a shallow baking dish—for 7 minutes, shaking the pan frequently. In-shell peanuts can be roasted in a shallow pan for about 15 minutes in a 180°C oven.

Sunflower &
Pumpkin seeds

Sunflower Seeds
PER 30G

Kilojoules	716
Fibre	2,0g
Protein	7g
Total Fat	15g
Saturated Fat	1,6g
Cholesterol	0mg
Sodium	1mg

NUTRIENTS
% RDA for people older than 10 years

Vitamin E	148%
Thiamin	49%
Magnesium	35%
Vitamin B6	19%
Folate	17%

Pumpkin Seeds
PER 30G

Kilojoules	679
Fibre	1,1g
Protein	7g
Total Fat	14g
Saturated Fat	2,6g
Cholesterol	0mg
Sodium	5mg

NUTRIENTS
% RDA for people older than 10 years

Magnesium	54%
Phosphorus	44%
Iron	32%

Sunflower Drop Scones

PREP: 10 MINUTES / COOK: 15 MINUTES

Buttermilk in the batter keeps these drop scones, or flapjacks, light and tender. They're a delicious addition to breakfast or brunch and are also tasty with soup and salad as a lunch or light supper.

375 ml flour
8 ml baking powder
2,5 ml each bicarbonate of soda
  and salt
0,6 ml cayenne pepper
30 ml each unsalted butter and solid
  vegetable shortening
125 ml dry-roasted sunflower seeds
175 ml low-fat cultured buttermilk

1. Preheat the oven to 230°C. Spray a large baking sheet with nonstick cooking spray; set aside.

2. In a large bowl, combine the flour, baking powder, bicarbonate of soda, salt and cayenne. With a pastry blender or two knives, cut in the butter and shortening until the mixture resembles coarse crumbs. Stir in the sunflower seeds. Stir in the buttermilk until the mixture forms a soft dough. Do not overmix.

3. Drop well-rounded tablespoons (15 ml) of the dough 5 centimetres apart onto the prepared baking sheet. Bake for 12 minutes or until the drop scones are golden brown and crusty. Makes 12 drop scones.

Per drop scone: Kilojoules 563; Fibre 1g; Protein 3g; Total Fat 8g; Saturated Fat 2g; Cholesterol 6mg; Sodium 159mg

Mexican Chicken with Pumpkin Seed Sauce

PREP: 15 MINUTES / COOK: 25 MINUTES

The sweet red pepper, chillies, tomato and lime juice in this dish combine to supply the daily adult requirement for vitamin C.

125 ml shelled pumpkin seeds
2 large green chillies, seeded and
  chopped
1 large tomato, cut into large pieces
125 ml chicken stock
125 ml chopped fresh coriander
  or parsley
10 ml olive oil
1 large red pepper, cut into 1-cm
  squares
450 g skinless, boned chicken thighs,
  cut into 2,5-cm pieces
2,5 ml salt
250 ml frozen corn kernels
15 ml lime or lemon juice

1. In a small frying pan, toast the pumpkin seeds over low heat for 3 minutes or until they begin to pop in the pan. Transfer to a blender or food processor. Add the chillies, tomato, stock and fresh coriander. Process until smooth.

2. In a large nonstick pan, heat the oil over moderate heat. Add the pepper and cook for 4 minutes or until crisp-tender. Add the chicken and sauté for 4 minutes or until browned all over. Stir in the pumpkin-seed mixture and salt and cook for 7 minutes or until the chicken is cooked through and the sauce is flavourful.

3. Stir in the corn kernels and lime juice and simmer for 5 minutes or until the corn kernels are piping hot. Serves 4.

*Per serving: Kilojoules 1 306; Fibre 3g;
Protein 37g; Total Fat 17g; Saturated Fat 4g;
Cholesterol 55mg; Sodium 543mg*

Crispy Seed-Topped Flat Breads

PREP: 1 HOUR 10 MINUTES
COOK: 15 MINUTES

These Near Eastern-style 'crackers' are sprinkled with pumpkin seeds, sunflower seeds and grated Parmesan.

560ml flour
3,5ml salt
1,25ml cayenne pepper
15ml each unsalted butter and solid vegetable shortening
1 egg white lightly beaten with 10ml water
60ml each shelled pumpkin seeds and shelled, dry-roasted sunflower seeds
30ml plus 10ml grated Parmesan cheese

1. In a medium bowl, combine the flour, salt and cayenne. With a pastry blender or two knives, cut in the butter and shortening until the mixture resembles coarse crumbs. Gradually add 150ml of water to make a soft, smooth dough. Knead for 5 minutes or until smooth and elastic. Transfer to a bowl that has been sprayed with nonstick cooking spray, cover, and let rest for 1 hour.

2. Preheat the oven to 220°C. Spray 2 large baking sheets with nonstick cooking spray (or use nonstick pans); set aside. Cut the dough into 4 pieces. Roll each piece out to a 23-cm round (about 2-mm thick). Transfer to the prepared baking sheets. Brush the dough with the egg-white mixture. Sprinkle the pumpkin and sunflower seeds over the dough. Sprinkle each dough round with 10ml of the Parmesan. Bake for 12 minutes or until the bread is lightly puffed, golden brown and crisp. Serves 12.

*Per serving: Kilojoules 582; Fibre 1g;
Protein 4g; Total Fat 5g; Saturated Fat 1g;
Cholesterol 4mg; Sodium 190mg*

At the market Pumpkin and sunflower seeds are sold in and out of their shells, plain or roasted.

Shelled sunflower seeds (left) and pumpkin seeds should be plump and meaty. Those shown here are unroasted.

Look for When buying in-shell pumpkin and sunflower seeds in bulk, look for clean, unbroken shells; there should be a minimum of debris in the bin.

Prep When cooking a pumpkin, don't throw out the seeds. Scoop them out, rinse them and let them dry. Then toast the seeds in a 180°C oven for 8 to 10 minutes or until crisp. To enhance their flavour, toast shelled pumpkin seeds in an ungreased pan over very low heat for 3 minutes or until they begin to pop.

Crispy Seed-Topped Flat Breads *Serve these savoury breads with dips or with dinner.*

Fish & Shellfish

Asian-Style Red Stumpnose

Salmo

Fresh Salmon*

PER 120 G COOKED	
Kilojoules	1034
Fibre	0 g
Protein	27 g
Total Fat	14,8 g
Saturated Fat	3 g
Cholesterol	76 mg
Sodium	73 mg

NUTRIENTS

% RDA for people older than 10 years

Vitamin B12	336 %
Niacin	54 %
Vitamin B6	39 %
Thiamin	29 %

* Atlantic, farmed

Tinned Red Salmon*

PER 100 G	
Kilojoules	642
Fibre	0 g
Protein	20,5 g
Total Fat	7,3 g
Saturated Fat	1,6 g
Cholesterol	44 mg
Sodium	538 mg

NUTRIENTS

% RDA for people older than 10 years

Vitamin B12	420 %
Niacin	31 %
Calcium	20 %

* drained solids

Salmon Steaks Veracruz-Style

PREP: 15 MINUTES / COOK: 55 MINUTES

Fresh salmon is an expensive, yet healthy, treat. A somewhat sharp tomato sauce, with the kick of capers and chilli, cuts the richness of the fish in this Mexican specialty.

10 ml olive oil
1 small onion, finely chopped
2 cloves garlic, finely chopped
5 ml chilli powder
1 tin (410 g) tomatoes, chopped with their juice
1 green chilli (or pickled jalapeño), finely chopped
60 ml pitted green olives, coarsely chopped
7,5 ml capers, rinsed and drained
1,25 ml dried oreganum
1,25 ml dried thyme
0,6 ml ground cinnamon
0,6 ml salt
4 salmon steaks (225 g each)
30 ml lime or lemon juice

1. In a large nonstick pan, heat the oil over moderate heat. Add the onion and garlic and sauté for 5 minutes or until soft. Add the chilli powder, stirring to coat. Add the tomatoes, fresh chilli, olives, capers, oreganum, thyme, cinnamon, salt and 60 ml of water and bring to a boil. Reduce to a simmer, cover and cook for 30 minutes or until the sauce is richly flavoured.

2. Preheat the oven to 180°C. Sprinkle the salmon with the lime juice and place in a 23 x 33-cm baking dish. Spoon 175 ml of the sauce over the fish and bake for 15 to 20 minutes or

until the salmon just flakes when tested with a fork. Reheat the remaining sauce and spoon over the fish before serving. Serves 4.

Per serving: Kilojoules 1 637; Fibre 2 g; Protein 36 g; Total Fat 26 g; Saturated Fat 5 g; Cholesterol 99 mg; Sodium 467 mg

Cold Poached Salmon with Herbed Mayonnaise

PREP: 10 MINUTES / COOK: 15 MINUTES

This elegant presentation is ideal for a summer dinner party.

1 medium onion, sliced
1 medium carrot, thinly sliced
6 whole black peppercorns
650 g salmon fillet, in one piece, skin on
60 ml light mayonnaise
45 ml sour cream
15 ml lime or lemon juice
60 ml chopped fresh basil
30 ml snipped chives or spring onions

1. In a large pan, bring 750 ml of water to a boil over moderate heat. Add the onion, carrot and peppercorns and reduce to a simmer. Slip in the fish, skin-side up; cover and simmer for 10 minutes or until the salmon is just cooked through. Cool in the poaching liquid. Reserving 30 ml of the poaching liquid, lift the fish out, transfer to a platter, cover and refrigerate until chilled. Discard the remaining poaching liquid and the solids.

Salmon Steaks Veracruz-Style A sophisticated fish dish with piquant Mexican flavours.

2. In a medium bowl, whisk together the reserved poaching liquid, the mayonnaise, sour cream and lime juice. Stir in the basil and chives. Refrigerate until serving time.

3. At serving time, remove the salmon skin and cut the fillet into 4 portions. Serve the chilled salmon with the sauce spooned on top. Serves 4.

Per serving: Kilojoules 1 416; Fibre 1g; Protein 26g; Total Fat 22g; Saturated Fat 5g; Cholesterol 87mg; Sodium 223mg

Baked Salmon Parcels with Baby Peas

PREP: 10 MINUTES / COOK: 15 MINUTES

This dinner party dish never fails to impress—it looks, smells and tastes great, but is simplicity itself to make. Parchment paper can be found in most supermarkets. If none is available, foil may be used instead. Parchment baking is suitable for most types of fish. See Techniques page 39 for instructions on baking food in packets.

360g frozen baby peas, thawed
2 spring onions, thinly sliced
60ml chopped fresh mint
30ml lemon juice
10ml olive oil
3,5ml salt
4 salmon fillets, skinned
   (175g each)

1. Preheat the oven to 230°C. In a medium bowl, toss together the peas, spring onions, mint, lemon juice, oil and 1,25ml of the salt.

2. Spray four 38-cm lengths of parchment paper or foil with nonstick cooking spray. Place the salmon fillets, rounded-side up, on one half of each piece of parchment paper. Sprinkle the salmon with the remaining salt and top with the pea mixture. Fold the other half of the paper over the salmon and fold the edges over once or twice to seal the parcels.

3. Lift the 'salmon parcels' carefully and place on a baking sheet. Bake for 12 to 15 minutes or until the parcels are puffed and the salmon is medium-rare to medium. Serves 4.

Per serving: Kilojoules 1 487 ; Fibre 8g; Protein 32g; Total Fat 18g; Saturated Fat 4g; Cholesterol 77mg; Sodium 504mg

Shopping & prep

At the market Fresh salmon is sold whole, in steaks and in fillets and originates mainly in Alaska or Canada. Most tinned salmon is pink salmon; tinned sockeye salmon is deeper in colour, richer in flavour and more expensive.

Look for Fresh salmon should smell like an ocean breeze, not 'fishy'. Steaks or fillets should look moist and slightly translucent; the flesh should feel resilient.

Prep Salmon steaks and fillets sometimes contain 'pin bones' firmly embedded in the flesh. Run your fingers over the surface of the fish to find them, then remove them with large tweezers.

To remove skin from a salmon fillet, slip a knife between skin and flesh and 'saw' it gently along, pulling the skin taut as you go.

Basic cooking Poach salmon in a large covered pan of simmering water for 10 minutes or until the fish barely flakes when tested with a knife.

Tuna

Fresh Tuna
PER 120 G COOKED

Kilojoules	924
Fibre	0 g
Protein	36 g
Total Fat	7,5 g
Saturated Fat	1,9 g
Cholesterol	80 mg
Sodium	60 mg

NUTRIENTS

% RDA for people older than 10 years

Vitamin B12	1305 %
Niacin	70 %
Vitamin B6	32 %
Magnesium	26 %

Tinned Tuna*
PER 120 G

Kilojoules	584
Fibre	0 g
Protein	31 g
Total Fat	1 g
Saturated Fat	0,3 g
Cholesterol	36 mg
Sodium	406 mg

NUTRIENTS

% RDA for people older than 10 years

Vitamin B12	360 %
Niacin	89 %
Vitamin B6	21 %

water-packed white, drained

Tuna with Roasted Onion Relish
PREP: 10 MINUTES / COOK: 50 MINUTES

- 12 ml sugar
- 5 ml salt
- 6,25 ml dried oreganum
- 2,5 ml pepper
- 0,6 ml allspice
- 650 g large onions (red, if available), cut into 1-cm cubes
- 20 ml olive oil
- 1 large tomato, diced
- 30 ml red wine vinegar
- 4 tuna steaks (175 g each)

1. Preheat the oven to 180°C. In a medium bowl, combine the sugar, 2,5 ml of the salt, the oreganum, pepper and allspice. Add the onions and 10 ml of the oil, tossing well to coat. Transfer to a 23 x 33-cm baking dish, cover with foil and bake for 30 minutes, stirring occasionally. Uncover and bake for 10 minutes. Transfer to a bowl, stir in the tomato and vinegar and cool to room temperature.

2. On a grill pan or in a large nonstick pan, heat the remaining 10 ml oil over moderately high heat. Sprinkle the remaining 2,5 ml salt over the tuna and cook, turning the fish over midway, for 5 minutes or until medium-rare. Serve with the relish spooned on top. Serves 4.

Per serving: Kilojoules 1521; Fibre 3 g; Protein 38 g; Total Fat 13 g; Saturated Fat 3 g; Cholesterol 82 mg; Sodium 688 mg

Chilli-Garlic Grilled Tuna
PREP: 10 MINUTES / COOK: 10 MINUTES

Fresh tuna is so dense, meaty and flavourful that it makes a welcome alternative to beef steaks at a braai. If you can't find green jalapeño pepper sauce at your local supermarket, use the regular red-coloured hot pepper sauce—adjust the amount according to your taste.

- 2 cloves garlic, finely chopped
- 2,5 ml crushed red chilli flakes
- 2,5 ml salt
- 4 tuna steaks, 2,5 cm thick (225 g each)
- 15 ml green jalapeño pepper sauce
- 20 ml olive oil

1. Heat the grill or prepare the braai. In a small bowl, combine the garlic, chilli flakes and salt. With a sharp, thin knife, make several horizontal slits into the sides of each tuna steak. Insert the garlic-pepper flake mixture into the slits.

2. Rub each tuna steak all over with the green jalapeño pepper sauce and oil. Grill or braai the tuna steaks 15 centimetres from the heat for 3 minutes per side or until the tuna is cooked to medium-rare. Serves 4.

Per serving: Kilojoules 1419; Fibre 0 g; Protein 47 g; Total Fat 15 g; Saturated Fat 3 g; Cholesterol 106 mg; Sodium 402 mg

Tuna Salad Niçoise

PREP: 15 MINUTES / COOK: 20 MINUTES

Tinned tuna is the traditional choice for this summery salad from Provence.

- 3 cloves garlic, peeled
- 225 g green beans, cut into 2,5-cm lengths
- 350 g small potatoes (red, if available), halved
- 60 ml balsamic or red wine vinegar
- 30 ml light mayonnaise
- 15 ml olive oil
- 2,5 ml salt
- 60 ml packed fresh basil leaves
- 450 g tomatoes, cut into 1-cm-thick wedges
- 2 tins (185 g each) water-packed tuna, drained
- 180 g torn cos lettuce (3 cups)
- 60 ml black olives

1. In a large pot of boiling water, cook the garlic for 3 minutes to blanch. With a slotted spoon, transfer the garlic to a food processor or blender; set aside. Add the green beans to the boiling water and cook for 4 minutes or until crisp-tender. Remove the beans with a slotted spoon, rinse under cold water and drain. Add the potatoes to the pot and cook for 12 minutes or until tender; drain.

2. Add the vinegar, mayonnaise, oil and salt to the garlic in the food processor and purée. Add the basil and 30 ml of water and purée.

3. Transfer the dressing to a large bowl. Add the tomatoes, green beans, potatoes and tuna, tossing to coat. Add the lettuce and toss again. Sprinkle the olives on top. Serves 4.

Per serving: Kilojoules 1 189; Fibre 6 g; Protein 24 g; Total Fat 8 g; Saturated Fat 1 g; Cholesterol 26 mg; Sodium 732 mg

Tuna Salad Niçoise *This light but satisfying salad features a heady basil dressing.*

At the market

Tuna is also known as 'tunny'. Yellowfin and longfin tuna are both available in summer and autumn, while bluefin and big eye are available during winter and spring. Tinned tuna is packed 'solid' (usually a single piece of tuna), flaked or in chunks. It is tinned in brine, oil or spring water and in various combinations of flavours.

The distinctive patterning of tuna can be clearly seen in a tin of solid-packed tuna.

Look for Fresh tuna looks more like meat than fish. Yellowfin is deep red. The steaks should have a pleasant saltwater smell; they should look moist and dense and feel springy to the touch. Tins of tuna should not be dented or damaged.

Basic cooking Grill or braai tuna steaks for 3 minutes per side or until medium-rare, or bake for 7 to 10 minutes in a 200°C oven. Don't let the steaks get too dry.

Meaty fish

High-Fat Fish*
PER 120G COOKED

Kilojoules	988
Fibre	0g
Protein	24,1g
Total Fat	15,6g
Saturated Fat	3,9g
Cholesterol	96mg
Sodium	132mg

NUTRIENTS

% RDA for people older than 10 years	
Vitamin B12	600%
Vitamin B6	50%
Niacin	47%
Thiamin	17%
Magnesium	12%

Average for HIGH FAT FISH (11-30% fat)

The following fish are included in the category HIGH FAT FISH:
Barracuda
Butterfish
Eel
Herring
Mackerel
Salmon
Swordfish

Grilled Marinated Yellowtail Steaks

PREP: 10 MINUTES / MARINATE: 1 HOUR / COOK: 10 MINUTES

If you want to persuade someone to start eating fish, try this recipe for yellowtail. It is also suitable for swordfish, tuna or marlin.

60 ml tomato sauce
30 ml balsamic vinegar
10 ml light brown sugar
10 ml olive oil
5 ml red hot pepper sauce
2,5 ml each dried oreganum and ground ginger
1,25 ml salt
4 yellowtail steaks (175 g each)

1. In a shallow bowl, combine the tomato sauce, vinegar, brown sugar, oil, hot pepper sauce, oreganum, ginger and salt. Add the yellowtail and rub the tomato-sauce mixture into both sides. Cover and refrigerate for at least 1 hour.

2. Preheat the grill to medium. Reserving the marinade, grill the yellowtail 15 centimetres from the heat for 4 minutes. Turn the fish over, spoon on the reserved marinade and grill for 4 minutes or until the fish is just cooked through. Alternatively, braai the fish over medium coals about 20 centimetres from the heat, basting with the sauce. Serves 4.

Per serving: Kilojoules 1 021; Fibre 0g; Protein 35g; Total Fat 8g; Saturated Fat 2g; Cholesterol 69mg; Sodium 374mg

Yellowtail Kebabs with Lemon-Garlic Sauce

PREP: 20 MINUTES / COOK: 10 MINUTES

These kebabs can also be made with swordfish, geelbek or kabeljou. If using wooden skewers, soak them in cold water for 30 minutes to prevent them from scorching.

3 cloves garlic, peeled
60 ml lemon juice
20 ml olive oil
15 ml chopped parsley
60 ml chicken stock
2,5 ml each sugar and salt
1,25 ml pepper
650 g yellowtail steaks, skinned and cut into 24 pieces
16 cherry tomatoes
1 medium onion (red, if available), cut into 8 pieces

1. In a small pot of boiling water, cook the garlic for 2 minutes to blanch. Finely chop the garlic and transfer it to a small bowl along with the lemon juice, 15 ml of the oil and the parsley. Set the sauce aside.

2. Preheat the grill. In a medium bowl, combine the stock, sugar, salt and pepper. Add the fish, tomatoes and onion, tossing gently to coat. Reserving the stock, alternately thread the fish, tomatoes and onions onto eight 20-cm skewers.

3. Add the remaining 5 ml oil to the reserved stock mixture. Brush the

At the market Marlin and swordfish are becoming increasingly popular. Yellowtail and geelbek (Cape Salmon) are freshly available from October to January. Kabeljou, yellowtail and geelbek are caught by skiboat fisherman and are often available as 'catch of the day'. Kingklip is the most popular fish in South Africa and the season lasts from April to October, peaking in July.

Look for Fish should smell clean and look almost translucent. The flesh should spring back when pressed.

Prep Steaks and fillets come ready to cook, except for monkfish fillets, which have a tough membrane on one side which must be peeled off.

Slide a knife between the monkfish fillet and the membrane, and pull the membrane off.

Basic cooking Measure the thickness of the fish and cook it about 10 minutes per 2,5 centimetres of thickness.

Yellowtail Kebabs with Lemon-Garlic Sauce *Serve over orzo tossed with vegetables.*

stock-oil mixture on the skewered fish and vegetables. Grill 15 centimetres from the heat for 6 minutes, turning the skewers over once or until the fish is just cooked through and the onion is lightly browned. Spoon the lemon-garlic sauce over the kebabs. Alternately, braai the kebabs over medium coals, basting with the sauce. Serves 4.

Per serving: Kilojoules 1 079; Fibre 1g; Protein 33g; Total Fat 11g; Saturated Fat 2g; Cholesterol 64mg; Sodium 517mg

Sautéed Parmesan-Crusted Monkfish

PREP: 20 MINUTES / COOK: 15 MINUTES

Rare to the South African table, fresh monkfish is so meaty and delicately sweet that it is sometimes called 'poor man's crayfish'. Monkfish fillets are sheathed in a tough membrane, which should be removed before cooking (see how-to photo at right). Kingklip can also be used in this recipe.

650g monkfish fillets (2,5 cm thick), thinly sliced into 16 slices
125ml grated Parmesan cheese
4 egg whites
175ml plain dry bread crumbs
2,5ml salt

20ml vegetable oil
4 lemon wedges

1. Preheat the oven to 200°C. Spray a baking sheet with nonstick cooking spray; set aside. Place the monkfish slices between 2 sheets of greaseproof paper and pound the fish to a 5-mm thickness.

2. Spread the Parmesan on a sheet of greaseproof paper. In a shallow dish, lightly beat the egg whites with 45ml of water. In another shallow dish combine the bread crumbs and salt. Dip the fish slices first in the Parmesan, then into the egg whites, then into the bread-crumb mixture, patting the bread crumbs onto the fish.

3. In a large nonstick pan, heat 5ml of the oil over moderately high heat. Sauté 4 slices of the fish for 1 minute per side or until golden brown and crispy. Transfer to the prepared baking sheet. Repeat with the remaining oil and fish. Bake the fish for 5 minutes or until just cooked through. Serve with the lemon wedges for squeezing. Serves 4.

Per serving: Kilojoules 1 145; Fibre 1g; Protein 36g; Total Fat 10g; Saturated Fat 3g; Cholesterol 89mg; Sodium 749mg

Mushroom-Smothered Baked Kabeljou

PREP: 20 MINUTES / COOK: 40 MINUTES

The dried mushrooms called porcini (or cèpes, in French) have especially good flavour and aroma, but less expensive dried mushrooms will do just fine for this recipe.

10 g dried porcini or other dried mushrooms
250 ml boiling water
20 ml olive oil
450 g button mushrooms, coarsely chopped
3 cloves garlic, finely chopped
60 ml chopped parsley
3,5 ml salt
650 g kabeljou fillet, skinned and cut into 4 pieces
30 ml lemon juice
1,25 ml pepper
30 ml plain dry bread crumbs

1. In a small heatproof bowl, combine the dried mushrooms and boiling water and let stand for 10 minutes or until softened. Reserving the soaking liquid, scoop out the porcini and coarsely chop. Strain the soaking liquid through a coffee filter or a paper towel-lined sieve.

2. In a large nonstick pan, heat 10 ml of the oil over moderate heat. Add the chopped porcini, the button mushrooms and garlic and sauté for 4 minutes or until the fresh mushrooms are tender. Add the mushroom soaking liquid, increase the heat to high and cook for 5 minutes or until the liquid has evaporated. Stir in the parsley and 1,25 ml of the salt.

3. Preheat the oven to 180°C. Spray a 23-cm square glass baking dish with nonstick cooking spray and arrange the fish pieces in a single layer. Sprinkle with the remaining salt, the lemon juice

and pepper. Spoon the mushroom mixture on top. Sprinkle on the bread crumbs; drizzle the remaining 10 ml oil over the crumbs. Bake for 30 minutes or until the fish is just cooked through. Serves 4.

Per serving: Kilojoules 930; Fibre 3 g; Protein 30 g; Total Fat 7 g; Saturated Fat 1 g; Cholesterol 80 mg; Sodium 571 mg

Provençal Fish Stew

PREP: 25 MINUTES / COOK: 20 MINUTES

Both kabeljou (kob) and hake are fish which are known for their tasty, firm flesh. Firm flesh is an important requisite when making a fish stew.

15 ml olive oil
1 medium onion, finely chopped
4 cloves garlic, finely chopped
1 red pepper, cut into 1-cm squares
1 tin (410 g) tomatoes, chopped with their juice
70 ml chicken stock
2,5 ml each fennel seeds and salt
1,25 ml cayenne pepper
60 ml Calamata or other brine-cured olives, pitted and coarsely chopped
350 g filleted, skinned kabeljou, cut into 2,5-cm pieces
350 g filleted, skinned hake, cut into 2,5-cm pieces
70 ml chopped fresh basil

Provençal Fish Stew
*Tomatoes, garlic,
fennel seeds, olives,
and fresh herbs give
this stew a true
French flavour.*

Did you know? . . .
Red roman, kingklip
and kabeljou all have
less than half the fat
of an equivalent serv-
ing of fillet, one of the
leanest cuts of beef.

1. In a large nonstick frying pan, heat
the oil over moderate heat. Add the
onion and garlic and sauté for 5 minutes or until the onion is soft. Add the
pepper and cook for 4 minutes or until
crisp-tender.

2. Add the tomatoes and their juice,
the stock, fennel seeds, salt, cayenne
and olives and bring to a boil. Reduce
to a simmer, add the kabeljou and hake,
cover and cook for 7 minutes or until
the fish is cooked through. Stir in
the basil. Serves 4.

*Per serving: Kilojoules 907; Fibre 2 g;
Protein 30 g; Total Fat 7 g; Saturated Fat 1 g;
Cholesterol 86 mg; Sodium 835 mg*

Orange-Poached Kingklip

PREP: 10 MINUTES / COOK: 25 MINUTES
*Kingklip is a firm but delicate-tasting fish
which is easily overcooked. It's delicious in
this citrusy wine sauce.*

**15 ml olive oil
8 spring onions, thinly sliced
2 cloves garlic, finely chopped
125 ml dry white wine or chicken
   stock
2,5 ml grated orange rind
250 ml orange juice
70 ml chicken stock
2,5 ml salt**

**1,25 ml pepper
4 kingklip fillets (175 g each), skinned
30 ml chopped parsley**

1. In a large pan, heat 5 ml of the oil
over low heat. Add the spring onions
and garlic and sauté for 2 minutes or
until the spring onions are soft. Add
the wine, increase the heat to high and
cook for 3 minutes or until the wine is
evaporated by half.

2. Add the orange rind, orange juice,
stock, salt and pepper. Bring to a boil.
Reduce to a simmer, add the fish, cover
and cook for 10 minutes or until the
fish is just cooked through.

3. Remove the fish from the poaching
liquid and transfer to a platter or serving plates. Increase the heat under the
pan to high, add the remaining 10 ml oil
and cook for 5 minutes or until the
sauce is slightly thickened and syrupy.
Stir in the parsley and spoon the sauce
over the fish. Serves 4.

*Per serving: Kilojoules 938; Fibre 0 g;
Protein 29 g; Total Fat 6 g; Saturated Fat 1 g;
Cholesterol 86 mg; Sodium 540 mg*

According to one study,
the Japanese—who
consume perhaps five
times as much fish
as Americans do—
have about one-sixth
the incidence of heart
disease.

Ocean fish, including
swordfish, monkfish,
kingklip and kabeljou,
are the best dietary
source of iodine, a
mineral required for
proper thyroid function.

Despite the fact that
they live in salt water,
marine fish are natu-
rally low in sodium.

Seafood is a good
source of fluorine,
which, in addition to its
well-known role in
keeping teeth healthy,
also helps prevent cal-
cium loss from bones.

Mild fish

Low-Fat Fish*
PER 120 G COOKED

Kilojoules	554
Fibre	0 g
Protein	27,8 g
Total Fat	1,6 g
Saturated Fat	0,3 g
Cholesterol	84 mg
Sodium	126 mg

NUTRIENTS

% RDA for people older than 10 years	
Vitamin B12	180 %
Magnesium	14 %
Vitamin B6	14 %
Niacin	14 %
Thiamin	7 %

Average for LOW-FAT FISH (0,1-2,9% fat)

The following fish are included in the category LOW FAT FISH:
Angelfish
Geelbek
Hake
Kingklip
Kabeljou (Kob)
Monkfish
Red Roman
Sole
Squid
Stumpnose

Grilled Sole with Herb Butter

PREP: 15 MINUTES / COOK: 5 MINUTES

Fillets of sole are a health-conscious cook's answer to fast food. Sole is also popular because of its delicate flavour and versatility—it can be grilled or used in complicated dishes. Remove the fish from the pan as soon as it is done or it may overcook from the heat of the pan.

30 ml unsalted butter, softened
10 ml low-fat cream cheese
15 ml snipped fresh dill
5 ml snipped fresh chives or spring onions
5 ml bottled horseradish, drained
2,5 ml grated lemon rind
4 sole fillets (175 g each)
30 ml lemon juice
1,25 ml salt

1. Preheat the grill. In a medium bowl, beat together the butter and cream cheese until well combined. Stir in the dill, chives, horseradish and lemon rind.

2. Sprinkle the sole with the lemon juice and salt. Grill 15 centimetres from the heat, without turning the fish over, for 5 minutes or until the sole is cooked through. Serve the fish topped with the herb butter. Serves 4.

Per serving: Kilojoules 864; Fibre 0g; Protein 30g; Total Fat 9g; Saturated Fat 4g; Cholesterol 102mg; Sodium 287mg

Asian-Style Red Stumpnose

PREP: 10 MINUTES / COOK: 20 MINUTES

This Chinese-restaurant-style presentation of a whole stumpnose is a real dinner-party showstopper. Serve with white or brown rice. White stumpnose or red steenbras can also be used in this recipe.

1 whole stumpnose (850 g)
30 ml light soya sauce
15 ml sherry
5 ml light brown sugar
1,25 ml salt
4 spring onions, thinly sliced
15 ml finely chopped fresh ginger
15 ml sesame oil

1. Preheat the oven to 200°C. With a large knife, make several slashes on both sides of the fish. Line a 23 x 33-cm metal baking tin (or small roasting pan) with foil, leaving a 5-cm overhang on both short ends. Fill the baking tin with water to come up 5 millimetres. Place the fish in the tin, cover the tin with foil and bake for 17 minutes or until the fish is just cooked through.

2. Meanwhile, in a bowl, combine the soya sauce, sherry, brown sugar and salt.

3. Using the overhang, lift the fish from the baking tin and pour off the liquid. Transfer the fish to a serving platter. Spoon the soya mixture over the fish. Sprinkle with the spring onions and ginger.

4. In a small saucepan, heat the sesame oil. Pour the hot oil over the fish. Serves 4.

Per serving: Kilojoules 795; Fibre 0g; Protein 30g; Total Fat 5g; Saturated Fat 1g; Cholesterol 89mg; Sodium 715mg

Baked Rolled Sole with Lemon & Oreganum

PREP: 15 MINUTES / COOK: 10 MINUTES

Despite its elegant appearance, this is an easy, recipe. Just be sure to lay the fillets smooth-side up (see how-to photo at right) so they will roll easily.

60ml plain dry bread crumbs
60ml grated Parmesan cheese
30ml chopped parsley
30ml seedless raisins or currants
2,5ml dried oreganum
2,5ml grated lemon rind

1,25ml each salt and pepper
4 sole fillets (175g each)
10ml lemon juice
10ml olive oil

1. Preheat the oven to 200°C. In a small bowl, combine the bread crumbs, Parmesan, parsley, raisins, oreganum, lemon rind, salt and pepper.

2. Place the fish, smooth-side up, on a work surface. Sprinkle the mixture over the fish and roll up from one short end. Place the rolls seam-side down in a 23-cm square glass baking dish. Drizzle the lemon juice and oil over the fish.

3. Bake, uncovered, for 10 minutes or until the fish is just cooked through and the filling is piping hot. Serves 4.

Per serving: Kilojoules 918; Fibre 1g; Protein 33g; Total Fat 6g; Saturated Fat 2g; Cholesterol 88mg; Sodium 411mg

At the market Both east and west coast sole are available—the east coast sole is said to be smaller and tastier. Frozen sole fillets are very convenient. Stumpnose is very seasonal. Hake (commonly known as 'stokvis') is plentiful and popular. Apart from fresh hake, supermarkets stock plain frozen hake and a large variety of frozen hake dishes. Fresh and frozen farm-raised rainbow trout is sold.

Look for Fillets should appear translucent and glistening fresh. Gutted whole fish should have bright, clear, bulging eyes; the gills should be bright red or pink.

Basic cooking Follow the Canadian rule for cooking any fish: measure the thickness of the fish with a ruler, and cook it about 10 minutes per 2,5 centimetres of thickness.

Baked Rolled Sole with Lemon & Oreganum *Perfect with asparagus for a spring dinner.*

When rolling fillets, place the fish on the work surface with the smooth side up and the muscled (ribbed) side down and the rolling will go more easily.

205

Sesame-Coated Hake with Spicy Tomato Sauce

PREP: 25 MINUTES / COOK: 25 MINUTES

Hake is often served dipped in batter and deep-fried. In this recipe, a thin coating of flour and sesame seeds gives the fish fillets a delicately crunchy crust and the firm flesh of hake makes it ideal for baking.

75ml sesame seeds
60ml flour
2,5ml salt
2,5ml paprika
2 egg whites
650g hake fillets, skinned and cut crosswise into 2,5-cm-wide strips
10ml olive oil
3 cloves garlic, finely chopped
250ml tinned tomatoes, finely chopped, with their juice
2,5ml grated orange rind
1,25ml ground ginger
1,25ml crushed red chilli flakes
30ml orange juice

1. Preheat the oven to 200°C. Spray a large baking sheet with nonstick cooking spray. On a plate or a sheet of greaseproof paper, combine the sesame seeds, flour, 1,25ml of the salt and the paprika. In a shallow bowl, lightly beat the egg whites with 15ml of water. Dip the fish first in the egg whites, then in the sesame mixture, pressing the sesame mixture into the fish. Place the fish on the prepared baking sheet.

2. In a large nonstick pan, heat the oil over low heat. Add the garlic and sauté for 2 minutes or until soft. Add the tomatoes and their juice, orange rind, ginger, red chilli flakes and the remaining 1,25ml salt. Bring to a boil, reduce to a simmer, cover and cook for 10 minutes or until the flavours have developed. Add the orange juice and cook for 1 minute.

3. Meanwhile, place the baking sheet in the oven and bake the fish, turning the pieces over once, for 10 minutes or until cooked through and crispy. Spoon the sauce alongside the fish. Serves 4.

Per serving: Kilojoules 1548; Fibre 1g; Protein 29g; Total Fat 24g; Saturated Fat 5g; Cholesterol 91mg; Sodium 582mg

Grilled 'Buffalo' Fish

PREP: 15 MINUTES / COOK: 5 MINUTES

This unusual fish dish picks up on the idea of Buffalo wings (spicy chicken wings served with a rich blue cheese sauce and celery sticks). For this variation, spice-rubbed fish fillets are accompanied with a relish made with celery, carrot and parsley tossed with a light blue cheese sauce.

2,5ml sugar
1,25ml dried oreganum
1,25ml thyme
1,25ml salt
0,6ml each cayenne and black pepper
4 steenbras or kingklip fillets, skinned (170g each)
35g blue cheese, crumbled
15ml red wine vinegar
15ml sour cream
30ml plain low-fat yoghurt
1 stalk celery, quartered lengthwise and thinly sliced (1 cup)
1 small carrot, quartered lengthwise and thinly sliced (¼ cup)
15ml chopped parsley

1. Preheat the grill. In a small bowl, combine the sugar, oreganum, thyme, salt, cayenne and black pepper. Rub the mixture into one side of the fish; set the fillets aside.

2. In a medium bowl, whisk together the blue cheese, vinegar, and sour cream until well combined. Stir in the yoghurt. Stir in the celery, carrot and parsley.

Rainbow Trout à la Meunière A whole trout with a crusty-brown 'coat' is a delectable country-style dish.

Did you know? . . .
The South African Heart Foundation recommends a well-balanced diet that includes fish (rather than fish-oil supplements) as a means of preventing heart disease.

3. Grill the fish, coated-side up, 15 centimetres from the heat for 4 to 5 minutes or until just cooked through. Serve the celery relish on the side. Serves 4.

Per serving: Kilojoules 770; Fibre 0g; Protein 30g; Total Fat 5g; Saturated Fat 3g; Cholesterol 95mg; Sodium 444mg

Rainbow Trout à la Meunière

PREP: 20 MINUTES / COOK: 20 MINUTES
Meunière means 'miller's wife' and describes foods sautéed with a light coating of flour.

- 4 whole rainbow trout (about 280g each)
- 125ml low-fat (2%) milk
- 60ml flour
- 10ml vegetable oil
- 70ml lemon juice
- 125ml chicken stock
- 3,5ml cornflour
- 1,25ml salt
- 20ml unsalted butter
- 15ml chopped parsley

1. Preheat the oven to 200°C. Dip the trout in the milk and then in the flour, shaking off the excess.

2. In a large nonstick pan, heat 5ml of the oil over moderately high heat. Add two trout to the pan and sauté, turning once, for 4 minutes or until lightly browned. Transfer to a baking sheet. Repeat with the remaining 5ml oil and two trout. Bake the trout for 10 minutes or until golden brown and cooked through.

3. Meanwhile, wipe the pan dry. Pour in the lemon juice and cook for 1 minute. Whisk the stock into the cornflour, add it to the pan and bring to a boil over moderate heat. Stir in the salt. Cook, stirring, for 1 minute or until slightly thickened.

4. Remove the sauce from the heat and swirl in the butter and parsley. Spoon the lemon sauce over the fish. Serves 4.

Per serving: Kilojoules 1353; Fibre 0g; Protein 39g; Total Fat 13g; Saturated Fat 4g; Cholesterol 115mg; Sodium 403mg

A health study begun in 1957 included a survey of the dietary habits of its 2107 male subjects. A follow-up 30 years later revealed that the men who ate the most fish had the lowest risk of heart disease— nearly 40 per cent lower than those who ate no fish at all.

A compound called DHA—one of the omega-3 fatty acids found in fish—is vital for brain development in early childhood, especially before the age of two. Researchers suspect that a deficit of DHA in adulthood may be a factor in depression.

Sardines

Potato & Sardine Salad

PREP: 20 MINUTES / COOK: 15 MINUTES

The addition of sardines turns this German-style potato salad into a satisfying main dish. Drained tinned tuna may be substituted for the sardines.

- 650 g potatoes (red, if available), cut into 1-cm pieces
- 70 ml cider vinegar
- 10 ml sugar
- 15 ml grainy mustard
- 2,5 ml salt
- 175 ml plain fat-free yoghurt
- 1 Granny Smith apple, cut into 1-cm pieces
- 1 red pepper, cut into 5-mm dice
- 1 stalk celery, halved lengthwise and thinly sliced
- 60 ml finely chopped onion (red, if available)
- 60 ml snipped fresh dill
- 2 tins (105 g or 120 g) sardines packed in oil, drained

1. In a large pot of boiling water, cook the potatoes for 12 minutes or until tender; drain.

2. Meanwhile, in a small saucepan, combine the vinegar and sugar and heat for 1 minute to dissolve the sugar. Transfer the vinegar mixture to a large bowl and whisk in the mustard and salt. Add the hot potatoes to the dressing, tossing to combine. Let stand for 10 minutes to absorb the dressing.

3. Stir in the yoghurt, apple, pepper, celery, onion and dill, tossing to combine. Add the sardines, gently toss. Serve at room temperature or chilled. Serves 4.

Per serving: Kilojoules 1 244; Fibre 4 g; Protein 17 g; Total Fat 6 g; Saturated Fat 1 g; Cholesterol 65 mg; Sodium 684 mg

Fish Cakes with Chutney Mayonnaise

PREP: 15 MINUTES / COOK: 10 MINUTES

Spicy sardine cakes are a tasty new idea (tuna would also work in this recipe). Their gentle curry flavour is complemented by a creamy mango-chutney sauce. A great way to increase calcium intake!

- 1 slice firm white sandwich bread, crumbled
- 30 ml low-fat (2%) milk
- 4 tins (105 g or 120 g) sardines packed in oil, drained
- 5 ml curry powder
- 2,5 ml ground ginger
- 1,25 ml each salt and pepper
- 10 ml vegetable oil
- 30 ml light mayonnaise
- 30 ml plain fat-free yoghurt
- 15 ml mango chutney, finely chopped
- 5 ml Dijon mustard
- 5 ml lemon juice
- 0,6 ml cayenne pepper

1. Preheat the oven to 200°C. In a medium bowl, combine the bread and milk until completely moistened. Add the sardines, curry powder, ginger, salt and pepper, stirring to combine. Shape into 4 patties.

Sicilian Pasta features an interplay of sweet and spicy flavours and appetizing aromas.

2. In a large nonstick pan, heat the oil over moderate heat. Add the fish cakes and cook for 2 minutes per side or until golden brown. Transfer to a baking sheet and bake for 5 minutes or until heated through.

3. Meanwhile, in a small bowl, combine the mayonnaise, yoghurt, chutney, mustard, lemon juice and cayenne. Serve the fish cakes with the chutney mayonnaise. Serves 4.

Per Serving: Kilojoules 1146; Fibre 0g; Protein 24g; Total Fat 16g; Saturated Fat 2g; Cholesterol 131mg; Sodium 790mg

Sicilian Pasta

PREP: 20 MINUTES / COOK: 30 MINUTES

The quintessentially Sicilian combination of fennel and raisins brings a lovely, subtle sweetness to this pasta toss. If you can't get fennel, substitute 3 stalks of celery, diced, and 5 millilitres crushed fennel seeds.

10ml olive oil
1 small onion, finely chopped
3 cloves garlic, finely chopped
450g bulb fennel, stalks and fronds removed, cut into 5-mm dice (or 3 stalks celery and 5ml fennel seeds)
2 tins (410g) tomatoes, chopped with their juice
2 tins (105g or 120g) sardines packed in oil, drained
125ml sultanas
2,5ml salt
0,6ml cayenne pepper
280g macaroni
15ml pine nuts, toasted

1. In a large nonstick frying pan, heat the oil over moderate heat. Add the onion and garlic and sauté for 5 minutes or until soft. Add the fennel and sauté for 5 minutes or until soft. Add the tomatoes, sardines, sultanas, salt and cayenne and bring to a boil. Reduce to a simmer, cover and cook for 15 minutes or until the sauce is highly flavoured.

2. Meanwhile, in a large saucepan of boiling water, cook the pasta according to package directions until *al dente*. Drain. Toss the hot pasta with the sardine-fennel sauce and pine nuts. Serves 4.

Per serving: Kilojoules 2254; Fibre 10g; Protein 24g; Total Fat 10g; Saturated Fat 1g; Cholesterol 64mg; Sodium 1022mg

At the market Most supermarkets offer a variety of tinned sardines. They are usually sold with the skin on and the soft, edible bones in. They may be packed in oil or in a variety of sauces such as tomato or mustard sauce. Tinned sardines are sometimes lightly smoked. The fresh sardines found on restaurant menus are usually imported from Portugal as local sardines are inferior in size, flavour and texture. Untinned 'fresh' sardines are usually sold frozen.

Look for Read and compare the nutrition labelling on tins of sardines: fat and sodium content varies considerably among the different types.

Basic cooking After cooking the boned fish, (sauté them briefly on both sides) you can use them in any of the recipes here.

Fresh sardines are milder in flavour than the tinned fish, but they boast the same nutritional assets.

Tinned Pilchards

Tinned in Tomato Sauce

PER 100 G

Kilojoules	531
Fibre	0 g
Protein	19 g
Total Fat	5,4 g
Saturated Fat	1,6 g
Cholesterol	70 mg
Sodium	370 mg

NUTRIENTS

% RDA for people older than 10 years

Vitamin B12	1200 %
Vitamin D	80 %
Niacin	42 %
Calcium	25 %
Iron	19 %
Zinc	11 %

Did you know? . . .

Pilchards are classified as oily fish, that is, they are also rich in omega-3 fatty acids which maintain cell membranes, transport fats around the body and are needed to make hormone-like chemicals.

Pilchard Cakes with Tomato Salsa

PREP: 15 MINUTES / COOK: 15 MINUTES

FISH CAKES:
- 3 slices (100 g) bread, crusts removed
- 1 tin (425 g) pilchards in tomato sauce
- 40 g finely chopped onion
- 1 egg, beaten
- 2,5 ml salt
- 2,5 ml hot pepper sauce
- 90 ml vegetable oil

SALSA:
- 4 medium tomatoes, seeded and diced
- 1 medium onion (red, if available), finely diced
- 2 cloves garlic, finely chopped
- 2 green chillies, seeded and finely chopped
- 30 ml lemon or lime juice
- 60 ml chopped fresh coriander leaves
- 2,5 ml salt

1. Soak the bread in a little water and squeeze dry. In a medium bowl, mash the pilchards and the tomato juice together. (Do not remove any bones.) Add the onions. Mix the egg and bread into the mashed pilchards and season with the salt and pepper.

2. Heat 45 ml of the oil in a frying pan. Using 2 dessert spoons, shape the fish-mixture into fish cakes and lower into the hot oil. Fry the fish cakes until brown on both sides. Repeat with the remaining fish-cake mixture and add the remaining oil to the pan as needed. Drain the fish cakes on paper towels and keep warm in the oven while making the salsa.

3. To make the salsa, mix all the salsa ingredients together in a bowl and season with the salt. Serve the fish cakes with the salsa. Makes 20 fish cakes.

Per serving: Kilojoules 328; Fibre 1 g; Protein 5 g; Total Fat 5 g; Saturated Fat 1 g; Cholesterol 25 mg; Sodium 229 mg

Pilchards on Red Peppers

PREP: 15 MINUTES / COOK: 30 MINUTES
Serve this dish on brown rice.

- 30 ml light vegetable oil
- 1 medium onion, sliced
- 2 cloves garlic, finely chopped
- 500 g red peppers, seeds removed and cut into strips
- 300 g tomatoes, chopped
- 2,5 ml salt
- 1 tin (425 g) pilchards in hot chilli sauce
- 60 ml fresh coriander or flat-leaf parsley

1. Heat the oil in a frying pan and saute the onions and garlic for about 1 minute. Add the peppers and tomatoes to the pan and cook for 10 minutes, stirring from time to time. Season with the salt.

2. Preheat the oven to 190°C. Transfer the pepper-tomato mixture to a flat ovenproof dish. Halve the pilchards lengthwise and arrange on the bed of peppers and tomatoes. Pour over the sauce from the tin. Place in the oven and bake for 15 minutes. Sprinkle with chopped coriander or parsley. Serves 4.

Per serving: Kilojoules 1 134; Fibre 3g; Protein 22g; Total Fat 14g; Saturated Fat 3g; Cholesterol 74mg; Sodium 704mg

---

Pilchard Pizza

PREP: 15 MINUTES / COOK: 20 MINUTES

An up-to-date way to get the family to eat healthy pilchards!

30 ml plus 15 ml light olive oil
300 g onions, peeled and sliced
1 clove garlic, finely chopped
30 ml fresh thyme leaves
2,5 ml sea salt

2,5 ml black pepper
1,25 ml sugar
1 ready-made pizza base (30 cm)
1 tin (425 g) pilchards in tomato sauce
100 g black olives
15 ml fresh oreganum leaves
2,5 ml crushed sea salt

1. Heat 30ml of the oil in a frying pan and saute the onions and garlic until golden brown. Reduce the heat to low and add 15ml of the thyme, the salt, black pepper and sugar and cook, stirring occasionally, until all the liquid has evaporated and the mixture is soft and quite brown.

2. Preheat the oven to 200°C. Heat a baking sheet in the oven. Spread the onions over the pizza base. Drain the pilchards and halve lengthwise. Arrange the pilchards, olives, oreganum and remaining thyme on the onions. Drizzle with the pilchard sauce and 15ml olive oil. Place the pizza base on the hot baking sheet and bake for 8 minutes or until the pastry is golden brown. Sprinkle with the sea salt. Serves 4.

Per serving: Kilojoules 1 741; Fibre 4g; Protein 20g; Total Fat 23g; Saturated Fat 6g; Cholesterol 59mg; Sodium 1 157mg

At the market Tinned pilchards are sold in all food shops. They are available in three flavours—tomato, hot chilli and plain in water with salt.

When making fish cakes, mash the pilchards with a fork, making sure to include the bones as well.

Look for As with all tinned goods, check that the tin is not badly dented, rusted or damaged in any way. Once the tin has been opened, any leftover fish should be covered with plastic wrap and kept in the refrigerator, but only for a day or two.

Prep Apart from opening the tin, tinned pilchards need no other preparation. In fact, many people believe that pilchards taste best eaten from the tin with a slice of brown bread! Pilchards are a cheap and easy way of obtaining a good calcium intake—but only if the soft bones are eaten as well.

Pilchard Cakes with Tomato Salsa *Salsa gives these fish cakes a new twist.*

Mussels & Oysters

Mussels
PER 100 G SHELLED

Kilojoules	721
Fibre	0g
Protein	24g
Total Fat	4,5g
Saturated Fat	0,9g
Cholesterol	56mg
Sodium	369mg

NUTRIENTS

% RDA for people older than 10 years

Vitamin A	989%
Vitamin E	22%
Zinc	18%

Oysters
PER 100 G SHELLED

Kilojoules	287
Fibre	0g
Protein	7g
Total Fat	2,5g
Saturated Fat	0,6g
Cholesterol	55mg
Sodium	112mg

NUTRIENTS

% RDA for people older than 10 years

Vitamin B12	1910%
Zinc	606%
Iron	48%

Pasta with Mussels in Marinara Sauce

PREP: 15 MINUTES / COOK: 20 MINUTES

Mussels in the shell top tomato-sauced linguine for an attractive but simple meal.

- 350g linguine pasta
- 20ml unsalted butter
- 10ml olive oil
- 1 small onion, finely chopped
- 5 cloves garlic, finely chopped
- 2 tins (410g each) tomatoes, chopped with their juice
- 650g mussels, well scrubbed and debearded (frozen mussels may also be used)
- 70ml chopped fresh basil
- 60ml chopped parsley
- 1,25ml each salt and pepper

1. In a large pot of boiling water, cook the pasta according to package directions until *al dente*. Drain, transfer to a large bowl, add the butter and toss to coat.

2. Meanwhile, in a large pan, heat the oil over low heat. Add the onion and garlic and sauté for 5 minutes or until soft. Add the tomatoes and cook, stirring occasionally, for 5 minutes or until the sauce is richly flavoured.

3. Add the mussels, cover and cook for 5 minutes or until the mussels have opened. (Start checking after 2 minutes and remove the mussels as they open; discard any that do not.)

4. When all the mussels have opened, return them to the pan. Add the basil, parsley, salt and pepper and cook for 1 minute. Add to the pasta, tossing gently to combine. Serves 4.

Per serving: Kilojoules 2215; Fibre 6g; Protein 26g; Total Fat 11g; Saturated Fat 3g; Cholesterol 41mg; Sodium 784mg

Pan-Fried Oysters with Spicy Mustard Sauce

PREP: 10 MINUTES / COOK: 5 MINUTES

Browned in just 10 millilitres of oil, these delicate crusty oysters barely fit the definition of 'fried'.

- 20ml Dijon mustard
- 15ml chilli sauce
- 5ml lemon juice
- 0,6ml red hot pepper sauce
- 7,5ml honey
- 1,25ml ground ginger
- 60ml flour
- 30ml fine yellow maize meal (fine polenta would be ideal)
- 1,25ml each baking powder and salt
- 1 egg white
- 12 oysters, shelled
- 10ml olive oil

1. In a small bowl, combine the mustard, chilli sauce, lemon juice, red pepper sauce, honey and ginger; set aside.

2. On a sheet of greaseproof paper, combine the flour, maize meal, baking powder and salt. In a small bowl, beat the egg white with 15 ml of water. Dip the oysters first in the egg white, then in the flour mixture.

3. In a nonstick pan, heat the oil over moderately high heat. Cook the oysters for 2 minutes per side or until golden brown and crisp. Serve with the mustard sauce spooned alongside. Serves 4.

Per serving: Kilojoules 444; Fibre 0g; Protein 4g; Total Fat 4g; Saturated Fat 1g Cholesterol 17mg; Sodium 364mg

Creamy Oyster Stew

PREP: 10 MINUTES / COOK: 10 MINUTES

South Africans usually eat oysters raw, but those who live in areas where oysters are plentiful will enjoy this stew. When you shell the oysters, work over a bowl to catch the liquid which you will need for the stew.

4 large slices (50g) Italian bread, without seeds
10 ml unsalted butter
750 ml low-fat (2%) milk

60 ml flour
3,5 ml salt
1,25 ml cayenne pepper
24 oysters, shelled, liquor reserved
60 ml chopped parsley

1. Toast the bread and spread with the butter; set aside.

2. In a large saucepan, whisk the milk into the flour. Stir over low heat until smooth. Add the salt and cayenne pepper and cook, stirring frequently, for 3 minutes or until slightly thickened and no floury taste remains.

3. Stir in 125 ml of the reserved oyster liquor. If there is not enough, make up the balance with chicken stock. Bring the mixture to a simmer, add the oysters, cover and cook for 3 minutes or just until the edges of the oysters begin to curl. Stir in the parsley.

4. Spoon the stew into individual soup bowls and serve with the buttered toast. Serves 4.

Per serving: Kilojoules 888; Fibre 1g; Protein 12g; Total Fat 8g; Saturated Fat 2g; Cholesterol 46mg; Sodium 638mg

At the market Mussels are 'farmed' at Saldanha Bay and imported from New Zealand and are always available. Saldanha mussels are smaller but tastier than the larger New Zealand variety. Oysters are 'farmed' in the Knysna Lagoon and are harvested all year; wild oysters are harvested after the spring tide.

Look for Mussels are sold live in the shell, or frozen or tinned; oysters are sold live in the shell or shelled (frozen or tinned). The shells should be tightly closed. Shelled oysters are packed in their 'liquor' which should be clear.

Prep To clean mussels, pull out the 'beards' and then scrub under running water. To shell oysters, use a knife with a short, sturdy blade. Protect your hands and insert the knife at the hinge and twist to break the hinge; work the knife around to sever the muscle, then cut the meat from the shell.

To clean a mussel, grab the 'beard' and pull out .

Creamy Oyster Stew One of the fastest, tastiest ways to serve oysters.

Crayfish

PER 120G COOKED	
Kilojoules	719
Fibre	0g
Protein	32g
Total Fat	2,3g
Saturated Fat	0,4g
Cholesterol	108mg
Sodium	272mg

NUTRIENTS	
% RDA for people older than 10 years	
Vitamin B12	144%
Zinc	58%
Niacin	33%
Vitamin E	22%
Magnesium	16%
Iron	12%

Did you know? . . .

Crayfish is an excellent source of selenium. Not only is selenium an antioxidant which may have cancer-fighting properties, but it also protects against toxic substances such as mercury—it binds with the toxic substance and is excreted from the body.

California Crayfish Roll

PREP: 15 MINUTES / COOK: 20 MINUTES

A popular sushi-bar selection, the California roll is a tidy assemblage of rice, crayfish, cucumber and avocado. Traditionally the filling would be wrapped in a sheet of nori (dried seaweed); these heartier rolls are made with tortillas. Try to use Japanese rice, which is available at large supermarkets, although it is not essential.

70 ml rice
1,25 ml salt
45 ml rice vinegar
7,5 ml sugar
8 tortillas (18 cm)
8 large butter lettuce leaves
450 g crayfish meat, cooked, shelled, cleaned and cut into small pieces
1 cucumber, peeled, halved lengthwise, seeded and cut into 5 cm x 5 mm strips
half an avocado, cut lengthwise into eighths
1 large red pepper, roasted and cut into 8 strips
30 ml plus 10 ml lemon juice

1. In a saucepan, bring 150 ml of water to a boil. Add the rice and salt, cover and simmer for 17 minutes or until tender. Sprinkle the vinegar and sugar over the rice and stir to combine. Let cool to room temperature.

2. Top each tortilla with a lettuce leaf. Spread the rice over the lettuce. Sprinkle the crayfish over the lettuce, then place a cucumber strip, an avocado slice and a roasted pepper strip on top. Sprinkle each with 5 ml of the lemon juice. Roll up. Serves 4.

Per serving: Kilojoules 1 752; Fibre 6g; Protein 35g; Total Fat 11g; Saturated Fat 2g; Cholesterol 101mg; Sodium 501mg

Curried Crayfish Salad

PREP: 15 MINUTES

Curried crayfish was fairly common in the days when crayfish was plentiful and cheap. Crayfish is no longer plentiful or cheap, but this recipe will make a small amount of crayfish go a long way. Served with other salads, it could stretch to serve six people.

5 ml curry powder
2,5 ml ground coriander
1,25 ml ground ginger
60 ml light mayonnaise
30 ml sour cream
15 ml lemon juice
1,25 ml salt
1,25 ml red hot pepper sauce
450 g crayfish meat, cooked, shelled, cleaned and cubed
1 red apple, cut into 5-mm dice
160 g torn butter lettuce (4 cups)
60 ml chopped fresh coriander or parsley

1. In a small pan, combine the curry powder, coriander and ginger and heat over low heat, shaking the pan occasionally, for 1 minute or until lightly toasted. Transfer to a medium bowl and stir in the mayonnaise, sour cream, lemon juice, salt and hot pepper sauce. Add the crayfish and apple, tossing to coat.

2. Line plates with the lettuce, top with the crayfish mixture and sprinkle with the fresh coriander. Serves 4.

Per serving: Kilojoules 1 121; Fibre 2 g; Protein 31 g; Total Fat 9 g; Saturated Fat 2 g; Cholesterol 114 mg; Sodium 561 mg

Grilled Crayfish

PREP: 10 MINUTES / COOK: 20 MINUTES

Many people believe that the only way to eat a crayfish fresh from the sea is to grill it and serve it with seasoning and lemon juice.

125 ml chopped coriander leaves
100 g soft butter
2 cloves garlic, crushed
60 ml lemon juice
5 ml coarse sea salt

2,5 ml ground black pepper
4 raw crayfish, prepared and cleaned and halved lengthwise

1. Mix the coriander, butter, garlic, lemon juice, salt and black pepper together in a food processor.

2. Preheat the grill. Brush the cut-sides of the crayfish with one quarter of the coriander-mixture and place cut side up on the grill rack. Keep the crayfish at least 10 centimetres from the heat to avoid charring or burning. Grill the crayfish, brushing frequently with the coriander-mixture for about 15 minutes or until the flesh is white and opaque.

3. To braai the crayfish, cook cut-side down briefly then turn the crayfish so that the cut side faces up. Baste the flesh with the coriander-mixture while it is braaing. Serve with the remaining coriander-mixture as a sauce. Serves 4.

Per serving: Kilojoules 1 453; Fibre 0 g; Protein 33 g; Total Fat 23 g; Saturated Fat 12 g; Cholesterol 167 mg; Sodium 1 096 mg

At the market You're most likely to find live crayfish in speciality fish shops; crayfish tails are available frozen. Crayfish have become an expensive delicacy and many recreational divers dive for their own during the season which runs from mid-November to the end of April. A permit is a legal requirement.

Look for West Coast rock lobster is smaller than the more expensive East Coast lobster. Ready-cooked fresh or frozen crayfish should look bright in colour and smell fresh.

Prep Put the live crayfish in a pot of cold salted water. Place a weight on the lid and bring to a boil. The crayfish will become comatose and then die.

Curried Crayfish Salad embellishes luxurious crayfish meat with a well-seasoned sauce.

Add crayfish shell to crayfish bisque as it is cooking—it enhances the flavour greatly. Sieve the bisque when cooked to remove the shell once more.

Prawns

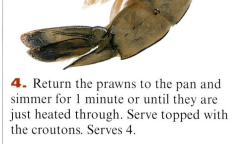

Prawn Bisque with Croutons

PREP: 20 MINUTES / COOK: 20 MINUTES

A bisque usually derives its richness from heavy cream. This version is rendered 'creamy' with low-fat milk and flour. Either fresh or frozen prawns may be used.

- **4 slices (1cm thick) French or Italian bread**
- **1 clove garlic, halved**
- **250ml chicken stock**
- **450g medium prawns, peeled and deveined**
- **250g crushed strained tomatoes**
- **500ml low-fat (2%) milk**
- **30ml flour**
- **2,5ml dried tarragon**
- **2,5ml salt**
- **2,5ml pepper**
- **60ml chopped parsley**

1. Preheat the oven to 200°C. Rub the bread with the cut sides of the halved garlic, then cut the bread into 1-cm cubes. Place on a baking sheet and bake for 5 minutes or until lightly toasted. Remove and set aside.

2. In a medium saucepan, bring the stock and 60ml of water to a simmer. Add the prawns and cook for 3 minutes or until just done. With a slotted spoon, transfer the prawns to a bowl. Stir the crushed, strained tomatoes into the saucepan.

3. In a medium bowl, whisk the milk into the flour, then whisk the mixture into the saucepan. Cook over moderate heat, stirring constantly, for 5 minutes or until the mixture is slightly thickened and no floury taste remains. Stir in the tarragon, salt, pepper and parsley.

4. Return the prawns to the pan and simmer for 1 minute or until they are just heated through. Serve topped with the croutons. Serves 4.

Per serving: Kilojoules 974; Fibre 1g; Protein 30g; Total Fat 4g; Saturated Fat 1g; Cholesterol 228mg; Sodium 1045mg

Cajun-Style Grilled Prawns

PREP: 25 MINUTES / MARINATE: 30 MINUTES / COOK: 5 MINUTES

- **7,5ml dried oreganum**
- **5ml granulated sugar**
- **3,5ml each dried thyme and salt**
- **2,5ml black pepper**
- **1,25ml cayenne pepper**
- **650g large prawns, peeled and deveined**
- **7,5ml vegetable oil**
- **70ml tomato sauce**
- **30ml plus 10ml red wine vinegar**
- **3,5ml light brown sugar**
- **2,5ml ground ginger**
- **380g frozen corn kernels, thawed**
- **4 spring onions, thinly sliced**

1. In a medium bowl, combine the oreganum, granulated sugar, thyme, salt, black pepper and cayenne. Add the prawns and oil, tossing to coat. Cover and refrigerate for 30 minutes.

Asian Stuffed Prawns Butterflied prawns are crowned with a gingery vegetable topping.

At the market Prawns are available all year round as they are harvested locally and imported from all over the world. They can be bought fresh (actually frozen on board ship and later thawed) or frozen. They may be sold in-shell, peeled and deveined or cooked. Prawns come in a wide range of sizes; the bigger they are, the pricier.

Look for Frozen prawns should be solidly frozen; thawed prawns should smell fresh and have firm, glossy shells.

Prep In-shell prawns need to be peeled and deveined for some recipes (see below).

To peel and devein prawns, make a cut along the centre back with kitchen shears or a sharp knife. Remove the shell and legs. Then pick out and remove the black vein which runs down the back.

2. Meanwhile, combine the tomato sauce, vinegar, brown sugar and ginger. Stir in the corn kernels and spring onions.

3. Preheat the grill. Grill the prawns 15 centimetres from the heat, turning them over once, for 4 minutes or until cooked through. Toss the hot prawns with the corn kernel mixture. Serves 4.

Per serving: Kilojoules 1 320; Fibre 3 g; Protein 37 g; Total Fat 4 g; Saturated Fat 1 g; Cholesterol 317 mg; Sodium 891 mg

Asian Stuffed Prawns

REP: 30 MINUTES / COOK: 10 MINUTES

- **16 large prawns (650 g), peeled and deveined**
- **70 ml chopped fresh coriander**
- **1 clove garlic, finely chopped**
- **15 ml olive oil**
- **2 medium carrots, julienned**
- **4 spring onions, cut into 2 x 5-mm strips**
- **15 ml finely chopped fresh ginger**
- **30 ml light soya sauce**
- **30 ml chilli sauce**
- **20 ml lime or lemon juice**
- **5 ml sugar**
- **360 g torn cos lettuce leaves (6 cups)**
- **1 cucumber, peeled, halved lengthwise, seeded and sliced**
- **30 ml chopped fresh mint**

1. With a paring knife, make a cut along the back of each prawn until you have cut almost, but not quite through, to the other side. In a large bowl, toss together the prawns, coriander, garlic and 5 ml of the oil; set aside.

2. In a large nonstick pan, heat the remaining 10 ml oil over moderate heat. Add the carrots and spring onions and sauté for 2 minutes. Add the ginger and cook for 2 minutes. Cool the vegetable mixture to room temperature.

3. Preheat the grill. Place the prawns, cut-side up, on a grill pan, pressing them down to flatten slightly. Spoon the vegetable mixture onto the shrimp and grill 15 centimetres from the heat for 4 minutes or until the prawns are just cooked through.

4. Meanwhile, in a large bowl, combine the soya sauce, chilli sauce, lime juice and sugar. Add the lettuce, cucumber and mint, tossing to combine. Serve the prawns on a bed of the salad mixture. Serves 4.

Per serving: Kilojoules 1 013; Fibre 3 g; Protein 37 g; Total Fat 6 g; Saturated Fat 1 g; Cholesterol 317 mg; Sodium 854 mg

Lean Meats

Grilled Flank Steak with Chimichurri Sauce

Beef sirloin

Sirloin
PER 100 G COOKED

Kilojoules	1142
Fibre	0g
Protein	29g
Total Fat	16,6g
Saturated Fat	6,8g
Cholesterol	74mg
Sodium	79mg

NUTRIENTS

% RDA for people older than 10 years

Vitamin B12	200%
Niacin	29%
Zinc	25%
Vitamin B6	18%
Thiamin	15%
Iron	14%
Riboflavin	11%

Did you know? . . .

Due to consumer demand, the meat industry, from the producer to the trade, has reacted by intro-ducing leaner meat. The average fat con-tent of South African beef carcasses dropped from 32 per cent in 1949 to 13 per cent in 1993.

Quick Beef Burgundy
PREP: 25 MINUTES / COOK: 40 MINUTES

- 55g lean, rindless back bacon, coarsely chopped
- 450g well-trimmed beef sirloin, cut into 1-cm pieces
- 30ml flour
- 100g pearl or pickling onions (1 cup)
- 4 cloves garlic, peeled and halved
- 2 medium carrots, halved lengthwise and cut into 5-cm lengths
- 340g small button mushrooms, quartered
- 150ml each dry red wine and chicken stock
- 15ml tomato paste
- 2,5ml each dried thyme and salt

1. In a flameproof casserole, heat the bacon and 60ml of water over moder-ate heat for 4 minutes or until the bacon has rendered its fat. Leave bacon in pan. Dredge the beef in the flour, shaking off the excess. Sauté the beef for 3 minutes or until lightly browned on both sides. Transfer the beef and bacon to a plate.

2. Add the onions and garlic to the pan and sauté for 5 minutes. Add the carrots and sauté for 7 minutes. Add the button mushrooms and cook for 4 minutes.

3. Add the wine, increase the heat to high and cook for 5 minutes or until reduced by half. Add the stock, tomato paste, thyme and salt and simmer for 10 minutes. Return the beef to the pan and simmer for 3 minutes. Serves 4.

Per serving: Kilojoules 1 361; Fibre 4g; Protein 27g; Total Fat 14g; Saturated Fat 6g; Cholesterol 61mg; Sodium 783mg

Double-Pepper Steak
PREP: 10 MINUTES / COOK: 10 MINUTES

- 10ml coarsely ground black pepper
- 4 well-trimmed sirloin steaks (115g each)
- 10ml vegetable oil
- 1 large red or yellow pepper, cut into 5 x 1-cm strips
- 1 large green pepper, cut into 5 x 1-cm strips
- 30ml brandy or whiskey
- 250ml chicken stock
- 1,25ml salt
- 30ml sour cream
- 3,5ml flour

1. Pat the black pepper onto both sides of the steaks. In a large nonstick pan, heat the oil over moderately high heat. Add the beef and cook for 2 minutes per side for medium-rare. Transfer the steaks to a plate.

2. Reduce the heat to moderate, add the peppers to the pan and cook for 3 minutes or until crisp-tender. Off the heat, add the brandy, then cook for 30 seconds. Add the stock and salt, bring to a boil and cook for 1 minute.

3. In a small bowl, combine the sour cream and flour. Stir the sour cream mixture into the pan and cook, stirring, for 1 minute or until slightly thickened. Reduce to a simmer, return the steaks to the pan and cook just until reheated. Serve the steaks with the sauce and peppers spooned on top. Serves 4.

Per serving: Kilojoules 1174; Fibre 1g; Protein 23g; Total Fat 17g; Saturated Fat 7g; Cholesterol 62mg; Sodium 593mg

Beef Stroganoff

PREP: 15 MINUTES / COOK: 10 MINUTES

As elegant as it may sound, beef Stroganoff (named for a Russian diplomat) can be a quick dish to prepare. Only 60 millilitres of sour cream is used.

15 ml vegetable oil
450 g well-trimmed beef sirloin, cut into 8 x 2,5-cm strips
1 small onion, thinly sliced
225 g mushrooms, thinly sliced
70 ml tinned tomatoes, chopped with their juice
15 ml tomato paste
2,5 ml dried tarragon
2,5 ml salt
1,25 ml black pepper
0,6 ml cayenne pepper
60 ml sour cream
4 slices Italian or French bread, toasted

Double-Pepper Steak *Coarsely ground black pepper coats the steaks; colourful peppers, cooked in stock, brandy and sour cream, serve as the sauce.*

1. In a large nonstick pan, heat 10 ml of the oil over moderately high heat. Add the beef and sauté for 2 to 3 minutes or until lightly browned and just cooked through. With a slotted spoon, transfer the meat to a plate.

2. Add the remaining 5 ml oil, the onion and mushrooms to the pan and cook, stirring frequently, for 3 minutes or until the mushrooms begin to release their juice. Add the tomatoes, tomato paste, tarragon, salt, black pepper and cayenne and bring to a boil. Cook for 1 minute. Remove from the heat and stir in the sour cream.

3. Return the meat to the pan, stirring to combine. Serve the stew with the toasted bread. Serves 4.

Per serving: Kilojoules 1 461; Fibre 3 g; Protein 25 g; Total Fat 20 g; Saturated Fat 8 g; Cholesterol 67 mg; Sodium 501 mg

Grilled Herb-Rubbed Steak

PREP: 5 MINUTES / COOK: 10 MINUTES

5 ml dried rosemary, crumbled
2,5 ml dried thyme
2,5 ml salt
1,25 ml sugar
1,25 ml pepper
4 well-trimmed sirloin steaks (115 g each)
10 ml olive oil

1. Preheat the grill to medium.

2. In a small bowl, combine the rosemary, thyme, salt, sugar and pepper. Rub the mixture into the steaks. Rub the oil over the beef.

3. Grill the steaks 20 centimetres from the heat for 3 minutes per side for medium-rare. Serves 4.

Per serving: Kilojoules 954; Fibre 0 g; Protein 22 g; Total Fat 15 g; Saturated Fat 5 g; Cholesterol 56 mg; Sodium 360 mg

At the market Sirloin is a cut from the loin and is most often sold as steak cuts. Entrecote steaks come from the end of the sirloin nearest the rib cage. Sirloin is tightly grained and more chewy than fillet, but richer in flavour. T-bone steaks contain soft fillet as well as finer-textured sirloin, separated by a T-shaped bone.

Look for The meat should be lean. The beef should be bright red and any fat around the edge of the steak should be white, not yellowish.

Prep Sirloin steak is often sold with a thin layer of fat around the edge. Trim this off before cooking the meat. (For these recipes, weigh the meat after trimming.)

Use a sharp knife with a sawing motion to trim any external fat from steaks.

Basic cooking Though lean, sirloin is tender enough to be grilled. It's also excellent when briefly braised and is suitable for roasting.

Steak & Potato Salad *To turn a warm potato salad into a hearty, low-fat main dish, add sliced sirloin, extra helpings of vegetables and a light vinaigrette.*

Did you know? . . .
Twenty-five grams of lean beef supplies more protein than two egg whites.

Iron-deficiency anaemia is a common nutrient-deficiency problem. This nutritional shortfall can result in fatigue, irritability and lowered immunity. Women and young children are especially susceptible to this condition and should pay particular attention to their intake of iron-rich foods. In children iron deficiency is also associated with impaired development and learning ability.

Beef is an excellent source of zinc which is readily available to the body. Zinc plays an important role in a number of metabolic processes and a deficiency adversely affects all body systems. Phytate and dietary fibre inhibit the availablity of zinc in plant products, but beef provides a source of readily available zinc.

Steak & Potato Salad
PREP: 20 MINUTES / COOK: 20 MINUTES
STANDING TIME: 10 MINUTES

- **650 g small potatoes**
- **2 large red peppers, cut lengthwise into flat panels**
- **1 clove garlic, peeled and halved**
- **70 ml chicken stock**
- **30 ml balsamic vinegar**
- **15 ml Dijon mustard**
- **15 ml honey**
- **2,5 ml salt**
- **2,5 ml black pepper**
- **1 large onion (red, if available), halved and thinly sliced**
- **2 well-trimmed sirloin steaks (225 g each)**
- **360 g torn cos or iceberg lettuce (6 cups)**

1. In a medium pot of boiling water, cook the potatoes for 20 minutes, until tender. When cool enough to handle, peel and cut into 1-cm-thick slices.

2. Meanwhile, preheat the grill. Place the pepper pieces, skin-side up, on the grill rack and grill 10 centimetres from the heat for 12 minutes or until the skin is blackened. When the peppers are cool enough to handle, peel them and cut into 1-cm-wide strips. Leave the grill on.

3. Rub a salad bowl with the cut garlic; discard the garlic. Add the stock, vinegar, mustard, honey, 1,25 ml each of the salt and black pepper and whisk to combine. Add the peppers, potatoes and onion, tossing to coat.

4. Rub the sirloin with the remaining 1,25 ml each salt and black pepper. Grill 4 minutes per side for medium-rare. Let stand for 10 minutes, then thinly slice across the grain and cut the slices into 5-cm lengths. Add to the bowl along with the lettuce and toss well. Serves 4.

Per serving: Kilojoules 1 667; Fibre 6 g; Protein 26 g; Total Fat 13 g; Saturated Fat 5 g; Cholesterol 54 mg; Sodium 603 mg

Fajitas with Tomato Relish
PREP: 25 MINUTES / MARINATE: 1 HOUR
COOK: 15 MINUTES / STANDING TIME:
10 MINUTES

- **2 well-trimmed sirloin steaks (225 g each)**
- **60 ml lime or lemon juice**
- **2,5 ml salt**
- **1,25 ml black pepper**
- **10 ml vegetable oil**
- **450 g tomatoes, halved, seeded and coarsely chopped**
- **70 ml chopped fresh coriander**
- **2 spring onions, thinly sliced**
- **70 ml diced avocado**

Devilled Hamburger

Combine 650 g lean minced sirloin, 45 ml tomato sauce, 15 ml rinsed capers, 15 ml Dijon mustard and 2,5 ml each salt and pepper. Shape into 4 patties. Grill for 3 to 4 minutes per side for medium-rare. Serve on rolls with lettuce, mustard and tomato. Serves 4. *[kJ 1710; Fat 14 g; Sodium 872 mg]*

Argentinian Beef & Fruit Kebabs

Toss 350 g well-trimmed sirloin, cut into 2,5-cm pieces, with 2 finely chopped garlic cloves, 30 ml lime juice, 5 ml oreganum and 2,5 ml each salt, pepper and sugar. Soften 16 dried apricot halves in boiling water; drain. Thread beef and apricots on 8 skewers. Grill 15 centimetres from heat for 3 minutes per side for medium-rare. Serves 4. *[kJ 804; Fat 10 g; Sodium 347 mg]*

Barbecued Beef Sandwich

Combine 125 ml tomato sauce, 15 ml red wine vinegar, 10 ml brown sugar, 2,5 ml ground ginger and 2,5 ml yellow mustard. Brush half of mixture over one side of two well-trimmed 225-g sirloin steaks. Grill for 4 minutes. Turn, brush on remaining mixture and grill 3 minutes for medium-rare. Thinly slice and place on 4 rolls. Serves 4. *[kJ 1502; Fat 13 g; Sodium 504 mg]*

- 1 green chilli, finely chopped (or 1 pickled jalapeño pepper, chopped)
- 2 large red peppers, cut lengthwise into flat panels
- 1 large onion, sliced into 5-mm-thick rounds
- 2,5 ml chilli powder
- 240 g shredded iceberg lettuce (4 cups)
- 4 corn tortillas (18-cm diameter)

1. Sprinkle the steaks with 30 ml of the lime juice, 1,25 ml of the salt, the black pepper and the oil. Cover and refrigerate for 1 hour, turning the steak once.

2. Meanwhile, to make the relish, combine the tomatoes, coriander, spring onions, chilli, 15 ml of the lime juice and the remaining 1,25 ml salt. Fold in the avocado. Refrigerate.

3. Preheat the grill. Gently toss the peppers and onion with the remaining 15 ml lime juice and the chilli powder. Grill the onion slices and peppers, skin-side up, 15 centimetres from the heat for 8 minutes, turning the onions once. Peel the peppers and cut into strips.

4. Grill the steaks 15 centimetres from the heat for 3 minutes per side for medium-rare. Let stand for 10 minutes, then thinly slice across the grain. Serve with the relish, peppers, onion, lettuce and tortillas. Serves 4.

Per serving: Kilojoules 2000; Fibre 6 g; Protein 27 g; Total Fat 22 g; Saturated Fat 8 g; Cholesterol 54 mg; Sodium 695 mg

Silverside & topside

Nutritional power

Beef fillet, silverside and topside are the leanest cuts of beef. Excellent protein sources, they also supply many of the B vitamins as well as iron and zinc.

Silverside
PER 100 G COOKED

Kilojoules	868
Fibre	0g
Protein	31g
Total Fat	9,1g
Saturated Fat	4,8g
Cholesterol	89mg
Sodium	38mg

NUTRIENTS

% RDA for people older than 10 years

Vitamin B12	220%
Zinc	31%
Niacin	28%
Vitamin B6	20%
Iron	17%
Riboflavin	11%

Did you know? . . .

Meat can be part of a healthy diet if it is carefully selected and sensibly prepared. Unfortunately, South Africans increasingly eat a lot of their beef in the form of fast-food hamburgers and cheeseburgers, which may have up to 45 grams of fat per serving.

Beef and Tomato Stew

PREP: 25 MINUTES / COOK: 50 MINUTES

- 450 g well-trimmed topside stewing steak, cut into 1-cm pieces
- 30 ml flour
- 15 ml vegetable oil
- 1 small onion, finely chopped
- 2 cloves garlic, finely chopped
- 2 medium carrots, thinly sliced
- 450 g potatoes, peeled and cut into 1-cm pieces
- 750 ml tinned tomatoes, chopped with their juice
- 45 ml each molasses and red wine vinegar
- 3,5 ml each ground ginger and salt

1. Dredge the beef in the flour, shaking off the excess. In a flameproof casserole, heat the oil over moderately high heat. Cook the beef for 3 minutes or until lightly browned. Transfer the beef to a plate.

2. Reduce the heat to moderate, add the onion and garlic to the pan and sauté for 5 minutes. Add the carrots and cook for 3 minutes. Add the potatoes, the tomatoes and their juice, the molasses, vinegar, ginger and salt and bring to a boil. Reduce to a simmer, cover and cook for 30 minutes or until the potatoes are tender.

3. Return the beef to the pan, cover and simmer for 5 minutes or until the beef is cooked through. Serves 4.

Per serving: Kilojoules 1 502; Fibre 4g; Protein 26g; Total Fat 12g; Saturated Fat 4g; Cholesterol 64mg; Sodium 814mg

Pot Roast with Carrots & Sweet Potatoes

PREP: 15 MINUTES / COOK: 3 HOURS

This pot roast cooks for three hours, but it doesn't need any attention while it cooks.

- 1,1 kg well-trimmed piece of silverside (eyepiece)
- 2 cloves garlic, slivered
- 5 ml dried thyme
- 5 ml salt
- 1,25 ml pepper
- 1 large onion, thinly sliced
- 4 medium carrots, thickly sliced
- 550 g sweet potatoes, peeled and cut into 1-cm pieces
- 1 tin (410 g) tomatoes, chopped with their juice
- 125 ml chicken stock

1. Preheat the oven to 180°C. Cut slits all over the meat and insert the slivers of garlic. Rub the meat with the thyme, salt and pepper.

2. Place the meat in a covered casserole small enough to hold the meat and vegetables tightly. Add the onion, carrots and sweet potatoes. Pour the tomatoes and their liquid and the stock on top. Cover tightly with foil, place the lid on top and bake for 3 hours or until the meat is very tender.

Beef and Tomato Stew is tangy with wine vinegar and a touch of ground ginger.

3. Transfer the meat and vegetables to a platter. Skim fat from the pan juices. Slice the meat and serve with the vegetables; top with pan juices. Serves 6.

Per serving: Kilojoules 1 472; Fibre 4g; Protein 39g; Total Fat 11g; Saturated Fat 6g; Cholesterol 106mg; Sodium 773mg

Beef Moussaka

PREP: 20 MINUTES / COOK: 1 HOUR
Sweet spices and fresh mint flavour this wonderful Greek casserole.

650g aubergine (eggplant), peeled
   and sliced lengthwise into
   1-cm-thick slices
10ml olive oil
1 large onion, finely chopped
3 cloves garlic, finely chopped
450g lean beef mince
425ml crushed, strained tomatoes
60ml chopped fresh mint
2,5ml salt
1,25ml ground cinnamon
0,6ml allspice
425ml low-fat (2%) milk
30ml flour
55g feta cheese, crumbled
30ml grated Parmesan cheese

1. Place the aubergine (in several layers if necessary) on a heatproof plate that will fit in a large pan without touching the sides of the pan. Place a wire rack in the pan and fill the pan with 2,5 centimetres of water. (The rack should sit above, not in, the water.) Bring the water to a simmer, place the plate on the rack, cover and steam for 12 minutes or until tender. Remove from the pan.

2. Meanwhile, preheat the oven to 190°C. Spray a 18 x 28-cm baking dish with nonstick cooking spray. In a large nonstick pan, heat the oil over low heat. Add the onion and garlic and sauté for 5 minutes or until tender. Crumble in the beef and sauté for 5 minutes or until no longer pink. Add the crushed tomatoes, mint, salt, cinnamon and allspice and simmer for 5 minutes.

3. In a medium saucepan, whisk the milk into the flour, stirring until smooth. Cook, stirring constantly, for 5 minutes or until slightly thickened. Spoon half the meat mixture into the bottom of the baking dish. Top with half the aubergine and half the white sauce. Repeat with the remaining meat mixture, aubergine and white sauce. Sprinkle the feta and Parmesan cheese on top. Bake for 35 minutes or until the top is golden brown. Serves 6.

Per serving: Kilojoules 1 268; Fibre 3g; Protein 29g; Total Fat 14g; Saturated Fat 6g; Cholesterol 86mg; Sodium 430mg

At the market Topside and silverside are both boneless cuts from the top of the leg. Beef mince is sold as plain mince, lean or extra lean.

Look for Beef topside and silverside have very little marbling (streaks of fat) and should have little or no exterior fat. Mince should be lean or extra-lean.

Prep If any exterior fat remains on the meat, trim it off with a sharp knife. For the leanest possible minced beef, cut a piece of topside into cubes or pieces (roughly 4-cm square) and chop them in a food processor.

To make beef mince, drop the pieces of topside through the feed tube and chop by pulsing the processor on and off.

Basic cooking Silverside can be pot-roasted or stewed and is popular as corned beef. Topside is best braised or pot-roasted. It can be roasted, but tends to be dry unless it is taken out of the oven when very rare.

Shepherd's Pie *is a warming, meaty main dish with a garlic-scented potato crust.*

Did you know? . . .

The complete protein in beef helps your body utilize the incomplete protein in vegetables, legumes and grains when you eat these foods along with beef.

A 100-gram serving of cooked lean beef contributes less than a third of the daily recommended intake of cholesterol.

Many older people suffer from an insufficient intake of dietary protein, leading to a loss of muscle strength and impairment of immune function. Including even small amounts of beef in their meals would give such people a big protein bonus.

Because beef supplies two kinds of iron (haeme and non-haeme iron), while plant foods such as spinach contain only nonhaeme iron, eating a little beef with iron-rich vegetables or legumes will help you better absorb the non-haeme iron from the plant foods.

Shepherd's Pie

PREP: 20 MINUTES / COOK: 50 MINUTES

Shepherd's pie, as the name suggests, was originally made with lamb. Many cooks, however, prefer to use beef. The sweet Hungarian paprika used in this recipe can be found in the spice section of the supermarket—usually labelled 'paprika'.

650 g potatoes, peeled and thinly sliced
3 cloves garlic, peeled and crushed
3,5 ml salt
60 ml low-fat (2%) milk
10 ml vegetable oil
1 medium onion, finely chopped
2 medium carrots, thinly sliced
5 ml Hungarian paprika
5 ml ground coriander
5 ml cumin
2,5 ml ground cinnamon
2,5 ml pepper
450 g lean beef mince
225 ml crushed, strained tomatoes

1. In a medium pot, combine the potatoes, garlic, 1,25 ml of the salt and water to cover. Bring to a boil and cook for 12 minutes or until the potatoes are tender. Drain; transfer the potatoes and garlic to a bowl. Add the milk and mash the potatoes with a potato masher or handheld mixer until smooth; set aside.

2. Preheat the oven to 190°C. In a large nonstick pan, heat the oil over moderate heat. Add the onion and carrots and cook for 7 minutes. Add the paprika, coriander, cumin, cinnamon and pepper and cook for 1 minute. Remove from the heat and stir in the beef, crushed tomatoes and the remaining salt.

3. Spoon into a 23-cm pie dish. Spread the potato mixture on top. Place on a baking sheet and bake for 30 minutes or until the potato topping is golden brown. Serves 6.

Per serving: Kilojoules 1156; Fibre 3g; Protein 25g; Total Fat 10g; Saturated Fat 4g; Cholesterol 67mg; Sodium 354mg

Italian Beef Rolls

PREP: 25 MINUTES / COOK: 15 MINUTES

This Sicilian-style recipe features beef slices wrapped around a piquant filling made with black olives, capers and raisins. For a dressy occasion, you can slice each roll crosswise into about six pieces and arrange them atop a bed of rice or orzo pasta.

- **450 g well-trimmed beef topside, cut into 8 thin slices**
- **70 ml chopped parsley**
- **60 ml chopped fresh basil**
- **60 ml Calamata or other brine-cured black olives, pitted and coarsely chopped**
- **45 ml plain dry bread crumbs**
- **30 ml capers, rinsed and drained**
- **30 ml seedless raisins**
- **5 ml grated lemon rind**
- **1,25 ml pepper**
- **30 ml flour**
- **10 ml olive oil**
- **500 ml tinned tomatoes, finely chopped with their juice**

1. One at a time, place the meat slices between 2 layers of greaseproof paper and pound to a 3-mm thickness; set aside.

2. In a medium bowl, combine the parsley, basil, olives, bread crumbs, capers, raisins, lemon rind and pepper. Spread the mixture over the beef slices. Roll the slices up from one short end. Fasten with a toothpick. Dredge the beef rolls in the flour, shaking off the excess.

3. In a large nonstick frying pan, heat the olive oil over moderate heat. Cook the beef rolls, turning them as they brown, for 4 minutes or until browned all over. Add the crushed tomatoes and bring to a boil. Reduce to a simmer, cover and cook for 10 minutes or until the beef is cooked through. Serve the beef rolls with the sauce. Serves 4.

Per serving: Kilojoules 1 046; Fibre 2 g; Protein 24 g; Total Fat 12 g; Saturated Fat 4 g; Cholesterol 64 mg; Sodium 615 mg

Taco Salad Brown 450 g lean beef mince with 15 ml chilli powder, 2,5 ml each cumin and coriander in 10 ml oil. Stir in 60 ml salsa. For each serving, top 60 g shredded lettuce with 250 ml meat mixture, 60 ml diced tomato, 30 ml diced avocado and 125 ml baked tortilla chips. Serves 4. *[kJ 1 725; Fat 25 g; Sodium 436 mg]*

Beef & Tomato Pasta Sauce In a large pan, sauté 60 ml each finely chopped onion and carrot and 3 finely chopped garlic cloves in 15 ml oil. Add 625 ml chopped tinned tomatoes, 15 ml tomato paste and 2,5 ml salt; simmer 10 minutes. Add 350 g lean beef mince; simmer 2 minutes. Cook 350 g pasta; toss with sauce and 60 ml Parmesan. Sprinkle with parsley. Serves 4. *[kJ 2 284; Fat 14 g; Sodium 718 mg]*

Chunky Beef Chilli Sauté 1 finely chopped small onion, 2 finely chopped garlic cloves, 15 ml chilli powder, 5 ml ground cumin and 2,5 ml oreganum in 10 ml oil for 1 minute. Add 450 g lean beef mince, stir to brown. Add a 400 g tin red kidney beans, drained, a 410 g tin chopped tomatoes and 250 ml corn kernels; simmer 5 minutes. Serves 4. *[kJ 1 443; Fat 12 g; Sodium 280 mg]*

Rump & Flank

Rump

PER 100 G COOKED

Kilojoules	1125
Fibre	0 g
Protein	29 g
Total Fat	17 g
Saturated Fat	7,4 g
Cholesterol	113 mg
Sodium	67 mg

NUTRIENTS

% RDA for people older than 10 years

Vitamin B12	220 %
Zinc	29 %
Niacin	27 %
Iron	22 %
Vitamin B6	22 %
Thiamin	17 %

Did you know? . . .

Most people think of bananas when they think of potassium sources, but beef is a very good source of this mineral which helps maintain the body's fluid balance. A 100-gram portion of grilled rump steak supplies more potassium than a large banana.

Grilled Flank Steak with Chimichurri Sauce

PREP: 15 MINUTES / COOK: 10 MINUTES
STANDING TIME: 10 MINUTES

Chimichurri is an Argentinian condiment for meat. It's a thick vinaigrette rounded out with herbs, garlic and hot chillies. The flank can be substituted with rump.

3,5 ml salt
2,5 ml each ground coriander, cumin, and dried oreganum
1 well-trimmed thick flank steak (about 450 g)
2 garlic cloves, peeled
250 ml packed coriander leaves
125 ml packed parsley leaves
1 green chilli, seeded and finely chopped (or 1 pickled jalapeño, finely chopped)
70 ml chicken stock
30 ml red wine vinegar
10 ml olive oil

1. In a small bowl, combine 1,25 ml of the salt, the coriander, cumin and oreganum. Rub into both sides of the flank steak; set aside.

2. To make the sauce: in a small pot of boiling water, cook the garlic for 2 minutes to blanch. Transfer to a food processor and add the fresh coriander, parsley, chilli, stock, vinegar, oil and the remaining salt. Process until smooth.

3. Preheat the grill. Grill the steak 15 centimetres from the heat for 4 minutes per side for medium-rare. Let stand for 10 minutes, then slice thinly across the grain. Serve with the chimichurri sauce spooned on top. Serves 4.

Per serving: Kilojoules 853; Fibre 1 g; Protein 24 g; Total Fat 8 g; Saturated Fat 3 g; Cholesterol 64 mg; Sodium 487 mg

Steak & Pasta Salad

PREP: 15 MINUTES / COOK: 20 MINUTES
STANDING TIME: 10 MINUTES

Narrow strips of grilled steak are perfect for tossing with pasta and a pesto-like sauce.

1 well-trimmed rump steak (450 g)
5 ml salt
2,5 ml each pepper and dried thyme
4 cloves garlic, peeled
280 g fusilli pasta
250 ml packed fresh basil leaves
250 ml low-fat evaporated milk
45 ml red wine vinegar
500 ml cherry tomatoes, halved (2 cups)
500 ml frozen corn kernels, thawed

1. Preheat the grill. Sprinkle the steak with 1,25 ml of the salt, 1,25 ml of the pepper and the thyme. Grill the steak 15 centimetres from the heat for 4 minutes per side for medium-rare. Let stand for 10 minutes, then slice thinly across the grain. Cut the slices into 2,5-cm-wide strips.

2. Meanwhile, in a large pot of boiling water, cook the garlic for 2 minutes to blanch. Remove with a slotted spoon and transfer to a food processor. Add the pasta to the boiling water and cook according to package directions until *al dente*. Drain.

3. Add the basil, evaporated milk, vinegar, the remaining salt and pepper to the garlic and process to a smooth purée. Transfer the sauce to a large bowl. Add the hot pasta to the sauce along with the steak, tomatoes and corn kernels. Toss well. Serve at room temperature or chilled. Serves 4.

Per serving: Kilojoules 2 749; Fibre 7 g; Protein 39 g; Total Fat 17 g; Saturated Fat 7 g; Cholesterol 101 mg; Sodium 758 mg

Stir-Fried Steak with Vegetables

PREP: 20 MINUTES / COOK: 10 MINUTES

Just 350 grams of beef serves four handsomely when combined with plenty of vegetables—which is how meat is most often used in Asia, home of the stir-fry.

15 ml light soya sauce
15 ml dry sherry
15 ml plus 5 ml cornflour
0,6 ml bicarbonate of soda
350 g well-trimmed rump steak,
    cut for stir-fry (see how-to photos
    at right)
125 ml chicken stock
15 ml rice vinegar
3,5 ml sugar
15 ml vegetable oil
15 ml finely chopped fresh ginger
3 cloves garlic, finely chopped
1 large red pepper, cut into
    5 x 1-cm strips
225 g asparagus, trimmed and cut
    into 5-cm lengths
160 g shredded Chinese cabbage
    (2 cups)
4 spring onions, thinly sliced

1. In a medium bowl, combine the soya sauce, sherry, 15 ml of the cornflour and the bicarbonate of soda. Add the beef, tossing to coat. In a small bowl, whisk together the stock, vinegar, sugar and the remaining 5 ml cornflour; set aside.

2. In a large nonstick frying pan, heat 5 ml of the oil over moderately high heat. (A wok or electric frying pan can also be used.) Add the beef and stir-fry for 2 to 3 minutes or until just cooked through. With a slotted spoon, transfer the beef to a plate.

3. Add the remaining 5 ml oil, the ginger and garlic to the pan and stir-fry for 30 seconds. Add the pepper and asparagus and cook for 2 minutes. Add the Chinese cabbage and spring onions and cook for 2 minutes.

4. Stir the stock mixture to recombine, add to the pan and bring to a boil. Cook, stirring, for 1 minute. Reduce to a simmer, return the beef to the pan and cook for 30 seconds or until just heated through. Serves 4.

Per serving: Kilojoules 1 028; Fibre 3g; Protein 20g; Total Fat 14g; Saturated Fat 5g; Cholesterol 64mg; Sodium 450mg

At the market Rump steak, also known as top sirloin, is by far the most popular cut in South Africa as it is tasty and succulent. Thick flank is not a well-known cut.

Look for Buy rump which looks red and juicy and has little or no fat attached. Flank steak should have virtually no marbling of fat through the lean tissue.

Prep Cut rump steak into thin strips for stir-fries and sautés (see below).

First cut the whole steak in half lengthwise, with the grain. Then cut each piece crosswise (and across the grain) into thin strips.

Basic cooking Rump can be roasted or grilled. Cook flank steak only to medium-rare or it will become tough.

Stir-Fried Steak with Vegetables Serve with white or brown rice—and chopsticks.

Veal

Veal Rump

PER 100 G COOKED

Kilojoules	800
Fibre	0g
Protein	28g
Total Fat	8,7g
Saturated Fat	4,9g
Cholesterol	105mg
Sodium	79mg

NUTRIENTS

% RDA for people older than 10 years

Vitamin B12	210%
Niacin	44%
Zinc	20%
Riboflavin	16%
Vitamin B6	14%

Did you know? . . .

Because veal is so lean, it requires careful cooking to keep it from becoming tough. But you don't have to cover veal with fat to maintain its tenderness. Just use moderate heat and never overcook it. This will protect the meat's delicate texture.

Saltimbocca

PREP: 15 MINUTES / COOK: 10 MINUTES

So tasty that they seem to jump in your mouth—that's what 'saltimbocca' means in Italian—these delectable little rolls of veal, ham and cheese are worthy of the name.

- 8 slices veal schnitzel (350 g), pounded 3-mm thick
- 2,5 ml each dried sage and salt
- 8 very thin slices baked ham (about 55 g)
- 125 ml grated mozarella cheese
- 30 ml flour
- 10 ml olive oil
- 60 ml dry white wine
- 125 ml chicken stock
- 5 ml cornflour blended with 15 ml water
- 60 ml chopped parsley

1. Sprinkle one side of the veal with the sage and salt. Place a piece of ham on each piece of veal; sprinkle with the mozzarella. Roll up from one short end (see how-to photo, opposite page) and secure with toothpicks.

2. Dredge the veal rolls in the flour, shaking off the excess. In a large nonstick pan, heat the oil over moderate heat. Add the veal rolls and cook for 4 minutes or until lightly browned.

3. Add the wine to the pan, increase the heat to high and cook for 1 minute, scraping up any browned bits from the pan. Add the stock and simmer for 1 minute. Stir in the cornflour mixture and cook, stirring constantly, for 1 minute or until slightly thickened. Stir in the parsley. Serve the veal with the sauce spooned on top. Serves 4.

Per serving: Kilojoules 965; Fibre 0g; Protein 22g; Total Fat 13g; Saturated Fat 6g; Cholesterol 81mg; Sodium 783mg

Veal Schnitzel with Mushrooms

PREP: 15 MINUTES / COOK: 10 MINUTES

Schnitzel, or scaloppine, (pounded veal cutlets), cook in a matter of minutes.

- 8 slices veal schnitzel (350 g), pounded 3-mm thick
- 30 ml flour
- 15 ml olive oil
- 2 cloves garlic, finely chopped
- 350 g mushrooms, thinly sliced
- 1,25 ml each crumbled dried rosemary, salt and pepper
- 175 ml chicken stock
- 2,5 ml grated lemon rind
- 15 ml lemon juice
- 5 ml cornflour blended with 15 ml water

1. Dredge the veal in the flour, shaking off the excess. In a large nonstick pan, heat 5 ml of the oil over moderately high heat. Add half of the veal and sauté for 1 minute per side or until golden brown and just cooked through. Transfer to a platter. Repeat with another 5 ml oil and the remaining veal.

2. Add the remaining 5 ml oil and the garlic to the pan, reduce the heat to moderate and cook for 30 seconds. Add the mushrooms, rosemary, salt and

At the market Veal is something of a specialty. However, you'll find some veal cuts in most supermarkets. Schnitzels, also known as scaloppine (scallops), are thin slices from the fillet end of the leg. Stewing meat may come from any cut and the loin provides excellent veal chops.

Look for Only veal which is grain-fed is available in South Africa. Grain-fed veal is dark pink in colour (though not as red as mature beef). There should be very little or no fat around the veal.

Basic cooking Cook veal gently because it has no marbling or interior fat. Be extra careful when cooking it using dry heat methods such as grilling.

Veal Stew with Orange & Basil A lively jolt of citrus brightens the tomato flavour.

pepper to the pan and sauté for 4 minutes or until the mushrooms have released their juice.

3. Stir the stock, lemon rind and lemon juice into the pan and bring to a boil. Add the cornflour mixture and cook, stirring constantly, for 1 minute or until slightly thickened. Spoon the sauce over the veal. Serves 4.

Per serving: Kilojoules 796; Fibre 2g; Protein 18g; Total Fat 9g; Saturated Fat 3g; Cholesterol 60mg; Sodium 471mg

Veal Stew with Orange & Basil

PREP: 20 MINUTES / COOK: 1 HOUR

You can buy veal for stewing already cut up or buy 450 grams of boned stewing veal and cut it into pieces yourself.

10ml olive oil
**450g stewing veal, cut into
  1-cm pieces**
30ml flour
1 onion, finely chopped
2 cloves garlic, finely chopped
225g small mushrooms, quartered
**250ml tinned tomatoes, chopped with
  their juice**
5ml grated orange rind

125ml orange juice
2,5ml salt
250ml frozen peas
60ml chopped fresh basil

1. Preheat the oven to 180°C. In a flameproof casserole, heat the oil over moderate heat. Dredge the veal in the flour, shaking off the excess. Sauté the veal, working in batches if necessary, for 4 minutes or until golden brown. With a slotted spoon, transfer the veal to a plate.

2. Add the onion and garlic to the pan and sauté for 3 minutes or until the onion is crisp-tender. Add the mushrooms and sauté for 5 minutes or until they begin to release their juices.

3. Add the tomatoes and their juice, the orange rind, orange juice and salt to the pan and bring to a boil. Return the veal to the pan, cover and bake for 45 minutes or until the veal is tender. Stir in the peas and basil and cook for 5 minutes or until the peas are heated through. Serves 4.

Per serving: Kilojoules 1 118; Fibre 5g; Protein 25g; Total Fat 9g; Saturated Fat 4g; Cholesterol 77mg; Sodium 479mg

To prepare the Saltimbocca (opposite page), lay a similar-sized piece of ham on each veal schnitzel. Sprinkle with cheese and roll the schnitzels tidily but not too tightly.

Pork loin

Lean Loin
PER 100G COOKED

Kilojoules	**1099**
Fibre	**0g**
Protein	**30g**
Total Fat	**8,3g**
Saturated Fat	**3g**
Cholesterol	**85mg**
Sodium	**62mg**

NUTRIENTS
% RDA for people older than 10 years

Thiamin	**36%**
Niacin	**27%**
Vitamin B6	**20%**
Zinc	**15%**
Riboflavin	**14%**
Iron	**8%**

Did you know? . . .

There is a significant difference in fat content between cuts of pork. A 100-g cooked portion of lean loin has about 8g of fat, while the leg contains more than 15g of fat per 100-g serving. (The figures in the nutrient lists above are an average of several cuts.)

Sweet & Sour Pork
PREP: 10 MINUTES / COOK: 10 MINUTES

- 250 ml tinned pineapple pieces in juice, drained, juice reserved
- 60 ml chilli sauce
- 45 ml rice vinegar
- 60 ml chicken stock
- 15 ml plus 2,5 ml sugar
- 15 ml cornflour
- 1,25 ml salt
- 15 ml light soya sauce
- 15 ml dry sherry
- 1,25 ml pepper
- 450 g well-trimmed boned centre-cut pork loin, cut into 2,5-cm pieces
- 15 ml vegetable oil
- 15 ml finely chopped fresh ginger
- 1 large carrot, thinly sliced
- 225 g sugar snap peas, strings removed

1. In a small bowl, combine the reserved pineapple juice, chilli sauce, vinegar, stock, 15 ml of the sugar, 5 ml of the cornflour and the salt; set aside.

2. In a medium bowl, combine the soya sauce, sherry, the remaining 10 ml cornflour, remaining 2,5 ml sugar and the pepper. Add the pork and toss well to coat.

3. In a large nonstick pan, heat the oil over moderately high heat. Add the pork and stir-fry for 4 minutes or until golden brown and just cooked through. With a slotted spoon, transfer the pork to a plate.

4. Add the ginger to the pan and cook for 30 seconds. Add the carrot and sugar snaps and stir-fry for 3 minutes or until crisp-tender. Stir in the pineapple pieces. Pour in the pineapple-chilli sauce mixture and bring to a boil. Cook, stirring constantly, for 1 minute or until slightly thickened. Reduce to a simmer, return the pork to the pan and cook just until heated through. Serves 4.

Per serving: Kilojoules 1 291; Fibre 3g; Protein 21g; Total Fat 9g; Saturated Fat 2g; Cholesterol 53mg; Sodium 591mg

Stir-Fried Pork with Vermicelli
PREP: 20 MINUTES / COOK: 15 MINUTES

- 300 g vermicelli pasta
- 30 ml cornflour
- 15 ml light soya sauce
- 15 ml dry sherry
- 3,5 ml salt
- 2,5 ml sugar
- 350 g well-trimmed boned centre-cut pork loin, cut into 5 cm x 5-mm matchsticks
- 15 ml vegetable oil
- 4 spring onions, thinly sliced
- 30 ml finely chopped fresh ginger
- 3 cloves garlic, finely chopped
- 6 pattipan squashes, halved and thinly sliced
- 1 large red pepper, cut into 1-cm squares
- 175 ml chicken stock

At the market Pork loin chops are sold bone-in and boned. Pork loin steaks are sold in various-size cuts. Rolled, tied pork loin roasts look impressive and are easy to slice.

Look for Pork loin should be a soft pink colour, with a fine, velvety texture. If there is bone in the meat, it should be reddish rather than white.

Prep Pork requires little preparation except for the removal of any external fat.

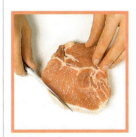

Pork loin chops can come with as much as a 5-mm layer of fat on the outside. Use a sharp paring knife to trim it before cooking.

Basic cooking Overcooking will toughen pork loin which is very lean. The meat should reach an internal temperature of 71°C, but you can remove a roast from the oven when the thermometer registers 68°C. Let stand for 15 minutes before serving; during this time, the temperature will rise to 71°C.

Barbecued Pork *is brushed with an herbed tomato-and-vinegar sauce as it grills.*

1. In a large pot of boiling water, cook the pasta according to package directions until *al dente*; drain.

2. Meanwhile, in a medium bowl, combine 25 ml of the cornflour, the soya sauce, sherry, 1,25 ml of the salt and the sugar. Add the pork, tossing well to coat.

3. In a large nonstick pan, heat 10 ml of the oil over moderate heat. Add the pork, spring onions, ginger and garlic and stir-fry for 3 minutes or until the pork is just cooked through. Transfer the pork to a plate.

4. Add the remaining 5 ml oil, the pattipans and pepper to the pan and sauté for 4 minutes or until the pattipans and pepper are crisp-tender. Add the drained vermicelli and the remaining salt and cook for 1 to 2 minutes, stirring constantly, until the noodles are lightly browned.

5. In a small bowl, combine the stock, 70 ml of water and the remaining 5 ml cornflour. Pour the stock mixture into the pan and bring to a boil. Return the pork to the pan and cook, stirring, for 1 minute or until the pasta is nicely coated. Serves 4.

Per serving: Kilojoules 2013; Fibre 4g; Protein 25g; Total Fat 9g; Saturated Fat 2g; Cholesterol 41mg; Sodium 936mg

Barbecued Pork

PREP: 10 MINUTES / COOK: 15 MINUTES

This pork dish can also be cooked on the braai quite successfully.

70 ml tomato sauce
30 ml red wine vinegar
30 ml molasses
5 ml dark brown sugar
2,5 ml red hot pepper sauce
1,25 ml each crumbled dried rosemary and sage
0,6 ml black pepper
0,6 ml liquid smoke (optional)
450 g well-trimmed boned centre-cut pork loin, cut into 4 slices

1. In a small saucepan, combine the tomato sauce, vinegar, molasses, brown sugar, hot pepper sauce, rosemary, sage, black pepper and liquid smoke (if using). Cook over low heat for 5 minutes or until the barbecue sauce is slightly thickened.

2. Preheat the grill. Brush the pork with half of the barbecue sauce and grill 15 centimetres from the heat for 4 minutes. Turn the pork over, brush with the remaining sauce and grill for 4 minutes or until the pork is cooked through but still juicy. Serves 4.

Per serving: Kilojoules 855; Fibre 0g; Protein 19g; Total Fat 5g; Saturated Fat 2g; Cholesterol 53mg; Sodium 147mg

Pork Enchiladas are baked in a creamy green-chilli sauce and topped with melted feta cheese.

Did you know? . . .
Pork loin has less total fat than loin cuts of beef, as well as less saturated fat.

Advances in the breeding and raising of pigs have resulted in a marked drop in the fat content of the meat.

Many people overcook pork because health authorities formerly recommended that it be cooked to 76°C to avoid any danger of trichinosis. However, the risk of trichinosis in commercially raised pork is now virtually nil, so it's safe to cook pork to 71°C and serve it when it is still deliciously juicy and slightly pink.

Pork is actually a lean meat—a 100g portion of lean roast leg of pork contains 7 per cent fat compared with 100g skinless roast chicken with 5,5 per cent fat.

Maple Pork Chops

PREP: 10 MINUTES / COOK: 10 MINUTES

4 well-trimmed centre-cut loin pork chops (175g each)
30 ml orange juice
2,5 ml each dried sage and salt
1,25 ml pepper
30 ml maple syrup
15 ml orange marmalade
2,5 ml light brown sugar

1. Preheat the grill. Sprinkle both sides of the pork chops with the orange juice, sage, salt and pepper.

2. In a small bowl, combine the maple syrup, marmalade and brown sugar. Brush the chops with half of the maple-syrup mixture and grill 15 centimetres from the heat for 3 to 4 minutes or until lightly browned.

3. Turn the chops over and brush with the remaining maple-syrup mixture. Grill for 3 minutes or until browned and cooked through but still juicy. Serves 4.

Per serving: Kilojoules 1210; Fibre 0g; Protein 29g; Total Fat 8g; Saturated Fat 3g; Cholesterol 82mg; Sodium 369mg

Pork Enchiladas

PREP: 20 MINUTES / COOK: 30 MINUTES

15 ml vegetable oil
4 spring onions, thinly sliced
3 cloves garlic, finely chopped
2 large green chillies, seeded and chopped
150 ml chopped fresh coriander
30 ml lime or lemon juice
150 ml low-fat (2%) milk
15 ml flour
350 g well-trimmed boned centre-cut pork loin, cut into 5cm x 5mm strips
2,5 ml salt
1 large tomato, coarsely chopped
125 ml frozen corn kernels, thawed
8 corn tortillas (15-cm diameter)
70 ml crumbled feta cheese

1. In a large nonstick pan, heat 10ml of the oil over moderate heat. Add the spring onions, garlic and chillies and cook for 2 minutes or until the spring onions and garlic are tender. Transfer the mixture to a food processor; add 75ml of the fresh coriander and the lime juice and process until smooth. Add the milk and flour and process until well combined.

2. Preheat the oven to 180°C. In the same pan, heat the remaining 5ml oil over moderate heat. Add the pork, sprinkle with the salt and sauté for 3 minutes or until just cooked through.

Remove the pan from the heat and stir in the tomato, corn kernels and the remaining 75 ml fresh coriander. Spoon the pork mixture down the centre of each tortilla and roll up.

3. Spoon 60 ml of the sauce into a 18 x 28-cm baking dish. Place the enchiladas, seam-side down, in the dish and spoon the remaining sauce on top. Cover with foil and bake for 15 minutes. Uncover, sprinkle the feta on top and return to the oven for 5 minutes or until the cheese is just melted. Serves 4.

Per serving: Kilojoules 1 632; Fibre 4g; Protein 23g; Total Fat 20g; Saturated Fat 5g; Cholesterol 53mg; Sodium 575mg

---

Mustard & Honey-Glazed Roast Pork

PREP: 10 MINUTES / COOK: 35 MINUTES
STANDING TIME: 10 MINUTES

No fat is added to the meat, but it comes out of the oven juicy and temptingly glossy.

- **2,5 ml salt**
- **1,25 ml dried rosemary, crumbled**
- **1 clove garlic, finely chopped**
- **450 g well-trimmed boned centre-cut pork loin**
- **30 ml honey**
- **20 ml Dijon mustard**
- **5 ml lemon juice**

1. Preheat the oven to 220°C. Rub the salt, rosemary and garlic into the pork. Place the roast in a small roasting tin lined with foil and roast for 20 minutes.

2. Meanwhile, in a small bowl, combine the honey, mustard and lemon juice. Brush half of the honey-mustard mixture over the top of the roast. Return the pork to the oven and roast, basting twice with the honey-mustard mixture, for 15 minutes or until the pork is just cooked through and nicely glazed. Let stand for 10 minutes before slicing. Serves 4.

Per serving: Kilojoules 844; Fibre 0g; Protein 19g; Total Fat 6g; Saturated Fat 2g; Cholesterol 53mg; Sodium 487mg

Spicy Pork Sandwich

In a saucepan, heat 70 ml cider vinegar, 30 ml water, 3 chopped garlic cloves, 60 ml chopped fresh coriander, 2,5 ml salt and 1,25 ml pepper. Add 450 g pork loin in 4 pieces. Cook until tender, slice, return to pan; stir in 30 ml tomato sauce. Serve on rolls with tomato slices. Serves 4. *[kJ 1257; Fat 6g; Sodium 630mg]*

Pork Satay with Curry Sauce

Toss 450 g well-trimmed pork loin, cut into 1-cm cubes, with 10 ml curry powder and 2,5 ml each sugar, salt and pepper. Thread on 4 skewers. Stir together 175 ml plain low-fat yoghurt, 15 ml chopped mango chutney and 2,5 ml curry powder. Grill skewers for 5 minutes, turning once. Serve with yoghurt mixture. Serves 4. *[kJ 823; Fat 6g; Sodium 399mg]*

Pork Piccata

Dredge 8 thin slices pork loin (450 g) in 30 ml flour. Heat 15 ml oil in large nonstick pan. Add pork, cook until browned on both sides; remove. Stir together 5 ml cornflour, 125 ml chicken stock, 45 ml lemon juice, 45 ml chopped parsley and 2,5 ml salt. Add to pan, simmer 1 minute. Spoon over pork. Serves 4. *[kJ 909; Fat 9g; Sodium 381mg]*

Pork fillet

PER 100 G COOKED	
Kilojoules	685
Fibre	0g
Protein	28g
Total Fat	4,8g
Saturated Fat	1,6g
Cholesterol	79mg
Sodium	56mg

NUTRIENTS	
% RDA for people older than 10 years	
Vitamin B12	100%
Thiamin	71%
Niacin	29%
Vitamin B6	26%
Riboflavin	24%
Zinc	20%
Iron	10%

Did you know? . . .

Fresh pork is a healthier choice by far than pork sausages, which may have more than 30g of fat (and sometimes more than 1 000 mg of sodium) per serving. This is true of frankfurters, salami and polony as well as fresh pork sausage.

Pork Rolls Stuffed with Apricots

PREP: 25 MINUTES / COOK: 40 MINUTES

For this guest-worthy dish, you first flatten two 225-gram pieces of pork into thin schnitzels (see how-to photographs, opposite page), then add a stuffing of beta carotene-rich dried apricots.

- **125 ml fresh bread crumbs**
- **60 ml plus 30 ml chopped dried apricots**
- **45 ml finely chopped onion (red, if available)**
- **45 ml finely chopped fresh basil**
- **30 ml grated Parmesan cheese**
- **450 g well-trimmed pork fillet**
- **125 ml apricot juice**
- **125 ml chicken stock**
- **15 ml lemon juice**
- **5 ml Worcestershire sauce**
- **10 ml cornflour blended with 15 ml water**
- **1,25 ml salt**

1. Preheat the oven to 180°C. Spray a small baking dish with nonstick cooking spray. In a small bowl, combine the bread crumbs, 60 ml of the apricots, the onion, basil and Parmesan.

2. Halve the fillet lengthwise. Working with one half at a time, place between 2 sheets of plastic wrap. With the flat side of a small pan or a meat pounder, pound the pork to a 5-mm thickness. Halve each piece crosswise for a total of 4 pieces.

3. Spread the apricot mixture over the pork and press to flatten. Roll up each piece of pork from one short end. Place the pork rolls, seam-side down, in the prepared baking dish and bake for 35 to 40 minutes or until the meat is cooked through but still juicy.

4. Meanwhile, in a small saucepan, combine the remaining 30 ml apricots, the apricot juice, stock, lemon juice, Worcestershire sauce, cornflour mixture and salt. Bring to a simmer, stirring, and cook for 1 minute or until slightly thickened. Cut the pork rolls into 4 to 6 slices each and serve with the apricot sauce. Serves 4.

Per serving: Kilojoules 852; Fibre 1g; Protein 24g; Total Fat 5g; Saturated Fat 2g; Cholesterol 61mg; Sodium 461mg

Orange-Glazed Roast Pork

PREP: 10 MINUTES / COOK: 30 MINUTES
STANDING TIME: 10 MINUTES

As roasts go, this one is super-fast, because pork fillet is a cut that cooks quickly.

- **60 ml orange marmalade**
- **15 ml tomato sauce**
- **10 ml cider vinegar**
- **1,25 ml Worcestershire sauce**
- **2,5 ml each ground coriander, cumin and salt**
- **1,25 ml ground ginger**
- **450 g well-trimmed pork fillet**

1. Preheat the oven to 220°C. Press the marmalade through a fine-mesh sieve to remove any solid bits. In a small bowl, combine the strained marmalade, tomato sauce, vinegar and Worcestershire sauce. In another small bowl, combine the coriander, cumin, salt and ginger. Rub the spice mixture into the pork.

2. Line a small roasting tin with foil. Place the pork in the tin and roast for 10 minutes. Brush half of the marmalade mixture over the pork and roast for 10 minutes. Brush with the remaining marmalade mixture and roast for

10 minutes or until the pork is cooked through but still juicy. Let stand for 10 minutes before slicing. Serves 4.

Per serving: Kilojoules 696; Fibre 0g; Protein 21g; Total Fat 4g; Saturated Fat 1g; Cholesterol 59mg; Sodium 367mg

Pork Medallions Milanese

PREP: 10 MINUTES / COOK: 20 MINUTES

This adaptation of a classic veal recipe substitutes a minimal amount of olive oil for the usual copious quantities of butter.

- 60 ml grated Parmesan cheese
- 70 ml plain dry bread crumbs
- 1 egg white
- 450 g well-trimmed pork fillet, cut crosswise into 4 pieces
- 15 ml olive oil
- 4 lemon wedges

1. Preheat the oven to 200°C. Place the Parmesan on a sheet of greaseproof paper. Place the bread crumbs on another sheet of greaseproof paper. In a small bowl, beat the egg white with 15 ml of water.

2. Dredge the pork in the Parmesan, pressing it on. Dip the pork in the egg white, then in the bread crumbs, patting the crumbs onto the pork.

3. In a large nonstick pan, heat the oil over moderate heat. Add the pork and cook for 3 minutes per side or until golden brown and crisp. Transfer to a baking sheet and bake for 10 to 15 minutes or until cooked through but still juicy. Serve with the lemon wedges. Serves 4.

Per serving: Kilojoules 955; Fibre 0g; Protein 31g; Total Fat 9g; Saturated Fat 3g; Cholesterol 81mg; Sodium 149mg

At the market Pork fillet is quite small and can only be removed from larger carcasses. A fillet will weigh about 500g. Supermarkets and butcheries sell pork fillet, although you might have to order it in advance.

Look for The fillet is a long, slender piece of meat, only about 5cm in diameter. Fillet is darker in colour than other cuts of pork.

Prep To make the Pork Rolls Stuffed with Apricots (opposite page), the fillet needs to be pounded thin (see below).

Pork Rolls Stuffed with Apricots are prettiest when the slices are fanned over the sauce.

Halve a 450-g piece of fillet lengthwise. Place each piece of pork between sheets of plastic wrap. Working from the centre out, use a meat pounder to thin the pork to a 5-mm thickness (top photo). Then cut each pounded portion crosswise (bottom).

237

Ham

Lean Ham	
PER 100 G	
Kilojoules	532
Fibre	0 g
Protein	19 g
Total Fat	5 g
Saturated Fat	1,6 g
Cholesterol	47 mg
Sodium	1 429 mg

NUTRIENTS	
% RDA for people older than 10 years	
Vitamin B12	80 %
Thiamin	66 %
Niacin	27 %
Vitamin B6	23 %
Riboflavin	14 %
Zinc	13 %

Did you know? . . .

Ham is usually made from the cured hind leg of pork. The flavour varies according to the curing process, but the basic ingredients are salt, sodium nitrate and soldium nitrite. Various flavourings may be added, such as molasses, honey and spices.

Peppery Ham & Swiss Strata

PREP: 15 MINUTES / SOAK: 30 MINUTES
COOK: 55 MINUTES

A strata is a layered casserole of bread, beaten eggs and cheese; ham adds extra protein and a wealth of flavour. Rye bread complements the Swiss cheese and ham.

- **6 slices (140 g total) rye bread, cut into 2,5-cm-wide strips**
- **1 large tomato, seeded and coarsely chopped**
- **175 g thinly sliced ham, slivered**
- **115 g Swiss cheese (Gruyère or Emmenthaler), grated**
- **500 ml low-fat (2%) milk**
- **1 egg**
- **4 egg whites**
- **45 ml grated Parmesan cheese**
- **2,5 ml cayenne pepper**

1. Using one-third of the bread, make a layer in the bottom of a 20-cm square glass baking dish. Top with half of the tomato, half of the ham and half of the Swiss cheese. Repeat with another one-third of the bread and the remaining tomato, ham and Swiss cheese. Top with a final layer of bread.

2. In a medium bowl, whisk together the milk, whole egg, egg whites, Parmesan and cayenne. Pour the mixture over the bread mixture, cover with foil and let soak for 30 minutes in the refrigerator.

3. Preheat the oven to 180°C. Bake the strata, covered, for 30 minutes. Uncover and bake for 25 minutes or until the strata is nicely puffed, golden brown and set. Serves 4.

Per serving: Kilojoules 1 536; Fibre 3g; Protein 29g; Total Fat 25g; Saturated Fat 7g; Cholesterol 110mg; Sodium 1 164mg

Ham & Sweet Potato Salad

PREP: 30 MINUTES / COOK: 15 MINUTES

The sweet potatoes and ginger-lime dressing set this salad apart from the ordinary.

- **450 g sweet potatoes (2 medium), peeled and cut into 1-cm pieces**
- **45 ml grated fresh ginger**
- **70 ml lime or lemon juice**
- **30 ml honey**
- **15 ml olive oil**
- **5 ml Dijon mustard**
- **1,25 ml black pepper**
- **2 pears (about 175 g each), peeled, quartered lengthwise, cored and sliced 5 mm thick**
- **225 g baked ham, cut into 1-cm pieces**
- **1 large red pepper, cut into 5-cm-long matchsticks**
- **125 ml thinly sliced onion (red, if available)**
- **360 g torn butter lettuce (6 cups)**

1. In a medium pot of boiling water, cook the sweet potatoes for 12 minutes or until tender.

2. Meanwhile, working over a large bowl, squeeze the ginger with your fingers to extract the ginger juice; discard the solids. Whisk in the lime juice, honey, oil, mustard and black pepper.

Ham & Sweet Potato Salad is equally delicious served warm or chilled.

3. Drain the sweet potatoes well and add to the bowl with the lime mixture, tossing to coat. Add the pears, ham, pepper and onion and toss again. Serve the salad on a bed of lettuce. Serves 4.

Per serving: Kilojoules 1 306; Fibre 7g; Protein 14g; Total Fat 7g; Saturated Fat 1g; Cholesterol 26mg; Sodium 972mg

Bow Ties with Smoked Ham & Asparagus

PREP: 25 MINUTES / COOK: 25 MINUTES

- **280 g** bow-tie pasta
- **350 g** asparagus, trimmed and cut into 2,5-cm lengths
- **10 ml** olive oil
- **2 large** onions, halved and thinly sliced
- **5 ml** sugar
- **2,5 ml** dried oreganum
- **1,25 ml** black pepper
- **1 large** red pepper, cut into 1-cm squares
- **115 g** smoked ham, cut into 5-mm dice
- **150 ml** chicken stock
- **3,5 ml** grated lemon rind
- **1,25 ml** salt

- **5 ml** cornflour blended with 15 ml water
- **70 ml** chopped fresh basil
- **15 ml** lemon juice

1. In a large pot of boiling water, cook the pasta according to package directions until *al dente*. Add the asparagus for the last 2 minutes of cooking time. Drain.

2. Meanwhile, in a large nonstick pan, heat the oil over moderate heat. Add the onions, sugar, oreganum and black pepper and sauté for 12 minutes or until the onions are light golden and very tender. Add the pepper and ham and cook for 5 minutes or until the pepper is crisp-tender.

3. Add the drained pasta and asparagus, the stock, lemon rind and salt and simmer until the pasta is heated through. Stir in the cornflour mixture and cook for 1 minute, stirring constantly, until slightly thickened. Remove from the heat and stir in the basil and lemon juice. Serves 4.

Per serving: Kilojoules 1 575; Fibre 6g; Protein 17g; Total Fat 6g; Saturated Fat 1g; Cholesterol 14mg; Sodium 797mg

At the market Baked ham can be found at the supermarket cold-meat counter. Other hams you may find there are country-style ham, Black Forest and Westphalian (two German smoked hams), and prosciutto (or Parma), which you can have sliced to order. In the past hams were cured in order to preserve the meat, but these days they are cured because people like the flavour. Cured meats have a very high sodium content.

Turkey ham—cooked, cured turkey meat—can be substituted for ham.

Look for All baked hams should have a good pink colour and be finely grained.

Prep Trim any external fat from ham before cooking or serving.

Basic cooking These recipes call for ready-to-eat ham.

Lamb

Grilled Lamb Chops with Mint Salsa

PREP: 20 MINUTES / COOK: 10 MINUTES

A pourable vinegar-based mint sauce is traditional with lamb; this update features a chunky mint salsa made with peppers, spring onions, garlic and lemon.

2 cloves garlic, peeled
125 ml chopped fresh mint
60 ml diced red pepper
2 spring onions, thinly sliced
5 ml grated lemon rind
45 ml rice vinegar
2,5 ml lemon juice
6 ml sugar
2,5 ml salt
2,5 ml dried oreganum
4 well-trimmed loin lamb chops
(140 g each)

1. In a small pot of boiling water, cook the garlic for 2 minutes to blanch. Drain. When cool enough to handle, finely chop and transfer to a medium bowl. Add the mint, pepper, spring onions, lemon rind, vinegar, lemon juice, 5 ml of the sugar and 1,25 ml of the salt; set aside.

2. In a small bowl, combine the oreganum, the remaining sugar and the remaining 1,25 ml salt. Rub the mixture onto both sides of the chops and let stand for 10 minutes.

3. Preheat the grill to medium. Grill the chops 20 centimetres from the heat for 3½ minutes per side for medium-rare. Serve the chops with the mint salsa spooned on top. Serves 4.

Per serving: Kilojoules 863; Fibre 0g; Protein 27g; Total Fat 9g; Saturated Fat 3g; Cholesterol 86mg; Sodium 378mg

Szechuan Lamb with Spring Onions

PREP: 20 MINUTES / COOK: 10 MINUTES

30 ml light soya sauce
15 ml dry sherry or white wine
15 ml cornflour
1,25 ml crushed red chilli flakes
350 g well-trimmed leg of lamb, thinly sliced and then cut into 1-cm-wide strips
15 ml vegetable oil
1 large yellow pepper, cut into 5-cm-long matchsticks
1 large red pepper, cut into 5-cm-long matchsticks
1 green chilli, seeded and chopped (or 1 pickled jalapeño pepper, finely chopped)
3 cloves garlic, finely chopped
15 ml finely chopped fresh ginger
10 spring onions, cut into 5-cm lengths
1,25 ml each salt and sugar

1. In a medium bowl, combine the soya sauce, sherry, cornflour and red chilli flakes. Add the lamb, tossing to coat. In a large nonstick pan, heat 10 ml of the oil over moderately high heat. Add the lamb to the pan and stir-fry for 2 minutes or until just cooked through. With a slotted spoon, transfer the lamb to a plate.

Grilled Lamb Chops with Mint Salsa *A tangy pepper relish accompanies the chops.*

2. Add the remaining 5 ml oil to the pan along with the peppers, chilli, garlic and ginger and stir-fry for 2 minutes or until the peppers are crisp-tender. Add the spring onions, salt and sugar and cook for 1 minute. Return the lamb to the pan and cook for 1 minute or just until heated through. Serves 4.

Per serving: Kilojoules 825; Fibre 2 g; Protein 21 g; Total Fat 9 g; Saturated Fat 2 g; Cholesterol 62 mg; Sodium 624 mg

Lamb Curry

PREP: 15 MINUTES / COOK: 1 HOUR

This unusual curry cooks in a coconut-almond sauce flavoured with curry spices

- **10 ml vegetable oil**
- **450 g well-trimmed boned lamb shoulder, cut into 1-cm pieces**
- **1 large onion, finely chopped**
- **1 large red pepper, diced**
- **5 ml turmeric**
- **3,5 ml each ground cumin and coriander**
- **2,5 ml ground ginger**
- **1,25 ml each ground cardamom and sugar**
- **60 ml dessicated coconut**
- **60 ml sliced natural almonds**
- **310 ml plain low-fat yoghurt**
- **125 ml tomato purée**
- **3,5 ml salt**
- **175 ml frozen peas**
- **125 ml chopped fresh coriander or parsley**

1. In a large nonstick pan, heat the oil over moderately high heat. Working in batches, add the lamb and sauté for 4 minutes or until browned. Transfer the lamb to a plate.

2. Reduce the heat to moderate, add the onion and pepper, and sauté for 7 minutes or until the onion is golden brown. Add the turmeric, cumin, coriander, ginger, cardamom and sugar and cook for 2 minutes or until the spices are fragrant. Transfer the mixture to a blender; add the coconut, almonds and 150 ml of water and process until smooth. Return to the pan, stir in 60 ml of the yoghurt, the tomato purée and salt and bring to a simmer.

3. Return the lamb to the pan, cover and cook for 35 minutes. Stir in the peas, cover and cook for 10 minutes or until the lamb is tender. Stir in the fresh coriander and the remaining 250 ml yoghurt. Serves 4.

Per serving: Kilojoules 1 588; Fibre 6 g; Protein 33 g; Total Fat 18 g; Saturated Fat 6 g; Cholesterol 85 mg; Sodium 533 mg

At the market Lamb loin chops, leg of lamb and boned shoulder of lamb are all popular cuts and easily obtainable. Lamb chops are especially popular in South Africa for braais.

Look for Fresh lamb should be pinkish red and firm; any bones should be reddish at the centre. Lamb can be very fatty—choose the leanest piece you can.

Prep There shouldn't be much external fat on a lean piece of lamb, but do trim off any that you see.

Although the layer of fat on most chops these days is minimal, it's more healthy to trim it to nothing before cooking.

Basic cooking When roasting or grilling lamb, don't cook it beyond medium-rare or it will lose its rich flavour. Lamb cooked by moist-heat methods such as stewing or braising, can be cooked longer.

Venison

PER 100G	
Kilojoules	632
Fibre	0g
Protein	30g
Total Fat	3,2g
Saturated Fat	1,3g
Cholesterol	112mg
Sodium	54mg

NUTRIENTS	
% RDA for people older than 10 years	
Vitamin B12	90%
Niacin	38%
Riboflavin	38%
Iron	32%
Vitamin B6	29%
Zinc	18%
Thiamin	13%

Did you know? . . .
Game is always on the move and as a result does not build up fat reserves. Therefore, the meat has little fatty tissue compared with that of domesticated animals.

Venison with Dried Fruit

SOAKING FRUIT: OVERNIGHT
PREP: 15 MINUTES
COOK: 1 HOUR 35 MINUTES

Any venison would be suitable for this casserole.

125 ml orange juice
500 g mixed dried fruit
30 ml vegetable oil
1 medium onion, chopped
2 cloves garlic, finely chopped
45 ml chopped fresh ginger
750 g venison, cut into 2,5 cm cubes
10 ml cumin seeds
5 ml salt
2 cinnamon sticks
5 cloves
10 ml grated orange rind
1 tin (400 ml) coconut milk

1. Add 125 ml of water to the orange juice. Pour over the dried fruit, cover and soak overnight.

2. Preheat the oven to 160°C. Heat the oil in an ovenproof casserole and saute the onion, garlic and ginger until slightly coloured.

3. Add the meat to the casserole and brown. Add the cumin seeds, salt, cinnamon sticks and cloves, stir to mix and cook for 2 minutes.

4. Add the dried fruit and orange juice mixture, the orange rind and the coconut milk. Bring to a simmer, cover with a lid and transfer to the oven. Cook for 60 minutes or until the meat is tender and most of the liquid is absorbed. Serves 6.

Per serving: Kilojoules 2217; Fibre 7g; Protein 29g; Total Fat 21g; Saturated Fat 15g; Cholesterol 91mg; Sodium 469mg

Springbok Goulash

PREP: 10 MINUTES
COOK: 1 HOUR 40 MINUTES

Serve this goulash with either boiled baby potatoes or noodles.

15 ml vegetable oil
400 g onions, sliced
800 g deboned springbok loin, cut into 2,5 cm cubes
5 ml salt
5 ml ground black pepper
5 ml mild paprika
250 ml beef stock or red wine
400 g tomatoes, coarsely chopped
15 ml tomato purée
1 clove garlic, chopped
5 ml caraway seeds
5 ml grated lemon rind

1. Heat the oil in a large saucepan and saute the onions until soft, but not coloured. Add the meat, cover the saucepan and cook over a low heat for 10 minutes.

2. Remove the lid, season with the salt and pepper and the paprika. Stir well to mix the seasonings and boil down the cooking juices. This will give the sauce flavour and colour.

3. Add the beef stock or red wine to the meat, cover and simmer on low heat for 60 minutes.

4. Add the tomatoes and tomato purée and cook for a further 20 minutes. Stir in the garlic, caraway seeds and lemon rind before serving.
Serves 6.

Per serving: Kilojoules 731; Fibre 2g; Protein 28g; Total Fat 6g; Saturated Fat 1g; Cholesterol 97mg; Sodium 598mg

Venison Bobotie

PREP: 20 MINUTES / COOK: 55 MINUTES

Bobotie was originally a dish which used leftover meat, but this bobotie will be the talking point of any dinner party. Serve it with the traditional accompaniments of fruit chutney, sliced bananas, white or yellow rice and a selection of sambals.

MEAT LAYER:
- 30 ml vegetable oil
- 2 medium onions chopped
- 1 clove garlic, finely chopped
- 20 ml curry powder
- 10 ml tumeric
- 1 kg venison, finely minced (kudu or gemsbok)
- 250 ml soft bread crumbs
- 5 ml grated lemon rind
- 30 ml lemon juice
- 1 cooking apple, peeled and grated
- 45 ml fruit chutney
- 100 ml chicken stock
- 5 ml salt

TOPPING:
- 30 ml smooth apricot jam
- 1 egg
- 250 ml low-fat milk
- 2,5 ml tumeric

1. Heat the oil in a large frying pan and saute the onions until soft. Add the garlic, curry powder and tumeric and saute for about 30 seconds for the flavours to develop. Add the mince to the pan and mix well with the onion and spices. Cook for 5 minutes.

2. Add the bread crumbs, lemon rind, lemon juice, apple, fruit chutney, chicken stock and salt. Lower the heat and simmer for 30 minutes.

3. Preheat the oven to 190°C. Transfer the entire contents of the pan to a large ovenproof dish. Spread the apricot jam over the top of the meat mixture. In a jug, mix the egg, milk and tumeric together and pour over the meat. Place the dish in the oven and bake for 15 minutes or until the custard layer on top is firm to the touch. Serves 6.

Per serving: Kilojoules 1 372; Fibre 2g; Protein 39g; Total Fat 11g; Saturated Fat 2g; Cholesterol 169mg; Sodium 695mg

At the market Venison is most freely available during the winter hunting season (from May to August), and supply is most limited during summer. Availability depends on the size of the herds. Game which is available throughout the year comes from private game farms which are fully fenced. Generally, availability cannot be guaranteed. Venison is usually sold in specialized butcheries, but if there is a surplus, supermarkets may carry it as well. Warthog, springbok, gemsbok, kudu, eland, blesbok and impala are all sold as venison.

Tougher cuts of meat can be tenderized by marinating in buttermilk for a few hours.

Look for The animal should be shot first thing in the morning or at night before it has had time to run around and certainly never after a long chase as running alters the texture and taste of the meat. Discuss the quality of the venison with your butcher.

Venison with Dried Fruit *What could be more South African than this hearty dish?*

Ostrich

Nutritional power

Ostrich meat is increasingly popular because it has low cholesterol and less fat than any other red meat.

PER 100 G	
Kilojoules	561
Fibre	0g
Protein	25g
Total Fat	3,5g
Saturated Fat	1,1g
Cholesterol	77mg
Sodium	52mg

NUTRIENTS	
% RDA for people older than 10 years	
Iron	16%

Did you know? . . .

When a 100-gram serving of various roasted meats is compared, ostrich has only 1,1g of saturated fat, whereas mutton has 6,9g, beef has 7,4g and pork has 6,5 grams.

Ostrich is lower in kilojoules than other red meats—although cooking methods can change this dramatically.

Ostrich Steaks with Balsamic Vinegar and Herb Marinade

PREP: 15 MINUTES
MARINATE: 30 MINUTES
COOK: 15 MINUTES

500 g piece extra-trim ostrich steak
20 ml balsamic vinegar
2 cloves garlic, finely chopped
10 ml Dijon mustard
120 ml light vegetable oil (Canola)
15 ml chopped rosemary
15 ml thyme leaves
5 ml dried oreganum
2,5 ml coarsely ground black pepper
5 ml coarse sea salt, crushed

1. Cut the meat in half, then slice across into thin steaks. Place between two layers of plastic wrap and beat lightly to an even thickness. Trim and place in a flat glass dish.

2. In a small bowl, whisk together the vinegar, garlic, mustard and 90 ml of the oil until well blended. Add the rosemary, thyme, oreganum, salt and pepper, stir to mix and pour over the meat. Marinate at room temperature for 30 minutes.

3. Heat the remaining 30 ml oil in a large pan over medium heat. Remove the meat from the marinade and shake off any excess marinade. Place the meat in the pan and brown well on one side before turning (it should still be pink inside). Remove the steaks to a warm platter and sprinkle with salt. Pour the marinade into the pan and add 125 ml of hot water. Bring to a boil, scraping the bits stuck to the pan loose. Strain and serve with the steaks. Serves 4.

Per serving: Kilojoules 1 727; Fibre 0g; Protein 27g; Total Fat 34g; Saturated Fat 5g; Cholesterol 71mg; Sodium 730mg

Ostrich Bolognaise Sauce

PREP: 10 MINUTES / COOK: 20 MINUTES

Serve this low-saturated fat version of a classic meat sauce over freshly cooked pasta—spaghetti is best.

30 ml vegetable oil
1 onion, chopped
1 clove garlic, finely chopped
450 g ostrich mince
1 green pepper, seeded and diced
2 red chillies, seeded and finely chopped
250 ml tomato sauce
5 ml salt
60 ml chopped parsley

1. Heat the oil in a large pan and saute the onion and garlic until golden brown. Add the ostrich mince, green pepper and chillies and cook until the meat changes colour.

2. To the meat mixture add the tomato sauce, 125 ml hot water and 5 ml salt. Lower the heat, cover the pan and simmer for 10 minutes. Stir in the parsley. Serves 4.

Per serving: Kilojoules 1 143; Fibre 2g; Protein 25g; Total Fat 11g; Saturated Fat 2g; Cholesterol 64mg; Sodium 1 022mg

Ostrich and Vegetable Kebabs

PREP: 15 MINUTES / COOK: 15 MINUTES

The trick with these kebabs is to keep basting and to keep turning. They can be grilled or braaied.

450 g ostrich fillet, cut into 4-cm cubes
2 medium onions, quartered lengthwise
2 mealies, cut into 2,5 cm slices

At the market Ostrich can be purchased at large supermarkets and butcheries. Various cuts are available such as fillet, steaks, neck and mince.

To prevent kebab sticks from catching fire and collapsing long before the meat is cooked, soak them in water for an hour or two beforehand.

Look for Ostrich meat should have a good deep red colour. Check the sell-by date if buying at a supermarket. Take the meat straight home and place it in the refrigerator or freezer.

Prep Apart from cutting the meat into the required size, ostrich meat does not need any preparation.

Ostrich and Vegetable Kebabs *A colourful and healthy meat dish.*

- 1 red pepper, seeds removed and cut into squares
- 1 yellow pepper, seeds removed and cut into squares
- 30 ml light soya sauce
- 30 ml sesame oil
- 30 ml lemon juice
- 5 ml coarse chilli paste

1. Thread the ostrich cubes, layers of onion, mealie slices and pepper slices alternately onto kebab skewers.

2. Preheat the grill (or prepare the braai fire). In a small bowl, mix together the soya sauce, sesame oil, lemon juice and chilli paste.

3. Brush over the kebabs and cook under the grill for 15 minutes turning repeatedly. Baste the kebabs frequently with the soya sauce mixture, until the ostrich meat is brown and cooked and the vegetables are slightly charred. Serves 4.

Per serving: Kilojoules 1 461; Fibre 4g; Protein 28g; Total Fat 19g; Saturated Fat 3g; Cholesterol 64mg; Sodium 539mg

Ostrich Salad

PREP: 15 MINUTES / COOK: 15 MINUTES

- 350 g ostrich steaks
- 15 ml light vegetable oil (Canola)
- 2,5 ml salt
- 2,5 ml pepper
- 6 spring onions
- 250 g cherry tomatoes, halved
- 2 sticks celery, trimmed and halved
- 1 tin (400 g) chickpeas, drained
- 1 avocado, sliced

DRESSING:
- 60 ml light vegetable oil (Canola)
- 15 ml balsamic vinegar
- 5 ml dried oreganum

1. Brush the steaks lightly with oil and season with salt and pepper. Heat a griddle pan until smoking and cook the steaks until brown on both sides. Set aside to cool, then cut into thin strips. Mix all the dressing ingredients. Place the salad ingredients in a bowl with the ostrich strips, pour the dressing over and toss lightly. Serves 4.

Per serving: Kilojoules 2 122; Fibre 8g; Protein 26g; Total Fat 30g; Saturated Fat 5g; Cholesterol 50mg; Sodium 901mg

Poultry

Roasted Baby Chickens with Garlic Potatoes

Whole chicken

Whole Chicken*

PER 100 G COOKED

Kilojoules	796
Fibre	0 g
Protein	29 g
Total Fat	7,4 g
Saturated Fat	2 g
Cholesterol	89 mg
Sodium	86 mg

NUTRIENTS

% RDA for people older than 10 years

Niacin	51 %
Vitamin B6	24 %
Zinc	14 %

roasted meat only, no skin

Did you know? . . .

A study has found that no significant fat is transferred from the skin to the meat when chicken is cooked. So when roasting, grilling or braaing chicken, it's okay to leave the skin on during cooking as long as you remove it before eating and don't use the fat for gravy.

Roasted Baby Chickens with Garlic Potatoes

PREP: 15 MINUTES / COOK: 1 HOUR

Potatoes roasted with chicken absorb lots of fat—unless the birds are skinned first. A full-sized chicken can also be used, simply adjust the roasting time.

- 900 g small new potatoes, quartered (a mixure of red and ordinary baby potatoes looks good)
- 15 ml olive oil
- 8 cloves garlic, peeled
- 3,5 ml salt
- 5 ml each dried oreganum and chilli powder
- 1,25 ml pepper
- 2 baby chickens (about 500 g each), skinned

1. Preheat the oven to 220°C. In a large pot of boiling water, cook the potatoes for 5 minutes to blanch. Drain.

2. Meanwhile, place the oil and garlic in a large roasting pan and bake for 5 minutes. Add the drained potatoes to the pan, sprinkle with 1,25 ml of the salt and bake for 15 minutes, shaking the pan occasionally and turning the potatoes as they brown.

3. In a small bowl, combine the oreganum, chilli powder, pepper and the remaining salt. Rub the chickens with the spice mixture. Place, breast-side up, on the potatoes and cook for 30 to 35 minutes or until the chickens are cooked through. Halve the chickens to serve. Serves 4.

Per serving: Kilojoules 1 691; Fibre 3 g; Protein 33 g; Total Fat 11 g; Saturated Fat 3 g; Cholesterol 89 mg; Sodium 513 mg

Braised Lemon Chicken

PREP: 20 MINUTES / COOK: 35 MINUTES

- 1 chicken (1,3 to 1,6 kg)
- 45 ml flour
- 15 ml vegetable oil
- 4 cloves garlic, finely chopped
- 1 small onion, thinly sliced
- 175 ml chicken stock
- 5 ml grated lemon rind
- 70 ml lemon juice
- 30 ml sugar
- 2,5 ml salt
- 5 ml cornflour blended with 15 ml water
- 60 ml chopped fresh coriander

1. Cut the chicken into 8 pieces (2 thighs, 2 drumsticks and 2 breasts cut in half; discard the wings and back or save for stock). Skin the chicken and dredge in the flour, shaking off the excess. In a large nonstick frying pan, heat the oil over moderate heat. Sauté the chicken for 3 minutes per side or until golden. Transfer the chicken to a plate.

2. Add the garlic and onion to the frying pan and sauté for 1 minute or until the onion is tender. Add the stock, 125 ml of water, the lemon rind, lemon juice, sugar and salt and bring to a boil. Return the drumsticks and thighs to the pan; reduce to a simmer, cover and cook for 10 minutes. Return the chicken breasts to the pan, re-cover and cook for 15 minutes or until the chicken is tender. Transfer the chicken to a platter.

3. Return the liquid in the pan to a boil, stir in the cornflour mixture and cook, stirring constantly, for 1 minute or until slightly thickened. Stir in the coriander and spoon the sauce over the chicken. Serves 4.

Per serving: Kilojoules 1 289; Fibre 0g; Protein 33g; Total Fat 12g; Saturated Fat 3g; Cholesterol 99mg; Sodium 665mg

Herb-Roasted Chicken

PREP: 10 MINUTES
COOK: 1 HOUR 5 MINUTES

1 chicken (1,3 to 1,6 kg), trimmed of excess fat
3,5 ml dried rosemary
5 ml salt
2,5 ml each dried marjoram and sage
6 large cloves garlic, unpeeled
125 ml chicken stock
10 ml lemon juice
15 ml flour

1. Preheat the oven to 220°C. Sprinkle the cavity of the chicken with 2,5 ml of the rosemary and 1,25 ml each of the salt, marjoram and sage. Place the garlic in the cavity.

2. In a small bowl, combine the remaining salt, rosemary, marjoram and sage. Carefully lift the skin of the breast and thighs and rub the herb mixture underneath.

3. Place the chicken, breast-side down, on a rack in a roasting pan and roast for 30 minutes. Turn breast-side up and roast for 30 minutes or until cooked through. Transfer to a platter.

4. Add the stock, lemon juice and 60 ml of water to the roasting pan and stir, scraping up the browned bits. Pour the drippings into a gravy separator, then pour the defatted juices into a small saucepan. Blend the flour with 60 ml of water, add to the pan and cook over medium heat, stirring, until the gravy is thickened. Serve the gravy alongside the chicken. Remove the skin before eating. Serves 4.

Per serving: Kilojoules 985; Fibre 0g; Protein 34g; Total Fat 9g; Saturated Fat 2g; Cholesterol 103mg; Sodium 893mg

At the market Whole chickens come in various sizes—the most popular is the medium size (1,3 to 1,4 kg, including giblets). Baby chickens may be more difficult to find, but they are available.

Look for Choose a chicken with a meaty breast. The skin colour will depend on the chicken's breed and diet and does not affect nutritional value.

Prep Thaw frozen chickens thoroughly. Rinse the chicken under cold running water. Remove any visible fat. To reduce the risk of food poisoning, wash utensils, work surfaces and hands with hot, soapy water after preparing raw chicken.

To halve a baby chicken, cut through the breastbone, then along the backbone.

Basic cooking To avoid salmonella risk, cook a whole chicken until a thermometer inserted in the thigh reads 82°C (the meat will be white and juices will run clear—not pink—when the meat is pierced).

Herb-Roasted Chicken *is redolent with rosemary, marjoram, sage and garlic.*

Chicken is almost always a good menu choice, but beware of what fast-food restaurants do to it: batter-dipped chicken has more than 20g of fat per serving, while commercial chicken pies may have as much as 40g of fat.

It's safer not to cook poultry with stuffing in the cavity. However, 'stuffing' a bird under the skin with a flavouring mixture is perfectly safe.

Dark chicken meat contains twice as much iron and zinc as light meat.

Chicken livers are a rich source of iron and vitamin A. However, chicken livers have a very high cholesterol content and should be avoided by people on a low-cholesterol diet.

A 100-g portion of roast chicken meat (no skin) contains 5g fat, compared with turkey with 3g, duck with 10g and goose with 22g fat.

Coq au Vin Blanc

PREP: 25 MINUTES / COOK: 1 HOUR

Our white-wine version of this French country stew is much lower in fat than the original.

2 slices bacon, chopped
1 chicken (1,3 to 1,6 kg)
45 ml flour
500 ml pearl onions
2 carrots, halved lengthwise and cut into 2,5-cm lengths
225 g small mushrooms, halved
175 ml dry white wine
175 ml chicken stock
3,5 ml salt
2,5 ml dried rosemary, crumbled
1,25 ml each dried sage and pepper
7,5 ml cornflour blended with 15 ml water
60 ml chopped parsley

1. In a flameproof casserole, combine the bacon and 60 ml of water over moderate heat. Cook for 4 minutes or until the bacon has rendered its fat and is lightly crisped. Cut the chicken into 8 pieces (2 thighs, 2 drumsticks and 2 breasts cut in half; discard the wings and back or save for stock). Skin the chicken and dredge in the flour, shaking off the excess. Sauté the chicken in the bacon drippings for 3 minutes per side or until golden brown. Transfer the chicken to a plate.

2. Add the pearl onions and carrots to the pan and cook for 10 minutes or until the onions are golden. Add the mushrooms and cook for 4 minutes or until they begin to release their juices.

3. Add the wine to the pan, increase the heat to high and cook for 3 minutes, scraping up any browned bits that cling to the bottom of the pan. Add the stock, salt, rosemary, sage and pepper and bring to a boil. Return the chicken thighs and drumsticks to the pan; reduce to a simmer, cover and cook for

15 minutes. Add the breasts, re-cover and cook for 15 minutes or until the chicken is cooked through.

4. Transfer the chicken to a serving platter. Bring the sauce to a boil, stir in the cornflour mixture and cook, stirring constantly, for 1 minute or until slightly thickened. Stir in the parsley and spoon over the chicken. Serves 4.

Per serving: Kilojoules 1501; Fibre 3g; Protein 37g; Total Fat 11g; Saturated Fat 3g; Cholesterol 103mg; Sodium 892mg

Grilled Poussins Diablo

PREP: 15 MINUTES / MARINATE: 1 HOUR
COOK: 15 MINUTES

'Poussins' is French for 'baby chickens'. The 'devillish' touch here is the marinade, made with chilli sauce and hot pepper sauce.

75 ml chilli sauce
10 ml olive oil
5 ml red hot pepper sauce
2,5 ml each salt and black pepper
2,5 ml grated lemon rind
3 cloves garlic, finely chopped
2 baby chickens (about 500g to 550g each), halved (see how-to photo, page 249) and skinned
30 ml red wine vinegar
1 medium red pepper, diced
1 stalk celery, cut into 5-mm dice

1. In a shallow dish, combine 30 ml of the chilli sauce, the oil, hot pepper sauce, salt, black pepper, lemon rind and garlic. Add the chickens, turn to coat, cover and refrigerate for 1 hour.

2. Meanwhile, in a medium bowl, combine the remaining 45 ml chilli sauce, the vinegar, pepper and celery. Set aside.

3. Preheat the grill to medium. Reserving the marinade, grill the

Greek-Style Roasted Baby Chickens *A 'stuffing' made with Greek olives, sun-dried tomatoes, garlic and mint is rubbed under the skin before roasting.*

Did you know? . . .
Skinless light-meat chicken may be as much as 60 per cent leaner than trimmed beef (the difference depends on the cut and grade of the beef).

chickens, breast-side down, 20 centimetres from the heat for 8 minutes (or braai the chickens, breast-side down over medium coals); brush with the reserved marinade as they cook. Turn the chickens over and brush with the marinade. Grill for 6 minutes or until the chickens are just cooked through. Serve with the pepper-celery relish. Serves 4.

Per serving: Kilojoules 1 018; Fibre 1g; Protein 30g; Total Fat 10g; Saturated Fat 2g; Cholesterol 89mg; Sodium 460mg

Greek-Style Roasted Baby Chickens

PREP: 20 MINUTES / COOK: 30 MINUTES
The chickens have a savoury tomato-olive mixture stuffed under the skin which gives them a wonderful flavour.

- **60 ml sun-dried tomato halves (not oil-packed)**
- **70 ml chopped fresh mint**
- **60 ml Calamata or other brine-cured black olives, pitted and chopped**
- **60 ml sultanas**
- **2 cloves garlic, finely chopped**
- **2,5 ml grated lemon rind**
- **1,25 ml salt**
- **2 baby chickens (550 g each), halved (see how-to photo, page 249)**

1. Preheat the oven to 220°C. In a small saucepan, bring 250ml of water to a boil. Add the sun-dried tomatoes and cook for 5 minutes to blanch. Reserving 30ml of the cooking liquid, drain the tomatoes. Place the reserved cooking liquid in a medium bowl. When cool enough to handle, coarsely chop the sun-dried tomatoes and add them to the bowl.

2. Add the mint, olives, sultanas, garlic, lemon rind and salt to the sun-dried tomatoes, stirring to combine. Using your fingers, carefully lift the chickens' breast skin and as much of the thigh skin as you can without tearing it. Place one-quarter of the sun-dried tomato stuffing mixture under the skin of each chicken half.

3. Place the chickens, skin-side up, on a rack in a roasting pan and roast for 25 minutes or until they are cooked through. Remove the skin before eating. Serves 4.

Per serving: Kilojoules 1 029; Fibre 1g; Protein 30g; Total Fat 9g; Saturated Fat 2g; Cholesterol 89mg; Sodium 390mg

Chicken is rich in niacin (vitamin B3), which may play a role in cancer protection. Laboratory experiments at the University of Kentucky in the United States suggest that niacin may help prevent certain precancerous changes at the cellular level.

It's best to roast a whole chicken on a rack which allows the fat to drip off as the bird cooks.

Chickens sold in stores are inspected by 'in-house' inspectors from the Department of Agriculture. Some shops also sell 'free-range' chickens.

Chicken breasts

Baked Moroccan Chicken & Couscous

PREP: 20 MINUTES / COOK: 35 MINUTES

This dish offers a satisfying and healthy balance of carbohydrate and protein.

5 ml each ground cumin and coriander
3,5 ml salt
2,5 ml each ground ginger, cinnamon and pepper
4 skinless, bone-in chicken breasts (225g each)
10 ml olive oil
1 small onion, finely chopped
3 cloves garlic, finely chopped
250 ml couscous
375 ml boiling water
60 ml chopped fresh coriander or parsley
60 ml chopped dates or raisins
30 ml lemon juice

1. In a small bowl, combine the cumin, coriander, 2,5 ml of the salt, the ginger, cinnamon and pepper. Rub the spice mixture onto the chicken.

2. Preheat the oven to 190°C. In a large nonstick pan, heat the oil over moderate heat. Add the chicken and cook for 3 minutes per side. Transfer the chicken to a plate.

3. Add the onion and garlic to the pan and sauté for 5 minutes. Add the couscous, boiling water and the remaining salt; stir, cover, remove from the heat and let stand for 5 minutes. With a fork, gently stir in the fresh coriander and chopped dates.

4. Make 4 mounds of the couscous mixture in a 23 x 33-cm baking dish and place a chicken breast on each mound. Sprinkle the chicken with lemon juice, cover with foil and bake for 10 minutes. Uncover and bake for 10 minutes or until the chicken is cooked through. Serve each person a mound of couscous topped with a chicken breast. Serves 4.

Per serving: Kilojoules 1655; Fibre 3g; Protein 44g; Total Fat 9g; Saturated Fat 2g; Cholesterol 70mg; Sodium 489mg

Chicken Strips with Two Sauces

PREP: 15 MINUTES / COOK: 15 MINUTES

125 ml plain dry bread crumbs
1,25 ml salt
2 egg whites
550 g skinless, boned chicken breasts, cut into 2,5-cm-wide strips
20 ml vegetable oil
70 ml tomato sauce
30 ml mango chutney, finely chopped
25 ml lime or lemon juice
2,5 ml ground ginger
70 ml plain low-fat yoghurt
30 ml light mayonnaise
2 spring onions, thinly sliced
2,5 ml dried tarragon

1. Preheat the oven to 180°C. On a sheet of greaseproof paper, combine the bread crumbs and salt. In a shallow bowl, beat the egg whites with 30 ml of water. Dip the chicken first into the egg whites, then into the bread crumbs.

2. In a large nonstick pan, heat 10 ml of the oil over moderate heat. Add half the chicken and cook for 2 minutes on one side, then transfer to a large baking sheet, browned-side up. Repeat with the remaining 10 ml oil and chicken. Bake the chicken for 10 minutes or until cooked through.

3. Meanwhile, in a bowl, combine the tomato sauce, chutney, 15 ml of the lime juice and the ginger. In another bowl, combine the yoghurt, mayonnaise, spring onions, the remaining 10 ml lime juice and the tarragon. Serve the chicken with the two sauces. Serves 4.

Per serving: Kilojoules 1 247; Fibre 1g; Protein 35g; Total Fat 13g; Saturated Fat 3g; Cholesterol 62mg; Sodium 524mg

Grilled Chicken with Parsley Sauce

PREP: 10 MINUTES / COOK: 10 MINUTES

This chicken dish can also be cooked on the braai with great success.

- **4 skinless, boned chicken breasts (140 g each)**
- **2,5 ml each salt, paprika and ground coriander**
- **1,25 ml sugar**
- **250 ml packed parsley leaves, preferably flat-leaf**
- **60 ml chicken stock**
- **15 ml lemon juice**
- **10 ml olive oil**

1. Preheat the grill to medium. Rub the chicken with 1,25 ml of the salt and

Southern 'Fried' Chicken *is briefly sautéed, then oven-baked.*

all of the paprika, coriander and sugar. Grill the chicken 20 centimetres from the heat for 6 to 8 minutes per side, until cooked through.

2. Meanwhile, in a food processor, purée the parsley, stock, lemon juice, oil and the remaining 1,25 ml salt. Spoon the sauce over the chicken. Serves 4.

Per serving: Kilojoules 834; Fibre 1g; Protein 32g; Total Fat 7g; Saturated Fat 2g; Cholesterol 57mg; Sodium 451mg

Southern 'Fried' Chicken

PREP: 10 MINUTES / MARINATE: 30 MINUTES / COOK: 30 MINUTES

- **250 ml low-fat cultured buttermilk**
- **15 ml honey**
- **2,5 ml each cayenne pepper and salt**
- **1,25 ml black pepper**
- **4 skinless, bone-in chicken breasts (225 g each)**
- **125 ml flour**
- **15 ml vegetable oil**

1. In a large bowl, whisk together the buttermilk, honey, cayenne, 1,25 ml of the salt and the black pepper. Add the chicken, turning to coat. Cover and marinate in the refrigerator for at least 30 minutes.

2. Preheat the oven to 200°C. Lift the chicken from its marinade and dredge in the flour, shaking off the excess. In a large nonstick pan, heat the oil over moderate heat. Sauté the chicken, bone-side up, for 4 minutes or until golden brown. Turn the chicken over and cook for 3 minutes. Transfer to a baking sheet lined with foil and bake, bone-side down, for 20 minutes or until the chicken is cooked through. Sprinkle with the remaining 1,25 ml salt. Serves 4.

Per serving: Kilojoules 1 240; Fibre 0g; Protein 35g; Total Fat 9g; Saturated Fat 2g; Cholesterol 60mg; Sodium 418mg

At the market Perennially popular chicken breasts come in several forms: bone-in with skin, boned with skin and boned, skinless. You can even buy skinless chicken breasts cut into bite-size pieces—though at a premium price.

Look for Chicken should look plump and smell fresh.

Prep For some recipes, you'll need to pound boned chicken breasts to flatten them to a uniform thickness.

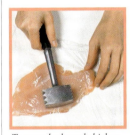

To pound a boned chicken breast, place it between two sheets of plastic wrap and pound it gently with the flat side of a meat pounder or a small, heavy pan.

Basic cooking To preserve the juiciness of chicken breasts, cook them quickly (especially when grilling or baking), but long enough that the meat is fully tender and the juices run clear when the meat is pierced.

Grilled Wine-Marinated Chicken Breasts *calls for just seven ingredients, but they add up to a bold, sophisticated flavour.*

Did you know? . . .

In South Africa the thigh and drumstick of the chicken is more popular than the breast. This is probably because breasts tend to dry out quickly when cooked too long. The leg portion is also more popular for braais.

When meat or poultry is grilled or braaied, carcinogenic substances can form as fat drips onto the fire; these substances are deposited back on the food in the form of smoke. But a study funded by the National Cancer Institute in the United States demonstrated that when chicken is marinated (the researchers used a marinade based on oil, vinegar, lemon juice and mustard), the amount of these substances formed is greatly reduced.

Chicken Parmigiana

PREP: 10 MINUTES / COOK: 20 MINUTES

- **125 ml grated Parmesan cheese**
- **125 ml plain dry bread crumbs**
- **2 egg whites**
- **4 skinless, boned chicken breasts (140 g each)**
- **15 ml olive oil**
- **60 ml grated mozzarella**
- **30 ml tomato purèe**

1. Preheat the oven to 200°C. Place the Parmesan on one sheet of greaseproof paper and the bread crumbs on another. In a shallow bowl, beat the egg whites with 30 ml of water. Dip the chicken into the Parmesan, then into the egg whites and then the bread crumbs.

2. In a large nonstick pan, heat the oil over moderate heat. Sauté the chicken for 3 minutes per side. Transfer the chicken to a baking sheet, sprinkle with the mozzarella; spoon the tomato sauce on top. Bake for 10 minutes or until the chicken is cooked through. Serves 4.

Per serving: Kilojoules 1 320; Fibre 1 g; Protein 40 g; Total Fat 14 g; Saturated Fat 5 g; Cholesterol 72 mg; Sodium 410 mg

Grilled Wine-Marinated Chicken Breasts

PREP: 10 MINUTES / MARINATE: 3 HOURS / COOK: 15 MINUTES

- **125 ml dry white wine**
- **15 ml olive oil**
- **4 cloves garlic, peeled and slightly crushed**
- **3,5 ml each crumbled dried rosemary and salt**
- **2,5 ml pepper**
- **3 strips orange rind (7,5 x 1 cm)**
- **4 skinless, bone-in chicken breasts (225 g each)**

1. In a shallow glass dish, combine the wine, oil, garlic, rosemary, salt, pepper and orange rind. Add the chicken, turning to coat. Cover and marinate in the refrigerator for at least 3 hours, turning the chicken several times.

2. Preheat the grill to medium. Reserving the marinade, grill the chicken, bone-side up, 20 centimetres from the heat for 8 minutes. Turn the chicken over, brush with the marinade and grill for 7 minutes or until the chicken is cooked through. Alternatively, braai over medium coals. Serves 4.

Per serving: Kilojoules 946; Fibre 0 g; Protein 32 g; Total Fat 8 g; Saturated Fat 2 g; Cholesterol 57 mg; Sodium 475 mg

Parchment-Baked Chicken Parcels

PREP: 30 MINUTES / COOK: 40 MINUTES

This dish is also called 'à la forestière'— prepared with mushrooms, potatoes and ham or bacon—simple ingredients which a hunter in Northern Europe might have had on hand.

- **650 g potatoes (red, if available), cut into 1-cm cubes (about 6 medium)**
- **3,5 ml salt**
- **2,5 ml pepper**
- **10 ml olive oil**
- **3 cloves garlic, finely chopped**
- **225 g mushrooms, thinly sliced**
- **60 g smoked ham, chopped**
- **2,5 ml dried sage**
- **4 skinless, boned chicken breasts (140 g each)**
- **8 parsley sprigs**
- **4 thin lemon slices, seeded**

1. In a medium pot of boiling water, cook the potatoes for 5 minutes to blanch. Drain; toss with 2,5 ml of the salt and 1,25 ml of the pepper.

2. Meanwhile, preheat the oven to 200°C. In a large nonstick pan, heat the oil over moderate heat. Add the garlic and sauté for 1 minute. Add the mushrooms and sauté for 5 minutes. Add the potatoes, ham and sage, tossing to coat.

3. Cut four 50-centimetre lengths of parchment paper or foil. Make a mound of mushroom-potato mixture on one half of each sheet. Place the chicken on top and sprinkle with the remaining 1,25 ml each salt and pepper. Top each breast with 2 parsley sprigs and a lemon slice. Fold the parchment or foil over the chicken and make several folds to seal the parcels.

4. Place the parcels on a baking sheet and bake for 20 to 25 minutes or until the chicken and potatoes are cooked through. Serves 4.

Per serving: Kilojoules 1 518; Fibre 4 g; Protein 38 g; Total Fat 9 g; Saturated Fat 2 g; Cholesterol 66 mg; Sodium 679 mg

Chinese Chicken Salad Cook 225 g linguine. Combine 45 ml light soya sauce, 30 ml rice vinegar, 15 ml sesame oil, 3,5 ml each sugar and ginger and 1,25 ml salt. Toss with 350 g cooked shredded chicken breast, 2 grated carrots, 1 slivered red pepper, 2 sliced spring onions and the pasta. Serves 4. *[kJ 1690; Fat 8 g; Sodium 845 mg]*

Chicken Sandwich with Lemon-Basil Mayo In a food processor, purée 125 ml fresh basil, 30 ml lemon juice, 60 ml light mayonnaise and 1,25 ml salt. Dredge 4 chicken breasts (115 g each) in 30 ml flour. Sauté in 15 ml oil for 3 minutes per side or until done. Place 4 lettuce leaves on 4 hard rolls. Top with tomato slices, breast and basil mixture. Serves 4. *[kJ 1619; Fat 9 g; Sodium 589 mg]*

Chicken & White Bean Soup In a saucepan, combine a tin (410 g) rinsed white kidney beans, mashed with 625 ml chicken stock, 30 ml tomato paste, 10 ml red wine vinegar, 1 diced red pepper, 70 ml chopped onion, 3 cloves chopped garlic, 1,25 ml each salt and red chilli flakes and 350 g skinless, boned chicken breasts, cut into pieces. Simmer until chicken is cooked. Serves 4. *[kJ 932; Fat 4 g; Sodium 1 141 mg]*

Chicken & Egg Noodle Stir-Fry

PREP: 20 MINUTES / COOK: 15 MINUTES

Sliced chicken and vegetables are served over a crisp Asian-style noodle 'pancake'.

- **225 g thin egg noodles**
- **15 ml vegetable oil**
- **1 large onion, thinly sliced**
- **2 cloves garlic, finely chopped**
- **1 large carrot, thinly sliced**
- **1 red pepper, cut into 1-cm-wide strips**
- **280 g skinless, boned chicken breasts, thinly sliced crosswise**
- **500 ml chicken stock**
- **30 ml dry sherry**
- **15 ml cornflour**
- **5 ml sugar**
- **3,5 ml ground ginger**
- **2,5 ml salt**

1. In a large pot of boiling water, cook the noodles according to package directions until *al dente*. Drain.

2. Meanwhile, in a large nonstick frying pan, heat 10 ml of the oil over moderately high heat. Add the onion and garlic and sauté for 3 minutes or until crisp-tender. Add the carrot and pepper and sauté for 3 minutes. Add the chicken and cook for 3 minutes or until just done.

3. In a small bowl, whisk together the stock, 125 ml of water, the sherry, cornflour, sugar, ginger and salt. Add to the frying pan and bring to a boil. Cook, stirring constantly, for 1 minute or until slightly thickened. Transfer the chicken and vegetable mixture to a bowl.

4. Add the remaining 5 ml oil to the pan along with the noodles. Cook without stirring for 3 minutes or until the noodles begin to brown on the bottom. Turn the noodles over and continue cooking, pressing down, until they are golden brown and have formed a flat cake. Slide the cake onto a serving platter. Return the chicken mixture to the pan and cook just until heated through. Pour over the noodle cake and cut into wedges to serve. Serves 4.

Per serving: Kilojoules 1 628; Fibre 5 g; Protein 27 g; Total Fat 9 g; Saturated Fat 2 g; Cholesterol 81 mg; Sodium 1 112 mg

Creole-Style Chicken
Chicken in a spicy tomato sauce, cooked with peppers and served with rice, is real comfort food.

Creole-Style Chicken

PREP: 15 MINUTES / COOK: 40 MINUTES

Cooked tomatoes are a rich source of lycopene, a phytochemical that is a promising cancer-fighter.

- 250 ml rice
- 3,5 ml salt
- 20 ml olive oil
- 5 ml paprika
- 4 skinless, bone-in chicken breasts (225 g each)
- 1 small onion, finely chopped
- 4 cloves garlic, finely chopped
- 1 medium red pepper, cut into 5 x 1-cm strips
- 1 medium green pepper, cut into 5 x 1-cm strips
- 1,25 ml each dried thyme and black pepper
- 0,6 ml cayenne pepper
- 1 tin (410 g) stewed tomatoes, chopped with their juice
- 125 ml chicken stock

1. In a medium saucepan, bring 625 ml of water to a boil. Add the rice and 1,25 ml of the salt, reduce to a simmer, cover and cook for 17 minutes or until the rice is tender.

2. Meanwhile, in a large nonstick pan, heat 10 ml of the oil over moderate heat. Add the paprika and stir for 10 seconds. Add the chicken and cook for 2 minutes per side or until richly browned. Transfer the chicken to a plate. Add the remaining 10 ml oil, the onion and garlic to the pan and sauté for 3 minutes or until the onion is slightly browned.

3. Add the peppers, thyme, black pepper, cayenne and the remaining salt to the pan and cook, stirring, for 5 minutes or until the peppers are crisp-tender. Add the tomatoes and stock, and bring to a boil. Reduce to a simmer, return the chicken to the pan, cover and cook for 20 minutes or until the chicken is just cooked through. Serve over the rice. Serves 4.

Per serving: Kilojoules 1 819; Fibre 3g; Protein 37g; Total Fat 10g; Saturated Fat 2g; Cholesterol 57mg; Sodium 885mg

Spicy Chicken Combine 1 small onion, finely chopped, 30 ml red wine vinegar, 10 ml brown sugar, 3,5 ml each black pepper and salt and 2,5 ml each allspice and cayenne. Rub onto 4 skinless, bone-in chicken breasts (225 g each). Grill 7 minutes per side or until done. Serves 4. *[kJ 1075; Fat 6g; Sodium 497mg]*

Grilled Chicken with Caper Dressing Combine 2,5 ml each salt and oreganum, 1,25 ml each sugar and pepper. Rub mixture onto 4 skinless, boned chicken breasts (140 g each). Grill 15 centimetres from heat for 4 minutes per side or until done. Combine 45 ml lemon juice, 15 ml olive oil and 15 ml rinsed capers. Spoon on top. Serves 4. *[kJ 863; Fat 8g; Sodium 479mg]*

Mustard Crumb Chicken Combine 30 ml Dijon mustard with 2,5 ml each honey and lemon juice. Sprinkle 2,5 ml each salt and pepper over 4 skinless, boned chicken breasts (140 g each). Brush with mustard mixture. Grill, mustard-side up, for 7 minutes. Sprinkle 60 ml dry bread crumbs over, pressing gently. Drizzle with 15 ml oil; grill until cooked through. Serves 4. *[kJ 949; Fat 9g; Sodium 600mg]*

Chicken legs

Chicken Thighs*

PER 100G COOKED

Kilojoules	874
Fibre	0g
Protein	26g
Total Fat	10,9g
Saturated Fat	2,8g
Cholesterol	93mg
Sodium	88mg

NUTRIENTS

% RDA for people older than 10 years

Niacin	36%
Zinc	17%
Riboflavin	14%

*meat only, no skin

Did you know? . . .

Chicken drumsticks and thighs offer richly flavoured meat similar to that of goose. However, chicken is considerably lower in fat than goose.

Mushroom-Stuffed Chicken Thighs

PREP: 20 MINUTES / COOK: 40 MINUTES

- 2 slices bacon, chopped
- 1 small onion, finely chopped
- 2 cloves garlic, finely chopped
- 115g mushrooms, chopped
- 2,5ml dried rosemary, crumbled
- 1,25ml each salt and pepper
- 2 slices firm white sandwich bread, toasted and crumbled
- 60ml chopped parsley
- 4 skinless, boned chicken thighs (115g each)
- 10ml olive oil
- 125ml dry white wine
- 150ml chicken stock
- 5ml cornflour blended with 15ml water

1. In a large nonstick pan, cook the bacon over low heat for 2 minutes or until it begins to render its fat. Add the onion and garlic and sauté for 5 minutes. Add the mushrooms, 1,25ml of the rosemary, the salt and pepper and sauté for 4 minutes. Transfer to a bowl and stir in the bread and parsley. Cool to room temperature.

2. Place a chicken thigh between 2 sheets of plastic wrap and pound to a 3-mm thickness. Repeat for all the thighs. Spoon the stuffing over them and roll up from one short end to form packages. Secure with toothpicks.

3. In a large nonstick pan, heat the oil over moderate heat. Add the chicken rolls and cook for 5 minutes or until golden. Add the wine, increase the heat to high and cook for 3 minutes. Add the stock and the remaining 1,25ml rosemary. Cover and simmer for 15 minutes or until the chicken is cooked through.

4. Transfer the chicken to plates. Bring the liquid to a boil, add the cornflour mixture and cook, stirring, for 1 minute or until slightly thickened. Spoon the sauce over the chicken. Serves 4.

Per serving: Kilojoules 1257; Fibre 2g; Protein 25g; Total Fat 14g; Saturated Fat 4g; Cholesterol 86mg; Sodium 612mg

Chicken with Plum Sauce

PREP: 10 MINUTES / COOK: 35 MINUTES

Give your grilled chicken an unusual and healthy twist with this plum sauce.

- 225g tomato purée
- 70ml plum jam
- 15ml cider vinegar
- 2 cloves garlic, finely chopped
- 2,5ml red hot pepper sauce
- 2,5ml ground ginger
- 2,5ml salt
- 5ml each chilli powder, ground cumin and coriander
- 8 chicken drumsticks (900g total), skinned

1. In a medium saucepan, combine the tomato purée, jam, vinegar, garlic, hot pepper sauce, ginger and salt and bring to a boil. Reduce to a simmer, cover and cook for 10 minutes. Uncover and cook for 5 minutes or until the plum sauce is thick enough to coat a spoon and the flavours have blended. Cool to room temperature. Measure out 125ml of the plum sauce and set aside; use the rest as a baste.

2. Preheat the grill. In a small bowl, stir together the chilli powder, cumin and coriander. Rub the chicken with the spice mixture. Grill the chicken 15 centimetres from the heat for 3 minutes per

Chicken with Plum Sauce *Spicy chicken is brushed with a tangy-sweet sauce.*

side. Brush with half of the basting mixture and grill for 5 minutes longer. Turn the chicken over, brush with the remaining baste and grill for 7 minutes or until cooked through. Serve the chicken with the reserved sauce. Serves 4.

Per serving: Kilojoules 1049; Fibre 1g; Protein 29g; Total Fat 6g; Saturated Fat 2g; Cholesterol 93mg; Sodium 409mg

Risotto with Chicken & Mushrooms

PREP: 15 MINUTES / COOK: 55 MINUTES

Arborio is an Italian rice which makes the creamiest risotto. If you can't get Arborio, regular rice can be used instead.

10 ml olive oil
450g skinless, boned chicken thighs, cut into 2,5-cm pieces
1 small onion, finely chopped
450g fresh button mushrooms, sliced
310 ml Arborio rice
150 ml dry white wine
375 ml chicken stock
1,25 ml salt
45 ml Parmesan cheese
2,5 ml pepper

1. In a large nonstick saucepan, heat the oil over moderate heat. Add the chicken and cook for 5 minutes. Transfer the chicken to a plate.

2. Add the onion to the pan and sauté for 5 minutes. Add the button mushrooms and sauté for 4 minutes.

3. Add the rice, stir to coat then add the wine. Cook until the wine has been absorbed, about 4 minutes. Combine the stock with 500 ml of water. Add 375 ml of stock mixture to the rice along with the salt and cook, stirring occasionally, for 12 minutes or until the liquid has been absorbed. Add 250 ml of the stock mixture and cook, stirring occasionally, for 10 minutes or until the liquid has been absorbed.

4. Add the remaining 250 ml stock mixture, return the chicken to the pan and cook for 7 minutes or until the rice is creamy but not mushy. Stir in the Parmesan and pepper. Serves 4.

Per serving: Kilojoules 2064; Fibre 4g; Protein 30g; Total Fat 14g; Saturated Fat 4g; Cholesterol 85mg; Sodium 899mg

Shopping & prep

At the market
Chicken thighs and drumsticks are sold separately. You can also buy whole legs and cut the drumstick and thighs apart.

Look for Chicken legs should be plump and firm, with unblemished skin. The colour of the skin (yellow or white) does not affect the flavour or nutritional value.

Prep To prepare the chicken for Mushroom-Stuffed Chicken Thighs (opposite page), the boned thighs are first pounded thin and then stuffed and rolled (see below).

After pounding boned chicken thighs to a uniform thickness, spoon the stuffing over them, leaving a border. Then roll up from one short side; secure with toothpicks.

Basic cooking
Chicken thighs and legs can stand up to fairly long braising. After cooking, even though the meat is dark, the juices should run clear when the meat is pierced with a sharp knife or skewer.

Chicken-Cashew Stir-Fry *This boldly flavourful Chinese-style dish includes broccoli and red pepper.*

Did you know? . . .
Chicken legs and thighs supply more zinc than do chicken breasts. Zinc plays a key role in cell growth and division. In this capacity, zinc helps your body heal itself when you are injured.

The dark meat (legs and thighs) of chicken contains more cholesterol than the white meat.

Chicken Paprikash
PREP: 20 MINUTES / COOK: 35 MINUTES

- 10 ml vegetable oil
- 4 chicken legs (drumsticks and thighs), split and skinned (350 g each leg)
- 30 ml plus 10 ml flour
- 1 medium onion, finely chopped
- 4 cloves garlic, finely chopped
- 15 ml paprika
- 1 green pepper, coarsely chopped
- 125 ml dry white wine
- 125 ml chicken stock
- 30 ml tomato paste
- 2,5 ml salt
- 1,25 ml caraway seeds (optional)
- 1 roasted red pepper
- 60 ml sour cream

1. In a large nonstick pan, heat the oil over moderate heat. Dredge the chicken in 30 ml of the flour. Sauté for 3 minutes per side or until golden; transfer the chicken to a plate.

2. Add the onion and garlic to the pan and sauté for 5 minutes. Stir in the paprika. Add the pepper and 60 ml of water and cook, stirring, for 5 minutes. Add the wine, increase the heat to high and cook for 2 minutes.

3. Add the stock, tomato paste, salt and caraway seeds and bring to a boil. Return the chicken to the pan, cover and simmer for 15 minutes or until the chicken is cooked through.

4. Meanwhile, in a food processor, combine the roasted pepper, sour cream and the remaining 10 ml flour and purée. Stir the mixture into the pan and cook for 3 minutes or until slightly thickened. Serves 4.

Per serving: Kilojoules 1 607; Fibre 2g; Protein 35g; Total Fat 19g; Saturated Fat 6g; Cholesterol 120mg; Sodium 593mg

Chicken-Cashew Stir-Fry
PREP: 20 MINUTES / COOK: 15 MINUTES

- 250 g broccoli florets (3 cups)
- 15 ml light soya sauce
- 15 ml dry sherry
- 20 ml cornflour
- 350 g skinless, boned chicken thighs, cut into 1-cm pieces
- 10 ml vegetable oil
- 15 ml finely chopped fresh ginger
- 3 cloves garlic, finely chopped
- 1 medium pepper, coarsely diced
- 125 ml chicken stock
- 45 ml chilli sauce
- 1,25 ml salt
- 4 spring onions, thinly sliced
- 60 ml cashew nuts, coarsely chopped

1. In a steamer, cook the broccoli for 3 minutes or until crisp-tender; set aside. In a medium bowl, combine the soya sauce, sherry and 15 ml of the cornflour. Add the chicken and toss.

2. In a large nonstick pan, heat the oil. Add the chicken and stir-fry for 3 minutes. Transfer to a plate. Add the ginger and garlic and stir-fry for 30 seconds. Add the broccoli and pepper and stir-fry for 2 minutes.

3. Add the stock, chilli sauce and salt and bring to a boil. In a small bowl, combine the remaining 5 ml cornflour with 15 ml water; add to the pan and stir for 1 minute or until slightly thickened. Return the chicken to the pan; add the spring onions and cook for 1 minute. Stir in the cashew nuts. Serves 4.

Per serving: Kilojoules 1 271; Fibre 3g; Protein 25g; Total Fat 16g; Saturated Fat 3g; Cholesterol 74mg; Sodium 703mg

Thai-Style Chicken

PREP: 25 MINUTES / COOK: 20 MINUTES

- 10 ml vegetable oil
- 4 skinless, boned chicken thighs (115 g each)
- 3 cloves garlic, finely chopped
- 30 ml finely chopped fresh ginger
- 150 ml chicken stock
- 30 ml tomato sauce
- 1 green chilli, seeded and chopped
- 2,5 ml salt
- 30 ml lime or lemon juice
- 60 ml each chopped basil and mint
- 175 g vermicelli, broken in thirds
- 160 g finely shredded Chinese cabbage or iceberg lettuce (2 cups)
- 2 spring onions, thinly sliced

1. In a large nonstick pan, heat the oil over moderate heat. Add the chicken and cook for 3 minutes per side or until golden brown. Transfer to a plate.

2. Add the garlic and ginger to the pan and cook for 1 minute. Add the stock, tomato sauce, chilli and salt. Return the chicken to the pan, cover and simmer for 12 minutes or until the chicken is cooked through. Stir in the lime juice, basil and mint.

3. Meanwhile, in a large pot of boiling water, cook the pasta according to package directions until *al dente*; drain. Divide the vermicelli among 4 plates. Top with the cabbage, spoon the chicken and sauce on top and sprinkle with the spring onions. Serves 4.

Per serving: Kilojoules 1 564; Fibre 3g; Protein 27g; Total Fat 12g; Saturated Fat 3g; Cholesterol 74mg; Sodium 650mg

Baked Walnut Chicken In a food processor, grind 70 ml walnuts, 60 ml dry bread crumbs and 2,5 ml each salt and grated lemon rind. Dip 4 each skinned chicken drumsticks and thighs in 2 egg whites, then in walnut mixture, patting it on. Bake at 200°C for 25 to 30 minutes or until done. Serves 4. *[kJ 1379; Fat 19g; Sodium 435mg]*

Mom's Chicken-Noodle Soup In a medium saucepan, combine 500 ml water, 250 ml chicken stock, 1 sliced celery stalk, 1 sliced carrot, 1 finely chopped garlic clove and 1,25ml salt. Bring to boil. Add 70 ml small pasta and 450 g skinless, boned chicken thighs, cut into 1-cm pieces. Cover and simmer 10 minutes or until pasta and chicken are done. Serves 4. *[kJ 868; Fat 9g; Sodium 606mg]*

Yoghurt Chicken Combine 500 ml plain low-fat yoghurt, 125 ml chopped fresh coriander, 5 ml each cumin, coriander, ginger, salt and pepper. Set half of mixture aside. To remaining mixture add 4 each skinned chicken drumsticks and thighs; marinate 1 hour. Discard marinade; grill chicken for 7 minutes per side or until done. Serve with reserved yoghurt mixture. Serves 4. *[kJ 1347; Fat 15g; Sodium 770mg]*

Turkey

PER 100 G COOKED*	
Kilojoules	683
Fibre	0 g
Protein	29 g
Total Fat	5 g
Saturated Fat	1,6 g
Cholesterol	76 mg
Sodium	70 mg

NUTRIENTS	
% RDA for people older than 10 years	
Niacin	30 %
Vitamin B6	23 %
Zinc	21 %
Iron	13 %

meat only, no skin

Did you know? . . .

Skinless turkey has about the same amount of protein, vitamin B6 and niacin as beef silverside, but only about half the fat.

Turkey Gumbo

PREP: 15 MINUTES / COOK: 50 MINUTES

When sliced okra is cooked, a substance in the vegetable thickens its cooking liquid much as cornflour would.

- 10 ml olive oil
- 450 g skinless, boned turkey breast, cut into 2,5-cm cubes
- 55 g smoked ham, chopped
- 2 medium onions, finely chopped
- 1 large red pepper, coarsely chopped
- 15 ml flour
- 250 g finely sliced okra
- 250 ml chicken stock
- 160 g spinach, shredded (4 cups)
- 2,5 ml each dried thyme and marjoram
- 1,25 ml salt
- 0,6 ml cayenne pepper

1. In a flameproof casserole, heat the oil over moderately high heat. Add the turkey and ham and cook for 5 minutes or until the turkey is lightly browned. Transfer the turkey and ham to a plate.

2. Add the onions to the pan and sauté for 5 minutes. Add the pepper and sauté for 4 minutes. Stir in the flour. Add the okra and stir until it has broken up and is well combined. Gradually add the stock and 150 ml of water, stirring constantly, until the sauce is smooth.

3. Add the spinach, thyme, marjoram, salt and cayenne. Bring to a boil, reduce to a simmer, cover and cook, stirring occasionally, for 30 minutes or until the gumbo is slightly thickened. Return the turkey and ham to the pan and cook for 2 minutes. Serves 4.

Per serving: Kilojoules 1 154; Fibre 4g; Protein 36g; Total Fat 7g; Saturated Fat 2g; Cholesterol 75mg; Sodium 834mg

Cajun-Spiced Turkey

PREP: 15 MINUTES / COOK: 3 HOURS

Rub this herb and spice mixture under the skin of your Christmas turkey and give your dinner guests a surprise. Rubbing the mixture under the skin means that when the fatty skin is removed, the flavour remains.

- 30 ml green hot pepper sauce
- 30 ml vegetable oil
- 5 ml salt
- 10 ml each dried oreganum, dried thyme and sugar
- 2,5 ml black pepper
- 2,5 ml cayenne pepper
- 1 turkey (5,8kg), thawed
- 1 lemon, pricked with a fork
- 30 ml flour
- 500 ml chicken or turkey stock

1. In a small bowl, combine the hot pepper sauce, oil, salt, oreganum, thyme, sugar, black pepper and cayenne pepper. Rub the spice mixture under the skin of the turkey's breast meat and drumsticks. Place the lemon in the cavity of the turkey.

2. Roast according to the roasting instructions in 'Basic cooking', opposite page.

3. Transfer the turkey to a cutting board; discard the lemon. Pour the pan juices into a gravy separator and then pour the defatted juices into a small saucepan. Whisk together the flour and stock and add to the pan juices. Cook, stirring, for 4 minutes or until the gravy is slightly thickened. Remove turkey skin before eating. Serves 12.

Per serving: Kilojoules 1 804; Fibre 0g; Protein 71g; Total Fat 13g; Saturated Fat 4g; Cholesterol 186mg; Sodium 584mg

Turkey Satay These turkey kebabs can be grilled in the oven or cooked over a braai.

Teriyaki Turkey

PREP: 15 MINUTES / COOK: 3 HOURS

- 70 ml light soya sauce
- 30 ml honey
- 30 ml sesame oil
- 5 ml grated orange rind
- 1,25 ml ground cinnamon
- 1 turkey (5,8 kg), thawed
- 1 head of garlic, unpeeled
- 30 ml flour
- 1,25 ml salt
- 500 ml chicken or turkey stock

1. In a small bowl, combine the soya sauce, honey, sesame oil, orange rind and cinnamon. Rub the mixture under the skin of the turkey's breast and drumsticks. Place the garlic in the cavity of the turkey.

2. Roast according to the roasting instructions in 'Basic cooking', at right.

3. Transfer the turkey to a cutting board; discard the garlic. Pour the pan juices into a gravy separator and then pour the defatted juices into a small saucepan. Whisk together the flour, salt and stock and add to the pan juices. Cook, stirring, for 4 minutes or until the gravy is slightly thickened. Remove turkey skin before eating. Serves 12.

Per serving: Kilojoules 1913; Fibre 0g; Protein 72g; Total Fat 14g; Saturated Fat 4g; Cholesterol 186mg; Sodium 667mg

Turkey Satay

PREP: 15 MINUTES / MARINATE: 1 HOUR
COOK: 10 MINUTES

- 125 ml lime or lemon juice
- 30 ml honey
- 30 ml peanut butter
- 2,5 ml crushed red chilli flakes
- 2,5 ml salt
- 450 g skinless, boned turkey breast, cut into 1-cm pieces
- 1 large cucumber, peeled, halved, seeded and cut into 16 pieces
- 1 large red pepper, cut into 16 pieces
- 30 ml finely chopped fresh basil or mint
- 16 fresh or tinned pineapple pieces

1. In a medium bowl, whisk together the lime juice, honey, peanut butter, red chilli flakes and salt. Set aside 60 ml of the mixture. Add the turkey, cucumber, pepper and basil to the mixture remaining in the bowl, tossing well. Cover and refrigerate for 1 hour.

2. Preheat the grill. Thread the turkey, vegetables and pineapple onto eight 25-cm skewers. Grill 15 centimetres from the heat for 6 minutes, turning once. To serve, spoon the reserved sauce over the kebabs. Serves 4.

Per serving: Kilojoules 1154; Fibre 2g; Protein 33g; Total Fat 7g; Saturated Fat 2g; Cholesterol 69mg; Sodium 407mg

At the market Frozen turkeys are usually only available at Christmas. They are all imported from The United States and Europe. Turkey drumsticks and mince are often on sale after Christmas. Check whether they were previously frozen.

Look for Turkeys should be solidly frozen.

Prep Thaw the frozen turkey thoroughly. Remove the giblets from the cavity. Rinse the turkey under cold running water and remove any pinfeathers.

To season the turkey, carefully lift the skin over the breast and drumsticks and rub the seasoning mixture underneath.

Basic cooking Have the turkey at room temperature. Place on a rack in a roasting pan and pour 500 ml of water into the pan. Roast, covered, in a preheated 180°C oven for 12 minutes per 450 grams or until the thigh meat registers 76,7°C. Uncover for the last 40 minutes of roasting.

Fruits & Berries

Honeydew-Lime Tart

Apples & Pears

Apples*
PER 1 MEDIUM (150 G)

Kilojoules	413
Fibre	3,8 g
Protein	0 g
Total Fat	0 g
Saturated Fat	0 g
Cholesterol	0 mg
Sodium	9 mg

NUTRIENTS

% RDA for people older than 10 years

Vitamin C	18 %

with skin, Golden Delicious variety

Did you know? . . .

Some of the fibre in apples is pectin which may help lower blood cholesterol.

Apples should be stored in the refrigerator. At room temperature they quickly begin to decline in quality: their flesh becomes mushy and they lose some of their vitamin content.

Butternut & Apple Soup

PREP: 25 MINUTES / COOK: 40 MINUTES

Garnish this autumnal purée with very thin, unpeeled apple slices which have been dipped in a little lemon juice to prevent them from going brown.

- 15 ml olive oil
- 1 small onion, halved and thinly sliced
- 3 cloves garlic, crushed and peeled
- 15 ml finely chopped fresh ginger
- 1 green chilli, finely chopped (or 1 pickled jalapeño)
- 650 g butternut squash, peeled, seeded and thinly sliced
- 10 ml sugar
- 900 g Granny Smith apples, peeled and thinly sliced
- 7,5 ml chilli powder
- 2,5 ml salt
- 1,25 ml dried thyme
- 375 ml chicken stock

1. In a large saucepan, heat the oil over moderate heat. Add the onion, garlic, ginger and chilli and sauté for 5 minutes or until the onion is soft. Add the butternut, sprinkle with the sugar and sauté for 5 minutes or until the butternut is crisp-tender.

2. Add the apples, chilli powder, salt and thyme, stirring to coat. Add the stock and 375 ml of water and bring to a boil. Reduce to a simmer, partially cover and cook for 30 minutes or until the butternut is very tender. Transfer to a food processor and purée. If necessary, reheat gently. Serves 4.

Per serving: Kilojoules 1 257; Fibre 9 g; Protein 4 g; Total Fat 4 g; Saturated Fat 1 g; Cholesterol 0 mg; Sodium 886 mg

Pork Chops with Fresh Pear Salsa

PREP: 20 MINUTES / COOK: 10 MINUTES

Try this tangy salsa with roast chicken or turkey or on a roast-beef sandwich.

- 350 g firm pears (Bosc or Bartlett would be suitable)
- 1 red pepper, cut into 1-cm squares
- 70 ml finely chopped onion (red, if available)
- 45 ml honey
- 30 ml apple cider vinegar
- 2,5 ml red hot pepper sauce
- 3,5 ml each salt and dried sage
- 2,5 ml black pepper
- 1,25 ml ground ginger
- 2 cloves garlic, finely chopped
- 4 trimmed pork chops (175 g each)

1. Peel the pears and cut them into 1-cm pieces. Transfer to a large bowl. Add the pepper, onion, honey, vinegar, hot pepper sauce and 1,25 ml of the salt. Toss to combine. Refrigerate until serving time.

2. Preheat the grill. In a small bowl, combine the sage, black pepper, ginger, garlic and the remaining salt. Rub the mixture into both sides of the chops. Grill 15 centimetres from the heat for 3 to 4 minutes per side or until cooked through but still juicy. Serve with the pear salsa. Serves 4.

Per serving: Kilojoules 1 636; Fibre 3 g; Protein 31 g; Total Fat 8 g; Saturated Fat 3 g; Cholesterol 85 mg; Sodium 489 mg

Apple Tart with Cheddar Crust *Apples are concealed beneath a savoury crust.*

Apple Tart with Cheddar Crust

PREP: 30 MINUTES / CHILL: 1 HOUR
COOK: 40 MINUTES

A slice of double-crust tart topped with a slab of Cheddar is very high in fat. Try this single-crust tart with the grated Cheddar cheese mixed into the dough.

CRUST:
- 250 ml cake flour
- 15 ml sugar
- 2,5 ml baking powder
- 1,25 ml salt
- 0,6 ml cayenne pepper
- 45 ml cold unsalted butter, cut up
- 30 ml solid vegetable shortening
- 250 ml grated sharp Cheddar cheese (115 g)
- 70 ml iced water

FILLING:
- 1,2 kg Granny Smith apples, peeled and thinly sliced
- 125 ml sugar
- 30 ml flour
- 15 ml lemon juice
- 2,5 ml ground cinnamon

1. For the crust: in a medium bowl, combine the flour, sugar, baking powder, salt and cayenne. With a pastry blender or two knives, cut in the butter and shortening until the mixture resembles coarse crumbs. Stir in the cheese until well combined. Sprinkle on the iced water and stir just until the dough leaves the sides of the bowl. Shape into a flat disc, wrap in plastic wrap and refrigerate for at least 1 hour.

2. Preheat the oven to 230°C. For the filling: in a large bowl, toss together the apples, sugar, flour, lemon juice and cinnamon. Spoon into a 23-cm glass pie dish.

3. On a lightly floured surface, roll the dough out to a 33-cm round and drape over the apples. Crimp the edges to seal. Make 2 slashes in the dough for steam vents. Place on a baking sheet with sides and bake for 20 minutes. Reduce the heat to 180°C and bake for 20 minutes or until the crust is golden brown and the apples are tender. If the crust begins to brown too much before the apples are tender, tent with foil. Serves 8.

Per serving: Kilojoules 1 412; Fibre 5 g; Protein 5 g; Total Fat 12 g; Saturated Fat 6 g; Cholesterol 29 mg; Sodium 218 mg

At the market Markets now offer numerous apple varieties in addition to the more common Granny Smith, Golden Delicious and Starking. Try Braeburn, Fuji or Starkrimson both for cooking and eating fresh. Bartlett and Comice are well-known as excellent eating pears but Packham's Triumph is the most popular. New varieties such as Flamingo have also come onto the market.

Granny Smith apples are most versatile. Sweet, juicy Bon Rouge pears are a treat for the eye as well as the palate.

Look for Choose hard apples with unbruised skin. Heavy waxing indicates that the apples are past their best. Buy firm, unblemished pears a few days before you'll eat them; pears are often sold underripe and need time to ripen at room temperature. Store ripe pears and apples in the refrigerator.

Prep Sprinkle cut apple and pear slices with lemon juice to prevent browning.

Chicken Normandy
Apples, sage and a touch of apple brandy in a cream sauce are lovely complements to sautéed chicken.

Did you know? . . .

Most of the vitamin C in pears is found in the skin.

Dried apples and pears are both high in kilojoules and have useful amounts of fibre, but some of the vitamin C is destroyed in the drying process. Most commercially dried fruit in South Africa has been exposed to sulphur to prevent browning.

Most of the fibre in pears is insoluble—the kind that helps prevent diverticulosis and colon cancer.

Pears tinned in juice have less vitamin C than fresh pears.

Chicken Normandy

PREP: 10 MINUTES / COOK: 30 MINUTES

Normandy is home to bountiful orchards and lush pastures for dairy cows. Dishes from this French region often include apples and cream. Calvados is an apple spirit made from distilled apple cider.

- **10 ml vegetable oil**
- **4 skinless, boned chicken breasts (450 g total)**
- **30 ml plus 5 ml flour**
- **1 small onion, thinly sliced**
- **700 g Granny Smith apples, peeled, halved and thinly sliced (or half Granny Smith and half any other firm cooking apple)**
- **45 ml Calvados or brandy**
- **175 ml chicken stock**
- **2,5 ml each salt and pepper**
- **1,25 ml dried sage**
- **45 ml sour cream**
- **30 ml chopped parsley**

1. In a large nonstick pan, heat the oil over moderate heat. Dredge the chicken in 30 ml of the flour, shaking off the excess. Sauté the chicken for 3 minutes per side or until golden brown. Transfer the chicken to a plate.

2. Add the onion to the pan and cook for 1 minute or until tender. Add the apples and sauté for 5 minutes or until lightly browned. Remove the pan from the heat and add the Calvados or brandy. Return the pan to the heat and cook for 30 seconds or until the liquid has evaporated. Add 60 ml of the stock and 1,25 ml each of the salt and pepper to the pan and simmer gently for 4 minutes or until the apples are tender but not falling apart. Remove with a slotted spoon; set aside.

3. Add the remaining stock to the pan along with the sage and the remaining 1,25 ml each salt and pepper. Bring to a boil. Reduce to a simmer, return the chicken to the pan, cover and cook for 5 to 7 minutes or until the chicken is cooked through. Return the apples to the pan and simmer gently for 1 minute or until heated through.

4. In a small bowl, whisk together the sour cream and the remaining 5 ml flour. Stir it into the pan and simmer, stirring constantly, for 2 minutes or until slightly thickened. Stir in the parsley. Serves 4.

Per serving: Kilojoules 1 542; Fibre 5 g; Protein 31 g; Total Fat 9 g; Saturated Fat 3 g; Cholesterol 72 mg; Sodium 630 mg

Pear Strudel

PREP: 20 MINUTES / COOK: 50 MINUTES

You could also make this strudel with apples. Use Golden Delicious, Braeburn or any cooking variety that will hold its shape.

- 70 ml apple juice (or frozen apple juice concentrate)
- 15 ml lemon juice
- 1,25 ml each salt and pepper
- 900 g firm-ripe pears, such as Bartlett or Bosc, peeled and coarsely chopped
- 70 ml dried currants
- 6 sheets phyllo pastry
- 30 ml plus 5 ml unsalted butter, melted
- 30 ml plus 5 ml sugar

1. In a large pan, bring the apple juice, lemon juice, salt and pepper to a boil over moderate heat. Add the pears, reduce to a simmer and cook, uncovered, for 10 minutes or until the pears are crisp-tender and the liquid has evaporated. Stir in the currants. Cool to room temperature.

2. Preheat the oven to 200°C. On a work surface, lay 2 sheets of phyllo pastry on top of one another with the long side facing you. Brush with 10 ml of the butter and sprinkle with 10 ml of the sugar. Repeat two more times, using 2 sheets of phyllo, 10 ml of butter, and 10 ml of sugar for each layer.

3. Spoon the pear mixture along the lower third of the phyllo, leaving a 5-cm border at each end. Fold the short ends in over the filling, then roll up from the long side jamroll fashion. Brush the roll with the remaining 5 ml butter and sprinkle with the remaining 5 ml sugar.

4. Place the roll on an ungreased baking sheet; make several diagonal slashes on the top of the roll. Bake for 40 minutes or until crisp and golden brown. Cool for 10 minutes before serving. Serves 6.

Per serving: Kilojoules 1 061; Fibre 5 g; Protein 2 g; Total Fat 6 g; Saturated Fat 3 g; Cholesterol 13 mg; Sodium 198 mg

Pear & Hazelnut Salad In a large bowl, whisk 60 ml lime juice, 30 ml honey and 5 ml olive oil. Add 4 medium Bartlett pears, cut into thin wedges. Add 120 g watercress (4 cups); toss. Sprinkle salad with 60 ml coarsely chopped toasted hazelnuts. Serves 4. *[kJ 922; Fat 6 g; Sodium 18 mg]*

Chunky Apple & Pear Sauce In a medium saucepan, combine 2 large apples and 2 large pears, peeled and diced. Add 30 ml sugar (or more to taste), 30 ml lemon juice and 1,25 ml each cinnamon and ginger. Cook over low heat, stirring often, for 10 minutes or until tender. Lightly mash with a potato masher or immersion blender. Serve warm or chilled. Serves 4. *[kJ 595; Fat 0 g; Sodium 7 mg]*

Apple-Pear Crisp Preheat the oven to 190°C. In a 20-cm square baking tin, toss 650 g each peeled, sliced pears and peeled, sliced apples with 45 ml lemon juice, 30 ml sugar, 2,5 ml ginger and 1,25 ml salt. In small bowl, mix 45 ml each white and brown sugars, 2,5 ml cinnamon and 1,25 ml salt. Cut in 30 ml unsalted butter. Sprinkle over fruit. Bake 40 minutes. Serves 4. *[kJ 1 570; Fat 6 g; Sodium 319 mg]*

Apricots

Fresh Apricots
PER 5 (175 G)

Kilojoules	277
Fibre	3,2g
Protein	1,4g
Total Fat	0,2g
Saturated Fat	0g
Cholesterol	0mg
Sodium	7mg

NUTRIENTS

% RDA for people older
lthan 10 years

Vitamin A	15%
Vitamin C	12%

Dried Apricots
PER 60 G (¼ CUP)

Kilojoules	679
Fibre	5,4g
Protein	2g
Total Fat	0,3g
Saturated Fat	0g
Cholesterol	0mg
Sodium	6mg

NUTRIENTS

% RDA for people older
than 10 years

Iron	20%
Niacin	10%

Grilled Chicken with Fresh Apricot Sauce

PREP: 20 MINUTES / MARINATE: 1 HOUR
COOK: 15 MINUTES

You can make the sauce with drained tinned apricots when fresh apricots aren't available. Be sure to rinse the fruit if it's packed in syrup.

- 175 ml apricot juice
- 30 ml balsamic vinegar
- 15 ml sesame oil
- 2 spring onions, chopped
- 10 ml grated fresh ginger
- 2 cloves garlic, chopped
- 4 skinless, boned chicken breasts (450 g total)
- 5 ml cornflour blended with 15 ml water
- 2,5 ml salt
- 280 g fresh apricots, sliced
- 2 spring onions, sliced (optional)

1. In a medium bowl, whisk together the apricot juice, vinegar, sesame oil, spring onions, ginger and garlic. Measure out 125 ml, transfer to a medium saucepan and set aside. Add the chicken to the mixture remaining in the bowl, tossing to coat. Marinate at room temperature for 1 hour or in the refrigerator for up to 4 hours.

2. Preheat the grill. Grill the chicken 15 centimetres from the heat, turning halfway through, for 12 minutes or until cooked through.

3. Meanwhile, add the cornflour mixture and salt to the saucepan of reserved apricot juice mixture. Bring to a simmer over moderate heat, stirring.

Add the apricots and cook for 2 minutes or until the sauce is slightly thickened and the apricots are fork-tender. Serve the chicken with the sauce spooned on top, garnished with the spring onions. Serves 4.

Per serving: Kilojoules 984; Fibre 2g; Protein 30g; Total Fat 7g; Saturated Fat 2g; Cholesterol 62mg; Sodium 353mg

Apricot Bavarian

PREP: 20 MINUTES / CHILL: 4 HOURS

Fresh apricots have a short season; tinned fruit can stand in, if necessary. Try to find fruit tinned in juice and weigh the fruit without the juice..

- 350 ml low-fat evaporated milk
- 2 x 10 g envelopes unflavoured gelatine
- 60 ml boiling water
- 565 g sliced fresh apricots (4 cups)
- 75 ml light brown sugar
- 75 ml honey
- 60 ml heavy cream
- 15 ml lemon juice
- 0,6 ml ground cinnamon
- 1 pinch of nutmeg

1. Place the evaporated milk in a large metal bowl and place in the freezer for 1 hour or until semi-frozen (slushy).

2. Meanwhile, in a small bowl, sprinkle the gelatine over 60 ml of cold water and let stand for 5 minutes. Transfer the gelatine to a blender or food processor, add the boiling water and process for 30 seconds or until dissolved. Add 425 g (3 cups) of the sliced apricots,

60 ml each of the brown sugar and honey, the heavy cream, 10 ml of the lemon juice, the cinnamon and nutmeg and process until smooth. Refrigerate the apricot purée for 1 to 1½ hours or until the texture of raw egg whites. (Or quick-chill in a bowl set in a larger bowl of iced water.)

3. When the evaporated milk is slushy, beat with an electric mixer at high speed until soft peaks form. Fold the beaten milk into the chilled apricot mixture. Pour into a 2-litre serving bowl or 8 individual 250-ml bowls. Chill for at least 3 hours or until set.

4. Coarsely dice the remaining 140 g apricots and combine with the remaining 15 ml each brown sugar and honey and the remaining 5 ml lemon juice. Serve the sweetened diced apricots with the bavarian. Serves 8.

Per serving: Kilojoules 739; Fibre 0g; Protein 6g; Total Fat 4g; Saturated Fat 3g; Cholesterol 23mg; Sodium 70mg

Grilled Chicken with Fresh Apricot Sauce *is tangy with the flavour of balsamic vinegar, ginger and garlic.*

Apricot 'Poundcake'

PREP: 20 MINUTES / COOK: 45 MINUTES

With just 30 millilitres of butter, it's not a real poundcake, but it is a delicious cake.

- **190 g dried apricots, chopped (1⅔ cups)**
- **175 ml sweetened applesauce**
- **30 ml unsalted butter**
- **30 ml olive oil**
- **60 ml low-fat cultured buttermilk**
- **3 eggs**
- **10 ml vanilla essence**
- **10 ml grated orange rind**
- **375 ml sugar**
- **700 g cake flour (875 ml)**
- **5 ml each baking powder and salt**
- **2,5 ml bicarbonate of soda**

1. Preheat the oven to 180°C. Spray a 25-cm tube tin with a removable bottom with nonstick cooking spray.

2. In a medium saucepan, combine 50 g of the apricots, the applesauce and 125 ml of water. Simmer for 5 minutes or until the apricots are softened. Transfer to a food processor or blender. Add the butter, oil and buttermilk and process until smooth. Set the apricot mixture aside to cool slightly, then beat in the eggs, vanilla essence and orange rind, blending just until smooth. Transfer to a large bowl. Stir in the sugar.

3. In a medium bowl, stir together the cake flour, baking powder, salt and bicarbonate of soda. Fold the flour mixture into the apricot mixture in 3 additions. Fold in the remaining apricots and scrape into the prepared tin.

4. Bake for 40 minutes or until a cake tester inserted halfway between the sides and the centre comes out clean. Cool in the tin on a wire rack for 10 minutes. Loosen the cake from the tin, remove the sides and set the cake on the rack to cool completely. Serves 16.

Per serving: Kilojoules 728; Fibre 2g; Protein 5g; Total Fat 5g; Saturated Fat 2g; Cholesterol 44mg; Sodium 169mg

Shopping & prep

At the market Most apricots sold in South Africa are grown in the Ladismith area of the Western Cape; they're available from November to the end of summer. Dried apricots are available as loose fruit, mebos and fruit rolls. Sulphur is used in the production of most commercially dried fruit.

Look for Apricots are highly perishable, so they're usually picked underripe to help them withstand shipping. Buy fruits that are firm but not rock-hard; the skin should be orangy-gold, with no greenish tinge. Ripen apricots at home in a paper bag at room temperature; when they're ripe, eat them immediately or refrigerate for a few days.

Prep Apricots are easy to peel if you drop them in boiling water for about 20 seconds; cool in cold water.

It's easiest to chop or dice dried apricots with kitchen scissors if you spray the blades with nonstick cooking spray. Cut the apricots into strips, then cut the strips into bits.

Apricot Danish

Layers of flaky phyllo pastry frame a cream-cheese filling topped with apricot purée and chopped nuts.

Tinned apricots may be substituted for fresh in most recipes; juice-packed fruit is the best choice. Apricots packed in heavy or extra-heavy syrup have double the kilojoules that juice-packed do. The extra kilojoules are 'empty' kilojoules which come from sugar.

Drying concentrates the apricot's impressive nutrient value. Dried apricots make a good cereal topping as well as a healthy substitute for raisins in breads, cakes and biscuits.

Dried apricots are often treated with sulphur dioxide to keep their colour bright. Those allergic to sulphites should look for unsulphured apricots in health-food stores.

Apricot-Pecan Nut Stuffing

PREP: 20 MINUTES / COOK: 1 HOUR

340 g white and whole-wheat bread cut into 2-cm cubes (8 cups)
15 ml olive oil
2 stalks celery, chopped
1 large onion (red, if available), finely chopped
2,5 ml each dried thyme and sage
310 ml chicken stock
180 g chopped dried apricots (1½ cups)
1 egg
60 ml chopped parsley
60 ml chopped toasted pecan nuts
1,25 ml each salt and pepper

1. Preheat the oven to 190°C. Spread the bread on a baking sheet and bake for 8 to 10 minutes or until dried out. Remove the bread from the oven and lower the temperature to 180°C.

2. In a large pan, heat the oil over moderate heat. Add the celery, onion, thyme and sage and cook for 8 minutes. Add 250 ml of the stock and the apricots. Bring to a simmer and cook for 5 minutes or until the apricots are softened. Transfer the apricot mixture to a large bowl and set aside to cool.

3. In a small bowl, whisk together the egg and the remaining 60 ml stock. Stir the egg mixture into the cooled apricot mixture along with the parsley, pecan nuts, salt and pepper. Add the bread cubes, tossing until well combined.

4. Spray a 23 x 33-cm baking dish with nonstick cooking spray. Spoon the stuffing mixture in and cover with foil. Bake for 25 minutes. Remove the foil and bake for 10 minutes or until crisp and heated through. Serves 10.

Per serving: Kilojoules 739; Fibre 4 g; Protein 5 g; Total Fat 5 g; Saturated Fat 1 g; Cholesterol 21 mg; Sodium 407 mg

Apricot Danish

PREP: 25 MINUTES / COOK: 45 MINUTES

90 g dried apricots, chopped (¾ cup)
120 ml plus 30 ml packed light brown sugar
10 ml vanilla essence
2,5 ml ground ginger
115 g fat-free smooth cottage cheese
6 ginger biscuits (about 25 g), crushed
30 ml unsalted butter, melted
30 ml vegetable oil
12 sheets frozen phyllo pastry, thawed
45 ml chopped hazelnuts or walnuts
70 ml smooth apricot jam
15 ml icing sugar

1. In a small saucepan, combine the apricots, 60 ml of the brown sugar and 125 ml of water. Bring to a simmer over medium heat and cook for 10 minutes or until softened. Transfer the apricot mixture to a blender or food processor, add 5 ml of the vanilla essence and process to a smooth purée.

2. In a medium bowl, cream 60 ml of the brown sugar, the ground ginger, the remaining 5 ml vanilla and the cottage cheese with an electric mixer. In a small bowl, combine the ginger biscuit crumbs and the remaining 30 ml brown sugar.

3. In a small dish, combine the butter and oil. Place the phyllo on a work surface and cover with a towel. Spray a baking sheet with nonstick cooking spray. Lay 2 sheets of phyllo on the baking sheet and brush lightly with some of the butter mixture. Sprinkle with 15 ml of the ginger biscuit crumbs. Repeat the layering with more butter mixture (save some for the top of the pastry) and the remaining phyllo and crumbs.

4. Preheat the oven to 190°C. Spoon the cottage cheese mixture down the centre of the dough in a 4-cm-wide strip; stop 2,5 centimetres short of the short ends. Spoon the apricot purée in two 4-cm-wide strips, one on either side of the cheese. Roll the long sides of the pastry in toward the centre until they just begin to cover the apricot. Roll the short sides in and press firmly to seal (if not firmly sealed, the phyllo may start to unfold as it bakes). The finished size should be 33 x 17 centimetres.

5. Brush the crust lightly with the remaining butter mixture. Sprinkle the nuts over the filling and bake for 30 to 35 minutes or until golden and crisped. Meanwhile, in a small saucepan, melt the apricot jam with 15 ml of water over low heat. Brush the jam over the warm pastry. Sprinkle with the icing sugar. Serves 8.

Per serving: Kilojoules 1 267; Fibre 2g; Protein 5g; Total Fat 11g; Saturated Fat 3g; Cholesterol 10mg; Sodium 158mg

Chocolate-Dipped Apricots

In a double boiler, melt 55g dark chocolate with 2,5 ml solid vegetable shortening. Cool to room temperature. Dip 24 dried apricots into chocolate mixture, coating one half of each apricot. Dry on a wire rack before serving. Serves 6. *[kJ 354; Fat 3g; Sodium 9mg]*

Fresh Apricots Poached in Syrup

In a medium saucepan, bring 250 ml water, 125 ml sugar and 2,5 ml ground ginger to a boil. Boil for 3 minutes. Add 8 fresh apricots, cover and cook for 10 minutes or until tender. Remove from heat and stir in 5 ml vanilla essence. Cool apricots in syrup. Chill to serve. Serves 4. *[kJ 514; Fat 0g; Sodium 3mg]*

Warm Apricot Compote

In a medium saucepan, bring 125 ml apricot juice, 125 ml orange juice, 60 ml sugar, 30 ml lemon juice and 1,25 ml cardamom to a boil. Add 350g dried apricots. Simmer 20 minutes or until tender. Serve warm, at room temperature or chilled. *[kJ 1324; Fat 1g; Sodium 10mg]*

Avocado

PER 85G (CUBES) (½ CUP)	
Kilojoules	868
Fibre	4,5g
Protein	1g
Total Fat	20g
Saturated Fat	4,1g
Cholesterol	0mg
Sodium	3mg

NUTRIENTS	
% RDA for people older than 10 years	
Vitamin C	20%
Magnesium	9%
Vitamin B6	8%
Folate	6%

Did you know? . . .

The avocado is a source of lutein, a carotenoid that seems to help prevent age-related macular degeneration, an eye disease that affects the elderly.

A medium avocado supplies 20 per cent of the daily adult requirement of vitamin E, which is a potent antioxidant.

Avocado & Ham Antipasto with Guacamole Dressing

PREP: 20 MINUTES

The favourite Mexican dip is used as a sauce in this inventive first-course dish. Cucumber provides a crunchy contrast to the velvety avocado.

- 1 medium avocado, cut lengthwise into thin wedges
- 1 large tomato, diced
- 60ml finely chopped onion (red, if available)
- 60ml chopped fresh coriander or parsley
- 30ml red wine vinegar
- 2,5ml ground cumin
- 1,25ml salt
- 1 cucumber, peeled and thinly sliced
- 60g smoked ham, cut into matchsticks

1. Measure 60ml of the avocado and chop coarsely. Transfer to a bowl and stir in the tomato, onion, coriander, vinegar, cumin and salt. Set the dressing aside.

2. Divide the remaining avocado and the cucumber and ham among 4 serving plates. Spoon the guacamole dressing on top. Serves 4.

Per serving: Kilojoules 711; Fibre 4g; Protein 5g; Total Fat 14g; Saturated Fat 3g; Cholesterol 9mg; Sodium 359mg

Avocado 'Sushi' Salad

PREP: 20 MINUTES / COOK: 20 MINUTES

Authentic sushi rolls are tricky to make, but you can enjoy similar flavours in this appetizer, a simple presentation of rice on green salad leaves. Use soft lettuce in place of spinach if you prefer.

- 250ml rice (preferably jasmine)
- 1,25ml salt
- 60ml rice vinegar
- 30ml each light soya sauce and lime (or lemon) juice
- 20ml sugar
- 1 medium carrot, cut into 5-mm dice
- 2 small avocados, cut into 5-mm dice
- 24 small spinach leaves

1. In a medium saucepan, bring 500ml of water to a boil. Add the rice and salt, cover and simmer for 17 minutes or until tender.

2. Meanwhile, in a small saucepan, bring the vinegar, soya sauce, lime juice and sugar to a boil. Remove from the heat. Stir into the cooked rice. Transfer the seasoned rice to a bowl and let cool to room temperature.

3. Stir the carrot and avocado into the rice. Spray four 225-ml ramekins or bowls with nonstick cooking spray and, dividing evenly, spoon the mixture into

Mixed Greens with Creamy Avocado Dressing

PREP: 15 MINUTES

1 avocado, cut into pieces
60 ml plain low-fat yoghurt
2,5 ml grated lemon rind
15 ml lemon juice
2,5 ml salt
240 g sliced cos lettuce (4 cups)
120 g watercress or curly endive
    (4 cups)
2 spring onions, thinly sliced

1. In a food processor or blender, combine the avocado, yoghurt, lemon rind, lemon juice, salt and 15 ml of water and process until smooth.

2. Transfer the dressing to a large bowl. Add the lettuce, watercress and spring onions, tossing to coat. Serves 4.

Per serving: Kilojoules 622; Fibre 4g; Protein 3g; Total Fat 12g; Saturated Fat 3g; Cholesterol 1mg; Sodium 327mg

the bowls. Gently but firmly press down. Arrange the spinach on serving plates and invert the moulded rice salads onto the spinach. Serves 4.

Per serving: Kilojoules 1 600; Fibre 6g; Protein 6g; Total Fat 18g; Saturated Fat 4g; Cholesterol 0mg; Sodium 612mg

Avocado 'Sushi' Salad *features Japanese flavours in a sophisticated side dish.*

At the market Some varieties of avocado which are available are Fuerte, Hass, Pinkerton, Edranol and Ryan, although avocados are not usually bought by variety—ripeness seems to be the main criteria.

Look for Choose an avocado with unbroken skin. The fruit should yield to gentle pressure at the stalk. If necessary, leave it at room temperature for a few days to soften. Speed up the ripening process by placing in a brown paper bag with other fruit.

Prep Peel and slice avocados close to serving time; their flesh darkens when exposed to air. To halve the fruit, run a knife lengthwise around the avocado, sliding it around the pit, then twist the halves. Remove the pit by twisting it out with a knife blade (see below).

To pit an avocado, strike the pit lightly but sharply with the blade of a chef's knife. Then twist the blade to 'unscrew' the pit and lift it out (attached to the blade).

Bananas

PER 1 MEDIUM (75G)	
Kilojoules	287
Fibre	1,3g
Protein	1g
Total Fat	0,2g
Saturated Fat	0,1g
Cholesterol	0mg
Sodium	1mg

NUTRIENTS	
% RDA for people older than 10 years	
Vitamin C	15%
Vitamin B6	11%

Did you know? . . .

Your body's supply of vitamin B6 must be replenished each day and eating bananas is a good way to do it. Vitamin B6 plays a role in antibody production, so an adequate supply of this nutrient strengthens immunity.

Banana Raita

PREP: 10 MINUTES / COOK: 10 MINUTES
CHILL: 2 HOURS

A raita is a yoghurt-based Indian condiment meant to be served as a cooling contrast to highly spiced dishes.

- 10 ml vegetable oil
- 1 small onion, finely chopped
- 2,5 ml each ground coriander and cumin
- 1,25 ml ground cardamom
- 0,6 ml ground ginger
- 450 g bananas (4 to 5 large), mashed
- 2,5 ml salt
- 0,6 ml cayenne pepper
- 500 ml plain low-fat yoghurt

1. In a small pan, heat the oil over moderate heat. Add the onion and sauté for 5 minutes or until golden. Stir in the coriander, cumin, cardamom and ginger and cook for 1 minute or until fragrant.

2. Add the bananas and stir to incorporate the spices. Transfer the banana mixture to a bowl and stir in the salt, cayenne and yoghurt. Cover and refrigerate for 2 hours or until well chilled. Makes 900 millilitres.

Per 125 ml (½ cup): Kilojoules 498; Fibre 1g; Protein 4g; Total Fat 3g; Saturated Fat 1g; Cholesterol 6mg; Sodium 221mg

Banana-Pecan Bread

PREP: 15 MINUTES
COOK: 1 HOUR 25 MINUTES

If your banana-bread recipe calls for butter, try this one instead—it's made with just 45 millilitres of oil.

- 110 g rolled oats
- 70 ml pecan nuts
- 450 g very ripe bananas (4 to 5 large)
- 250 ml low-fat cultured buttermilk
- 45 ml vegetable oil
- 2 egg whites
- 5 ml vanilla essence
- 125 ml each granulated sugar and packed dark brown sugar
- 500 ml flour
- 12,5 ml baking powder
- 2,5 ml bicarbonate of soda
- 1,25 ml salt

1. Preheat the oven to 180°C. Spray a 23 x 13-cm loaf tin with nonstick cooking spray. In a small baking tin, toast the oats, stirring them occasionally, for 10 minutes or until lightly browned. At the same time, in another small baking tin, toast the pecan nuts for 7 minutes or until fragrant and lightly browned. When the pecan nuts are cool enough to handle, chop them coarsely.

2. In a large bowl, with a potato masher or fork, mash the bananas until

Banana Pudding Tart *A layer of apricot-glazed bananas sits atop a banana pudding.*

At the market You can buy bananas just about anywhere: the trick is finding them at the proper stage of ripeness. To be safe, buy them several days before you need them.

The starch in green bananas is 'resistant', that is, it cannot be digested in the small intestine and goes on to ferment in the large intestine, causing wind. Try to eat only ripe bananas.

Look for Buy firm, unblemished bananas, either green-tipped or fully yellow. Beware of greyish bananas as they will not ripen properly. Bananas in bunches with the stems still intact will keep longer.

Prep Store bananas in a paper bag at room temperature if they need ripening. Sliced bananas will darken when exposed to air; to keep them from turning brown, toss the slices with a little citrus juice. To prevent bananas from getting overripe, store them in the refrigerator. The skin will turn an alarming black, but the bananas themselves will be fine.

---

not quite smooth. Add the buttermilk, oil, egg whites, vanilla essence and granulated and brown sugars and mix until well blended; set aside.

3. In a small bowl, combine the flour, baking powder, bicarbonate of soda and salt. Fold the dry ingredients into the banana mixture along with the oats and pecan nuts until just combined. Do not overmix. Spoon the batter into the prepared tin, smoothing the top. Bake for 1 hour and 25 minutes or until a cake tester inserted in the centre comes out clean. Cool in the tin on a rack for 10 minutes. Turn out of the tin onto the rack to cool completely. Serves 8.

Per serving: Kilojoules 1703; Fibre 3g; Protein 7g; Total Fat 11g; Saturated Fat 1g; Cholesterol 1mg; Sodium 125mg

---

Banana Pudding Tart

PREP: 15 MINUTES / COOK: 10 MINUTES

This impressive single-crust tart is crowned with a layer of jam-glazed banana slices.

225 g sweet biscuits (Marie or vanilla wafers—about 48)
15 ml plus 125 ml sugar
15 ml vegetable oil
60 ml cornflour
0,6 ml each salt and nutmeg

750 ml low-fat (2%) milk
5 ml vanilla essence
10 ml unsalted butter
650 g large bananas (6 to 7 large), thinly sliced
60 ml apricot jam, melted

1. Preheat the oven to 180°C. In a food processor, combine the biscuits and 15 ml of the sugar and process to crumbs. Add the oil and 60 ml of water and process until well combined. Press the mixture into a 23-cm pie plate to form a pie shell. Bake for 10 minutes or until set.

2. Meanwhile, in a medium saucepan, combine the remaining 125 ml sugar, the cornflour, salt and nutmeg. Whisk in the milk until well combined. Cook over moderate heat, stirring, for 7 minutes or until the mixture has come to a boil and is thickened. Remove from the heat and stir in the vanilla essence and butter. Let cool slightly.

3. Fold 250 ml of the bananas into the cooled pudding. Spoon the pudding mixture into the pie shell and arrange the remaining bananas in a circular pattern on top. Brush the jam over the bananas. Serves 8.

Per serving: Kilojoules 1498; Fibre 2g; Protein 7g; Total Fat 9g; Saturated Fat 3g; Cholesterol 18mg; Sodium 197m

Berries

Blueberries

PER 160 G (1 CUP)	
Kilojoules	426
Fibre	4,3 g
Protein	1 g
Total Fat	0,6 g
Saturated Fat	0 g
Cholesterol	0 mg
Sodium	10 mg

NUTRIENTS	
% RDA for people older than 10 years	
Vitamin C	35 %

Did you know? . . .

In a US Department of Agriculture analysis of the antioxidant capacities of fruits, blueberries ranked first among fruits. A 100-g portion of blueberries has the same antioxidant power (in the test tube) as 1 270 mg of vitamin C.

The blueberry's colour comes from pigments called anthocyanosides which are antioxidants.

Blueberry Semifreddo

PREP: 10 MINUTES / COOK: 10 MINUTES
FREEZE: 4 HOURS / STAND: 30 MINUTES

This moulded frozen dessert is meltingly creamy. Semifreddo means 'half-frozen'.

- 640 g blueberries (4 cups)
- 125 ml sugar
- 0,6 ml allspice
- 250 ml low-fat (2%) milk
- 15 ml flour
- 425 g ricotta cheese
- 70 ml crème fraîche (or sour cream if crème fraîche is not available)
- 60 ml honey
- 3,5 ml vanilla essence

1. In a medium saucepan, combine the blueberries, sugar and allspice and simmer over moderate heat for 5 minutes or until slightly thickened. Cool to room temperature.

2. Meanwhile, in a small saucepan, whisk the milk into the flour. Cook, stirring, for 5 minutes or until the mixture is slightly thickened. Cool to room temperature, then transfer to a food processor. Add the ricotta, crème fraîche, honey and vanilla essence and process until smooth. Transfer to a bowl and fold in 500 ml of the blueberry sauce. (Refrigerate the remaining sauce until serving time.)

3. Line a 23 x 13-cm glass loaf dish with plastic wrap, leaving a 2-cm over-hang. Spoon the blueberry-ricotta mixture into the dish, smoothing the top. Cover with plastic wrap and freeze for 4 hours.

4. To serve, let stand for 30 minutes at room temperature, then unmould onto a serving platter. Cut into slices and serve with the reserved blueberry sauce. Serves 8.

Per serving: Kilojoules 1 103; Fibre 2g; Protein 8g; Total Fat 10g; Saturated Fat 6g; Cholesterol 37mg; Sodium 68mg

Fresh Blueberry Jam

PREP: 10 MINUTES / COOK: 20 MINUTES

The delicious flavour of this jam makes the effort worthwhile. Jam made by this method is not meant for long storage; refrigerate it and use it within about a week.

- 480 g blueberries (3 cups)
- 250 ml sugar
- 30 ml lemon juice
- 4 strips (7,5 x 1 cm) orange rind
- 2,5 ml ground cinnamon
- 1,25 ml salt
- 5 ml vanilla essence

1. In a pot of boiling water, sterilize 2 x 200-millilitre preserving jars and lids.

2. In a medium saucepan, combine the blueberries, sugar, lemon juice, orange rind, cinnamon and salt and cook over moderate heat, stirring frequently, for

20 minutes or until thick. Remove from the heat. Discard the rind and stir in the vanilla. Spoon the jam into the sterilized jars. Makes 375 millilitres.

Per 15 ml: Kilojoules 182; Fibre 0g; Protein 0g; Total Fat 0g; Saturated Fat 0g; Cholesterol 0mg; Sodium 25mg

Blueberry Scones

PREP: 15 MINUTES / COOK: 25 MINUTES

We've made our 'cream scones' with low-fat buttermilk instead of heavy cream. Scones are tastiest when served warm.

- 70 ml low-fat cultured buttermilk
- 1 egg, separated
- 375 ml flour
- 30 ml plus 10 ml sugar
- 7,5 ml baking powder
- 1,25 ml each bicarbonate of soda and salt
- 45 ml cold unsalted butter
- 240 g blueberries (1½ cups)
- 5 ml grated lemon rind

1. Preheat the oven to 190°C. In a small bowl, combine the buttermilk and egg yolk; set aside.

2. In a large bowl, combine the flour, 30 ml of the sugar, the baking powder, bicarbonate of soda and salt. With a pastry blender or two knives, cut in the butter until the mixture resembles coarse crumbs. Add the blueberries and lemon rind, stirring until well mixed.

3. Make a well in the centre of the dry ingredients, add the buttermilk mixture and, with a fork, combine until a soft dough is formed. (If the mixture is too dry, add up to 30 ml more buttermilk.)

4. Transfer the dough to a lightly floured surface and knead 4 or 5 times until well mixed. Transfer to an ungreased baking sheet and shape into a 18-cm round disc. Lightly beat the egg white and brush over the dough. Sprinkle with the remaining 10 ml sugar. Cut the round into 6 wedges. Bake for 25 minutes or until a cake tester inserted in the centre comes out clean. Cool on a wire rack. Serves 6.

Per serving: Kilojoules 946; Fibre 2g; Protein 4g; Total Fat 8g; Saturated Fat 4g; Cholesterol 52mg; Sodium 126mg

At the market You'll find blueberries at some supermarkets from December to early March. Frozen blueberries are also available.

Look for Choose plump berries; those with a waxy 'bloom' on the surface are freshest. If the box is stained with juice, the berries at the bottom may be spoiled or crushed.

Prep Pick over the berries, removing any green, withered or squashed ones. Pull off any berry stems with your fingers. Only rinse just before using or they will become soft. Blueberries will last for up to three weeks if kept in the refrigerator. They can also be successfully frozen for out-of-season treats.

Blueberry Scones A British institution, scones are delightful for afternoon tea or brunch.

Pat the dough for the Blueberry Scones (at left) into a 18-cm round disc, then cut the round into six wedges.

279

Youngberries
PER 160 G (1 CUP)

Kilojoules	391
Fibre	8,5g
Protein	1g
Total Fat	0,6g
Saturated Fat	0g
Cholesterol	0mg
Sodium	0mg

NUTRIENTS

% RDA for people older than 10 years

Vitamin C	56%

Raspberries
PER 160 G (1 CUP)

Kilojoules	376
Fibre	10,9g
Protein	1g
Total Fat	1g
Saturated Fat	0g
Cholesterol	0mg
Sodium	0mg

NUTRIENTS

% RDA for people older than 10 years

Vitamin C	67%

Raspberry Coffeecake

PREP: 30 MINUTES / COOK: 40 MINUTES

Crunchy walnut streusel covers juicy berries which, in turn, top a light, lemony cake.

- 60 ml packed light brown sugar
- 30 ml chopped walnuts
- 5 ml ground cinnamon
- 30 ml plus 500 ml flour
- 30 ml vegetable oil
- 30 ml unsalted butter, melted
- 250 ml granulated sugar
- 15 ml baking powder
- 3,5 ml salt
- 1 egg
- 250 ml low-fat cultured buttermilk
- 5 ml grated lemon rind
- 320 g fresh or frozen unsweetened raspberries (2 cups)
- 60 ml raspberry jam, strained to removed seeds

1. Preheat the oven to 200°C. Spray a 23-cm square baking tin with nonstick cooking spray.

2. In a small bowl, combine the brown sugar, walnuts, cinnamon and 30 ml of the flour. In another small bowl, blend the oil and butter. Add 15 ml of the butter mixture to the walnut mixture and stir until crumbly.

3. In a large bowl, stir together the remaining 500 ml flour, the granulated sugar, baking powder and salt until combined. Make a well in the centre. Add the egg, buttermilk, lemon rind and the remaining butter mixture. Blend the wet ingredients, then stir in the dry ingredients until just combined.

4. Scrape the batter into the prepared tin. Top with the fresh raspberries or thawed frozen raspberries and dab on the jam. Sprinkle with the walnut topping. Bake for 40 minutes or until a cake tester inserted in the centre comes out clean. Serves 8.

Per serving: Kilojoules 1 556; Fibre 4g; Protein 5g; Total Fat 10g; Saturated Fat 3g; Cholesterol 36mg; Sodium 255mg

No-Bake Raspberry Cheesecake

PREP: 30 MINUTES / COOK: 5 MINUTES
CHILL: 4 HOURS

This refrigerator cheesecake is always a spectacular and impressive dessert. Frozen raspberries can be used quite successfully once the short raspberry season is over.

- 250 ml low-fat evaporated milk
- 480 g fresh or frozen unsweetened raspberries, thawed (3 cups)
- 250 ml sugar
- 10 ml cornflour mixed with 15 ml water
- 2 x 10 g envelopes unflavoured gelatine
- 225 g fat-free smooth cottage cheese
- 225 g low-fat cream cheese
- 500 ml low-fat smooth cottage cheese
- 125 ml sour cream
- 10 ml grated lemon rind
- 30 ml lemon or lime juice

1. Pour the evaporated milk into a metal bowl; place in the freezer until ice crystals form. Spray a 23-cm spring-form with nonstick cooking spray.

2. In a blender or food processor, purée 160 g (1 cup) of the raspberries and strain through a sieve into a small saucepan. Add 60 ml of the sugar and the cornflour mixture. Bring to a simmer, stirring and cook for 1 minute or until thickened. Set aside to cool slightly.

3. Place the gelatine in a small bowl and sprinkle on 70 ml of cold water to soften. Place the bowl over a pan of simmering water and stir to dissolve the gelatine. In a food processor, combine the cream cheese, cottage cheeses, sour cream, lemon rind, lemon juice and the remaining sugar and process until smooth. Add the dissolved gelatine and process until smooth. Scrape into a large bowl and refrigerate until the mixture begins to mound.

4. With an electric mixer, whip the partially frozen evaporated milk until soft peaks form. Fold half of the raspberry sauce into the cottage-cheese mixture, then fold in the whipped milk. Fold in the remaining 320 g (2 cups)

At the market Indulge in these delicate fruits in midsummer when they're most plenti- ful—tayberries from mid-October to the end of December; young- berries from late Octo- ber to late January; English blackberries from mid-November to mid-March; boysenber- ries from early Novem- ber to late January; and raspberries from late October to the end of May. Out of season, most of these berries can be bought frozen. Unsweetened frozen berries can stand in for fresh in many recipes.

Look for Be sure that these fragile berries are in good condition, uncrushed and free of mould. If the bottom of the box is stained, some of the berries have been crushed.

Savoury Berry Salad The fruit flavour is underscored with a raspberry vinaigrette.

raspberries. Scrape the mixture into the prepared springform tin. Pour the remaining raspberry sauce on top and swirl it with a knife. Chill for 3 to 4 hours or until set. Remove the sides of the springform and slice. Serves 8.

Per serving: Kilojoules 1 488; Fibre 4g; Protein 17g; Total Fat 14g; Saturated Fat 7g; Cholesterol 58mg; Sodium 279mg

Savoury Berry Salad

PREP: 15 MINUTES

- 60ml raspberry vinegar or balsamic vinegar
- 20ml olive oil
- 10ml honey
- 10ml Dijon mustard
- 1,25ml each salt and pepper
- 480g torn mixed salad greens (8 cups)
- 170g thinly sliced fennel or celery (1 cup)
- 160g raspberries (1 cup)
- 160g youngberries or boysenberries (1 cup)
- 250ml yellow cherry tomatoes (red can be substituted), halved (1 cup)
- 55g mild soft goat cheese, crumbled

1. In a bowl, whisk together the vine- gar, oil, honey, mustard, salt and pepper.

Arrange the salad greens on 4 plates. Top with the fennel, raspberries, young- berries, tomatoes and goat cheese. Drizzle with the dressing. Serves 4.

Per serving: Kilojoules 735; Fibre 8g; Protein 5g; Total Fat 9g; Saturated Fat 3g; Cholesterol 6mg; Sodium 306mg

Versatile Berry Sauce

PREP: 15 MINUTES

Serve this berry sauce over various desserts such as pavlova or poached peaches.

- 125g berries (raspberries, or the other red berries such as tayberries or loganberries) or 125g frozen mixed berries, thawed
- 300g smooth low-fat cottage cheese
- 30ml icing sugar

1. Select a few berries for decoration and put aside. In a bowl, purée the rest of the berries.

2. Add the cottage cheese to the purée and stir well. Add the icing sugar and stir in. Chill. Serve as a topping, decorat- ed with the reserved berries. Serves 6.

Per serving: Kilojoules 267; Fibre 1g; Protein 5g; Total Fat 2g; Saturated Fat 0g; Cholesterol 2mg; Sodium 67mg

A seedless raspberry sauce is a delectable luxury. To eliminate the seeds, use a rubber spatula to press the berry purée through a sieve.

Raspberry-Topped Brownie Cake

Treat family or guests to this luscious combination of chocolate and berries.

Did you know? . . .

The high fibre content of raspberries and blackberries is due in large part to the fact that they are usually eaten seeds and all.

Along with ellagic acid and beta carotene, blackberries and raspberries contain other cancer-fighting phytochemicals: monoterpenes, catechins and phenolic acids. Monoterpenes also inhibit cholesterol production.

Blackberries are superior to blueberries, raspberries and strawberries in potassium content. This vital mineral helps to regulate blood pressure.

Fresh cranberries are not available, but cranberry juice is. The juice is high in vitamin C, and either the vitamin or some as-yet unidentified compound in the juice seems to have a protective effect against urinary tract infections.

Raspberry-Topped Brownie Cake

PREP: 15 MINUTES / COOK: 30 MINUTES

30 ml vegetable oil
30 ml cocoa powder
1 egg
175 ml sugar
125 ml flour
1,25 ml bicarbonate of soda
1,25 ml salt
60 ml coarsely chopped pecan nuts
480 g raspberries (3 cups)
**15 ml cornflour mixed with
   30 ml water**

1. Preheat the oven to 180°C. Spray a 20-cm round cake tin with nonstick cooking spray. In a large bowl, combine the oil, cocoa powder, egg, 60 ml of water, 125 ml of the sugar, the flour, bicarbonate of soda and salt. Mix until well combined. Fold in the nuts. Pour the batter into the prepared tin and bake for 20 minutes or until a toothpick inserted in the centre comes out clean. Cool in the tin on a rack.

2. Meanwhile, in a medium saucepan, combine 240 g of the raspberries and the remaining sugar and cook, stirring,

for 4 minutes or until the berries are juicy. Stir in the cornflour mixture and cook, stirring, for 4 minutes or until thickened. Strain through a sieve to remove the seeds. Cool for 10 minutes, then spoon over the brownie base. Arrange the remaining berries on top. Serves 8.

Per serving: Kilojoules 847; Fibre 5 g; Protein 3 g; Total Fat 8 g; Saturated Fat 1 g; Cholesterol 26 mg; Sodium 95 mg

Raspberry Swirl Sorbet

PREP: 25 MINUTES / FREEZE: 4 HOURS

2 mangoes, peeled and pitted
30 ml lime or lemon juice
125 ml sugar
60 ml plus 30 ml honey
**320 g fresh or frozen unsweetened
   raspberries (2 cups)**
70 ml raspberry jam

1. In a food processor, purée the mangoes with 175 ml of water, the lime juice, sugar and 60 ml of the honey. Place in a metal tin and freeze for 2 to 3 hours or until almost frozen.

2. Meanwhile, in the food processor, purée the raspberries, jam and the remaining honey. Strain to remove the seeds. Place in a metal tin and freeze for 2 to 3 hours or until almost frozen.

3. Cut the frozen mango purée into pieces and process in a food processor until smooth; transfer to a bowl. Repeat the process with the raspberry purée. Add the raspberry sorbet to the mango sorbet, swirl together and return to the freezer to refreeze. Serves 6.

Per serving: Kilojoules 1152; Fibre 6g; Protein 1g; Total Fat 1g; Saturated Fat 0g; Cholesterol 0mg; Sodium 4mg

---

Summer Pudding

PREP: 25 MINUTES / CHILL: 8 HOURS

This classic British dessert is a sort of uncooked bread pudding. Instead of the individual berries, a box of mixed frozen berries can be used.

320g blackberries (2 cups)
320g raspberries (2 cups)
160g blueberries (1 cup)
125ml raspberry jam (sieved to remove the seeds)
60ml honey
60ml sugar
15ml lemon juice
10 slices firm-textured white sandwich bread, crusts removed
70ml heavy cream, whipped

1. In a medium saucepan, combine the berries, jam, honey and sugar. Bring to a simmer and cook for 2 minutes. Stir in the lemon juice and set aside to cool.

2. Line a 1-litre soufflé dish or mixing bowl with plastic wrap, leaving a 13-cm overhang. Slice the bread in half on the diagonal and line the bottom and sides of the dish (there will be bread left over for the top).

3. Spoon the berries and juices into the bowl. Cover with the remaining bread, trimming all sides. Cover with plastic wrap and fold the overhang over the top. Weight down with a pan or heavy tin. Refrigerate for at least 8 hours. Unmould onto a serving plate, remove the plastic, cut into wedges and serve with the whipped cream. Serves 8.

Per serving: Kilojoules 1041; Fibre 7g; Protein 4g; Total Fat 4g; Saturated Fat 2g; Cholesterol 12mg; Sodium 191mg

Spicy Raspberry Vinegar In a medium bowl, crush 320g (2 cups) raspberries with 30ml sugar. Transfer to large jar with 750ml distilled white vinegar, 5ml red chilli flakes and let stand for 24 hours. Drain. Makes 750 millilitres.
[15ml serving: kJ 23; Fat 0g; Sodium 0mg]

Berry Fool In a food processor, purée 320g (2 cups) blackberries (or boysenberries or youngberries) with 125ml sugar. Stir in 125ml sour cream. Whip 250ml very well chilled evaporated whole milk until stiff peaks form. Fold in the berry mixture. Serves 4. *[kJ 1234; Fat 13g; Sodium 78mg]*

Raspberry Dessert Sauce Purée 350g thawed frozen unsweetened raspberries with 60ml honey, 30ml orange juice and 5ml vanilla essence. Strain out seeds. Serves 4. *[kJ 487; Fat 1g; Sodium 1mg]*

Cape Gooseberries

PER 170G (1 CUP)	
Kilojoules	423
Fibre	8,8g
Protein	3g
Total Fat	1,2g
Saturated Fat	0,1g
Cholesterol	0mg
Sodium	2mg

NUTRIENTS	
% RDA for people older than 10 years	
Vitamin C	32%
Niacin	26%
Vitamin A	15%
Thiamin	14%

Did you know? . . .

Cape gooseberries are not true berries, but are related to the tomato family. The variety known in South Africa originated in South America.

Two cups (340g) of cape gooseberries provide half of the fibre required every day.

Cape Gooseberry and Chicken Salad

PREP: 20 MINUTES

Not only do the cape gooseberries add wonderful colour to this salad, they also have a distinctive tart flavour. Arrange the salad on a bed of salad greens. Lower the fat content by using less oil.

DRESSING:
- 100 ml light vegetable oil (Canola)
- 5 ml grated lemon rind
- 30 ml lemon juice
- 5 ml dried tarragon
- 2,5 ml salt
- 5 ml Dijon mustard

SALAD:
- 350 g cooked chicken breasts, shredded
- 6 spring onions, sliced
- 125 g cape gooseberries, halved
- 100 g thinly sliced celery
- 100 g beansprouts (mung and lentil)

1. In a jar or plastic container with a lid, mix together all of the dressing ingredients.

2. Place the shredded chicken, spring onions, cape gooseberries and celery in a large bowl. Shake the salad dressing well, pour over the salad and toss thoroughly.

3. If using salad greens, arrange them on a platter and spoon the chicken mixture on top. Sprinkle with the sprouts and serve. Serves 4.

Per serving: Kilojoules 1 689; Fibre 3g; Protein 28g; Total Fat 29g; Saturated Fat 3g; Cholesterol 54mg; Sodium 345mg

Cape Gooseberry Muffins

PREP: 15 MINUTES / COOK: 25 MINUTES

- 2 eggs
- 250 ml orange juice
- 250 ml low-fat cultured buttermilk
- 125 ml light vegetable oil (Canola)
- 125 ml runny honey
- 400 g self-raising flour
- 200 g toasted muesli
- 40 g wheatgerm
- 250 ml cape gooseberries, halved
- 10 ml grated orange rind

1. Preheat the oven to 180°C. Spray 18 muffin cups with nonstick cooking spray. In a large bowl beat the eggs lightly. Add the orange juice, buttermilk, oil and honey to the eggs and mix thoroughly.

2. Fold the flour, muesli and wheatgerm into the orange juice-buttermilk mixture. Stir until the ingredients have just combined and make a lumpy batter.

3. Add the gooseberries and orange rind to the batter. Spoon the batter into the prepared muffin cups and bake for 20 to 25 minutes or until a cake tester inserted into the centre of a muffin comes out clean. Cool for a few minutes in the cups, then transfer to a rack to cool or serve while still warm. Makes 18 muffins.

Per muffin: Kilojoules 1 068; Fibre 2g; Protein 5g; Total Fat 10g; Saturated Fat 2g; Cholesterol 24mg; Sodium 46mg

Caramelized Bananas with Cape Gooseberries

PREP: 5 MINUTES / COOK: 15 MINUTES

- 15 ml unsalted butter
- 30 ml brown sugar
- 4 bananas, peeled and cut into slices
- 5 ml grated lemon rind
- 30 ml lemon juice
- 100 g cape gooseberries, halved
- 6 granadillas, pulp removed
- 6 mint leaves, finely shredded

1. Melt the butter in a frying pan. Add the sugar, banana slices and lemon rind and fry until the bananas are golden, turning once. Add the lemon juice and heat through.

2. Divide the bananas and cape gooseberries between 4 dessert bowls. Add the granadilla pulp to the pan, warm through and pour over the bananas and gooseberries. Sprinkle with the mint. Serves 4.

Per serving: Kilojoules 716; Fibre 6 g; Protein 2 g; Total Fat 4 g; Saturated Fat 2 g; Cholesterol 8 mg; Sodium 4 mg

Cape Gooseberry Topping

PREP: 5 MINUTES / COOK: 25 MINUTES

This cape gooseberry topping is ideal for flans and fruit tarts, but can be used over any dessert. Frozen cape gooseberries should be thawed before you use them.

- 250 ml water
- 125 g sugar
- 1 cinnamon stick
- 1 kg cape gooseberries (fresh or frozen)

1. In a saucepan, boil the water, sugar and cinnamon for 3 minutes. Add the gooseberries and simmer until they are soft. Remove the berries with a slotted spoon and allow to cool. Remove the cinnamon stick and discard.

2. Boil the syrup and watch it carefully until it has reduced to about 45 ml and is thick and glazed. (This should take about 20 minutes.) Place the gooseberries on top of the dessert and spoon the sugar glaze over. Serves 6 (as a topping).

Per serving: Kilojoules 751; Fibre 9 g; Protein 3 g; Total Fat 1 g; Saturated Fat 0 g; Cholesterol 0 mg; Sodium 2 mg

At the market These berries are harvested in November and December. Frozen berries are available, but can only be used for sauces or in desserts.

Cape gooseberries can be frozen successfully—be sure to spread them out so that they do not stick together. (See Techniques, page 36.)

Look for Round plump fruits which have not split or been damaged. Check for mouldy berries and look at the bottom of the punnet for squashed berries. Keep cape gooseberries in the refrigerator.

Prep The only preparation necessary is rinsing and, possibly, halving,

Cape Gooseberry and Chicken Salad *A colourful salad to serve as a light lunch.*

Cherries

Sweet Cherries
PER 150 G PITTED (1 CUP)

Kilojoules	411
Fibre	2,3 g
Protein	1,7 g
Total Fat	0,1 g
Saturated Fat	0 g
Cholesterol	0 mg
Sodium	8 mg

NUTRIENTS

% RDA for people older than 10 years

Vitamin C	23 %

Sour Cherries
PER 160 G PITTED (1 CUP)

Kilojoules	334
Fibre	2,5 g
Protein	1,6 g
Total Fat	0,5 g
Saturated Fat	0 g
Cholesterol	0 mg
Sodium	5 mg

NUTRIENTS

% RDA for people older than 10 years

Vitamin C	27 %

Did you know?. . .
Cherry juice may neutralize enzymes which cause tooth decay.

Chocolate & Cherry Pudding

PREP: 25 MINUTES / COOK: 10 MINUTES
CHILL: 30 MINUTES

The cherries are not cooked—just layered in—so they retain all of their vitamin C.

- 45 ml flour
- 45 ml cornflour
- 125 ml sugar
- 1,25 ml salt
- 750 ml low-fat (2%) milk
- 1 egg
- 10 ml vanilla essence
- 55 g dark chocolate, finely chopped
- 300 g fresh cherries, halved and pitted (2 cups)
- 12 Boudoir biscuits (or chocolate wafer biscuits), coarsely chopped

1. In a medium saucepan, whisk together the flour, cornflour, sugar and salt. Whisk in the milk. Bring to a simmer over moderate heat, stirring frequently. Simmer for 2 minutes or until the pudding has thickened slightly.

2. In a small bowl, lightly beat the egg. Gradually beat 175 ml of the hot pudding into the egg, then whisk the warmed egg mixture back into the pan and cook until the pudding starts to simmer. Remove from the heat and stir in the vanilla essence. Scrape the pudding into a bowl and place plastic wrap directly on the surface to prevent a skin from forming. Cool to room temperature and refrigerate for 30 minutes or until chilled, then whisk until smooth. Stir in all but 30 ml of the chopped chocolate.

3. Dividing the ingredients evenly among six 175-ml dessert dishes, make layers as follows: cherries (use half of the total), pudding (use half), all of the chopped biscuits, the remaining cherries and pudding. Sprinkle with the reserved chopped chocolate. Serves 6.

Per serving: Kilojoules 1 259; Fibre 1 g; Protein 8 g; Total Fat 7 g; Saturated Fat 3 g; Cholesterol 45 mg; Sodium 172 mg

Fresh Cherry Sundaes

PREP: 1 HOUR / COOK: 5 MINUTES
FREEZE: 1 HOUR 30 MINUTES

Unsweetened frozen cherries, which can be purchased from supermarkets or delicatessens, work perfectly well in this tempting treat.

- 560 ml low-fat frozen vanilla yoghurt
- 110 g chopped pitted cherries (¾ cup) plus 150 g halved pitted cherries (1 cup), from about 500 g unpitted cherries
- 60 ml chopped toasted almonds
- 125 ml cherry or raspberry jam
- 10 ml cornflour mixed with 15 ml water
- 5 ml vanilla essence
- 0,6 ml almond essence

1. Let the frozen yoghurt stand in the refrigerator for 30 minutes or until softened. Scoop the softened frozen yoghurt into a medium bowl and stir in the chopped cherries and 30 ml of the almonds. Return the bowl to the freezer and freeze for 1½ hours or until refrozen.

2. Meanwhile, in a medium saucepan, combine the halved cherries, jam and

Sour Cherry Tart This gently spiced tart is dressed up with biscuit-cutter cut-outs.

cornflour mixture. Bring to a simmer over moderate heat, stirring and cook for 1 minute or until thickened. Stir in the vanilla essence and almond essence.

3. Serve the frozen yoghurt with warm or room-temperature cherry sauce. Sprinkle with the remaining 30 ml almonds. Serves 4.

Per serving: Kilojoules 1 200; Fibre 1g; Protein 5g; Total Fat 7g; Saturated Fat 3g; Cholesterol 2mg; Sodium 81 mg

Sour Cherry Tart

PREP: 30 MINUTES / CHILL: 1 HOUR
COOK: 45 MINUTES

This tart has a top crust only. You can either cut simple steam vents in the tart top or dress it up with cut-outs as shown above. To make cut-outs, use 5-cm biscuit cutters to cut out shapes from the dough round before you put it over the tart. After placing the dough on the tart, position the cut-out pieces on top.

250 ml all-purpose flour (cake flour can be substituted)
20 ml plus 150 ml sugar
2,5 ml salt
45 ml unsalted butter
15 ml solid vegetable shortening
800 g frozen Morello cherries (or tinned sour cherries packed in light syrup, drained) (8 cups)
30 ml honey
15 ml lemon juice

60 ml cornflour
0,6 ml ground allspice (optional)
15 ml low-fat (2%) milk

1. In a medium bowl, combine the flour, 15 ml of the sugar and the salt. With a pastry blender or 2 knives, cut in the butter and shortening until the mixture resembles coarse crumbs. Stir 35 ml to 45 ml ice water into the flour mixture until just combined. Flatten the dough into a disc, wrap in plastic wrap and refrigerate for at least 1 hour.

2. Preheat the oven to 190°C. In a large bowl, stir together the cherries, honey, lemon juice, 150 ml of the sugar, the cornflour and allspice. Transfer to a 23-cm tart dish.

3. On a lightly floured surface, roll the dough out to a 30 cm round. Place the dough on top of the tart, crimping the edges to seal to the rim of the tart dish. Brush the crust with the milk and sprinkle with the remaining 5 ml sugar. With a sharp knife, cut 3 or 4 slits in the crust to act as steam vents.

4. Place the tart on a baking sheet with sides and bake for 45 to 50 minutes or until bubbly and hot in the centre. Serve warm or at room temperature. Serves 6.

Per serving: Kilojoules 1 407; Fibre 3g; Protein 3g; Total Fat 9g; Saturated Fat 4g; Cholesterol 17mg; Sodium 248mg

Shopping & prep

At the market Sweet cherries have an extremely short season—from November to December and are generally quite expensive. Many families embark on cherry-picking expeditions, but punnets of cherries can be purchased at supermarkets. Frozen Morello cherries are available at supermarkets and delicatessens. Various varieties of tinned cherries are also available.

Look for Fresh cherries should be plump, firm and shiny, with flexible green stems still attached. If the fruit is sticky, it's been damaged and is leaking juice.

Prep If you need to pit cherries for a recipe, a cherry pitter (see below) is the best tool. However, an old-fashioned hairpin or a paper clip can also be used for the job.

This handy little tool quickly pops the pits out of cherries. (It works nicely on olives, too.)

Dried Figs

Nutritional power

The tiny seeds that give figs their unique texture also supply a lot of dietary fibre. Potassium, manganese, iron and calcium are among figs' other benefits.

PER 40 G (2 LARGE)	
Kilojoules	484
Fibre	3,7 g
Protein	1,2 g
Total Fat	0,5 g
Saturated Fat	0,1 g
Cholesterol	0 mg
Sodium	4 mg

NUTRIENTS	
% RDA for people older than 10 years	
Iron	6 %
Calcium	5 %

Did you know? . . .

Although you may occasionally find them at small shops, fresh figs are highly perishable. Most figs are sold dried and are just as nutritious as fresh figs.

The medicinal use of figs goes back to ancient times. More recently, researchers in Tokyo have had some success using a chemical from figs to treat cancer.

Pasta with Bacon, Figs & 'Cream' Sauce

PREP: 20 MINUTES / COOK: 20 MINUTES

Figs, like raisins and prunes, are a delicious— and healthy—addition to savoury dishes.

- 225 g dried figs, cut into 5-mm pieces
- 500 ml boiling water
- 5 ml olive oil
- 2 slices bacon, cut crosswise into 5-mm-wide strips
- 1 medium onion, finely chopped
- 20 ml flour
- 350 ml low-fat evaporated milk
- 350 g penne pasta
- 30 ml low-fat cream cheese
- 3,5 ml salt
- 2,5 ml pepper
- 70 ml grated Parmesan cheese
- 60 ml chopped parsley

1. In a heatproof bowl, combine the figs and boiling water and let stand for 10 minutes or until softened. Drain, reserving 125 ml of the soaking liquid.

2. In a large nonstick pan, heat the oil over moderate heat. Add the bacon and cook for 4 minutes or until lightly crisped. Add the onion and sauté for 7 minutes or until lightly golden. Whisk in the flour until coated. Gradually add the evaporated milk and cook, stirring, for 3 minutes or until slightly thickened.

3. Meanwhile, in a large pot of boiling water, cook the penne according to package directions until *al dente*. Drain and transfer to a large bowl.

4. Whisk the cream cheese, the reserved fig soaking water, the salt and pepper into the pan and cook for

1 minute or until the cream cheese has melted. Add the sauce, drained figs, Parmesan and parsley to the hot pasta, tossing well to combine. Serves 4.

Per serving: Kilojoules 2861; Fibre 9 g; Protein 24 g; Total Fat 13 g; Saturated Fat 6 g; Cholesterol 43 mg; Sodium 776 mg

Fig & Almond Biscuits

PREP: 25 MINUTES / CHILL: 1 HOUR
COOK: 1 HOUR 5 MINUTES

- 560 ml flour
- 2,5 ml each bicarbonate of soda and salt
- 60 ml unsalted butter
- 30 ml solid vegetable shortening
- 150 ml sugar
- 1 egg
- 45 ml low-fat (2%) milk
- 5 ml grated lemon rind
- 450 g dried figs, cut into 5-mm pieces
- 60 ml whole almonds
- 30 ml honey
- 10 ml lemon juice
- 1,25 ml ground ginger

1. In a small bowl, combine the flour, bicarbonate of soda and salt. In a medium bowl, beat the butter and shortening with an electric mixer until creamy. Beat in the sugar until light and fluffy. Beat in the egg and milk until well combined. Beat in the lemon rind. Stir in the dry ingredients until just combined. Divide the dough in half, pat each half into a rectangle, wrap in plastic wrap and refrigerate for at least 1 hour.

Pasta with Bacon, Figs & 'Cream' Sauce *The sauce is made with evaporated milk.*

At the market Most of the dried figs which are now available, are imported Turkish Smyrna figs. The White Genoa and Adam's Fig are two of the varieties which are dried locally, mainly in the Little Karoo. Fig rolls are also a popular form of this dried fruit—most are produced by local farmers and sold at farm stalls.

2. In a medium saucepan, combine the figs and 375 ml of water. Bring to a boil, reduce to a simmer, cover and cook for 30 minutes or until the figs are soft. Uncover and cook for 5 minutes or until no liquid remains. Transfer the figs to a food processor along with the almonds. Process to a smooth purée. Stir in the honey, lemon juice and ginger. Cool to room temperature.

3. Preheat the oven to 180°C. Spray a baking sheet with nonstick cooking spray. On a lightly floured surface, roll each dough half to a 13 x 23-cm rectangle. Spoon half of the filling down the centre of one rectangle, leaving a 5-cm border on the long sides and a 1-cm border at each end. Fold the ends in over the filling, then starting on a long side, roll the dough over the filling, jamroll fashion. Repeat with the second dough half and remaining filling.

4. Place the rolls, seam-side down and 10 centimetres apart on the prepared baking sheet. Bake for 30 minutes or until golden brown and firm to the touch. Cool for 10 minutes on the baking sheet, then carefully transfer to a wire rack to cool completely. Cut each roll into 12 slices. Makes 24 biscuits.

Per biscuit: Kilojoules 673; Fibre 2g; Protein 1g; Total Fat 5g; Saturated Fat 2g; Cholesterol 14mg; Sodium 78mg

Dried Figs Poached in Red Wine

PREP: 5 MINUTES / COOK: 40 MINUTES

For a stylish dinner-party dessert, serve the figs in goblets accompanied with delicate wafer biscuits. For a more casual meal, partner the poached fruit with ginger biscuits.

- **500 ml dry red wine**
- **125 ml sugar**
- **6 whole black peppercorns**
- **1 bay leaf**
- **16 dried figs (about 300 g)**
- **60 ml crème fraîche (or sour cream)**

1. In a medium saucepan, combine the wine, sugar, peppercorns and bay leaf. Bring to a boil over moderate heat. Add the figs, reduce to a simmer, cover and cook for 35 minutes or until tender. With a slotted spoon, transfer the figs to a bowl and set aside.

2. Increase the heat to high and boil the liquid for 5 minutes or until reduced to a medium syrup (about 125 ml). Remove from the heat, discard the bay leaf and pour over the figs. Cool to room temperature and refrigerate.

3. Serve the figs topped with some of the syrup and a spoon of crème fraîche. Serves 4.

Per serving: Kilojoules 1589; Fibre 7g; Protein 3g; Total Fat 5g; Saturated Fat 3g; Cholesterol 13mg; Sodium 24mg

Dried figs, fresh figs and fig jam all contain useful amounts of fibre. Dried figs used to be a luxury item, but are now imported from Turkey and sold in all supermarkets.

Look for They may be dried, but figs should be plump and soft. Squeeze the package to make sure.

Prep To make chopping sticky figs easier, first spray the knife (or the blades of kitchen scissors) with nonstick cooking spray or coat lightly with vegetable oil.

Grapefruit

PER 1 MEDIUM (250 G)	
Kilojoules	413
Fibre	4,8 g
Protein	2 g
Total Fat	0,3 g
Saturated Fat	0 g
Cholesterol	0 mg
Sodium	8 mg

NUTRIENTS	
% RDA for people older than 10 years	
Vitamin C	142 %
Folate	8 %
Magnesium	7 %

Did you know? . . .

Grapefruit is rich in pectin, a type of dietary fibre which seems to reduce LDL cholesterol.

Researchers have found chemical compounds in grapefruit which cause the body to absorb more of certain medications. If you take medication with grapefruit juice, check with your doctor to be sure this is not a problem.

Grapefruit with Spiced Red-Currant Sauce

PREP: 15 MINUTES / COOK: 5 MINUTES
CHILL: 1 HOUR

Delicious as a dessert, this ruby-hued fruit cup also makes a pleasing addition to a brunch menu. You can prepare it a day or two ahead of time and keep it in a covered bowl in the refrigerator.

2 pink grapefruits
1 white grapefruit
70 ml red currant jam or jelly
2,5 ml ground ginger
1,25 ml white pepper
0,6 ml allspice
15 ml lemon juice

1. With a small paring knife, peel the grapefruits. Working over a bowl to catch the juice, separate the grapefruit sections from the membranes; reserve any juice that collects in the bowl.

2. In a small pan, combine the jam, ginger, pepper and allspice. Bring to a simmer and cook for 1 minute.

3. Pour the jam mixture into a medium bowl and stir in the lemon juice and 15 ml of the reserved grapefruit juice. Add the grapefruit and toss to combine. Serve chilled. Serves 4.

Per serving: Kilojoules 510; Fibre 4g; Protein 1g; Total Fat 0g; Saturated Fat 0g; Cholesterol 0mg; Sodium 8mg

Grapefruit-Grilled Salmon

PREP: 20 MINUTES / COOK: 10 MINUTES

Tart citrus is the perfect counterpoint to rich fish and lemon isn't the only fruit which fits the bill. Here, a lively grapefruit salad complements grilled salmon.

3 grapefruits
1 large red pepper, diced
1 celery stalk, cut into
    5-mm dice
60 ml finely chopped onion (red, if available)
10 ml olive oil
5 ml Dijon mustard
2,5 ml salt
4 boned salmon fillets, with skin
    (175 g each)
2,5 ml dried oreganum
1,25 ml black pepper

1. With a small paring knife, peel the grapefruits. Working over a bowl to catch the juice, separate the grapefruit sections from the membranes; reserve any juice that collects in the bowl. Halve the grapefruit sections crosswise and transfer to a salad bowl. Add the pepper, celery, onion, oil, mustard and 1,25 ml of the salt. Toss to combine and refrigerate until serving time.

2. Preheat the grill. Place the salmon, skin-side down, on a grill rack. Sprinkle 45 ml of the reserved grapefruit juice, the oreganum, black pepper and the remaining 1,25 ml salt over the salmon. Grill 15 centimetres from the heat for

8 minutes or until just cooked through. Serve the salmon with the grapefruit salad. Serves 4.

Per serving: Kilojoules 1 528; Fibre 4g; Protein 29g; Total Fat 18g; Saturated Fat 3g; Cholesterol 77mg; Sodium 421mg

Chicken & Grapefruit Salad

PREP: 25 MINUTES

Chicken and grapefruit make a clean, cool partnership. You could also opt for prawns with the grapefruit, or good-sized cubes of monkfish.

4 grapefruits
30 ml light mayonnaise
15 ml finely chopped mango chutney
10 ml Dijon mustard
5 ml sesame oil
1,25 ml each salt and pepper
350 g skinless, deboned chicken breast, poached and cubed
60 g watercress, tough stems trimmed
1 Belgian endive, cut crosswise into 1-cm-wide strips
1 head butter lettuce, separated into leaves

1. With a small paring knife, peel the grapefruits. Working over a bowl to catch the juice, separate the grapefruit sections from the membranes; reserve any juice that collects in the bowl.

2. In a medium bowl, whisk together the mayonnaise, chutney, mustard, sesame oil, salt, pepper and 45 ml of reserved grapefruit juice.

3. Add the chicken, tossing to combine. Add the watercress, endive and grapefruit sections and toss. Serve the salad on a bed of butter lettuce. Serves 4.

Per serving: Kilojoules 1 232; Fibre 6g; Protein 29g; Total Fat 7g; Saturated Fat 2g; Cholesterol 57mg; Sodium 390mg

At the market You'll find grapefruit in the supermarket all year round

Look for Choose nice round grapefruits that feel heavy in your hand (that means they'll be juicy). The skin should be glossy, but a few dull or brown patches are not a bad sign.

Prep To cut neat segments from a grapefruit, first peel the fruit, using a sharp knife to remove all the white pith, which is unpleasantly bitter. Also remove the outer layer of membrane which surrounds the fruit. Working over a bowl to catch the juice, free the segments from the membranes (see below).

Carefully slice between each dividing membrane and the grapefruit pulp to release the segments.

Chicken & Grapefruit Salad *Tart grapefruit and greens serve as foils for the chicken.*

Grapes & Raisins

Grapes
PER 180 G (1 CUP)

Kilojoules	540
Fibre	3,6 g
Protein	1 g
Total Fat	0,2 g
Saturated Fat	0,1 g
Cholesterol	0 mg
Sodium	4 mg

NUTRIENTS

% RDA for people older than 10 years	
Vitamin C	9 %
Thiamin	9 %

Raisins
PER 80 G (½ CUP)

Kilojoules	1097
Fibre	3,3 g
Protein	2,6 g
Total Fat	0,6 g
Saturated Fat	0,2 g
Cholesterol	0 mg
Sodium	12 mg

NUTRIENTS

% RDA for people older than 10 years	
Iron	11 %
Vitamin B6	10 %

Grapes are a good source of boron, which helps keep bones strong.

Grape & Raisin Coffeecake

PREP: 15 MINUTES / COOK: 55 MINUTES

- 320 ml flour
- 6 ml baking powder
- 2,5 ml bicarbonate of soda
- 1,25 ml salt
- 60 ml unsalted butter, at room temperature
- 150 ml plus 60 ml sugar
- 1 egg
- 2 egg whites
- 175 ml low-fat cultured buttermilk
- 5 ml vanilla essence
- 125 ml raisins
- 60 ml pecan nuts or walnuts
- 3,5 ml cinnamon
- 360 g seedless red and/or green grapes (2 cups)

1. Preheat the oven to 180°C. Spray a 23-cm square baking tin with nonstick cooking spray; set aside. In a small bowl, combine the flour, baking powder, bicarbonate of soda and salt.

2. In a large bowl, cream the butter and 150 ml of the sugar with an electric mixer until light and fluffy. Add the whole egg and egg whites, one at a time, beating until well combined. Beat in the buttermilk and vanilla essence. Fold the dry ingredients into the butter mixture. Fold in the raisins.

3. In a food processor, combine the remaining 60 ml sugar, the pecan nuts and cinnamon, pulsing until the nuts are coarsely ground. Spoon half of the batter into the tin and sprinkle with half of the nut mixture. Top with the remaining batter, the grapes and the remaining nut mixture. Bake for 55 minutes or until a cake tester inserted in the centre comes out clean. Serves 8.

Per serving: Kilojoules 1 323; Fibre 2g; Protein 5g; Total Fat 10g; Saturated Fat 4g; Cholesterol 44 mg; Sodium 119 mg

Chicken Véronique

PREP: 15 MINUTES / COOK: 20 MINUTES

This is a variation on the classic Sole Véronique. A combination of red and green grapes makes the prettiest dish.

- 10 ml olive oil
- 4 skinless, boned chicken breasts (140 g each)
- 30 ml flour
- 125 ml dry white wine
- 175 ml chicken stock
- 2,5 ml salt
- 1,25 ml each crumbled dried rosemary and black pepper
- 360 g seedless red and/or green grapes, halved (2 cups)
- 45 ml sour cream
- 60 ml chopped parsley

1. In a large nonstick pan, heat the oil over moderate heat. Dredge the chicken in the flour, shaking off and reserving the excess. Sauté the chicken for 2 min-

Chicken Véronique Serve the chicken with orzo and vegetables moulded in custard cups.

At the market The grape season extends from January to May during which time various varieties come onto the market. Among the seedless grapes are Thompson Seedless, Flame Seedless and Ruby Seedless (red).

Most raisins are made from Thompson Seedless , Hanepoort or Datal grapes. Raisins come in two colours: brown raisins are sun-dried and left as is after drying, while sultanas are dried in the shade and treated with sulphur dioxide to keep them from darkening.

utes per side or until golden brown. Add the wine, increase the heat to high and cook for 2 minutes.

2. Add the stock, salt, rosemary and pepper and bring to a boil. Reduce to a simmer, cover and cook for 5 minutes or until the chicken is cooked through. Add the grapes, cover and cook for 5 minutes or until tender.

3. In a small bowl, whisk together the sour cream and the reserved flour. Stir the mixture into the pan and cook, stirring constantly, for 2 minutes or until slightly thickened. Transfer the chicken to serving plates. Stir the parsley into the sauce and spoon over the chicken. Serves 4.

Per serving: Kilojoules 1 282; Fibre 2 g; Protein 31 g; Total Fat 9 g; Saturated Fat 3 g; Cholesterol 72 mg; Sodium 626 mg

Raisin Bars
PREP: 10 MINUTES / COOK: 25 MINUTES

- **320 g raisins (2 cups)**
- **500 ml boiling water**
- **310 ml flour**
- **2,5 ml baking powder**
- **1,25 ml bicarbonate of soda**
- **2,5 ml ground cinnamon**
- **1,25 ml ground nutmeg**
- **0,6 ml ground cloves**
- **60 ml unsalted butter, at room temperature**
- **125 ml packed dark brown sugar**
- **30 ml molasses**
- **1 egg**
- **1 egg white**

1. Preheat the oven to 180°C. Spray a 23-cm square metal baking tin with nonstick cooking spray. Dust with flour; set aside. In a small heatproof bowl, combine the raisins with the boiling water. Let stand for 5 minutes; drain.

2. In a small bowl, combine the flour, baking powder, bicarbonate of soda, cinnamon, nutmeg and cloves. In a large bowl, beat the butter, brown sugar and molasses with an electric mixer until creamy. Add the whole egg and egg white, one at a time, beating well after each addition. Stir in the dry ingredients.

3. Fold the raisins into the batter. Spread the batter in the prepared tin. Bake for 25 minutes or until the top is springy to the touch and lightly golden. Cool the cake in the tin on a rack, then cut into 24 bars. Makes 24 bars.

Per raisin bar: Kilojoules 448; Fibre 1 g; Protein 1 g; Total Fat 2 g; Saturated Fat 1 g; Cholesterol 14 mg; Sodium 9 mg

Look for Choose a well-shaped bunch of plump grapes, avoiding bunches with withered, shrivelled or crushed fruit. The grapes should not be pale around the stems, and the stems should be pliable. Grapes do not continue to ripen after picking. Raisin packets should show clearly whether the raisins are deseeded or not. The use of sulphur should also be indicated.

Prep Don't rinse grapes until shortly before serving. Store in the refrigerator.

Guavas

PER 1 LARGE (130 G)	
Kilojoules	377
Fibre	10,3 g
Protein	1 g
Total Fat	0,4 g
Saturated Fat	0,1 g
Cholesterol	0 mg
Sodium	1 mg

NUTRIENTS	
% RDA for people older than 10 years	
Vitamin C	752 %
Niacin	11 %
Folate	6 %
Vitamin B6	5 %

Did you know? . . .
One large guava contains five times more vitamin C than one medium orange.

Guava contains lycopene, the same beta carotene found in tomatoes, a cancer-fighting carotenoid.

Guava pips contain vitamin C and the soluble fibre, pectin.

Rosewater-Flavoured Guavas with Pistachio Nuts

PREP: 15 MINUTES / COOK: 10 MINUTES

Rosewater concentrate gives this dessert a taste of Turkish delight. Rosewater is available from pharmacies. Add the pistachio nuts just before serving to prevent them softening.

45 ml caster sugar
8 ripe guavas, peeled and halved
5 ml lemon juice
60 ml thickened cream
125 ml low-fat plain yoghurt
a few drops of rosewater concentrate
20 g chopped pistachio nuts

1. In a medium saucepan dissolve the sugar in 125 ml of water and bring to a boil.

2. Add the guavas, cover with the lid and simmer until the guavas are soft. Liquidize in a blender or processor, then push the pulp through a sieve and discard the seeds. Add the lemon juice to the pulp.

3. In a medium bowl, whisk the cream lightly, then add the yoghurt and whisk together until combined. Fold the cream mixture through the guava pulp. Flavour with the rosewater concentrate. Spoon into 4 dessert glasses and sprinkle with the pistachio nuts just before serving. Serves 4.

Per serving: Kilojoules 1 051; Fibre 16 g; Protein 4 g; Total Fat 7 g; Saturated Fat 3 g; Cholesterol 16 mg; Sodium 28 mg

Tropical Fruit Breakfast Cup

PREP: 15 MINUTES

Serve this fruit salad with granola and thick low-fat plain yoghurt for a really healthy start to the day.

1 tin (410 g) grapefruit segments in fruit juice
5 ripe guavas, peeled and quartered
1 pineapple, peeled and cut into pieces
2 medium bananas, peeled and sliced
5 ml lemon rind
20 ml lemon juice

1. Combine all the ingredients in a large bowl. Cover and chill for 30 minutes. Serves 4.

Per serving: Kilojoules 844; Fibre 13 g; Protein 2 g; Total Fat 1 g; Saturated Fat 0 g; Cholesterol 0 mg; Sodium 8 mg

Guava and Walnut Loaf

PREP: 15 MINUTES / COOK: 60 MINUTES

The unusual combination of spices and guavas give this loaf delicious flavour—spicy with a faint guava aroma. Serve with plain low-fat cream cheese for a really healthy teatime treat.

125 ml softened butter
175 ml sugar
2 eggs
250 ml all-purpose flour
250 ml whole-wheat flour
5 ml baking powder
5 ml bicarbonate of soda

Rosewater-flavoured Guavas with Pistachio Nuts *is a perfect ending to a meal.*

At the market Winter is guava season in South Africa. Guavas are also available tinned, as fruit juice and as dried fruit rolls, all of which are good sources of vitamin C.

Remove the seeds from cooked guavas by pushing the guavas through a sieve with a spoon.

Look for Guavas should have a smooth unblemished skin. Avoid bruised fruits. As guavas do bruise easily, do not pack them into a shopping bag with other groceries which have hard or sharp edges. Keep at room temperature until they are soft, then store in the refrigerator.

Prep Wash the raw fruit and eat the skin and seeds for fibre. To use in fruit salad, peel and dice (do not discard or remove the seeds). To poach guavas, peel the fruits and simmer in a little water with sugar to taste until they are soft.

2,5 ml salt
2,5 ml ground ginger
7,5 ml ground cinnamon
5 ml ground nutmeg
250 ml cooked guava pulp
10 ml vanilla essence
120 g chopped walnuts

1. Preheat the oven to 190°C. Spray a 20 x 10-cm loaf tin with nonstick cooking spray. In a medium bowl or food processor cream the butter and sugar. Beat in the eggs one at a time.

2. In a large bowl, sift together the all-purpose flour, whole-wheat flour, baking powder, bicarbonate of soda, salt and all the spices.

3. Blend the dry mixture into the butter mixture. Fold in the guava pulp, vanilla essence and walnuts. Mix well and spoon the dough into the loaf tin. Bake for 60 minutes or until a cake tester inserted in the centre of the loaf comes out clean. Leave the loaf to cool in the tin before turning out. Makes 1 loaf/12 slices.

Per slice: Kilojoules 1 228; Fibre 4g; Protein 5g; Total Fat 17g; Saturated Fat 6g; Cholesterol 58mg; Sodium 199mg

Guava Soft Serve

PREP: 15 MINUTES

Keep this dessert in the freezer and serve on hot summer days (either on its own or with a fruit salad), when guavas are out of season.

1 tin (180 g) evaporated milk
1 tin (410 g) guavas in fruit juice
15 ml caster sugar or fructose
4 drops almond essence

1. Chill the evaporated milk in the refrigerator for a few hours until very cold. When the milk is cold, purée the guavas (with the juice) in a food processor. Sieve the pulp to remove the pips and discard the pips. Whip the milk until it is quite firm and fold into the guava purée together with the caster sugar. Stir well and freeze.

2. Just before serving, place the frozen purée in a food processor and pulse to soften, adding the almond essence. Serve the soft serve immediately. Serves 6.

Per serving: Kilojoules 398; Fibre 3g; Protein 12g; Total Fat 2g; Saturated Fat 1g; Cholesterol 9mg; Sodium 32mg

Kiwifruit

Chicken Salad with Kiwi & Lime-Ginger Dressing

PREP: 25 MINUTES / COOK: 10 MINUTES

You might call this an updated Waldorf salad. In place of apples, walnuts and mayonnaise, this salad is made with kiwifruit and water chestnuts and tossed with a tangy chilli vinaigrette. Slices of grilled chicken make the salad a meal.

- 2,5 ml each dried tarragon, salt and pepper
- 4 skinless, boned chicken breasts (140 g each)
- 2,5 ml grated lime rind
- 45 ml lime juice
- 45 ml chilli sauce
- 15 ml honey
- 5 ml olive oil
- 3,5 ml ground ginger
- 240 g sliced cos lettuce (4 cups)
- 4 kiwifruit, peeled and cut into 1-cm cubes
- 125 ml tinned sliced water chestnuts, rinsed and cut into strips

1. Preheat the grill. Rub the tarragon, 1,25 ml of the salt and the pepper into the chicken breasts. Grill 15 centimetres from the heat for 4 minutes per side or until cooked through. Cool to room temperature and slice crosswise into 1-cm slices.

2. Meanwhile, in a large bowl, whisk together the lime rind, lime juice, chilli sauce, honey, oil, ginger and the remaining 1,25 ml salt.

3. Add the lettuce, kiwi and water chestnuts, tossing to combine. Add the chicken and toss again. Serves 4.

Per serving: Kilojoules 1 212; Fibre 4 g; Protein 32 g; Total Fat 6 g; Saturated Fat 1 g; Cholesterol 62 mg; Sodium 564 mg

Kiwi with Ricotta Cream

PREP: 15 MINUTES

Macerating kiwifruit in a mixture of sugar and lime juice produces a tasty syrup that forms the sauce for this dessert. The creamy topping is surprisingly low in fat.

- 60 ml plus 30 ml sugar
- 60 ml lime or lemon juice
- 8 kiwifruit, peeled and cut into 1-cm cubes
- 2,5 ml grated lime or lemon rind
- 125 ml ricotta cheese
- 30 ml crème fraîche (or sour cream)

1. In a medium bowl, combine 60 ml of the sugar and the lime juice. Add the kiwi, tossing to combine. Cover and refrigerate until serving time.

2. In a small bowl, combine the lime rind, ricotta, crème fraîche and the remaining 30 ml sugar. Serve the kiwi with its syrup, topped with the ricotta cream. Serves 4.

Per serving: Kilojoules 970; Fibre 4g; Protein 5g; Total Fat 5g; Saturated Fat 3g; Cholesterol 5mg; Sodium 34mg

Red Steenbras with Kiwi Relish

PREP: 10 MINUTES / COOK: 10 MINUTES

You don't need a thick, heavy sauce to turn basic fish fillets into a dressy dinner. This colourful uncooked relish, made with kiwifruit, cucumber, red pepper and spring onions, gives a wonderful flavour to simple grilled fish fillets.

- **4 kiwifruit, peeled and cut into 1-cm cubes**
- **1 red pepper, diced**
- **1 small cucumber, peeled and cut into 5-mm dice (125 ml)**
- **2 spring onions, thinly sliced**
- **30 ml honey**
- **3,5 ml each salt, ground coriander and cumin**
- **0,6 ml crushed red chilli flakes**
- **4 red steenbras fillets, with skin (175g each)**
- **30 ml lime or lemon juice**

1. In a medium bowl, combine the kiwi, pepper, cucumber, spring onion, honey, 1,25 ml each salt, coriander and cumin and the red chilli flakes. Cover and refrigerate.

2. Preheat the grill. Place the fish on a grill pan, skin-side down. Sprinkle the fillets with the lime juice and the remaining salt, coriander and cumin. Grill 15 centimetres from the heat for 7 minutes or until the fish is lightly browned and starts to flake. Serve the fish topped with the kiwi relish. Serves 4.

Per serving: Kilojoules 970; Fibre 3g; Protein 29g; Total Fat 2g; Saturated Fat 0g; Cholesterol 84mg; Sodium 554mg

Red Steenbras with Kiwi Relish *The fruit-and-vegetable relish is sweet and slightly hot.*

At the market

Kiwifruit are available all year round. Kiwis are imported from New Zealand from June to the end of September and from Italy from November to February. Locally grown fruits are on the shelves from late March to August.

Look for Kiwis are usually firm when sold, but they ripen readily at room temperature. (When ready to eat, a kiwi is about as yielding as a ripe peach.) Choose plump, unbruised fruits; avoid any with shrivelled skin.

Prep You can eat a kiwifruit skin and all; though it's a bit furry, the skin is good for you. Or peel it and then slice it. Instead of using a peeler to peel a kiwi, use a spoon (see below).

Cut the kiwi in half, then use a spoon to scoop out the flesh in one piece.

Basic cooking

Kiwifruit, like pineapple, contains an enzyme that keeps gelatine from setting, so it should not be used in gelatine desserts.

Lemons & Limes

Nutritional power

Bursting with vitamin C, these tart fruits serve as fat-free, virtually sodium-free seasonings for all sorts of foods and beverages.

Lemon
PER 1 MEDIUM (80 G)

Kilojoules	170
Fibre	3,8 g
Protein	1 g
Total Fat	0,2 g
Saturated Fat	0 g
Cholesterol	0 mg
Sodium	2 mg

NUTRIENTS

% RDA for people older than 10 years

Vitamin C	103 %

Lime
PER 1 MEDIUM (80 G)

Kilojoules	158
Fibre	2,2 g
Protein	1 g
Total Fat	0,2 g
Saturated Fat	0 g
Cholesterol	0 mg
Sodium	2 mg

NUTRIENTS

% RDA for people older than 10 years

Vitamin C	39 %

Did you know? . . .

Add fresh lemon or lime juice to bottled juice to boost the vitamin C content.

Lime Parfait

PREP: 1 HOUR 40 MINUTES
COOK: 5 MINUTES / CHILL: 2 HOURS

Limes are golf-ball-size, yellow or green-skinned fruits. Key or West Indian limes are yellow-skinned and very acidic, while the larger green-skinned Tahiti is not as acidic. Limes are imported from Swaziland.

**350 ml low-fat evaporated milk
1 envelope (10 g) unflavoured gelatine
125 ml icing sugar
125 ml sour cream
2,5 ml grated lime rind
125 ml fresh lime juice**

1. Pour the evaporated milk into a large mixing bowl and place in the freezer until ice crystals begin to form, about 1 hour.

2. In a glass measuring cup, sprinkle the gelatine over 60 ml cold water and let stand for 5 minutes or until softened. Place the cup in a pan of simmering water and heat for 4 minutes or until the gelatine has dissolved. Cool to room temperature.

3. Beat the partially frozen evaporated milk until soft peaks form. Gradually beat in the icing sugar and continue whipping until stiff peaks form. Beat in the sour cream. Beat in the lime rind and cooled gelatine mixture until well combined. Place the bowl in the refrigerator and chill for 30 minutes or until the mixture begins to mound.

4. Fold the lime juice into the milk mixture. Transfer to 8 parfait glasses and chill for 2 hours. Serves 8.

Per serving: Kilojoules 600; Fibre 0 g; Protein 5 g; Total Fat 5 g; Saturated Fat 3 g; Cholesterol 26 mg; Sodium 67 mg

Lemon-Limeade

PREP: 15 MINUTES / COOK: 10 MINUTES

'Simple syrup'—a boiled sugar syrup—is the secret to the best lemonade. This recipe has the extra advantage of lively lime juice.

**375 ml sugar
6 strips (7,5 x 1 cm) lemon rind
6 strips (7,5 x 1 cm) lime rind
175 ml fresh lemon juice
175 ml fresh lime juice**

1. In a small saucepan, combine the sugar, 250 ml of water and the lemon and lime rind. Bring to a boil over moderate heat and boil for 5 minutes. Let the syrup cool to room temperature; discard the rind. Transfer to a large jar or juice container, add the lemon and lime juices and shake to combine.

2. To serve: spoon 60 ml of the lemon-lime mixture into an 225-ml glass. Add 70 ml of water or soda water and stir to combine. Add 2 ice cubes and serve. Serves 12.

Per serving: Kilojoules 448; Fibre 0g; Protein 0g; Total Fat 0g; Saturated Fat 0g; Cholesterol 0mg; Sodium 1mg.

Tomato-Vegetable Salad with Lemon Vinaigrette

PREP: 20 MINUTES / COOK: 10 MINUTES

When you dice the lemons, pour the juice from the cutting board into a measuring cup and save it to use in the dressing. Have a third lemon on hand in case you need more juice.

- 1 large yellow or red pepper, cut lengthwise into flat panels
- 2 lemons
- 60 ml lemon juice
- 15 ml olive oil
- 2,5 ml salt
- 1,25 ml black pepper
- 1,25 ml sugar
- 3 large tomatoes, cut into 2,5-cm pieces
- 1 stalk celery, thinly sliced
- 60 ml chopped fresh basil

1. Preheat the grill. Place the pepper pieces, skin-sides up, on the grill pan and grill for 12 minutes or until the skin is charred. When cool enough to handle, peel and thinly slice.

2. With a paring knife, peel the lemons. Cut into 5-mm dice, discarding the seeds. In a large bowl, whisk together the lemon juice, oil, salt, black pepper and sugar.

3. Add the lemon pieces to the bowl along with the tomatoes, celery, basil and roasted pepper. Toss well to combine. Serves 4.

Per serving: Kilojoules 421; Fibre 4g; Protein 2g; Total Fat 4g; Saturated Fat 1g; Cholesterol 0mg; Sodium 311mg

Tomato-Vegetable Salad with Lemon Vinaigrette *Like oranges or grapefruit, lemons are delicious in salads. The slightly sweet dressing balances their tartness.*

At the market

Lemons are available throughout the year. Limes are imported and supply is less reliable.

Look for Pick firm, heavy, bright-coloured fruits that have fine-grained, glossy skins. Large-pored skin can be an indication of very thick pith and less juice.

Prep If a recipe calls for the rind as well as the juice or pulp of the lemon or lime, be sure to remove the rind first. Rolling the fruit under the palm of your hand (or warming it under hot water) will make it easier to squeeze the juice.

Here are two ways to peel off the rind (the outermost, coloured part of the peel) from a lemon or lime. You can use a vegetable peeler and then sliver the rind with a knife. Or you can use a special tool, which pulls the rind off in thin strands.

Mangoes

Mango & Prawn Salad

PREP: 20 MINUTES / COOK: 5 MINUTES

- 70 ml lemon juice
- 1 bay leaf
- 1,25 ml crushed red chilli flakes
- 1,25 ml salt
- 450 g medium prawns, peeled and deveined
- 60 ml chilli sauce
- 15 ml olive oil
- 1 large red pepper, slivered
- 170 g cherry tomatoes, halved (1 cup)
- 1 cucumber, halved lengthwise, seeded, and cut into half-rounds
- 2 mangoes (1 kg total), peeled and cut into 1-cm cubes
- 8 lettuce leaves
- coriander sprigs, for garnish

1. In a large pan, combine 500 ml of water, 15 ml of the lemon juice, the bay leaf, red chilli flakes and salt. Bring to a boil over moderate heat. Add the prawns, reduce to a simmer, cover and cook for 4 minutes or until pink and firm. Drain the prawns and set aside to cool to room temperature.

2. In a large bowl, whisk together the chilli sauce, oil and the remaining lemon juice. Add the prawns, pepper, tomatoes, cucumber and mangoes, tossing to combine. Line plates with the lettuce and top with the prawn mixture. Garnish with fresh coriander sprigs. Serves 4.

Per serving: Kilojoules 1 315; Fibre 5 g; Protein 24 g; Total Fat 6 g; Saturated Fat 1 g; Cholesterol 195 mg; Sodium 480 mg

Grilled Pork Chops with Mango Sauce

PREP: 15 MINUTES / COOK: 10 MINUTES

Well-trimmed pork chops can be quite dry when grilled—this tangy barbecue sauce will keep them juicy and flavourful.

- 1 mango (450 g), peeled and cut into large pieces
- 1 small onion, finely chopped
- 60 ml balsamic vinegar
- 45 ml packed dark brown sugar
- 30 ml tomato paste
- 2,5 ml salt
- 1,25 ml crushed red chilli flakes
- 4 well-trimmed pork chops (225 g each)

1. In a medium saucepan, combine the mango, onion, vinegar, brown sugar, tomato paste, salt and red chilli flakes. Bring to a boil over moderate heat. Reduce to a simmer, cover and cook for 10 minutes or until the sauce is thickened and the mango is very soft. Mash the mango with a spoon and set aside to cool to room temperature.

2. Preheat the grill. Set aside half of the mango sauce to be served with the pork chops. Brush one side of the chops with half of the remaining sauce and grill 15 centimetres from the heat for 4 minutes. Turn the chops over, brush with the remaining sauce and grill for 4 minutes or until cooked through but still juicy. Serve with the reserved sauce. Serves 4.

Per serving: Kilojoules 1 564; Fibre 2 g; Protein 31 g; Total Fat 9 g; Saturated Fat 5 g; Cholesterol 85 mg; Sodium 369 mg

At the market Mango months are from the end of November to late May. Although most mango varieties are now fibreless, the Peach mango, which appears early in the season, does have some fibres.

Look for Mangoes are picked unripe; choose a smooth, unbruised fruit with a reddish or orange tint to its skin.

Prep Ripen mangoes at room temperature until fragrant. To cut, hold the mango stem-end up and make two vertical cuts, one on either side of the large, flat pit. Remove these two side pieces, then cut off the band of flesh that remains around the edges of the pit.

Mango Mousse

PREP: 20 MINUTES / CHILL: 2 HOURS

This pretty, refreshing dessert is most welcome after a rich meal. And there's a nutritional bonus: mango plus lime juice equals lots of vitamin C.

2 mangoes (1 kg total), peeled and sliced
60 ml lime juice (lemon juice can be used, but the flavour will not be as tart)
2,5 ml ground ginger
1 envelope (10 g) unflavoured gelatine
45 ml sugar
125 ml crème fraîche or sour cream

1. In a food processor, purée the mangoes with the lime juice and ginger.

2. In a small bowl, sprinkle the gelatine over 60 ml of water. Let stand for 5 minutes or until softened. Meanwhile, in a small saucepan, combine the sugar and 60 ml of water and bring to a boil. Stir the gelatine into the sugar mixture and cook, stirring, for 1 minute or just until the gelatine is dissolved.

3. Add the sugar-gelatine mixture to the mango purée and process until well combined. Add the crème fraîche and process briefly just to blend.

4. Spoon into dessert bowls, cover and refrigerate until chilled and set. Serves 4.

Per serving: Kilojoules 1 053; Fibre 3g; Protein 4g; Total Fat 8g; Saturated Fat 5g; Cholesterol 28mg; Sodium 48mg

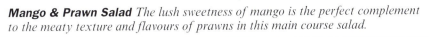

Mango & Prawn Salad *The lush sweetness of mango is the perfect complement to the meaty texture and flavours of prawns in this main course salad.*

To cube a mango, make criss-cross cuts down to, but not through, the skin of one of the side pieces (top photo). Pop the piece inside out and slice off the cubes.

301

Melons

Nutritional power

These delicious fruits provide plenty of vitamin C. Yellow- and orange-fleshed melons supply beta carotene; water-melon has lycopene, another carotenoid.

Spanspek
PER 160 G (1 CUP)

Kilojoules	278
Fibre	1,6 g
Protein	1 g
Total Fat	0,1 g
Saturated Fat	0 g
Cholesterol	0 mg
Sodium	27 mg

NUTRIENTS

% RDA for people older than 10 years	
Vitamin C	104 %
Vitamin A	23 %
Folate	9 %

Honeydew
PER 160 G (1 CUP)

Kilojoules	306
Fibre	1,0 g
Protein	1 g
Total Fat	0,3 g
Saturated Fat	0,1 g
Cholesterol	0 mg
Sodium	18 mg

NUTRIENTS

% RDA for people older than 10 years	
Vitamin C	72 %
Vitamin A	1 %

Festive Melon Bowl

PREP: 40 MINUTES

Use a small biscuit cutter or a melon baller to cut the holes in the watermelon 'bowl'.

- ½ small watermelon (3 kg)
- 640 g spanspek, cut into balls (4 cups)
- 480 g honeydew melon, cut into balls (3 cups)
- 180 g seedless red or green grapes (2 cups)
- 360 g fresh or tinned pineapple cubes (2 cups)
- 45 ml sugar
- 600 ml plain low-fat yoghurt
- 60 ml honey
- 10 ml lime juice or lemon juice
- 1 pinch of allspice

1. With a melon baller, cut the water-melon into balls, remove the seeds and transfer to a large bowl (reserve the shell). Add the melons, grapes and pineapple; sprinkle the fruit with 15 ml of the sugar. Chill the fruit and water-melon shell until serving time.

2. In a small bowl, combine the yoghurt, honey, remaining 30 ml sugar, the lime juice and allspice. Chill until serving time.

3. Spoon as much of the fruit mixture as will fit in the watermelon 'bowl', reserving the rest for refills. Serve the yoghurt sauce on the side. Serves 16.

Per serving: Kilojoules 579; Fibre 3 g; Protein 3 g; Total Fat 1 g; Saturated Fat 0 g; Cholesterol 3 mg; Sodium 39 mg

Honeydew-Lime Tart

PREP: 35 MINUTES / COOK: 15 MINUTES
CHILL: 3 HOURS

Lemons can be used instead of limes, but the flavour will be milder.

CRUST:
- 375 ml flour
- 22 ml sugar
- 3,5 ml salt
- 67 ml unsalted butter
- 22 ml solid vegetable shortening

FILLING & TOPPING:
- 105 ml sugar
- 45 ml flour
- 30 ml cornflour
- 1,25 ml salt
- 1,25 ml ground ginger (optional)
- 625 ml low-fat (2%) milk
- 1 egg
- 10 ml grated lime rind
- 5 ml vanilla essence
- 350 g peeled, seeded honeydew melon, cut into thin slices
- 8 lime or lemon wedges

1. For the crust: in a medium bowl, combine the flour, sugar and salt. With a pastry blender or 2 knives, cut in the butter and shortening until the mixture resembles coarse crumbs. Stir 37 ml to 45 ml iced water into the flour mixture until just combined. Flatten the dough into a disc, wrap in plastic wrap and refrigerate for at least 1 hour.

2. Preheat the oven to 200°C. Spray a 28-cm quiche tin with a removable bot-tom with nonstick cooking spray. On a lightly floured surface, roll out the dough to a 34-cm circle and fit into the tin. Prick the dough in several places with a fork and bake for 8 to 10 minutes or until crisped and golden. Cool on a rack for at least 10 minutes.

3. Meanwhile, for the filling: in a medium saucepan, whisk together the sugar, flour, cornflour, salt and ginger. Whisk in the milk. Bring to a simmer over medium heat, whisking constantly, and cook for 1 minute. In a small bowl, lightly beat the egg. Whisk in some of the hot milk mixture, then whisk the warmed egg back into the pan along with the lime rind and vanilla. Bring just to a simmer, remove from the heat and pour into the cooled tart shell. Place plastic wrap directly on the surface of the custard to keep a skin from forming. Refrigerate for 2 hours or until chilled.

4. Arrange the honeydew slices on top of the custard. Serve the tart with the lime wedges for squeezing. Serves 8.

Per serving: Kilojoules 1 243; Fibre 1g; Protein 6g; Total Fat 12g; Saturated Fat 5g; Cholesterol 50mg; Sodium 383mg

Orange-Spanspek Sherbet

PREP: 15 MINUTES
FREEZE: 2 TO 3 HOURS

125 ml sugar
640 g spanspek cubes, cut into 2-cm cubes (4 cups)
175 ml low-fat cultured buttermilk
60 ml orange juice
5 ml grated orange rind

1. Dissolve the 125 ml sugar in 125 ml water. In a food processor, purée the spanspek. Transfer to a bowl and stir in the buttermilk, the sugar solution, orange juice and orange rind.

2. Freeze in an ice cream machine or, to still-freeze, freeze for 2 to 3 hours until almost frozen. Cut into pieces and process in a food processor until smooth. If not serving right away, refreeze, but let soften in the refrigerator for 30 minutes before serving. Serves 4.

Per serving: Kilojoules 785; Fibre 2g; Protein 3g; Total Fat 1g; Saturated Fat 0g; Cholesterol 2mg; Sodium 74mg

In the market Summer is peak season for domestically grown melons. Imported fruits are sometimes available out of the normal peak season.

Look for All melons should sound hollow when tapped. Spanspeks should smell sweet. Spanspeks and honeydews should have a smooth indentation at the stem end (this indicates that the melon was picked ripe). A honeydew should have a velvety skin; the 'netting' on a spanspek should cover the whole surface, with no breaks. A watermelon's rind should look somewhat dull and waxy, rather than shiny; the pale underside should be yellowish, not greenish. Once a melon is picked, it won't get any sweeter; but if you leave a melon at room temperature for a day or two, it will get softer and juicier.

Festive Melon Bowl is a simply carved watermelon shell filled with a rainbow of fruit.

A melon baller makes it easy to prepare attractive fruit salads and desserts. This inexpensive gadget has a different-size scoop at each end.

Smoked Turkey & Melon Salad *This summertime salad is sparked with a honey-mustard dressing and fresh basil.*

Watermelon

PER 180 G (1 CUP)

Kilojoules	248
Fibre	2 g
Protein	2 g
Total Fat	0,2 g
Saturated Fat	0 g
Cholesterol	0 mg
Sodium	7 mg

NUTRIENTS

% RDA for people older than 10 years	
Vitamin C	18 %

Did you know? . . .

Watermelon is rich in lycopene, a carotenoid that seems to offer protection against prostate cancer. One large study showed that men who ate 10 or more servings per week of lycopene-rich foods had a 45 per cent reduction in prostate cancer risk.

Cut watermelons are a tempting choice because you can more easily judge their ripeness, but keep in mind that melons lose vitamin C when they are cut. If you do buy a half or quarter melon, choose one that's been tightly wrapped in plastic and kept chilled.

Watermelon Ice with Chocolate 'Seeds'

PREP: 15 MINUTES
FREEZE: 3 HOURS

This cool summer dessert looks like it's dotted with seeds, but they're actually chocolate chips. You can adjust the amount of honey used depending on the sweetness of the watermelon.

650 g cubed watermelon
125 ml honey
15 ml lemon juice
60 g mini chocolate chips

1. Remove as many seeds as possible from the watermelon cubes. In a food processor or blender, purée the watermelon and push through a strainer if there appear to be any seeds left. In a medium bowl, combine the watermelon purée, honey and lemon juice.

2. Freeze in an ice cream machine or, to still-freeze: pour into a 23 x 33 x 5-cm tin and freeze for 2 to 3 hours or until almost frozen. Cut into pieces and

process in a food processor until smooth. Fold in the chocolate chips, pack into a plastic container and refreeze until firm. Serves 6.

Per serving: Kilojoules 942; Fibre 1g; Protein 2g; Total Fat 3g; Saturated Fat 2g; Cholesterol 3mg; Sodium 18mg

Spicy Spanspek Antipasto

PREP: 20 MINUTES

Serve this salad soon after you make it; if you leave the spanspek in the vinaigrette for too long, the melon juice will dilute the dressing.

60 ml orange juice
30 ml red wine vinegar
15 ml olive oil
15 ml chopped fresh mint
5 ml honey
2,5 ml hot red pepper sauce
1,25 ml salt
640 g spanspek, cut into 2-cm cubes (4 cups)

175 g mozzarella cheese, cut into
   1-cm cubes
180 g thinly sliced cos lettuce (3 cups)
100 g thinly sliced red cabbage
   or red lettuce (1 cup)

1. In a large bowl, whisk together the orange juice, vinegar, oil, mint, honey, hot pepper sauce and salt. Add the spanspek and mozzarella, tossing well to coat.

2. Toss the cos lettuce and cabbage together and line 4 salad plates with the mixture. With a slotted spoon, top the lettuce with the melon-cheese mixture. Serve the remaining dressing on the side. Serves 4.

Per serving: Kilojoules 1 039; Fibre 3g; Protein 11g; Total Fat 14g; Saturated Fat 6g; Cholesterol 34mg; Sodium 349mg

---

Smoked Turkey & Melon Salad

PREP: 20 MINUTES

480 g honeydew and/or spanspek balls
   (3 cups)
350 g smoked turkey or chicken breast
   (or any other light meat), cut into
   1-cm cubes
125 ml thinly sliced celery
2 spring onions, sliced
30 ml slivered fresh basil
30 ml chopped toasted walnuts or
   pecan nuts
30 ml honey-mustard
15 ml white wine vinegar
10 ml olive oil
2,5 ml soya sauce

1. In a large bowl, toss together the melon balls, turkey, celery, spring onions, basil and walnuts.

2. In a small bowl, whisk together the honey-mustard, vinegar, oil and soya sauce. Toss the dressing with the melon mixture just before serving. Serves 4.

Per serving: Kilojoules 895; Fibre 2g; Protein 20g; Total Fat 7g; Saturated Fat 1g; Cholesterol 67mg; Sodium 1 435mg

Virgin Honeydew Margarita In a blender, combine 320g (2 cups) honeydew pieces, 125ml orange juice, 15ml lime or lemon juice, 15ml honey and 4 ice cubes. Purée. Pour into 2 tall glasses. Serves 2. *[kJ 523; Fat 0g; Sodium 19mg]*

Prosciutto & Melon with Honey-Lemon Dressing Halve and seed 1 spanspek (1,25 kg). Cut into 12 wedges. Drape each wedge with a thin slice of prosciutto using about 115g total. Whisk 70ml honey with 70ml lemon juice. Serve wedges with the lemon sauce. Serves 4. *[kJ 933; Fat 2g; Sodium 456mg]*

Melon in Syrup with Toasted Almonds In a small saucepan, bring 70ml water, 45ml sugar and 5ml grated lime or lemon rind to a boil. Boil 3 minutes. Cool. Add 240g (1½ cups) honeydew cubes and 240g (1½ cups) spanspek cubes. Serve sprinkled with 125ml toasted sliced almonds. Serves 4. *[kJ 672; Fat 7g; Sodium 18mg]*

Oranges & Naartjies

Naartjies

PER 1 MEDIUM (75 G)

Kilojoules	173
Fibre	1,7 g
Protein	1 g
Total Fat	0,2 g
Saturated Fat	0 g
Cholesterol	0 mg
Sodium	4 mg

NUTRIENTS

% RDA for people older than 10 years	
Vitamin C	46 %

Did you know? . . .

Naartjies and oranges contain compounds called terpenes, which seem to limit the body's production of cholesterol. Terpenes also fight cancer by deactivating carcinogens.

Citrus fruits contain pectin, a type of dietary fibre that can lower blood cholesterol levels.

Prawn & Naartjie Salad

PREP: 25 MINUTES / COOK: 5 MINUTES

This summer-bright salad is a treat in the winter—peak season for naartjies.

- 3,5 ml salt
- 2,5 ml each dried oreganum and black pepper
- 450 g medium prawns, peeled and deveined
- 6 naartjies, clementines or minneolas
- 45 ml light mayonnaise
- 30 ml sour cream
- 0,6 ml cayenne pepper
- 125 ml diced red pepper
- 125 ml diced green pepper
- 60 ml finely chopped onion (red, if available)
- 1 stalk celery, halved lengthwise and thinly sliced

1. In a large bowl, combine 1,25 ml of the salt, the oreganum and black pepper. Add the prawns, tossing well to coat; set aside.

2. Separate 5 of the naartjies into sections. Cut each section into thirds and remove the pips. Juice the remaining naartjie and measure out 60 ml. In a large bowl, whisk together the naartjie juice, mayonnaise, sour cream, cayenne and remaining salt. Add the naartjie sections, peppers, onion and celery.

3. Preheat the grill. Grill the prawns 15 centimetres from the heat for 2 minutes per side or until just cooked through. Cool to room temperature and add to the bowl, tossing to combine. Serve at room temperature or chilled. Serves 4.

Per serving: Kilojoules 965; Fibre 3 g; Protein 23 g; Total Fat 7 g; Saturated Fat 2 g; Cholesterol 206 mg; Sodium 765 mg

Naartjie & Lamb Stir-Fry

PREP: 25 MINUTES / COOK: 10 MINUTES

Bite-size bits of naartjie bring a burst of flavour to this spicy stir-fry. As is usually the case with stir-fries, the preparation takes some time, but the actual cooking time is quick.

- 30 ml cornflour
- 30 ml light soya sauce
- 5 ml ground coriander
- 5 ml grated naartjie rind
- 2,5 ml each sugar and salt
- 0,6 ml cayenne pepper
- 450 g well-trimmed boned leg of lamb, cut into 1-cm-wide strips
- 10 ml vegetable oil
- 1 red pepper, cut into 1-cm squares
- 3 cloves garlic, finely chopped
- 5 spring onions, thinly sliced

125 ml chicken stock
4 naartjies, peeled, separated into
  sections, halved and pitted
60 ml chopped coriander

1. In a medium bowl, combine 25 ml of the cornflour, the soya sauce, coriander, naartjie rind, sugar, 1,25 ml of the salt and the cayenne. Add the lamb, tossing well to coat.

2. In a large nonstick pan or wok, heat 5 ml of the oil over moderately high heat. Add the lamb and stir-fry for 2 minutes or until lightly browned. With a slotted spoon, transfer the lamb to a plate. Reduce the heat to moderate, add the remaining 5 ml oil, the red pepper, garlic, spring onions and the remaining 1,25 ml salt and stir-fry for 4 minutes or until the pepper is crisp-tender.

3. In a small bowl, whisk the stock into the remaining 5 ml cornflour. Add to the pan and bring to a boil. Return the lamb to the pan, add the naartjies

Prawn & Naartjie Salad The creamy dressing is made with naartjie juice.

and cook for 1 minute or until the sauce is slightly thickened and the lamb is heated through. Stir in the fresh coriander. Serves 4.

Per serving: Kilojoules 1 090; Fibre 3 g; Protein 27 g; Total Fat 9 g; Saturated Fat 3 g; Cholesterol 79 mg; Sodium 978 mg

Frozen Vanilla-Orange Mousse
PREP**: 1 H**OUR **20 M**INUTES
COOK**: 5 M**INUTES **/ C**HILL**: 2 H**OURS
This is reminiscent of that classic ice cream-frozen sucker duo: vanilla ice cream and orange sorbet.

250 ml evaporated milk
60 ml malt milk powder
5 ml grated orange rind
2 x 10 g envelopes unflavoured
  gelatine
625 ml orange juice
125 ml sugar
5 ml vanilla essence
0,6 ml salt

1. In a large bowl, combine the evaporated milk, malt milk powder and orange rind with an electric mixer. Place in the freezer until ice crystals begin to form, about 1 hour.

2. In a glass measuring jug, sprinkle the gelatine over 125 ml of the orange juice and let stand for 5 minutes or until softened. Place the jug in a pan of simmering water and heat for 4 minutes or until the gelatine has dissolved. Cool to room temperature.

3. Beat the partially frozen evaporated-milk mixture until thick. Gradually beat in the sugar. Add the gelatine mixture. Beat in the remaining 500 ml orange juice, the vanilla and salt. Spoon into 4 dessert bowls and chill for 2 hours or until set. Serves 4.

Per serving: Kilojoules 1 260; Fibre 0 g; Protein 10 g; Total Fat 6 g; Saturated Fat 3 g; Cholesterol 20 mg; Sodium 177 mg

At the market
Oranges are widely available all year round; naartjies and their kin are most bountiful in the winter.

Two members of the tangerine family: the diminutive clementine (left) and the Minneola tangelo (a naartjie-grapefruit cross).

Look for Select firm, heavy oranges and naartjies. Choose thin-skinned oranges such as Valencias for juicing; use navel oranges for snacking and cooking (they're seedless and easy to peel).

Prep Remove all the white pith when peeling an orange. Naartjies are easy to peel but must be seeded: snip the top of each segment and squeeze out the seeds.

To section an orange, cut along both sides of each dividing membrane to release the segments.

Chicken Bigarade *is a delectable, classic French dish which is made without butter or cream.*

Oranges

PER 1 MEDIUM (180 G)

Kilojoules	410
Fibre	5,8 g
Protein	1 g
Total Fat	0,2 g
Saturated Fat	0 g
Cholesterol	0 mg
Sodium	2 mg

NUTRIENTS

% RDA for people older than 10 years

Vitamin C	159 %
Folate	14 %

Did you know? . . .

Oranges contain a phytochemical called limonene, which seems to have an anticarcinogenic effect in the body. Oranges also contain glucarase, another cancer-fighting compound, as well as plenty of vitamin C, an antioxidant.

If you usually drink a small glass of orange juice at breakfast, consider eating a whole orange instead: You'll get the same amount of vitamin C, but the whole fruit also provides fibre.

Winter Fruit Shortcakes

PREP: 25 MINUTES / COOK: 15 MINUTES

A creamy, fresh orange filling is sandwiched in a homemade buttermilk scone.

- 4 navel oranges
- 30 ml packed light brown sugar
- 70 ml plain low-fat yoghurt
- 60 ml sour cream
- 2,5 ml vanilla essence
- 250 ml flour
- 30 ml granulated sugar
- 5 ml baking powder
- 1,25 ml bicarbonate of soda
- 1,25 ml salt
- 30 ml cold unsalted butter
- 15 ml solid vegetable shortening, chilled
- 70 ml low-fat cultured buttermilk
- 1 egg white

1. Preheat the oven to 220°C. With a small paring knife, peel the oranges. Working over a bowl to catch the juice, separate the orange sections from the membranes; reserve any juice which collects in the bowl.

2. Transfer the orange segments to a bowl with 60 ml of the reserved orange juice. Add the brown sugar, yoghurt, sour cream and vanilla essence, tossing well to combine all the ingredients.

Cover and refrigerate while you make the shortcakes.

3. In a medium bowl, combine the flour, 25 ml of the granulated sugar, the baking powder, bicarbonate of soda and salt. With a pastry blender or two knives, cut in the butter and shortening until the mixture resembles coarse crumbs. Add the buttermilk and stir just until combined.

4. Transfer the mixture to a lightly floured surface and knead 5 or 6 times until the mixture forms a dough. Pat out to a 1-cm-thick round 13 cm in diameter. Cut the round into quarters. Place the wedges on an ungreased baking sheet. Brush with the egg white and sprinkle with the remaining 5 ml sugar. Bake for 15 minutes or until golden brown and baked through.

5. Transfer the scones to a wire rack to cool completely. With a serrated knife, slice off the top one-third of the scones to create a bottom that is thicker than the top. Spoon the orange mixture over the bottom of each scone and add the top. Serves 4.

Per serving: Kilojoules 1 641; Fibre 3g; Protein 5g; Total Fat 14g; Saturated Fat 7g; Cholesterol 31mg; Sodium 264mg

Chicken Bigarade

PREP: 15 MINUTES / COOK: 20 MINUTES

A classic bigarade is made with tart Seville oranges. We add vinegar to recreate that zing.

- 15 ml olive oil
- 4 skinless, boned chicken breasts (115 g each)
- 30 ml flour
- 1 red pepper, diced
- 30 ml sugar
- 60 ml red wine vinegar
- 15 ml thinly slivered orange rind
- 125 ml orange juice
- 125 ml chicken stock
- 2,5 ml salt
- 1,25 ml each rosemary and black pepper
- 5 ml cornflour blended with 15 ml water
- 2 navel oranges

1. In a large pan, heat 10 ml of the oil over moderate heat. Dredge the chicken in the flour, shaking off the excess. Sauté the chicken for 2 minutes per side or until lightly golden. Transfer to a plate. Add the pepper and the remaining 5 ml oil and sauté for 3 minutes or until crisp-tender. Add to the plate with the chicken.

2. Add the sugar to the pan and cook for 3 minutes or until caramelized. Add the vinegar and cook for 30 seconds. Add the orange rind, orange juice, stock, salt, rosemary and black pepper and bring to a boil.

3. Return the chicken and pepper to the pan, reduce to a simmer, cover and cook for 7 minutes or until the chicken is just cooked through. Stir in the cornflour mixture and boil for 1 minute, stirring, until slightly thickened.

4. Meanwhile, with a small paring knife, peel the oranges. Separate the orange sections from the membranes and stir the segments into the pan. Serve the chicken with the sauce and oranges. Serves 4.

Per serving: Kilojoules 1 215; Fibre 3 g; Protein 31 g; Total Fat 8 g; Saturated Fat 2 g; Cholesterol 62 mg; Sodium 541 mg

Orange-Banana Breakfast Smoothie

In a blender, combine 175 ml orange juice, 125 ml sliced banana, 10 ml brown sugar and 0,6 ml almond essence. Add 2 ice cubes and blend until thick and smooth. Garnish with a mint sprig. Serves 1.
[kJ 773; Fat 1 g; Sodium 5 mg]

Modern Ambrosia

In a large bowl, combine 45 ml honey and 15 ml lime juice. Add 6 peeled and segmented minneolas or naartjies, 250 ml diced mango, 70 ml dessicated coconut and 60 ml sultanas. Toss well. Serves 4.
[kJ 1 158; Fat 4 g; Sodium 10 mg]

Caramelized Orange Compote

Place 4 peeled and segmented navel oranges in a gratin dish or shallow ovenproof baking dish. Sprinkle with 60 ml brown sugar, 1,25 ml ground cinnamon and 15 ml slivered orange rind. Grill for 2 minutes or until sugar melts. Serves 4.
[kJ 598; Fat 0 g; Sodium 4 mg]

Pawpaws

PER 160G (1 CUP)	
Kilojoules	**298**
Fibre	**2,7g**
Protein	**1g**
Total Fat	**0,2g**
Saturated Fat	**0,1g**
Cholesterol	**0mg**
Sodium	**11mg**

NUTRIENTS	
% RDA for people older than 10 years	
Vitamin C	**232%**
Vitamin A	**20%**
Magnesium	**10%**

Did you know? . . .

Pawpaws are a wise choice for snacking: gram for gram, pawpaws contain more than ten times as much vitamin C as apples and more than twice as much potassium.

An enzyme in uncooked pawpaw keeps gelatine from setting, so you shouldn't use pawpaw in gelatine desserts.

Tropical Fruit Salad

PREP: 30 MINUTES

If necessary, you can substitute two nectarines or peaches for the mango—a little less tropical but still delicious.

- 70 ml pawpaw or apricot juice
- 45 ml lime or lemon juice
- 30 ml honey
- 60 ml chopped fresh mint
- 1 mango (450 g), peeled and cut into 2,5 cm pieces
- 250 ml fresh or canned pineapple wedges
- 1 large banana, thickly sliced
- 2 kiwifruits, peeled and cut into 1-cm pieces
- 1 pawpaw (350 g), peeled and cut into 1-cm pieces

1. In a large bowl, whisk together the pawpaw juice, lime juice, honey and mint. Add the mango, pineapple, banana and kiwi, tossing to combine. Refrigerate until serving time.

2. At serving time, add the pawpaw and toss again. Serve immediately. Serves 4.

Per serving: Kilojoules 1016; Fibre 5g; Protein 2g; Total Fat 1g; Saturated Fat 0g; Cholesterol 0mg; Sodium 10mg

Pawpaw-Strawberry Crisp

PREP: 10 MINUTES / COOK: 15 MINUTES

The crunchy topping for this crisp covers a tempting combination of fruit which is accented with lemon and, surprisingly, salt and pepper.

- 2 pawpaws (650 g total), peeled and cut into 2,5-cm pieces
- 5 ml grated lemon rind
- 30 ml lemon juice
- 1,25 ml each salt and pepper
- 0,6 ml ground allspice
- 120 g strawberries
- 30 ml granulated sugar
- 30 ml packed light brown sugar
- 15 ml unsalted butter
- 45 ml flour

1. Preheat the oven to 230°C. In a 20-cm round ceramic or glass baking dish, toss together the pawpaws, lemon rind, lemon juice, salt, pepper and all-spice. Scatter the strawberries on top.

2. In a small bowl, combine the granulated sugar, brown sugar and butter with your fingers. Mix in the flour until the mixture is crumbly. Sprinkle the crumb mixture over the fruit. Bake for

Grilled Steak with Fresh Pawpaw Chutney *A burst of tropical colour and flavour.*

At the market Paw-paws have yellow flesh, but the Red Exotic variety with its reddish flesh is increasingly popular. The pawpaw season runs from August to November. Pawpaws can weigh anything from 250 g to 4 kg.

Look for A truly green pawpaw will never ripen, so choose one that's at least half yellow. The fruit should yield slightly to gentle thumb pressure. Sniffing won't help you pick: an uncut pawpaw has no fragrance.

Prep Ripen a pawpaw by leaving it at room temperature in a paper bag for a few days. When ripe, store it in the refrigerator and use as soon as possible. To serve, just halve the fruit lengthwise and spoon out the seeds, which are edible. Scoop out the flesh with a spoon or peel the pawpaw halves with a vegetable peeler.

Scoop out pawpaw seeds with a spoon; you can use them as an edible garnish.

---

12 to 15 minutes or until the top is lightly browned and set and the fruit is heated through. Serves 4.

Per serving: Kilojoules 798; Fibre 4g; Protein 2g; Total Fat 3g; Saturated Fat 2g; Cholesterol 8mg; Sodium 165mg

Grilled Steak with Fresh Pawpaw Chutney

PREP: 20 MINUTES / COOK: 10 MINUTES

This freshly made relish is very different from sticky-sweet bottled chutney. It supplies about 110 milligrams of vitamin C, more than any commercial chutney.

- **3,5 ml salt**
- **2,5 ml sugar**
- **2,5 ml dried oreganum**
- **1,25 ml black pepper**
- **4 well-trimmed sirloin steaks (175 g each)**
- **2 pawpaws (650 g total), peeled and cut into 1-cm pieces**
- **1 large red pepper, cut into 5-mm dice**
- **1 small onion (red, if available), cut into 5-mm dice**
- **60 ml lime or lemon juice**
- **30 ml apricot jam**

1. Preheat the grill. In a small bowl, combine 2,5 ml of the salt, the sugar, oreganum and black pepper. Rub the mixture into the steaks; set aside.

2. In a large bowl, combine the pawpaws, pepper, onion, lime juice, jam and the remaining salt. Cover and refrigerate the fresh chutney until serving time.

3. Place the steaks on the grill rack and grill 15 centimetres from the heat for 3 minutes per side for medium-rare. Thinly slice each steak on the diagonal and serve with the chutney. Serves 4.

Per serving: Kilojoules 1 781; Fibre 4g; Protein 34g; Total Fat 19g; Saturated Fat 8g; Cholesterol 84mg; Sodium 527mg

Peaches & Nectarines

White Peaches	
PER 1 MEDIUM (150 G)	
Kilojoules	**294**
Fibre	**3g**
Protein	**1g**
Total Fat	**0,2g**
Saturated Fat	**0g**
Cholesterol	**0mg**
Sodium	**6mg**
NUTRIENTS	
% RDA for people older than 10 years	
Vitamin C	**20%**

Nectarines	
PER 1 MEDIUM (150 G)	
Kilojoules	**335**
Fibre	**2,6g**
Protein	**1g**
Total Fat	**0,2g**
Saturated Fat	**0g**
Cholesterol	**0mg**
Sodium	**3mg**
NUTRIENTS	
% RDA for people older than 10 years	
Vitamin C	**13%**

Did you know? . . .
Peaches and nectarines contain more vitamin C when they are fully ripe.

Peach-Filled Dessert Crêpes

PREP: 15 MINUTES / COOK: 15 MINUTES

The crêpe batter can be made several hours ahead of time and refrigerated, covered.

175 ml flour
5 ml granulated sugar
1,25 ml salt
250 ml low-fat (2%) milk
1 egg
15 ml unsalted butter, melted
70 ml peach or apricot juice
30 ml plus 10 ml light brown sugar
1,25 ml ground ginger
450 g peaches or nectarines, sliced 5-mm thick
30 ml crème fraîche or sour cream

1. In a medium bowl, combine the flour, granulated sugar and salt. Whisk in the milk, egg and melted butter until well combined. Let the batter stand for at least 10 minutes.

2. Spray a 20-cm nonstick pan with nonstick cooking spray and heat over moderate heat. Spoon the batter, a scant 60 ml at a time, into the pan, swirling so that the batter covers the bottom. Cook for 30 seconds or until lightly browned on the bottom. Turn the crêpe over and cook for 10 seconds on the second side. Transfer the crêpe to a plate and cover with a sheet of greaseproof paper. Continue cooking and stacking the crêpes until you have used all the batter (you should have 8 crêpes).

3. In a large pan, bring the juice, 30 ml of the brown sugar and the ginger to a boil over moderate heat. Add the peaches, reduce to a simmer and cook for 4 minutes or until the peaches are tender. Reserving the juices in the pan, remove the peaches with a slotted spoon.

4. In a small bowl, stir together the crème fraîche and the remaining 10 ml brown sugar. Spoon one-eighth of the peaches (about 60 ml) in a strip down the centre of each crêpe. Fold the sides of the crêpes in over the peaches until they almost meet in the centre, then roll up from the short end. Serve drizzled with the reserved pan juices and with the sweetened crème fraîche spooned over. Serves 4.

Per serving: Kilojoules 1 333; Fibre 3g; Protein 8g; Total Fat 8g; Saturated Fat 3g; Cholesterol 72mg; Sodium 206mg

Peach Pandowdy

PREP: 25 MINUTES / COOK: 40 MINUTES

Pandowdy is a deep-dish fruit dessert with a sweet, scone-like topping. The topping can be simply spooned on (as shown here); or, for a less 'dowdy' pandowdy, it can be piped over the fruit in a lattice pattern.

- **1,3 kg large peaches or nectarines, sliced**
- **30 ml lemon juice**
- **125 ml finely chopped dried apricots**
- **150 ml packed light brown sugar**
- **375 ml flour**
- **3,5 ml ground cinnamon**
- **60 ml granulated sugar**
- **5 ml baking powder**
- **1,25 ml salt**
- **1 egg**
- **15 ml unsalted butter, melted**
- **5 ml vanilla essence**
- **500 ml low-fat frozen vanilla yoghurt**

1. Preheat the oven to 200°C. In a large bowl, combine the peaches, lemon juice and apricots. Sprinkle with the brown sugar, 60 ml of the flour and the cinnamon, tossing well to combine. Transfer to a 18 x 28-cm baking tin.

2. In a medium bowl, whisk together the remaining 310 ml flour with the granulated sugar, baking powder and salt. Make a well in the centre and add the egg, butter, vanilla essence and 70 ml of water. Whisk the liquid ingredients in the centre until blended. Then quickly incorporate the dry ingredients just until blended. Spoon or pipe the topping over the fruit.

3. Bake for 35 to 40 minutes or until the topping is golden and the fruit is bubbly. Serve warm with a scoop of frozen yoghurt. Serves 8.

Per serving: Kilojoules 1 426; Fibre 5 g; Protein 6 g; Total Fat 5 g; Saturated Fat 2 g; Cholesterol 31 mg; Sodium 128 mg

At the market
Domestically grown peaches and nectarines are available from late October to early March. Imported peaches and nectarines are available at other times of year. A nectarine is not a cross between a peach and a plum, but is a variety of smooth peach.

Look for Locally grown peaches and nectarines are tastiest. These fruits do not continue to ripen after they are picked, though they may become softer. Choose fruits with a yellow undertone (not greenish). They should yield slightly to thumb pressure along the 'seam'.

Prep If a recipe requires you to peel peaches, you'll need to blanch them in boiling water for about 2 minutes—not enough to cook them, but just enough to loosen the skin. Cool the fruit in a bowl of iced water, then peel them.

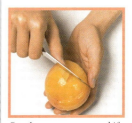

Peaches are easy to peel if you first blanch them briefly in boiling water.

Peach Pandowdy *Serve this old-fashioned dessert warm and 'à la mode'.*

Tuna Steaks with Fresh Nectarine Relish *The chunky fruit 'salsa' is sweet, spicy and touched with the freshness of mint.*

Yellow-Cling Peaches

PER 1 MEDIUM (150 G)

Kilojoules	353
Fibre	2,9g
Protein	1g
Total Fat	0,2g
Saturated Fat	0g
Cholesterol	0mg
Sodium	5mg

NUTRIENTS

% RDA for people older than 10 years	
Vitamin C	33%

Tinned peaches in fruit juice lose over 50 per cent of their vitamin C.

Dried peaches are five times higher in kilojoules than fresh, but they do contain useful amounts of iron and potassium

A 100g dried peaches provides nearly a third of your daily iron requirement.

Refrigerator Peach Jam

PREP: 20 MINUTES / COOK: 20 MINUTES

A special type of fruit pectin for making low-kilojoule preserves lets you create a thick fruit jam with relatively little sugar. If you can't find this type of pectin, you can make tasty refrigerator 'preserves' instead. Simply omit the pectin and cook the peaches until slightly thickened.

1,3 kg peaches
30 ml lemon juice
45 g fruit pectin for light jam
1,25 ml allspice
5 ml ground cinnamon
875 ml sugar

1. Bring a large pot of water to a boil. Add the peaches in batches and cook for 2 minutes to blanch. Peel and pit the peaches, transfer them to a large saucepan and mash them with a potato masher.

2. Add the lemon juice, pectin, allspice and cinnamon, stirring until the pectin is dissolved. Bring to a full boil over high heat. Add the sugar all at once, stirring constantly. Bring to a full rolling boil and cook for 1 minute. Skim off the foam.

3. Ladle the jam into four 500 ml containers rinsed in boiling water; fill to within 1 cm of the top. Cover with tight lids and let stand at room temperature overnight; then store in the refrigerator for up to 3 weeks. Makes 1,7 litres.

Per 15 ml: Kilojoules 123; Fibre 0g; Protein 0g; Total Fat 0g; Saturated Fat 0g; Cholesterol 0mg; Sodium 6mg

Peach-Cherry Oat Crumble

PREP: 15 MINUTES / COOK: 25 MINUTES

Although cherries are the ideal taste combination here, they can be replaced with other berries.

600 g sliced peaches (4 cups)
225 g cherries, pitted and halved
125 ml granulated sugar
15 ml cornflour
5 ml vanilla essence
2,5 ml grated lemon rind
70 ml rolled oats
45 ml packed light brown sugar
45 ml flour
22 ml unsalted butter, cut up

1. Preheat the oven to 190° C. Spray a 23-cm glass pie dish with nonstick cooking spray.

2. In a medium saucepan, combine the peaches, cherries, granulated sugar and cornflour and bring to a boil over moderate heat. Remove from the heat and stir in the vanilla essence and lemon rind. Spoon into the pie dish.

3. In a medium bowl, combine the oats, brown sugar and flour. With a pastry blender or 2 knives, cut in the butter until the mixture is crumbly. Scatter over the fruit, place the pie dish on a baking sheet and bake for 20 minutes or until the filling is bubbly and the top is browned. Serve warm or at room temperature. Serves 4.

Per serving: Kilojoules 1 430; Fibre 5 g; Protein 3 g; Total Fat 6 g; Saturated Fat 3 g; Cholesterol 12 mg; Sodium 13 mg

Tuna Steaks with Fresh Nectarine Relish

PREP: 20 MINUTES / COOK: 10 MINUTES

Swordfish steaks—or any other meaty fish— can be used instead of the tuna steaks.

30 ml honey
30 ml chilli sauce
30 ml red wine vinegar
1,25 ml salt
450 g nectarines or peaches, cut into 1-cm cubes
1 red pepper, cut into 1-cm squares
3 spring onions, thinly sliced
60 ml chopped fresh mint
4 tuna steaks (175 g each)
2,5 ml each ground coriander and cumin

1. In a medium bowl, whisk together the honey, chilli sauce, vinegar and salt. Add the nectarines, pepper, spring onions and mint, tossing to mix. Refrigerate until serving time.

2. Preheat the grill. Rub the tuna steaks with the coriander and cumin. Grill 15 centimetres from the heat for 3 minutes per side or until lightly browned and just cooked through. Serve topped with the relish. Serves 4.

Per serving: Kilojoules 1 409; Fibre 3 g; Protein 38 g; Total Fat 8 g; Saturated Fat 2 g; Cholesterol 82 mg; Sodium 260 mg

Amaretti-Stuffed Peaches Preheat oven to 180°C. Halve 4 peaches and place cut-sides up in 18 x 28-cm baking dish. Spoon 5 ml red currant jam or jelly into each hollow. Spoon 1 crushed amaretti biscuit into each hollow. Cover with foil and bake 25 minutes or until tender. Serves 4. *[kJ 472; Fat 1 g; Sodium 5 mg]*

Savoury Peach Salad with Watercress In a large bowl, combine 60 ml red wine vinegar, 15 ml Dijon mustard, 15 ml olive oil, 2,5 ml each salt and pepper. Add 2 bunches watercress, 4 peaches or nectarines cut into thick wedges and 125 ml sliced water chestnuts. Toss well. Serves 4. *[kJ 633; Fat 4 g; Sodium 425 mg]*

Nectarine Brûlée Preheat the oven to 180°C. Cut 4 peaches or nectarines into thin wedges. Toss with 15 ml lemon juice and 15 ml sugar. Spoon into a 20-cm ovenproof dish and bake 10 minutes. Preheat grill. Top fruit with 125 ml sour cream. Sprinkle with 70 ml brown sugar. Grill 5 minutes or until sugar is melted and bubbly. Serves 4. *[kJ 938; Fat 8 g; Sodium 19 mg]*

Pineapples

PER 180 G FRESH (I CUP)	
Kilojoules	445
Fibre	3,2 g
Protein	1 g
Total Fat	0,2 g
Saturated Fat	0 g
Cholesterol	0 mg
Sodium	2 mg

NUTRIENTS	
% RDA for people older than 10 years	
Vitamin C	129 %
Thiamin	10 %

Did you know? . . .

When buying tinned pineapple, opt for the juice-packed type. Pineapple packed in heavy syrup has lots of added sugar and about 200 kilojoules more per serving.

Fresh pineapple can be used as a meat tenderizer, as it contains the enzyme bromelain which breaks down protein.

Pineapple-Barbecued Prawns

PREP: 30 MINUTES / MARINATE: 30 MINUTES / COOK: 5 MINUTES

A grill topper—a smooth, flat, perforated metal grilling 'sheet'—is great for prawns.

45 ml honey
30 ml lime or lemon juice
3,5 ml chilli powder
2,5 ml salt
1,25 ml crushed red chilli flakes
540 g fresh pineapple chunks (5 mm) (3 cups)
125 ml diced red pepper
125 ml diced cucumber (5 mm)
60 ml diced onion (red, if available)
125 ml pineapple juice
10 ml olive oil
2,5 ml dried oreganum
450 g large prawns, peeled and deveined

1. In a large bowl, whisk together the honey, lime juice, 1,25 ml each of the chilli powder and salt and the red chilli flakes. Add the pineapple, pepper, cucumber and onion, tossing well to combine. Cover the salsa and refrigerate until serving time.

2. In a large bowl, whisk together the pineapple juice, oil, oreganum, the remaining chilli powder and salt. Add the prawns and toss well. Marinate for 30 minutes.

3. Preheat the grill (or preheat the grill with a grill topper). Grill the prawns 15 centimetres from the heat for 2 minutes per side or until just cooked through. Serve with the pineapple salsa. Serves 4.

Per serving: Kilojoules 1 163; Fibre 3g; Protein 22g; Total Fat 4g; Saturated Fat 1g; Cholesterol 195 mg; Sodium 532 mg

Pineapple Brown Betty

PREP: 10 MINUTES

Amaretti are Italian almond biscuits usually dunked in coffee. They are as light as air, as they're made without shortening.

115 g amaretti cookies (20 medium)
60 ml pecan nuts
70 ml packed light brown sugar
15 ml unsalted butter, cut up
2,5 ml ground cinnamon
5 ml vanilla essence
3 tins (425 g each) juice-packed pineapple pieces, drained

1. Preheat the oven to 180°C. In a food processor, combine the amaretti, pecan nuts, brown sugar, butter, cinnamon and vanilla essence and pulse until the biscuits are finely ground.

2. In an 20-cm square glass baking dish, toss the pineapple with the crumb mixture. Bake for 30 minutes or until the pineapple is piping hot and the crumbs are crusty. Serves 4.

Per serving: Kilojoules 1 555; Fibre 3g; Protein 3g; Total Fat 11g; Saturated Fat 3g; Cholesterol 8 mg; Sodium 194 mg

Pineapple Foster

PREP: 15 MINUTES / COOK: 10 MINUTES

Bananas Foster is a beloved New Orleans dessert, created in the 1950s at Brennan's Restaurant. This pineapple variation, in which the fruit is sautéed in butter and brown sugar and then flambéed, will bring raves.

20 ml unsalted butter
45 ml packed light brown sugar
1,25 ml ground nutmeg
6 slices (2-mm thick) fresh pineapple, cored and cut into thirds
45 ml dark rum
30 ml Grand Marnier or other orange liqueur
320 ml low-fat frozen vanilla yoghurt

1. In a large pan, melt the butter over moderate heat. When it begins to foam, add the brown sugar and nutmeg and heat until the sugar has melted. Add the pineapple and cook, tossing often, for 4 minutes or until the pineapple is warmed through.

2. Remove the pan from the heat, sprinkle the rum and Grand Marnier over the pineapple and ignite the alcohol with a long match. Return the pan to the heat and shake until the alcohol burns off.

3. Serve the pineapple slices and sauce with the frozen yoghurt. Serves 4.

Per serving: Kilojoules 1 012; Fibre 2g; Protein 2g; Total Fat 7g; Saturated Fat 4g; Cholesterol 12mg; Sodium 46mg

At the market Fresh pineapples are available all year round.

Look for Once picked, a pineapple won't get any sweeter. Choose a large, plump, heavy specimen with fresh green leaves and a sweet fragrance. The Queen pineapple is the most popular as it is very sweet, but it must be yellow to be ripe. The Cayenne pineapple is not as sweet and can still be green in appearance when it is ripe.

Prep To cut pineapple, first remove the crown. For crosswise slices, first cut off the skin with a sharp knife, then slice the fruit (cut out the woody core after slicing). For chopped fruit, it's simpler to quarter the unpeeled fruit lengthwise and then cut the fruit off the skin before chopping.

To remove the crown, grasp it in your hand and twist.

Basic cooking The bromelain in fresh pineapple will prevent gelatine from setting. So use only cooked (or tinned) pineapple in gelatine desserts.

Pineapple Foster is a seductive pairing of warm sautéed fruit and frozen yoghurt.

Plums

PER 140G (2 LARGE)	
Kilojoules	325
Fibre	2,5g
Protein	1g
Total Fat	0,1g
Saturated Fat	0g
Cholesterol	0mg
Sodium	6mg

NUTRIENTS	
% RDA for people older than 10 years	
Vitamin C	7%

Did you know? . . .

Lutein, which is also found in leafy green vegetables, red peppers, parsley and pumpkin, helps protect your retinas against the damaging effects of free radicals.

In the US Department of Agriculture's evaluation of total antioxidant capacity of fruits, plums won third place, behind blueberries and strawberries.

Plum Clafouti

PREP: 15 MINUTES / COOK: 45 MINUTES

Clafouti, a rustic recipe from the Limousin region of France, is a charmingly simple dessert best described as a moist oven-baked pancake. The fruit rises to the surface as the batter bakes.

650g black or red plums, cut into 5-mm-thick wedges
15ml plus 125ml granulated sugar
2 eggs
2 egg whites
125ml flour
250ml low-fat (2%) milk
60ml sour cream
5ml vanilla essence
5ml grated orange rind
1,25ml salt
15ml icing sugar

1. Preheat the oven to 200°C. In a medium bowl, toss the plums with 15ml of the granulated sugar; set the plums aside.

2. In another medium bowl, whisk together the whole eggs, egg whites and the remaining 125ml granulated sugar. Slowly beat in the flour, milk, sour cream, vanilla essence, orange rind and salt. Arrange the plums in a 25-cm quiche tin or pie dish. Pour the egg mixture over. Bake 30 minutes or until the custard is just set. Dust with the icing sugar and serve warm. Serves 6.

Per serving: Kilojoules 1051; Fibre 2g; Protein 6g; Total Fat 5g; Saturated Fat 2g; Cholesterol 82mg; Sodium 162mg

Spiced Plum Tart

PREP: 30 MINUTES / CHILL: 1 HOUR
COOK: 40 MINUTES

The plums are sprinkled with a mixture of flour, brown sugar, ginger and (surprisingly) black pepper. Used in many European gingerbreads and spice biscuits, pepper has a bite which enhances the ginger's flavour.

250ml plus 20ml flour
15ml granulated sugar
1,25ml salt
45ml unsalted butter, cut up
30ml low-fat cream cheese
30ml sour cream
1 egg white, lightly beaten
550g purple plums, cut into 5-mm-thick wedges
70ml packed light brown sugar
1,25ml ground ginger
0,6ml black pepper (optional)

1. In a large bowl, combine 250ml of the flour, the granulated sugar and salt. With a pastry blender or 2 knives, cut in the butter and cream cheese until the mixture resembles coarse crumbs. In a small bowl, combine the sour cream and 30ml iced water. Stir the sour-cream mixture into the flour mixture until just combined. Flatten the dough into a disc, wrap in plastic wrap and refrigerate for at least 1 hour.

2. Preheat the oven to 190°C. On a lightly floured surface, roll the dough out to a 33-cm round. Place on a baking sheet and roll the edges over once to form a neat edge and a 28-cm circle.

At the market Many varieties of plums are produced domestically. Plums are available from November to March.

Look for Red, yellow, purple or 'black' (really blue-black) plums offer many varieties to choose from. Pick firm (but not hard) plums which are full and plump, not shrivelled or bruised. Plums continue to ripen after they are picked—when they are soft near the stalk they are ready to be eaten. Keep ripe plums in the refrigerator. For recipes which require the plums to be pitted, choose freestone varieties such as Gaviota.

Spiced Plum Tart The secret of its tender low-fat crust is low-fat cream cheese.

3. Brush the dough with the egg white. Lay the plum wedges on top in overlapping concentric circles. In a small bowl, combine the brown sugar, ginger, pepper and the remaining 20 ml flour. Sprinkle evenly over the plums. Bake for 40 minutes or until the plums are tender and the crust is golden. Serves 6.

Per serving: Kilojoules 1 060; Fibre 2g; Protein 4g; Total Fat 9g; Saturated Fat 5g; Cholesterol 26mg; Sodium 130mg

Stir-Fried Pork with Plums

PREP: 20 MINUTES / COOK: 15 MINUTES

Pork with plums is a classic Chinese combination. Chinese plum sauce from a jar has little to offer nutritionally, but this stir-fry is made with fresh plums which supply beta carotene, potassium and vitamin C.

15 ml vegetable oil
450 g well-trimmed pork fillet, cut into 2,5 x 1-cm strips
15 ml plus 7,5 ml cornflour
1 large carrot, thinly sliced on the diagonal
1 small onion, thinly sliced
2 cloves garlic, finely chopped
450 g purple, red or black plums, cut into 1-cm-thick wedges
250 ml chicken stock
30 ml plum jam
15 ml rice or cider vinegar
15 ml light soya sauce
2,5 ml ground ginger

1. In a large nonstick frying pan or wok, heat the oil over moderately high heat. Toss the pork with 15 ml of the cornflour, rubbing it into the meat. Stir-fry the pork for 5 minutes or until lightly browned and just cooked through. With a slotted spoon, transfer the pork to a plate.

2. Reduce the heat to moderate. Add the carrot, onion and garlic to the pan and cook for 1 minute. Add the plums and cook for 4 minutes or until they begin to soften.

3. In a small bowl, whisk together the stock, jam, vinegar, soya sauce, ginger and the remaining 7,5 ml cornflour. Pour into the pan and bring to a boil. Boil for 1 minute. Reduce to a simmer, return the pork to the pan and cook for 2 minutes or until heated through. Serves 4.

Per serving: Kilojoules 1 723; Fibre 3g; Protein 32g; Total Fat 13g; Saturated Fat 4g; Cholesterol 57mg; Sodium 674mg

The black Angelino plum originated in the United States and was introduced to South Africa in 1995. The flesh is firm rather like that of an apple and, surprisingly, it has a sweet flavour.

Prunes

PER 100 G (½ CUP)	
Kilojoules	1124
Fibre	7,1 g
Protein	2,6 g
Total Fat	0,5 g
Saturated Fat	0 g
Cholesterol	0 mg
Sodium	4 mg

NUTRIENTS	
% RDA for people older than 10 years	
Iron	18 %
Magnesium	15 %
Vitamin B6	13 %

Did you know? . . .

Prune butter can replace up to half the fat in many baking recipes thus cutting fat and increasing fibre and nutrient content. Baked goods with intense flavours, such as chocolate biscuits or spice cake, are good candidates for this trick. To make 250 ml of prune butter, process 225 g pitted prunes with 90 ml water in a food processor.

Pork & Prunes with Port

PREP: 15 MINUTES / COOK: 30 MINUTES

The heady flavour of port—a sweet, fortified red wine—adds a deep, rich 'bass note' to the complex flavours of this dish. The pork and prunes are cooked in a sauce that also includes spring onions, garlic and mustard.

- 15 ml olive oil
- 450 g well-trimmed pork fillet, cut into 8 slices
- 30 ml flour
- 1 large yellow or red pepper, cut into 1-cm squares
- 2 spring onions, thinly sliced
- 1 clove garlic, finely chopped
- 125 ml dry red wine
- 125 ml ruby port
- 125 ml chicken stock
- 225 g pitted prunes
- 10 ml Dijon mustard
- 2,5 ml each salt and black pepper

1. In a large nonstick pan, heat the oil over moderate heat. Dredge the pork in the flour, shaking off the excess. Sauté for 2 minutes per side or until lightly browned. With a slotted spoon, transfer the pork to a plate.

2. Add the pepper, spring onions and garlic and sauté for 4 minutes or until the pepper is crisp-tender. Add the wine and port, increase the heat to high and cook for 3 minutes or until slightly reduced.

3. Add the stock, prunes, mustard, salt and black pepper; reduce the heat to low and cook for 5 minutes.

4. Return the pork to the pan and cook for 7 to 10 minutes or until the slices of pork are cooked through but still juicy and the prunes are tender. Serves 4.

Per serving: Kilojoules 1 715; Fibre 5 g; Protein 21 g; Total Fat 10 g; Saturated Fat 3 g; Cholesterol 53 mg; Sodium 612 mg

Curry Cream-Stuffed Prunes

PREP: 25 MINUTES / COOK: 10 MINUTES

For this tempting hors d'oeuvre, look for the extra-large prunes that are often sold loose (in delicatessens and health-food stores); the smaller packaged prunes can be tedious to stuff. If you don't have—or don't care for—crystallized ginger, substitute 30 millilitres of chopped mango chutney.

- 60 ml walnuts
- 85 g low-fat cream cheese
- 15 ml milk
- 30 ml finely chopped crystallized ginger
- 2,5 ml curry powder
- 1,25 ml black pepper
- 24 large pitted prunes

1. Preheat the oven to 180°C. In a small baking tin, toast the walnuts for 7 minutes or until fragrant and crisp.

When cool enough to handle, chop the walnuts finely.

2. In a medium bowl, stir the cream cheese and milk together until soft. Stir in the crystallized ginger, curry powder, pepper and toasted walnuts.

3. With a paring knife, make a slit in each prune. Spoon the cream cheese mixture into the prunes. Serves 6.

Per serving: Kilojoules 902; Fibre 4g; Protein 3g; Total Fat 7g; Saturated Fat 2g; Cholesterol 16mg; Sodium 46mg

Spiced Prunes

PREP: 15 MINUTES / COOK: 20 MINUTES

If you're looking for a change from apple-sauce, cook up a pot of these fragrant, exotically spiced prunes. Try them with roast chicken, turkey or pork. Try to buy prunes which are already pitted to avoid this tedious chore.

150ml red wine vinegar
70ml sugar
2,5ml ground ginger
2,5ml salt
2,5ml black pepper
2,5ml mustard seeds
0,6ml ground allspice
350g pitted prunes, halved
1 large red pepper, cut into 1-cm squares
1 large tomato, cut into 1-cm cubes
1 small onion (red, if available), cut into 1-cm cubes
5ml vanilla essence

1. In a medium saucepan, combine the vinegar, sugar, ginger, salt, black pepper, mustard seeds and allspice. Bring to a boil over moderate heat.

2. Stir in the prunes, pepper, tomato and onion. Return to a boil, reduce to a simmer, cover and cook for 10 minutes. Uncover and cook for 5 minutes or until the prunes are tender and the liquid is reduced to a thick syrup. Stir in the vanilla essence. Serve warm, at room temperature or chilled. Makes 875 millilitres.

Per 60ml (¼ cup): Kilojoules 381; Fibre 2g; Protein 1g; Total Fat 0g; Saturated Fat 0g; Cholesterol 0mg; Sodium 89mg

At the market Prunes are mainly of the Prune d'Agen variety—grown specially for drying. Dried prunes, whole or pitted, are sold in bags ready packaged either as prunes or as part of dried fuit salad.

Look for Check to be sure that the prunes are still plump and moist.

Prep To remove the pips, snip each prune with kitchen shears dipped in hot water (to keep the blades from sticking). Squeeze out the pips. Whole prunes can be reconstituted by soaking in water for an hour or two.

It's easier to snip prunes with scissors than to chop them with a knife. Dip the blades in hot water, or oil them lightly, to keep them from sticking.

Spiced Prunes are a fine accompaniment for roast meat or poultry.

Strawberries

PER 160 G SLICED (1 CUP)	
Kilojoules	251
Fibre	3g
Protein	1g
Total Fat	0,5g
Saturated Fat	0g
Cholesterol	0mg
Sodium	6mg

NUTRIENTS	
% RDA for people older than 10 years	
Vitamin C	155%
Folate	15%

Did you know? . . .

In the US Department of Agriculture's study of the antioxidant power of various fruits, strawberries placed second, after blueberries.

A 160-g serving of strawberries supplies more vitamin C than a small orange.

Strawberries contain respectable amounts of folate—a heart-healthy B vitamin—and potassium.

Strawberry-Ricotta Crêpes

PREP: 25 MINUTES / STAND: 30 MINUTES
COOK: 15 MINUTES

- 125 ml milk
- 70 ml flour
- 5 ml plus 60 ml granulated sugar
- 1 egg
- 1 egg white
- 10 ml unsalted butter, melted
- 1,25 ml salt
- 250 ml ricotta cheese
- 5 ml vanilla essence
- 480 g strawberries, hulled and thinly sliced (3 cups), plus 4 whole strawberries for garnish
- 15 ml icing sugar

1. In a blender, combine the milk, flour, 5 ml of the granulated sugar, the whole egg, egg white, melted butter and salt. Process until smooth. Let stand for 30 minutes.

2. Spray a 20-cm nonstick pan with nonstick cooking spray. Heat over moderate heat. Spoon the batter, a generous 30 ml at a time, into the pan and swirl to coat the bottom. Cook for 15 seconds or until lightly browned on the bottom. Lift and turn the crêpe over and cook for 5 seconds or until cooked through. Slide the crêpe onto a plate, cover with greaseproof paper and continue making crêpes and stacking them with sheets of greaseproof paper in between. You will need 8 crêpes (if you are adept at making crêpes, you may get more than 8).

3. In a large bowl, combine the ricotta, vanilla essence and the remaining 60 ml granulated sugar. Fold in the strawberries. Spoon the mixture onto the centre of each crêpe, fold the ends over and roll up. Place 2 crêpes on each of 4 dessert plates, sprinkle with the icing sugar and garnish with a whole strawberry. Serves 4.

Per serving: Kilojoules 1 278; Fibre 3g; Protein 12g; Total Fat 13g; Saturated Fat 7g; Cholesterol 88mg; Sodium 249mg

Strawberry Salad

PREP: 25 MINUTES / COOK: 10 MINUTES

If the idea of strawberries in a savoury salad sounds odd to you, remember that tomatoes, like strawberries, are juicy red fruits! Balsamic vinegar is said to bring out the flavour of strawberries.

- 60 ml pecan nut halves
- 640 g strawberries, hulled (4 cups)
- 30 ml balsamic vinegar
- 10 ml olive oil
- 5 ml light brown sugar
- 1,25 ml each salt and pepper
- 360 g Boston lettuce, torn into bite-size pieces (6 cups)
- 1 cucumber, peeled, halved lengthwise, seeded, and thinly sliced
- 60 ml snipped fresh dill
- 115 g mild goat cheese, thinly sliced

1. Preheat the oven to 180°C. In a small baking tin, toast the pecan nuts for 7 minutes or until crisp. When cool enough to handle, coarsely chop.

2. In a large salad bowl, mash 80 g of the strawberries. Slice the remaining strawberries thickly; set aside.

Strawberry Angel Tarts *A mint sprig is a fine finishing touch for this lovely dessert.*

3. Whisk the vinegar, oil, brown sugar, salt and pepper into the mashed strawberries. Add the lettuce, cucumber, dill and sliced strawberries, tossing to combine. Sprinkle the salad with the goat cheese and pecan nuts. Serves 4.

Per serving: Kilojoules 927; Fibre 5g; Protein 8g; Total Fat 13g; Saturated Fat 5g; Cholesterol 13mg; Sodium 276mg

Strawberry Angel Tarts

PREP: 30 MINUTES
COOK: 1 HOUR 5 MINUTES

These tarts are miniature versions of the meringue-based Pavlova or angel pie.

- 4 large egg whites
- 1,25ml cream of tartar
- 250ml sugar
- 45ml cocoa powder, sifted
- 5ml vanilla essence
- 640g strawberries, hulled (4 cups)
- 45ml raspberry jam (sieved to remove the seeds)
- 10ml cornflour blended with 15ml water
- 60ml heavy cream, whipped

1. Preheat the oven to 150°C. Line a baking sheet with greaseproof paper. Draw four 12-cm circles on the paper; set aside. In a large bowl, beat the egg whites and cream of tartar with an electric mixer until soft peaks form. Gradually add the sugar and beat until stiff peaks form. Fold in the cocoa and vanilla essence.

2. Spoon the mixture into a pastry bag without a tip or into a heavy-duty plastic bag with a small bit of one corner cut off. Pipe the mixture in a spiral on the 4 circles, making 4 flat discs. Bake the discs for 1 hour or until the meringue is set. Remove the tart shells and cool to room temperature.

3. Meanwhile, place 160g (1 cup) of the strawberries in a small saucepan and mash with a potato masher. Slice the remaining strawberries and set aside. Stir the jam into the mashed berries and bring to a boil over moderate heat. Stir in the cornflour mixture and cook, stirring constantly, for 1 minute. Off the heat, stir in the sliced berries.

4. Just before serving, beat the cream until stiff peaks form. With the back of a spoon, break the centre of the cooled meringue shells to create a depression. Spoon the strawberry mixture onto the shells. Top with the whipped cream. Serves 4.

Per serving: Kilojoules 1127; Fibre 4g; Protein 6g; Total Fat 7g; Saturated Fat 4g; Cholesterol 21mg; Sodium 88mg

At the market For the ultimate strawberry flavour, buy strawberries when they are in season locally—from September to December. Imported strawberries are sometimes available, but at a price.

Look for Choose strawberries that are plump, colourful and, most important, sweetly fragrant. The leafy caps should look fresh and green. Check the bottom of the box —stains there suggest that the berries at the bottom may be crushed or spoiled.

Prep Store unwashed berries in the refrigerator but eat as soon as possible as they will not last long. RInse berries in cold water, then hull them (see below). If you hull the berries *before* rinsing, they will absorb excess water.

Hulling a strawberry involves more than removing the leafy caps; you also need to remove the white 'core' attached to the cap. Use a small paring knife to dig it out.

C

D

E

R

T

watermelon ice with chocolate
'seeds', 304
Wheat, about, 152-153. *See also
Bulgur*
banana bran muffins, 153
crunchy dessert topping, 152
flour, whole-wheat, about,
152-153
mushroom roll-ups, 152
wheat bran, about, 153
wheat germ, about, 152-153
White beans. *See Kidney beans,
white*
Wild rice, about, 166-167
wild rice & pecan nut stuffing,
166
wild rice salad, 167
wild rice-brown rice pilaf, 166

Yellowtail
grilled marinated yellowtail steaks,
200
yellowtail kebabs with lemon-
garlic sauce, 200
Yoghurt, about, 124-126
banana raita, 276
fresh cherry sundaes, 286
fruit-topped yoghurt cheese tart, 124
fruity yoghurt parfait, 124
garlic-dill yoghurt cheese, 125
green goddess salad dressing, 127
lamb curry, 241
pear-yoghurt cake with yoghurt
topping, 126

raspberry yoghurt cheese, 125
spring onion-pepper yoghurt
cheese, 125
tandoori-style chicken, 127
tropical smoothie, 127
two-berry yoghurt frozen suckers,
127
yoghurt cheese, 125; how to make,
38
yoghurt chicken, 261
Youngberries. *See Berries*

Zeaxanthin, about, 27, 52
Zinc, about, 19, 27

PHOTO CREDITS

Cover photographs by Angelo Caggiano (pasta recipe), David Murray, Vernon
Morgan, Jules Selmes. All interior recipe photography by Mark Ferri, with the
following exceptions: Beatriz daCosta: 77-79, 81 (top & centre), 83, 87, 92-95, 97 (top),
137, 145-149, 271, 273 (top & centre), 301. Lisa Koenig: Pages 178-181, 183, 205-209,
212-213, 215 (left), 216-217, 238-241, 249-257, 266-269, 275-276, 277 (left), 278-279,
281-283, 301, 307, 309, 313-315, 319 (left). Steven Mark Needham: Pages 63 (centre),
67, 68-71. Henrique Wilding: 75, 211, 243, 245, 285, 295. All how-to and ingredient
identification photographs by Lisa Koenig, with the following exceptions: Henrique
Wilding: 39 (opening an oyster & checking live mussels), 66, 74, 98, 116, 129, 199, 208,
210, 211, 214, 215, 243, 245, 277, 284, 285, 289, 294, 295, 319.

Recommended Dietary Allowances (RDAs), 1989

Food and Nutrition Board, National Academy of Sciences – National Research Council, USA

	Age (years)	Protein (g)	Vitamin A (mcg RE)	Vitamin D (mcg)	Vitamin E (mg alpha TE)	Vitamin K (mcg)	Vitamin C (mg)	Thiamin (mg)	Riboflavin (mg)	Niacin (mg)	Vitamin B6 (mg)	Folate (mcg)	Vitamin B12 (mcg)	Calcium (mg)	Phosphorus (mg)	Magnesium (mg)	Iron (mg)	Zinc (mg)	Iodine (mcg)	Selenium (mcg)
Males	11-14	45	1000	10	10	45	50	1,3	1,5	17	1,7	150	2,0	1200	1200	270	12	15	150	40
	15-18	59	1000	10	10	65	60	1,5	1,8	20	2,0	200	2,0	1200	1200	400	12	15	150	50
	19-24	58	1000	10	10	70	60	1,5	1,7	19	2,0	200	2,0	1200	1200	350	10	15	150	70
	25-50	63	1000	5	10	80	60	1,5	1,7	19	2,0	200	2,0	800	800	350	10	15	150	70
	51+	63	1000	5	10	80	60	1,2	1,4	15	2,0	200	2,0	800	800	350	10	15	150	70
Females	11-14	46	800	10	8	45	50	1,1	1,3	15	1,4	150	2,0	1200	1200	280	15	12	150	45
	15-18	44	800	10	8	55	60	1,1	1,3	15	1,5	180	2,0	1200	1200	300	15	12	150	50
	19-24	46	800	10	8	60	60	1,1	1,3	15	1,6	180	2,0	1200	1200	280	15	12	150	55
	25-50	50	800	5	8	65	60	1,1	1,3	15	1,6	180	2,0	800	800	280	15	12	150	55
	51+	50	800	5	8	65	60	1,0	1,2	13	1,6	180	2,0	800	800	280	10	12	150	55
Pregnant		60	1300	10	10	65	70	1,5	1,6	17	2,2	400	2,2	1200	1200	320	30	15	175	65
Lactating 1st 6 mo		65	1300	10	12	65	95	1,6	1,8	20	2,1	280	2,6	1200	1200	355	15	19	200	75
2nd 6 mo		62	1200	10	11	65	90	1,6	1,7	20	2,1	260	2,6	1200	1200	340	15	16	200	75

Estimated safe and adequate daily dietary intakes

Age category	Biotin (mcg)	Pantothenic acid (mg)	Copper (mg)	Manganese (mg)	Fluoride (mg)	Chromium (mcg)
Adults	30-100	4-7	1,5-3,0	2,0-5,0	1,5-4,0	50-200